W9-CKR-992

STAR WARS™

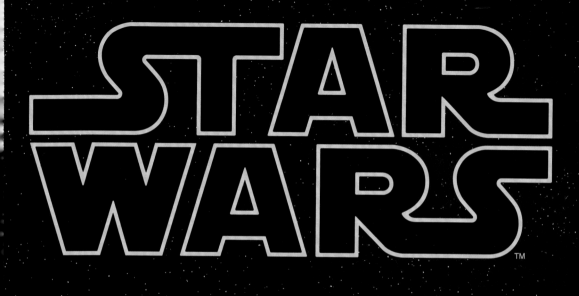

THE DESTINY PATH

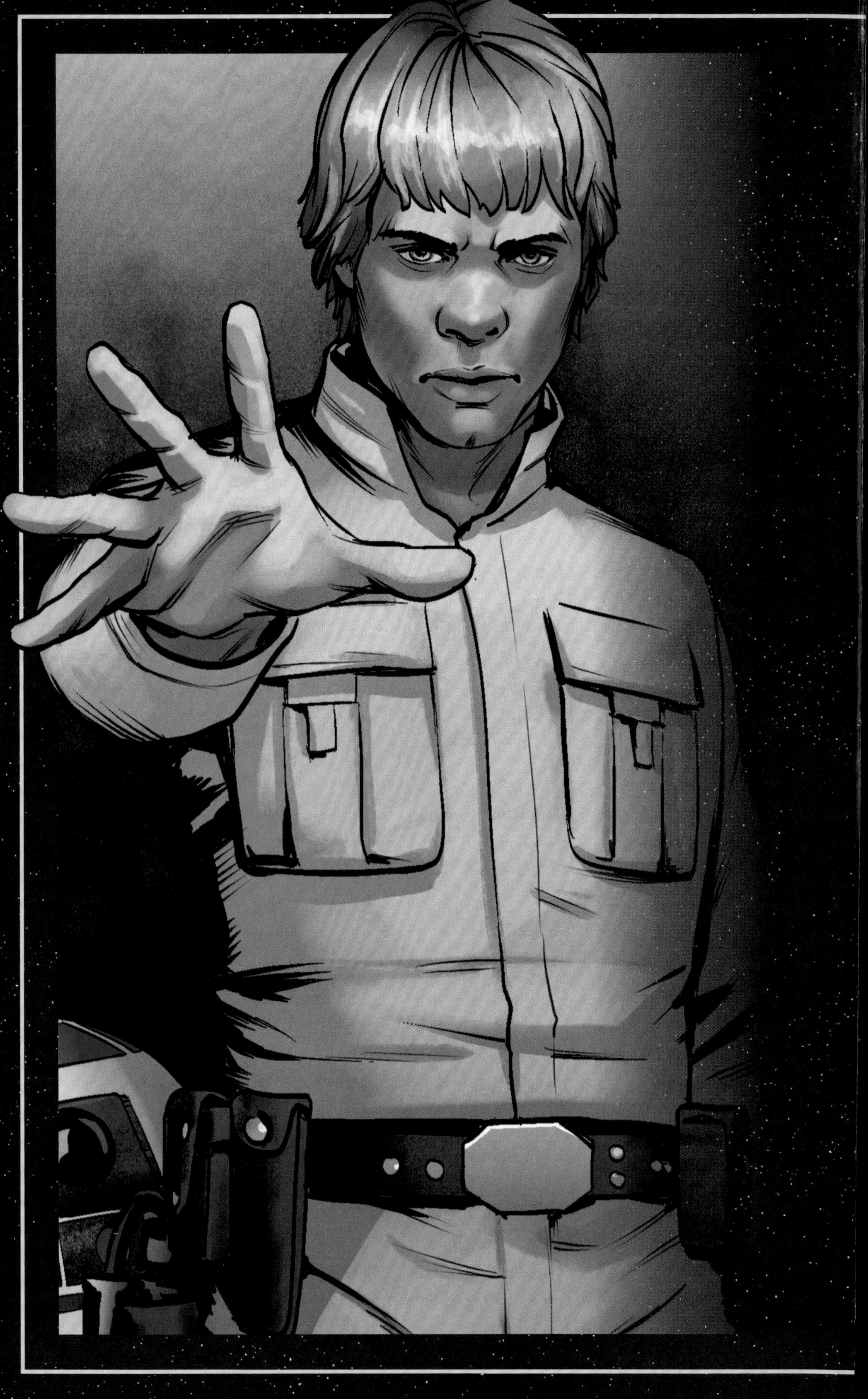

STAR WARS™

THE DESTINY PATH

Writer
CHARLES SOULE

Artist
JESÚS SAIZ

Color Artists
ARIF PRIANTO
with **JESÚS SAIZ** (#1), **RACHELLE ROSENBERG** (#4) & **DAN BROWN** (#5)

Letterer
VC's CLAYTON COWLES

Cover Art
R.B. SILVA & **GURU-eFX**

Assistant Editor
TOM GRONEMAN

Editor
MARK PANICCIA

Collection Editor **JENNIFER GRÜNWALD**
Assistant Managing Editor **MAIA LOY**
Assistant Managing Editor **LISA MONTALBANO**
Editor, Special Projects **MARK D. BEAZLEY**
duction & Special Projects **JEFF YOUNGQUIST**
Book Designer **ADAM DEL RE**
VP Print, Sales & Marketing **DAVID GABRIEL**
Editor in Chief **C.B. CEBULSKI**

For Lucasfilm:

Senior Editor **ROBERT SIMPSON**
Creative Director **MICHAEL SIGLAIN**
Art Director **TROY ALDERS**
Lucasfilm Story Group **MATT MARTIN**
PABLO HIDALGO
EMILY SHKOUKANI
JAMES WAUGH
Lucasfilm Art Department **PHIL SZOSTAK**

ARS VOL. 1: THE DESTINY PATH. Contains material originally published in magazine form as STAR WARS (2020) #1-6. First printing 2020. ISBN 978-1-302-92078-4. Published by MARVEL WORLDWIDE, subsidiary of MARVEL ENTERTAINMENT, LLC. OFFICE OF PUBLICATION: 1290 Avenue of the Americas, New York, NY 10104. STAR WARS and related text and illustrations are trademarks and/or copyrights, nited States and other countries, of Lucasfilm Ltd. and/or its affiliates. © & TM Lucasfilm Ltd. No similarity between any of the names, characters, persons, and/or institutions in this magazine with those ving or dead person or institution is intended, and any such similarity which may exist is purely coincidental. Marvel and its logos are TM Marvel Characters, Inc. **Printed in Canada.** KEVIN FEIGE, Chief Officer; DAN BUCKLEY, President, Marvel Entertainment; JOHN NEE, Publisher; JOE QUESADA, EVP & Creative Director; TOM BREVOORT, SVP of Publishing; DAVID BOGART, Associate Publisher & SVP of ffairs; Publishing & Partnership; DAVID GABRIEL, VP of Print & Digital Publishing; JEFF YOUNGQUIST, VP of Production & Special Projects; DAN CARR, Executive Director of Publishing Technology; ALEX S, Director of Publishing Operations; DAN EDINGTON, Managing Editor; RICKEY PURDIN, Director of Talent Relations; SUSAN CRESPI, Production Manager; STAN LEE, Chairman Emeritus. For information g advertising in Marvel Comics or on Marvel.com, please contact Vit DeBellis, Custom Solutions & Integrated Advertising Manager, at vdebellis@marvel.com. For Marvel subscription inquiries, please call 1-5480. **Manufactured between 9/9/2020 and 10/6/2020 by SOLISCO PRINTERS, SCOTT, QC, CANADA.**

6 5 4 3 2 1

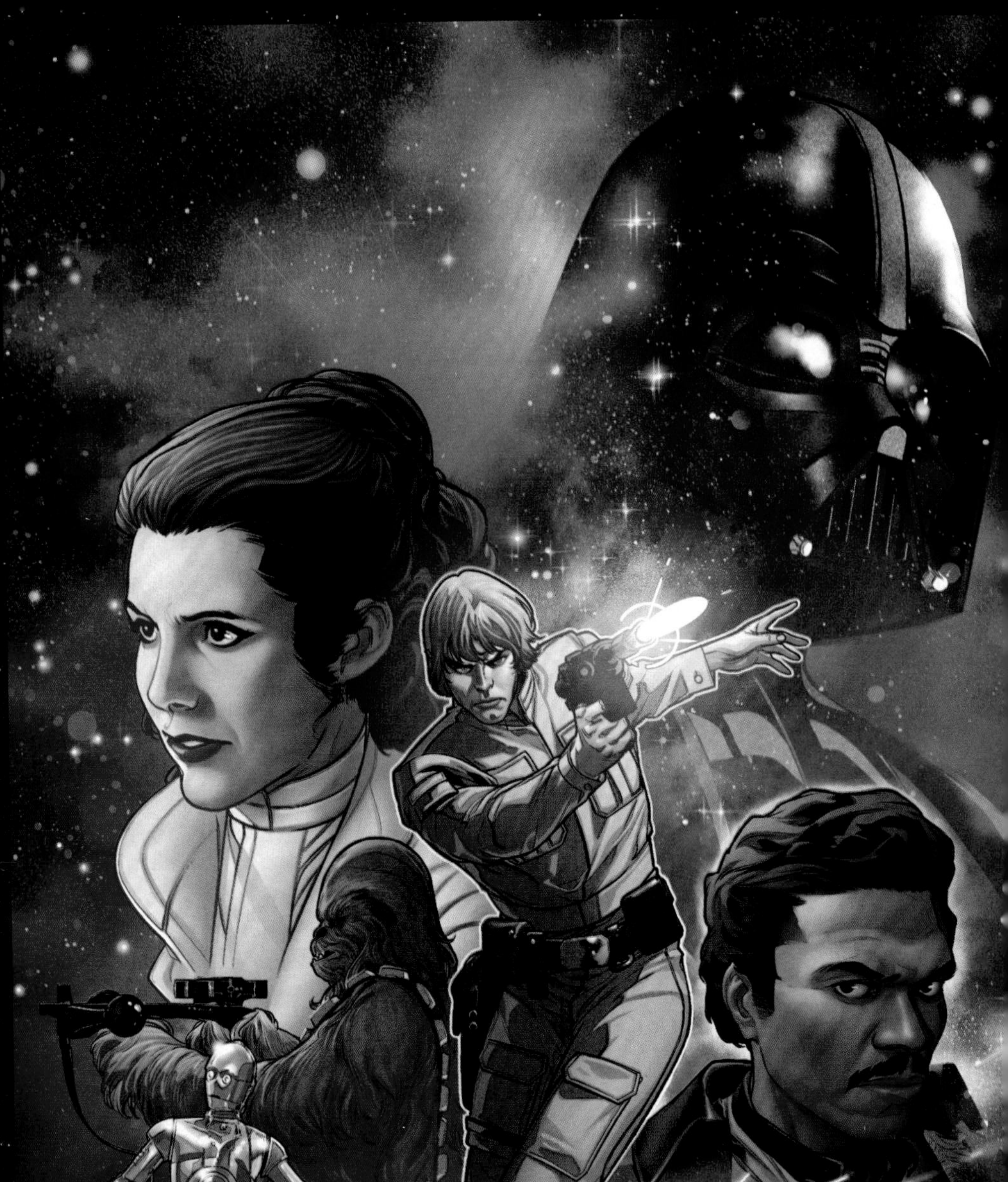

1

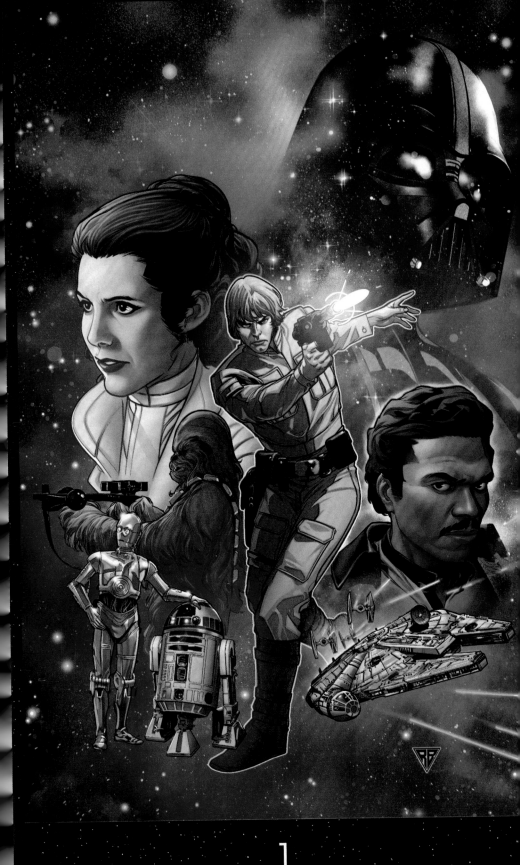

A long time ago in a galaxy far, far away....

AR
RS

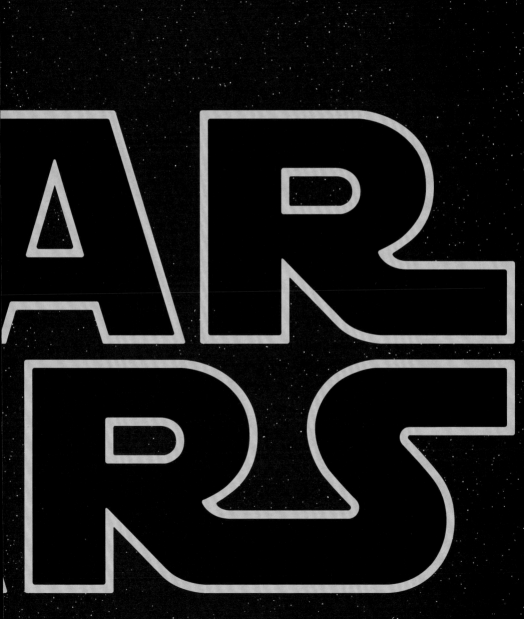

THE DESTINY PATH

The Rebel Alliance has been scattered following their defeat at Hoth. To evade the Empire, Han Solo, Princess Leia Organa, Chewbacca and C-3PO fled in the Millennium Falcon in hope of finding refuge with Han's old friend, Lando Calrissian.

But Darth Vader arrived at Cloud City first and forced Lando to take them prisoner as bait to lure Luke Skywalker into a trap. Leia managed to lead the others in a daring escape, though Han Solo was lost to Vader's bounty hunter.

And Luke now reels from his defeat at the hands of Darth Vader....

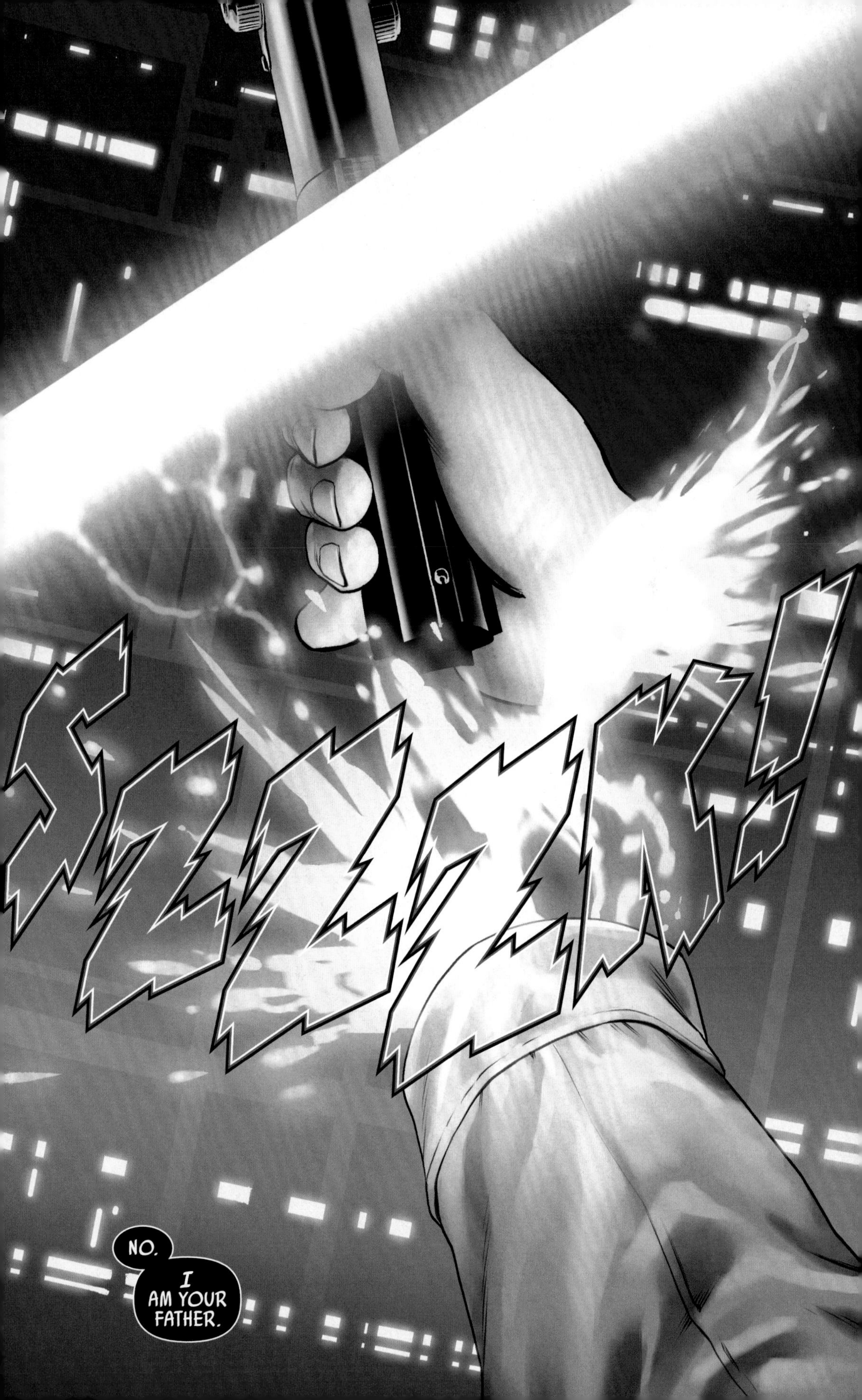
SZZZZN!
NO.
I AM YOUR FATHER.

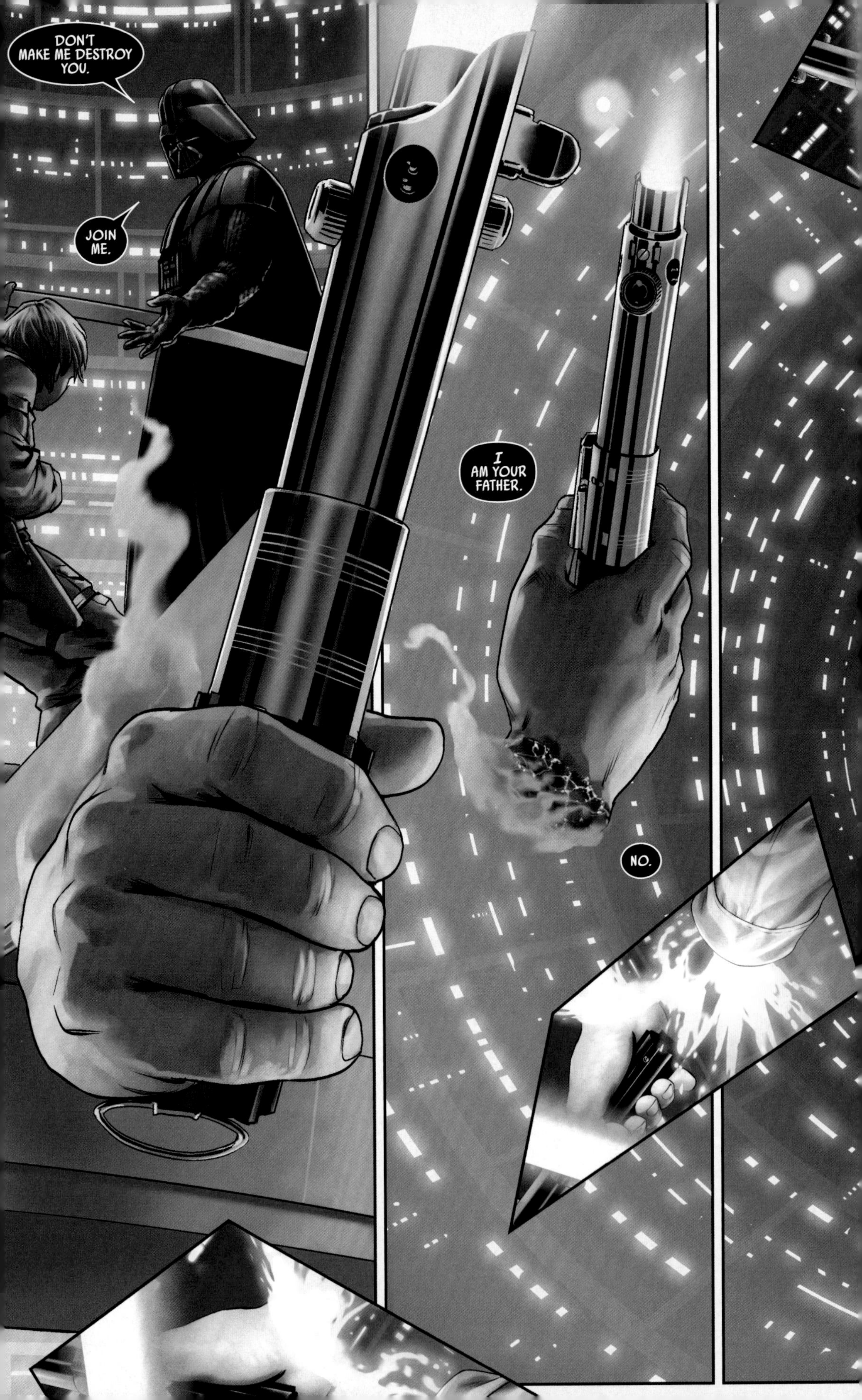
DON'T MAKE ME DESTROY YOU.
JOIN ME.
I AM YOUR FATHER.
NO.

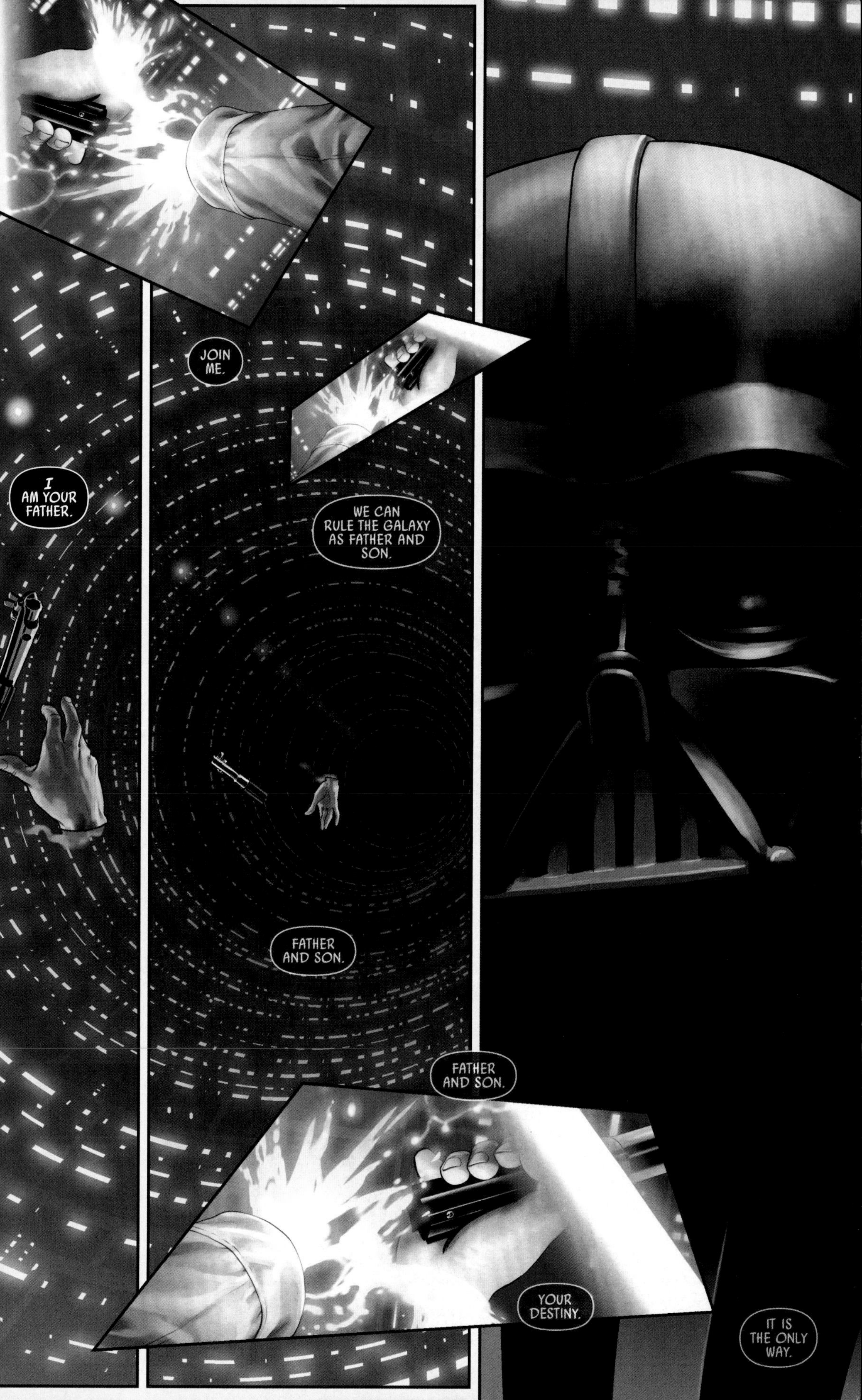
JOIN ME.
I AM YOUR FATHER.
WE CAN RULE THE GALAXY AS FATHER AND SON.
FATHER AND SON.
FATHER AND SON.
YOUR DESTINY.
IT IS THE ONLY WAY.

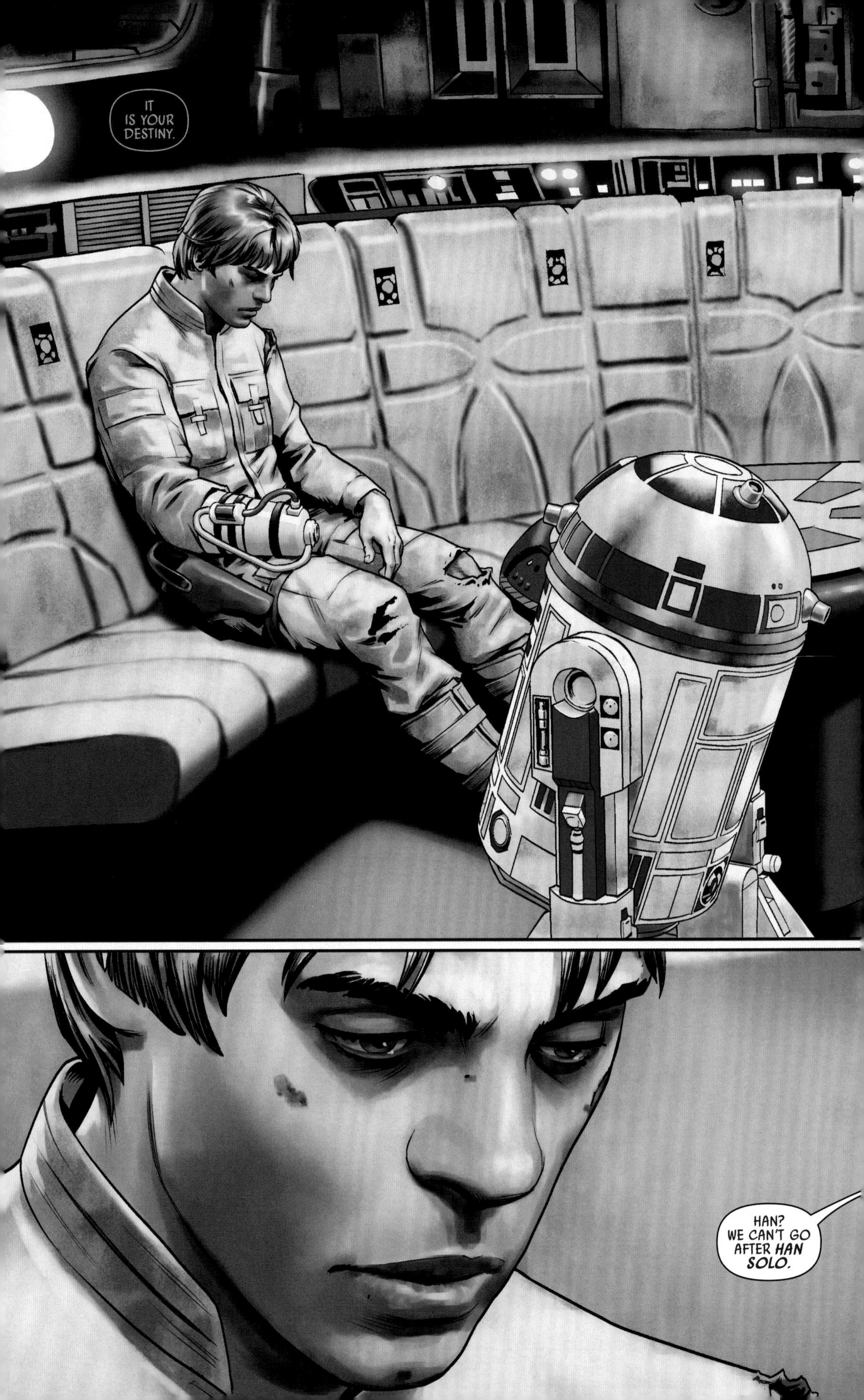
IT IS YOUR DESTINY.
HAN? WE CAN'T GO AFTER HAN SOLO.

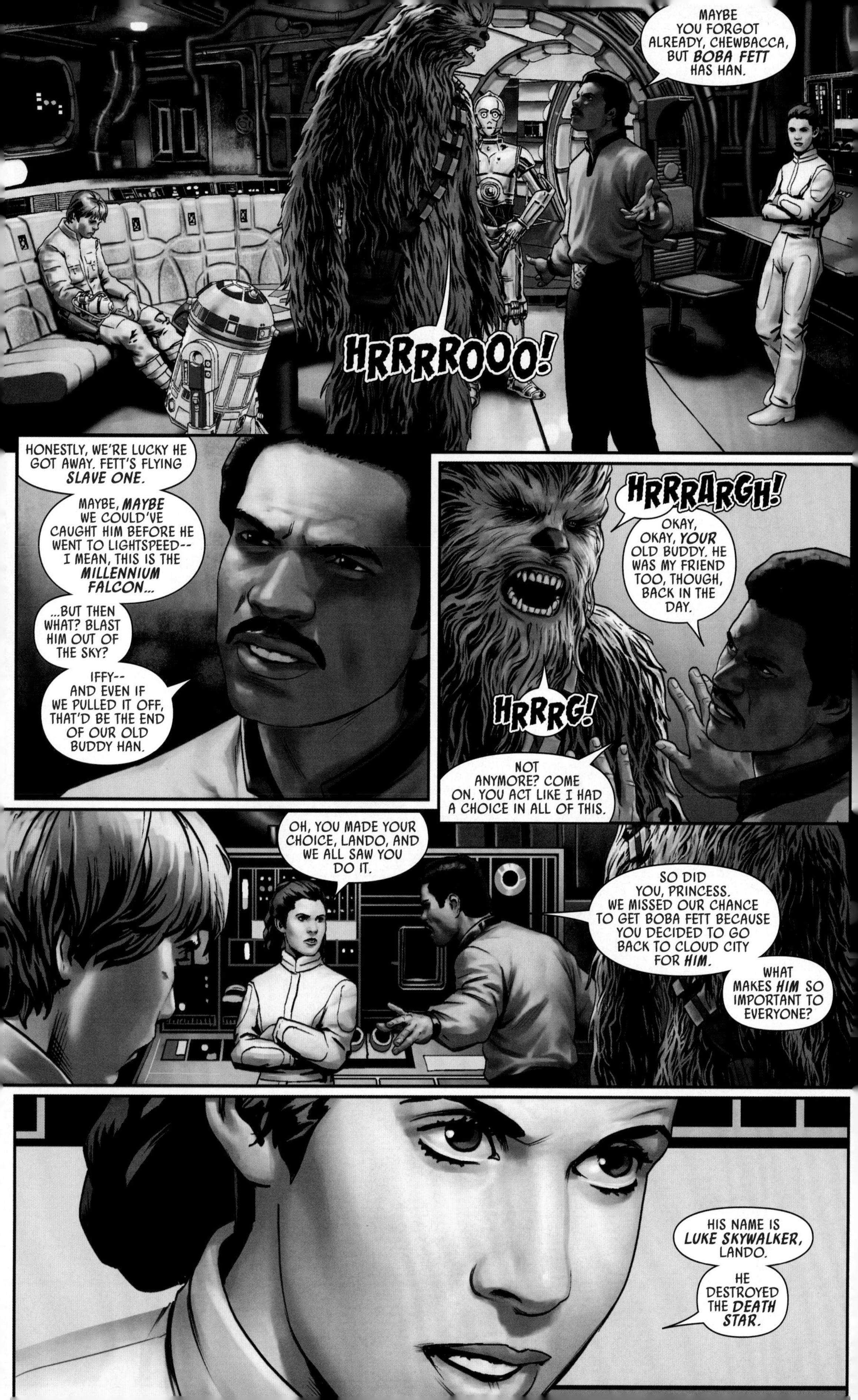
MAYBE YOU FORGOT ALREADY, CHEWBACCA, BUT BOBA FETT HAS HAN.
HRRRROOO!
HONESTLY, WE'RE LUCKY HE GOT AWAY. FETT'S FLYING SLAVE ONE.
MAYBE, MAYBE WE COULD'VE CAUGHT HIM BEFORE HE WENT TO LIGHTSPEED-- I MEAN, THIS IS THE MILLENNIUM FALCON...
...BUT THEN WHAT? BLAST HIM OUT OF THE SKY?
IFFY-- AND EVEN IF WE PULLED IT OFF, THAT'D BE THE END OF OUR OLD BUDDY HAN.
HRRRARGH!
OKAY, OKAY, YOUR OLD BUDDY. HE WAS MY FRIEND TOO, THOUGH, BACK IN THE DAY.
HRRRG!
NOT ANYMORE? COME ON. YOU ACT LIKE I HAD A CHOICE IN ALL OF THIS.
OH, YOU MADE YOUR CHOICE, LANDO, AND WE ALL SAW YOU DO IT.
SO DID YOU, PRINCESS. WE MISSED OUR CHANCE TO GET BOBA FETT BECAUSE YOU DECIDED TO GO BACK TO CLOUD CITY FOR HIM.
WHAT MAKES HIM SO IMPORTANT TO EVERYONE?
HIS NAME IS LUKE SKYWALKER, LANDO.
HE DESTROYED THE DEATH STAR.

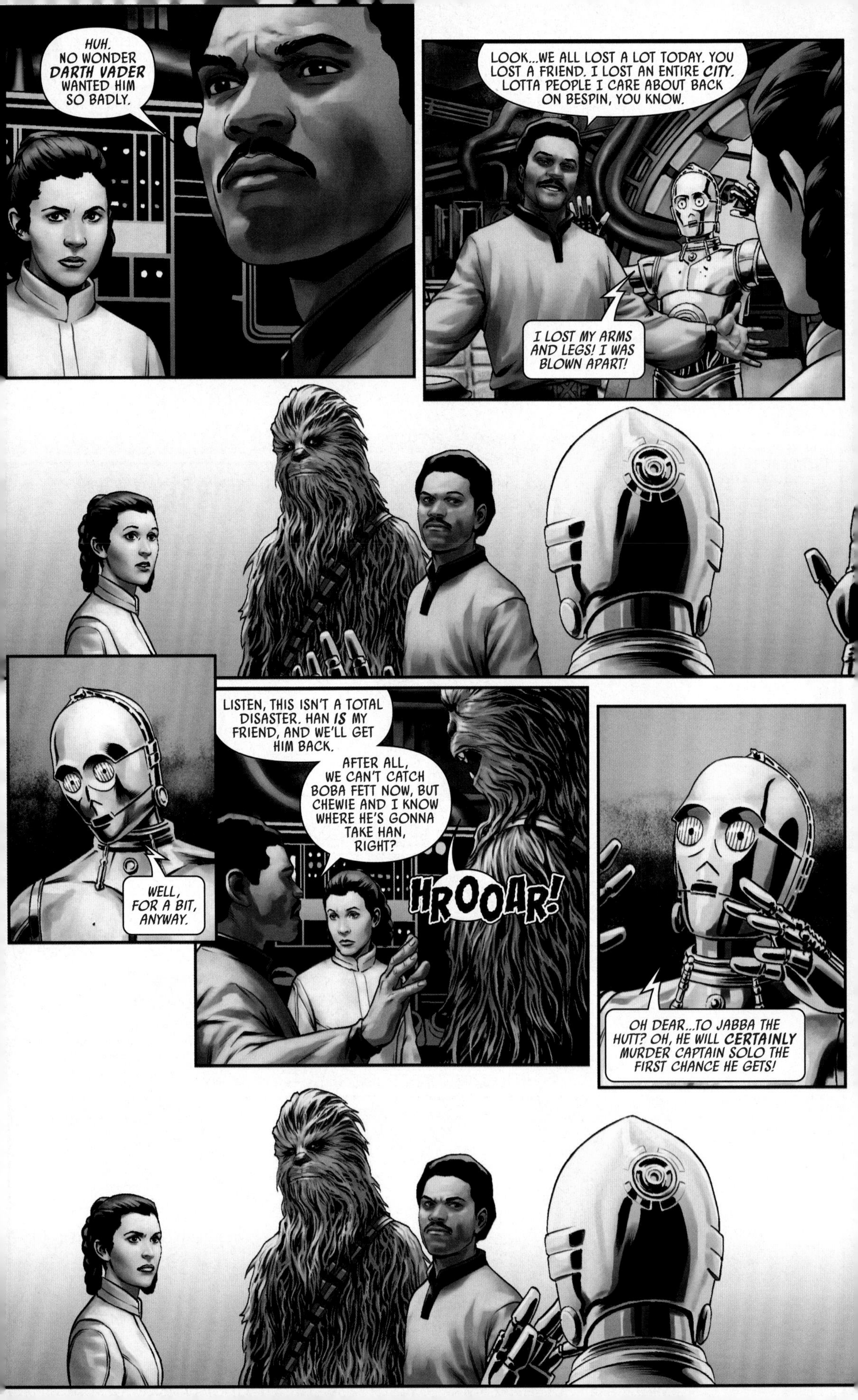
HUH. NO WONDER DARTH VADER WANTED HIM SO BADLY.
LOOK...WE ALL LOST A LOT TODAY. YOU LOST A FRIEND. I LOST AN ENTIRE CITY. LOTTA PEOPLE I CARE ABOUT BACK ON BESPIN, YOU KNOW.
I LOST MY ARMS AND LEGS! I WAS BLOWN APART!
WELL, FOR A BIT, ANYWAY.
LISTEN, THIS ISN'T A TOTAL DISASTER. HAN IS MY FRIEND, AND WE'LL GET HIM BACK.
AFTER ALL, WE CAN'T CATCH BOBA FETT NOW, BUT CHEWIE AND I KNOW WHERE HE'S GONNA TAKE HAN, RIGHT?
HROOAR!
OH DEAR...TO JABBA THE HUTT? OH, HE WILL CERTAINLY MURDER CAPTAIN SOLO THE FIRST CHANCE HE GETS!

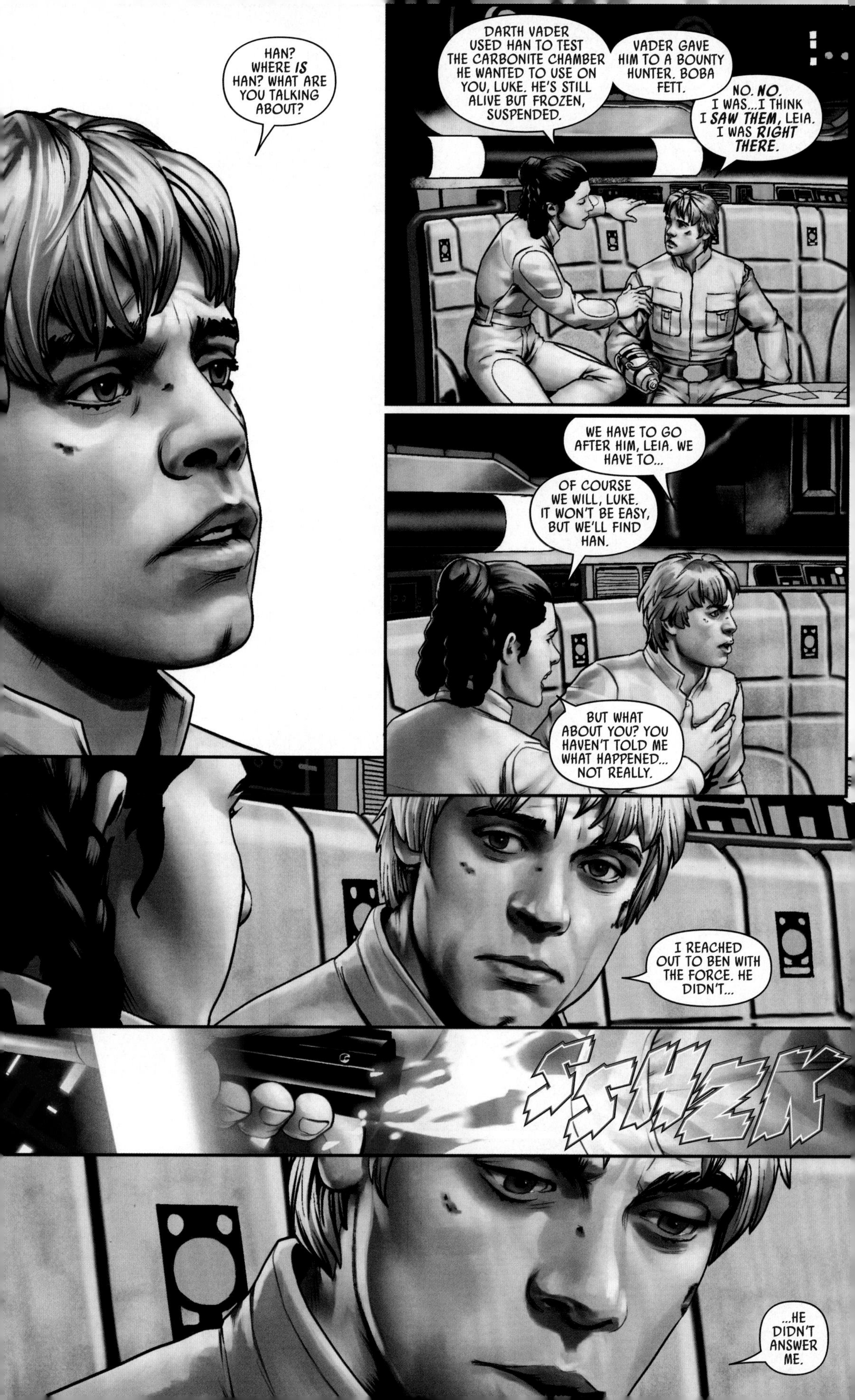
HAN? WHERE *IS* HAN? WHAT ARE YOU TALKING ABOUT?
DARTH VADER USED HAN TO TEST THE CARBONITE CHAMBER HE WANTED TO USE ON YOU, LUKE. HE'S STILL ALIVE BUT FROZEN, SUSPENDED.
VADER GAVE HIM TO A BOUNTY HUNTER. BOBA FETT.
NO. *NO.* I WAS...I THINK I *SAW THEM,* LEIA. I WAS *RIGHT THERE.*
WE HAVE TO GO AFTER HIM, LEIA. WE HAVE TO...
OF COURSE WE WILL, LUKE. IT WON'T BE EASY, BUT WE'LL FIND HAN.
BUT WHAT ABOUT YOU? YOU HAVEN'T TOLD ME WHAT HAPPENED... NOT REALLY.
I REACHED OUT TO BEN WITH THE FORCE. HE DIDN'T...
SSHZK
...HE DIDN'T ANSWER ME.

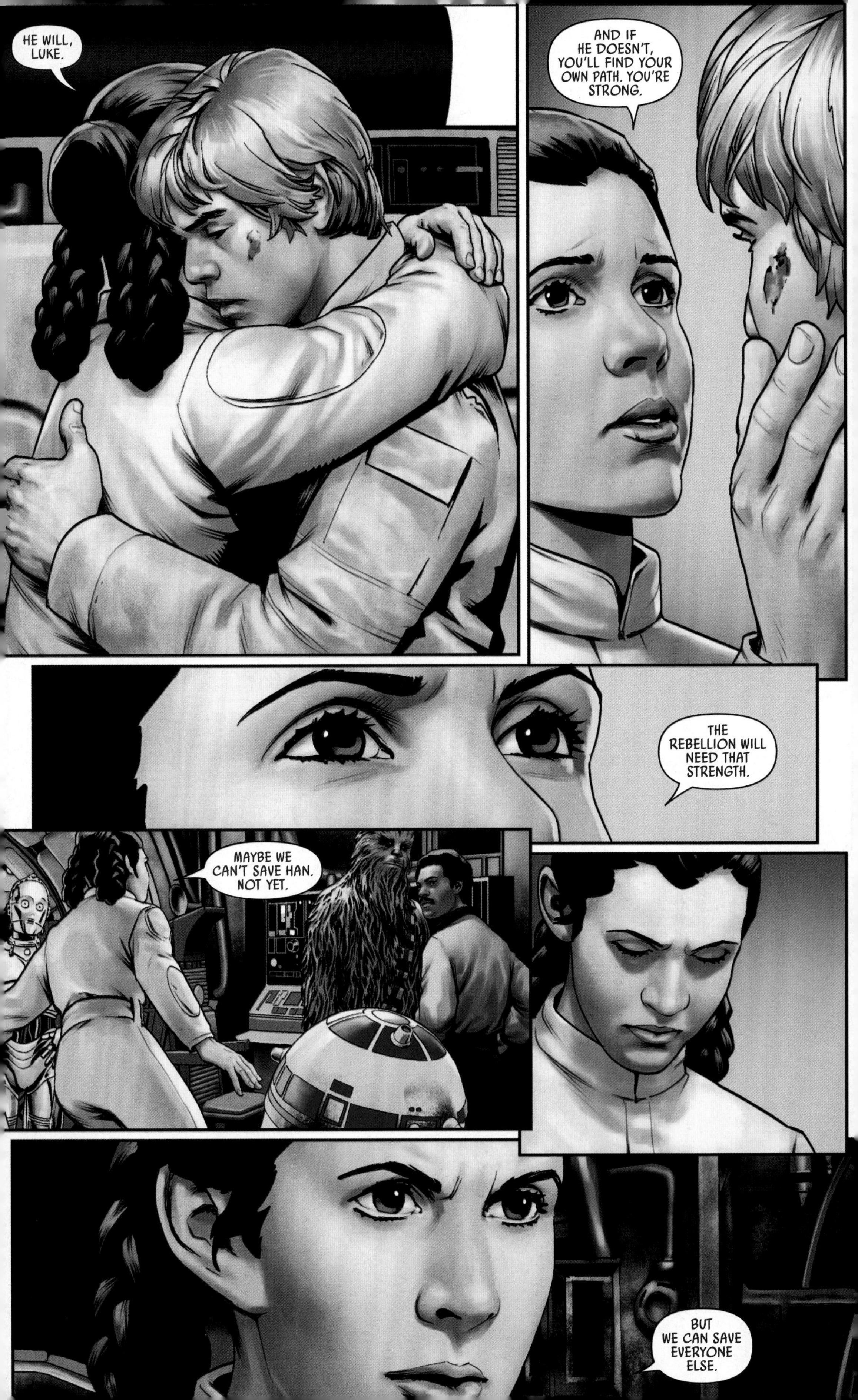
HE WILL, LUKE.
AND IF HE DOESN'T, YOU'LL FIND YOUR OWN PATH. YOU'RE STRONG.
THE REBELLION WILL NEED THAT STRENGTH.
MAYBE WE CAN'T SAVE HAN. NOT YET.
BUT WE CAN SAVE EVERYONE ELSE.

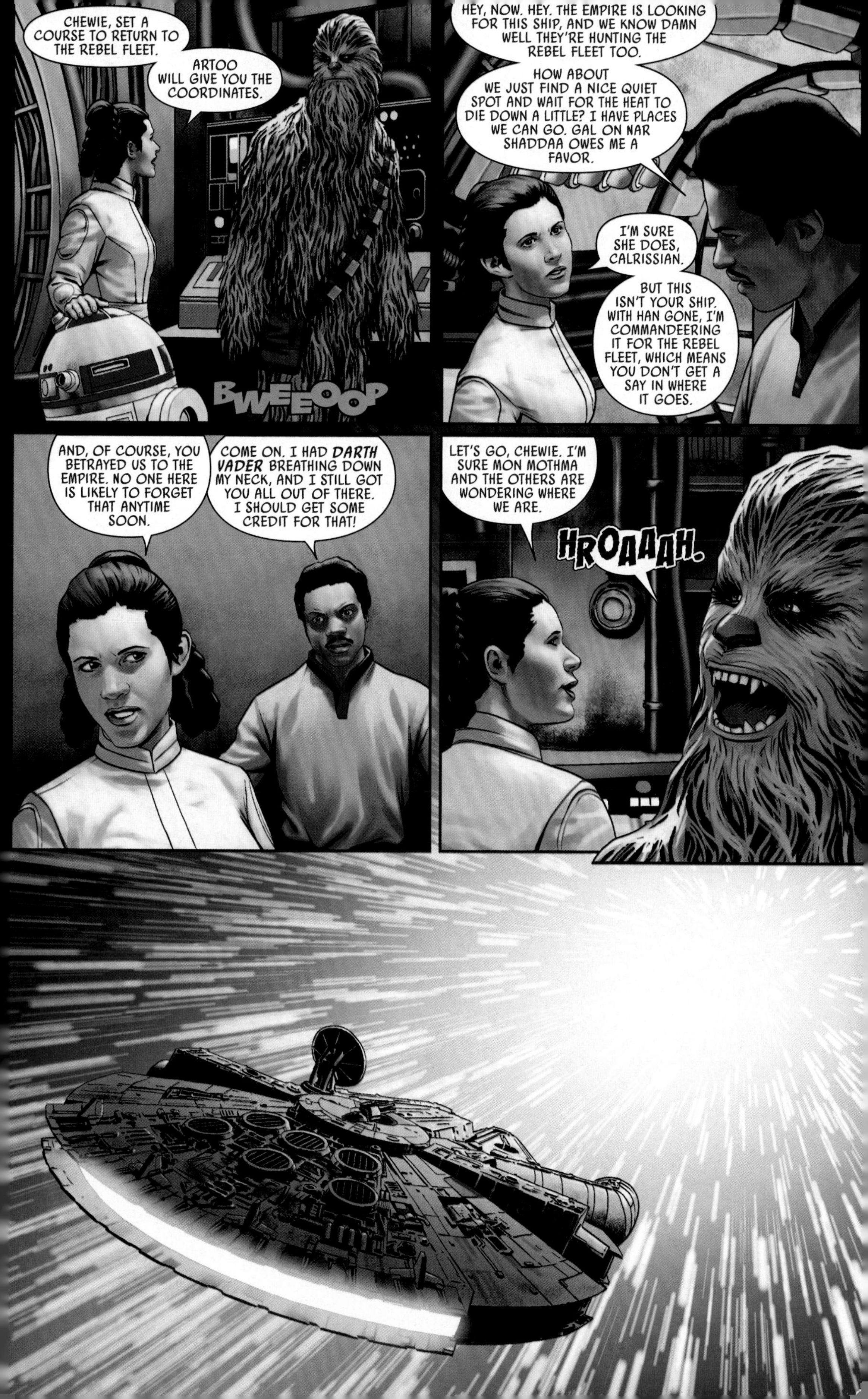
CHEWIE, SET A COURSE TO RETURN TO THE REBEL FLEET.
ARTOO WILL GIVE YOU THE COORDINATES.
BWEEOOP
HEY, NOW. HEY. THE EMPIRE IS LOOKING FOR THIS SHIP, AND WE KNOW DAMN WELL THEY'RE HUNTING THE REBEL FLEET TOO.
HOW ABOUT WE JUST FIND A NICE QUIET SPOT AND WAIT FOR THE HEAT TO DIE DOWN A LITTLE? I HAVE PLACES WE CAN GO. GAL ON NAR SHADDAA OWES ME A FAVOR.
I'M SURE SHE DOES, CALRISSIAN.
BUT THIS ISN'T YOUR SHIP. WITH HAN GONE, I'M COMMANDEERING IT FOR THE REBEL FLEET, WHICH MEANS YOU DON'T GET A SAY IN WHERE IT GOES.
AND, OF COURSE, YOU BETRAYED US TO THE EMPIRE. NO ONE HERE IS LIKELY TO FORGET THAT ANYTIME SOON.
COME ON. I HAD *DARTH VADER* BREATHING DOWN MY NECK, AND I STILL GOT YOU ALL OUT OF THERE. I SHOULD GET SOME CREDIT FOR THAT!
LET'S GO, CHEWIE. I'M SURE MON MOTHMA AND THE OTHERS ARE WONDERING WHERE WE ARE.
HROAAAH.

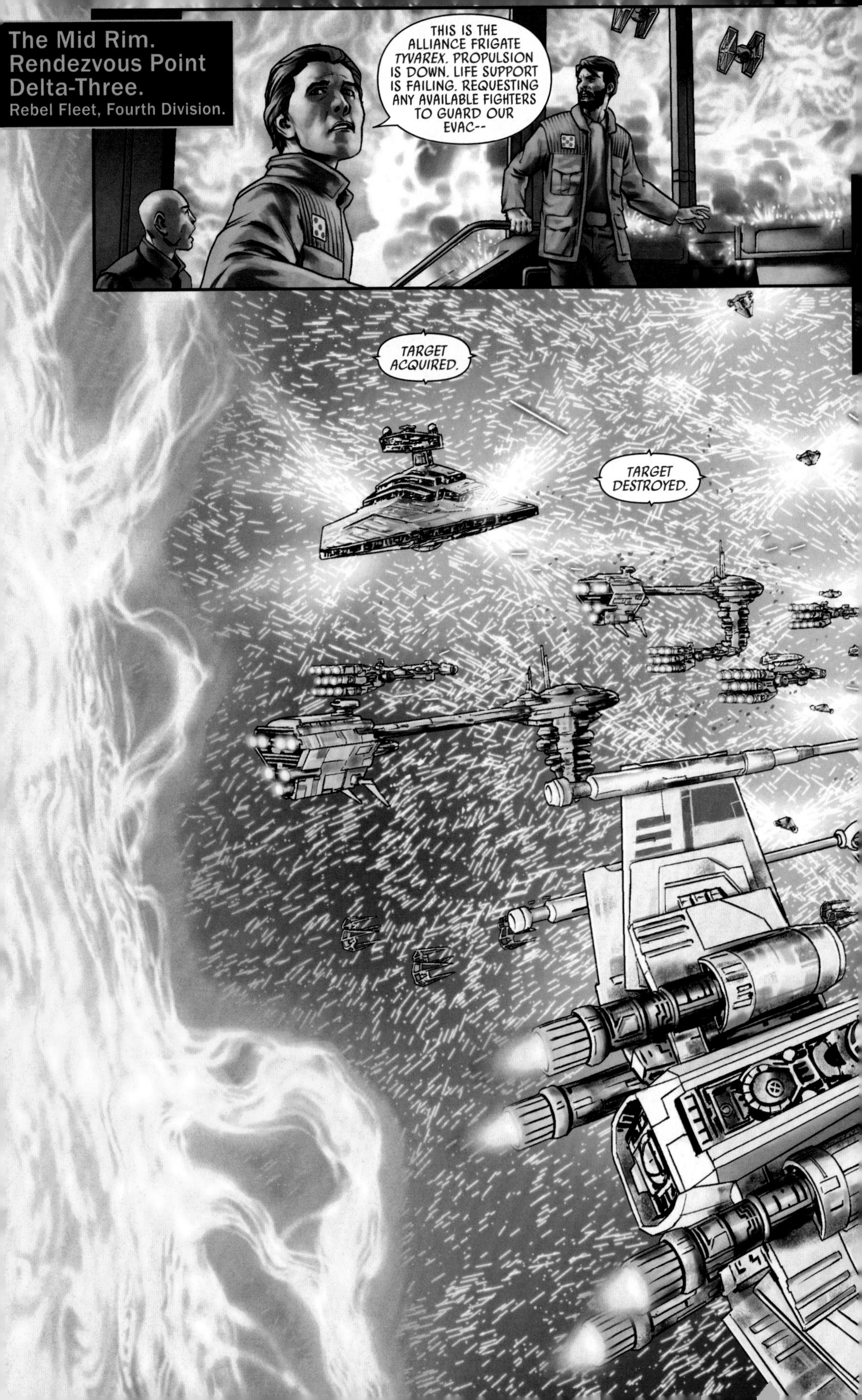

The Mid Rim.
Rendezvous Point
Delta-Three.
Rebel Fleet, Fourth Division.
THIS IS THE ALLIANCE FRIGATE *TYVAREX*. PROPULSION IS DOWN. LIFE SUPPORT IS FAILING. REQUESTING ANY AVAILABLE FIGHTERS TO GUARD OUR EVAC--
TARGET ACQUIRED.
TARGET DESTROYED.

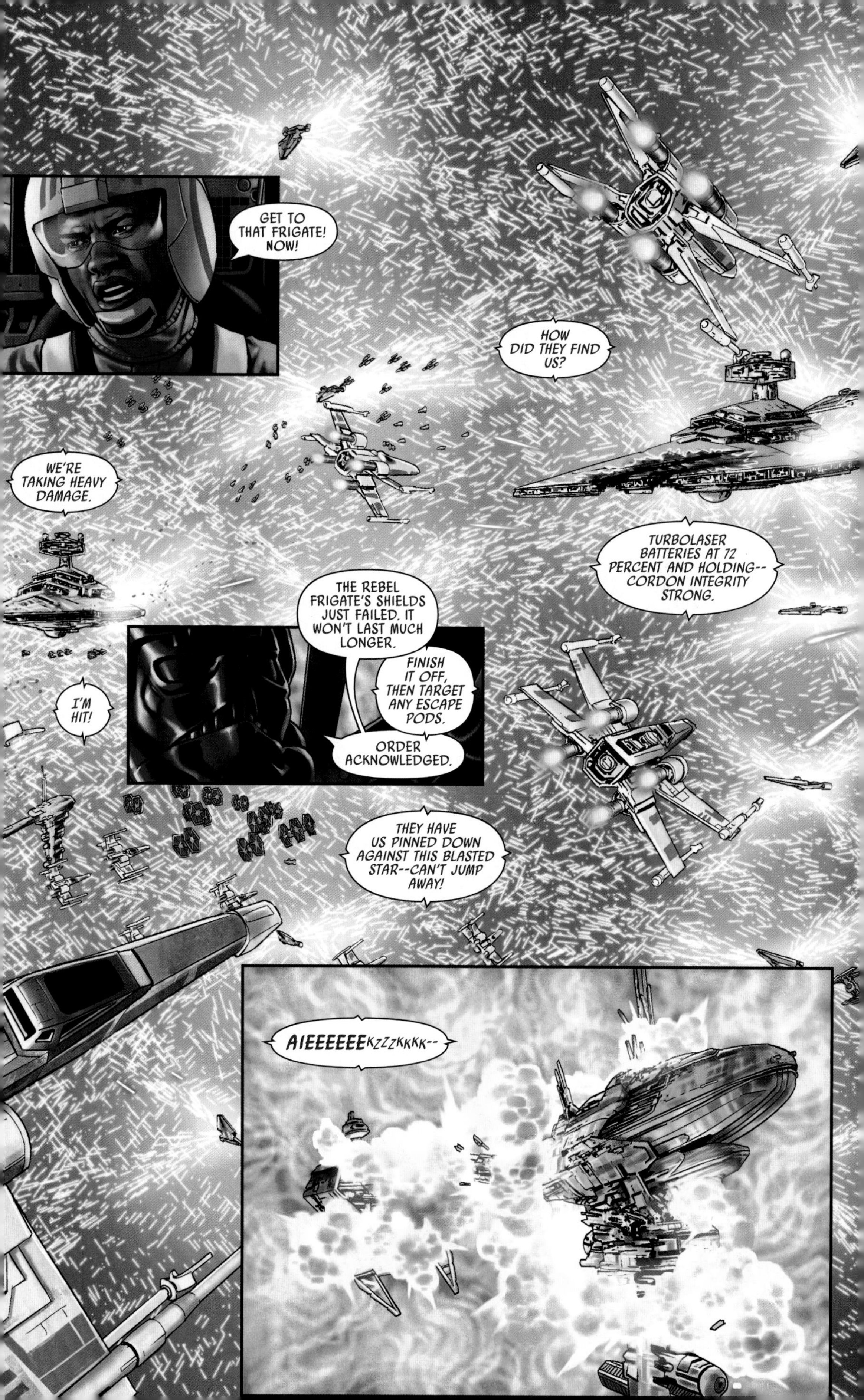
GET TO THAT FRIGATE! NOW!
HOW DID THEY FIND US?
WE'RE TAKING HEAVY DAMAGE.
TURBOLASER BATTERIES AT 72 PERCENT AND HOLDING-- CORDON INTEGRITY STRONG.
THE REBEL FRIGATE'S SHIELDS JUST FAILED. IT WON'T LAST MUCH LONGER.
FINISH IT OFF, THEN TARGET ANY ESCAPE PODS.
ORDER ACKNOWLEDGED.
I'M HIT!
THEY HAVE US PINNED DOWN AGAINST THIS BLASTED STAR--CAN'T JUMP AWAY!
AIEEEEEEKZZZKKKK--

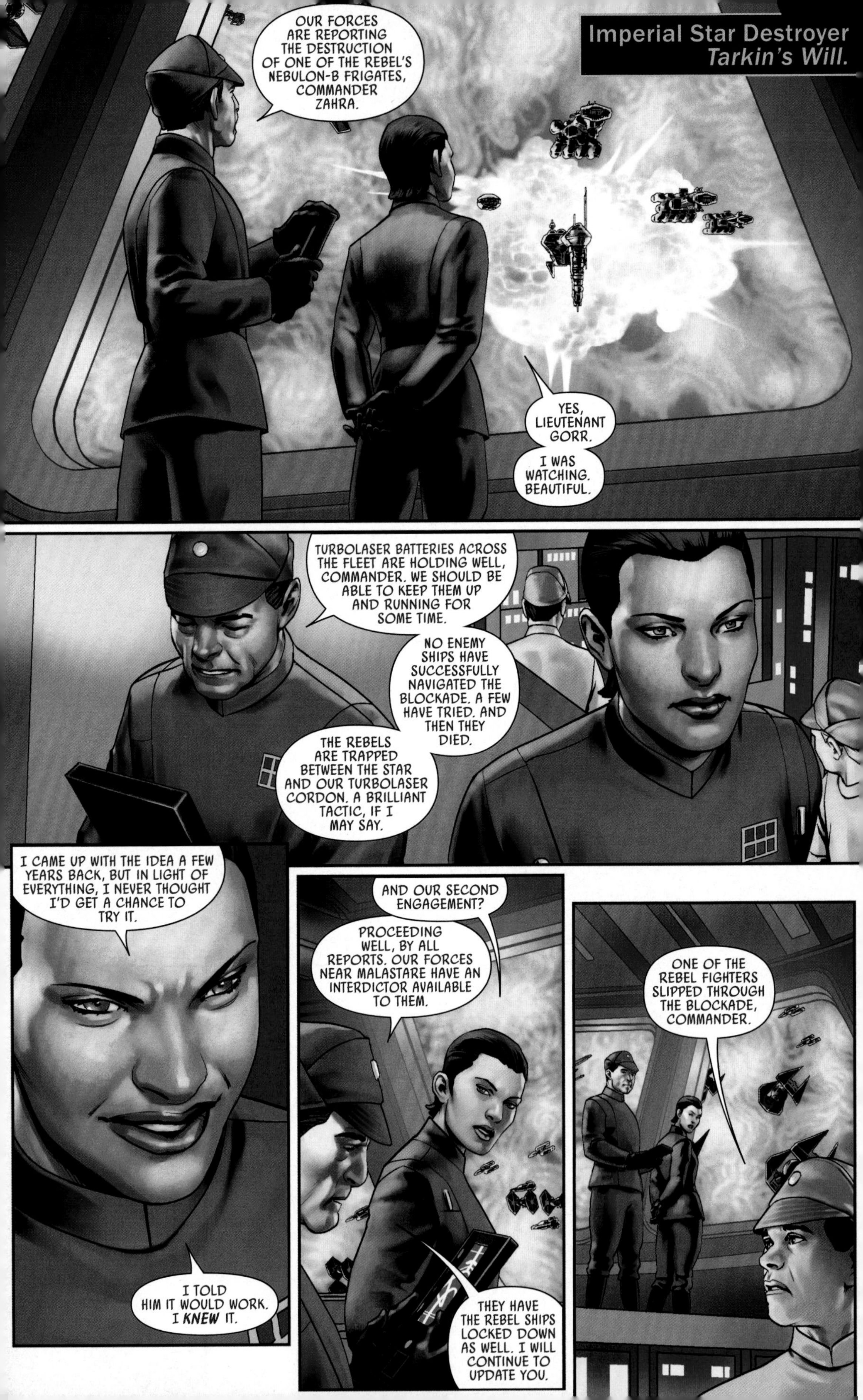
Imperial Star Destroyer Tarkin's Will.
OUR FORCES ARE REPORTING THE DESTRUCTION OF ONE OF THE REBEL'S NEBULON-B FRIGATES, COMMANDER ZAHRA.
YES, LIEUTENANT GORR.
I WAS WATCHING. BEAUTIFUL.
TURBOLASER BATTERIES ACROSS THE FLEET ARE HOLDING WELL, COMMANDER. WE SHOULD BE ABLE TO KEEP THEM UP AND RUNNING FOR SOME TIME.
NO ENEMY SHIPS HAVE SUCCESSFULLY NAVIGATED THE BLOCKADE. A FEW HAVE TRIED. AND THEN THEY DIED.
THE REBELS ARE TRAPPED BETWEEN THE STAR AND OUR TURBOLASER CORDON. A BRILLIANT TACTIC, IF I MAY SAY.
I CAME UP WITH THE IDEA A FEW YEARS BACK, BUT IN LIGHT OF EVERYTHING, I NEVER THOUGHT I'D GET A CHANCE TO TRY IT.
I TOLD HIM IT WOULD WORK. I *KNEW* IT.
AND OUR SECOND ENGAGEMENT?
PROCEEDING WELL, BY ALL REPORTS. OUR FORCES NEAR MALASTARE HAVE AN INTERDICTOR AVAILABLE TO THEM.
THEY HAVE THE REBEL SHIPS LOCKED DOWN AS WELL. I WILL CONTINUE TO UPDATE YOU.
ONE OF THE REBEL FIGHTERS SLIPPED THROUGH THE BLOCKADE, COMMANDER.

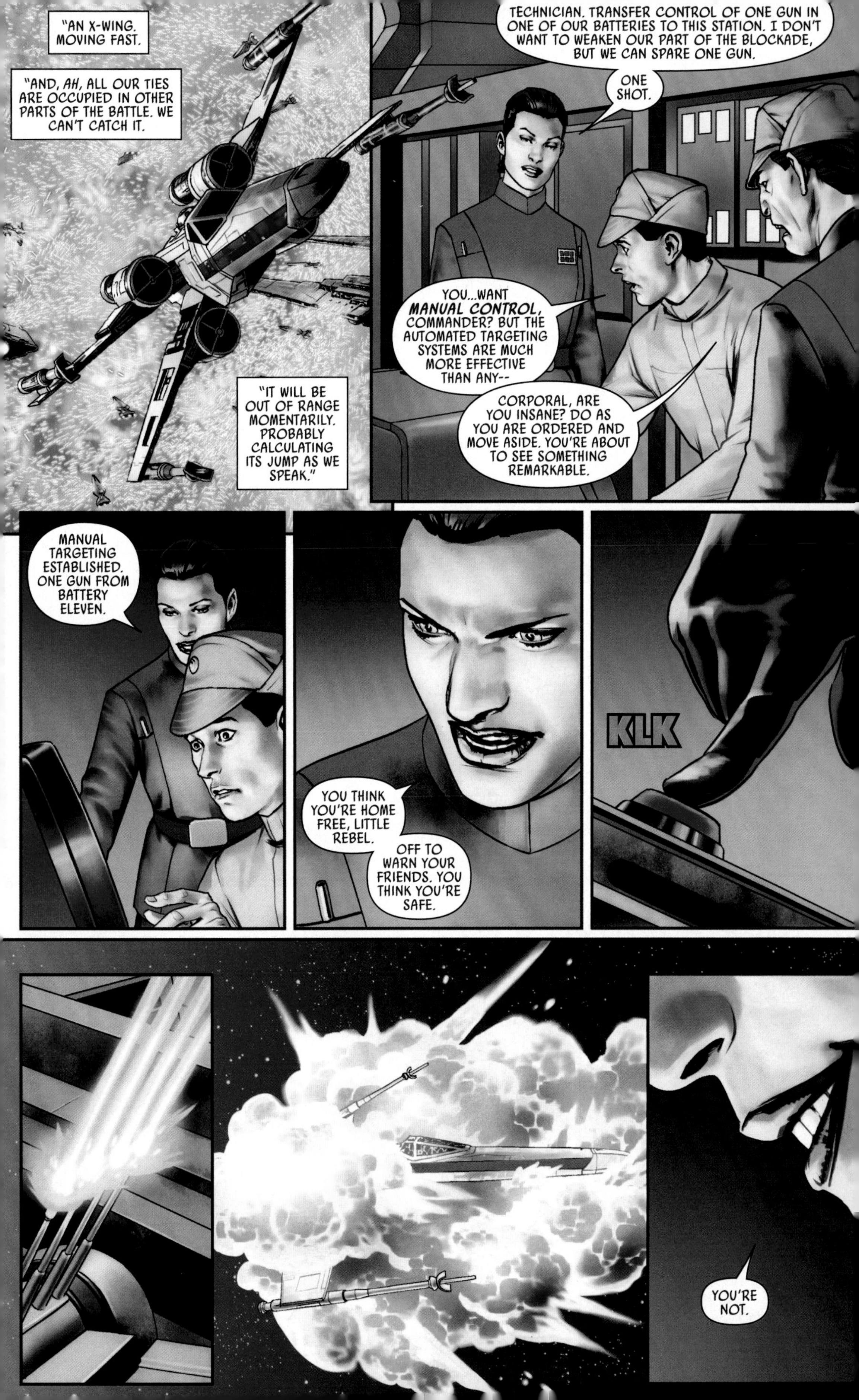
"AN X-WING. MOVING FAST.
"AND, AH, ALL OUR TIES ARE OCCUPIED IN OTHER PARTS OF THE BATTLE. WE CAN'T CATCH IT.
"IT WILL BE OUT OF RANGE MOMENTARILY. PROBABLY CALCULATING ITS JUMP AS WE SPEAK."
TECHNICIAN. TRANSFER CONTROL OF ONE GUN IN ONE OF OUR BATTERIES TO THIS STATION. I DON'T WANT TO WEAKEN OUR PART OF THE BLOCKADE, BUT WE CAN SPARE ONE GUN.
ONE SHOT.
YOU...WANT MANUAL CONTROL, COMMANDER? BUT THE AUTOMATED TARGETING SYSTEMS ARE MUCH MORE EFFECTIVE THAN ANY--
CORPORAL, ARE YOU INSANE? DO AS YOU ARE ORDERED AND MOVE ASIDE. YOU'RE ABOUT TO SEE SOMETHING REMARKABLE.
MANUAL TARGETING ESTABLISHED. ONE GUN FROM BATTERY ELEVEN.
YOU THINK YOU'RE HOME FREE, LITTLE REBEL.
OFF TO WARN YOUR FRIENDS. YOU THINK YOU'RE SAFE.
KLK
YOU'RE NOT.

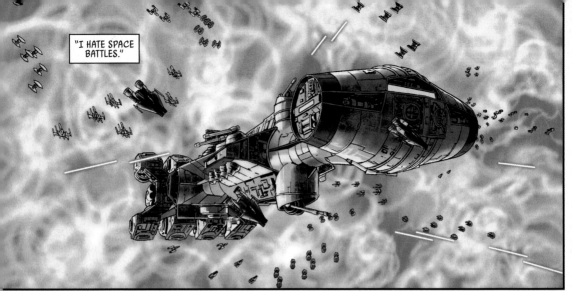

"I HATE SPACE BATTLES."

I MEAN, WE'RE *SOLDIERS*. PATHFINDERS. WE'RE USELESS UNLESS THE SHIP GETS BOARDED. ALL WE CAN DO IS WAIT TO SEE IF WE BLOW UP.

YOU'RE CRAZY, NEEDLE. THAT'S EXACTLY WHY I LOVE 'EM.

WE DON'T HAVE TO DO ANYTHING. SPACE BATTLES ARE THE ONLY TIME I GET TO RELAX.

SAY, FRELL, WHAT'S WITH DAMERON?

OH--HE'S WATCHING THE A-WINGS. WATCHING *ONE* A-WING, MORE LIKE.

OH *REALLY?* WHICH ONE?

GREEN THREE.

GREEN THREE? THAT'S...

SHARA BEY. ALSO KNOWN AS MY WIFE AND MY SON'S MOTHER.

CAN YOU GUYS SHUT UP? I'M TRYING TO FOCUS. THINGS ARE...MOVING PRETTY FAST OUT THERE.

ALL RIGHT, FINE. WAKE ME UP IF WE GET BOARDED.

OR IF THE SHIP BLOWS UP. WHICHEVER, REALLY.

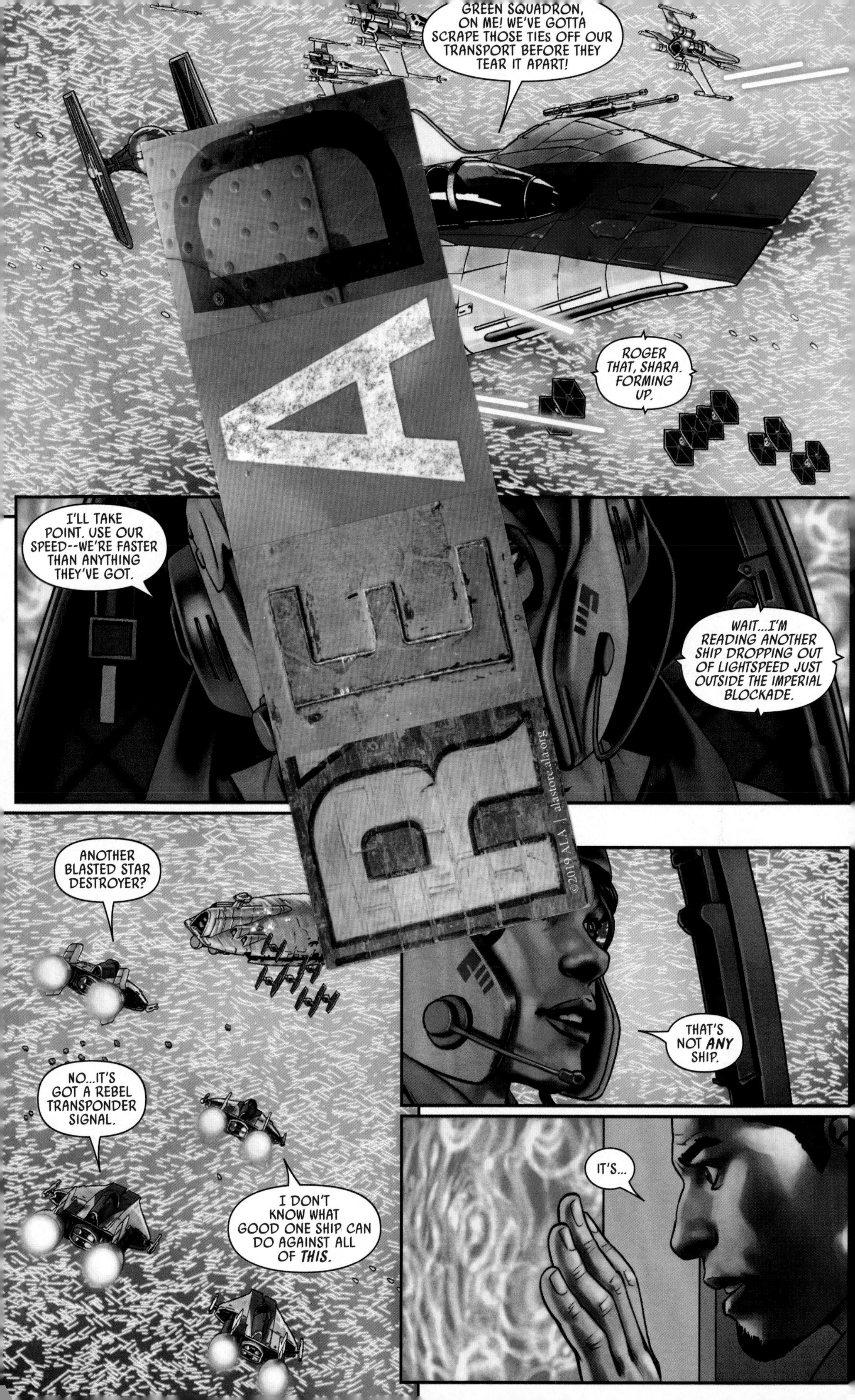
GREEN SQUADRON, ON ME! WE'VE GOTTA SCRAPE THOSE TIES OFF OUR TRANSPORT BEFORE THEY TEAR IT APART!
ROGER THAT, SHARA. FORMING UP.
I'LL TAKE POINT. USE OUR SPEED--WE'RE FASTER THAN ANYTHING THEY'VE GOT.
WAIT...I'M READING ANOTHER SHIP DROPPING OUT OF LIGHTSPEED JUST OUTSIDE THE IMPERIAL BLOCKADE.
ANOTHER BLASTED STAR DESTROYER?
THAT'S NOT *ANY* SHIP.
NO...IT'S GOT A REBEL TRANSPONDER SIGNAL.
I DON'T KNOW WHAT GOOD ONE SHIP CAN DO AGAINST ALL OF *THIS*.
IT'S...

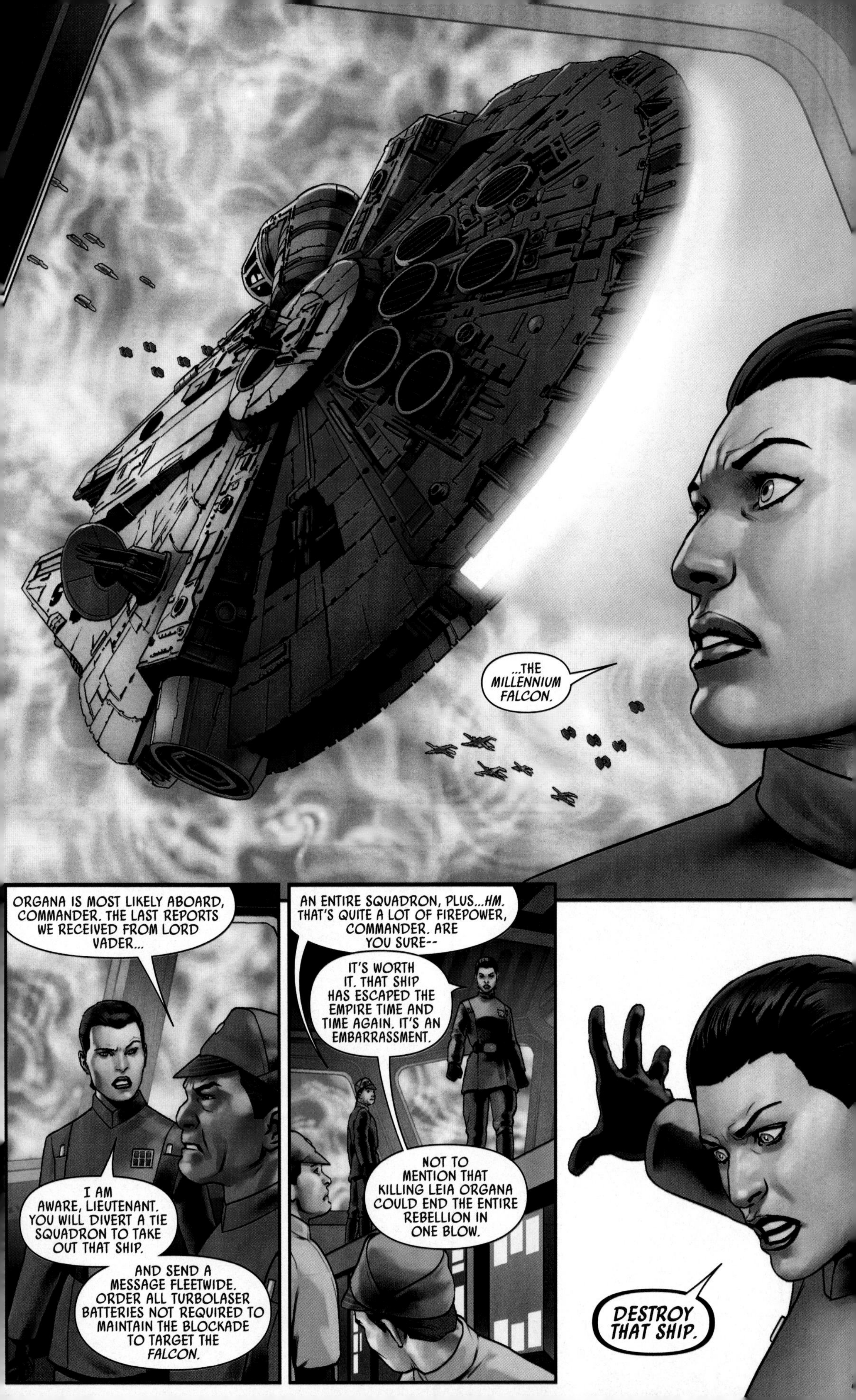
...THE MILLENNIUM FALCON.
ORGANA IS MOST LIKELY ABOARD, COMMANDER. THE LAST REPORTS WE RECEIVED FROM LORD VADER...
I AM AWARE, LIEUTENANT. YOU WILL DIVERT A TIE SQUADRON TO TAKE OUT THAT SHIP.
AND SEND A MESSAGE FLEETWIDE. ORDER ALL TURBOLASER BATTERIES NOT REQUIRED TO MAINTAIN THE BLOCKADE TO TARGET THE *FALCON.*
AN ENTIRE SQUADRON, PLUS...*HM.* THAT'S QUITE A LOT OF FIREPOWER, COMMANDER. ARE YOU SURE--
IT'S WORTH IT. THAT SHIP HAS ESCAPED THE EMPIRE TIME AND TIME AGAIN. IT'S AN EMBARRASSMENT.
NOT TO MENTION THAT KILLING LEIA ORGANA COULD END THE ENTIRE REBELLION IN ONE BLOW.
DESTROY THAT SHIP.

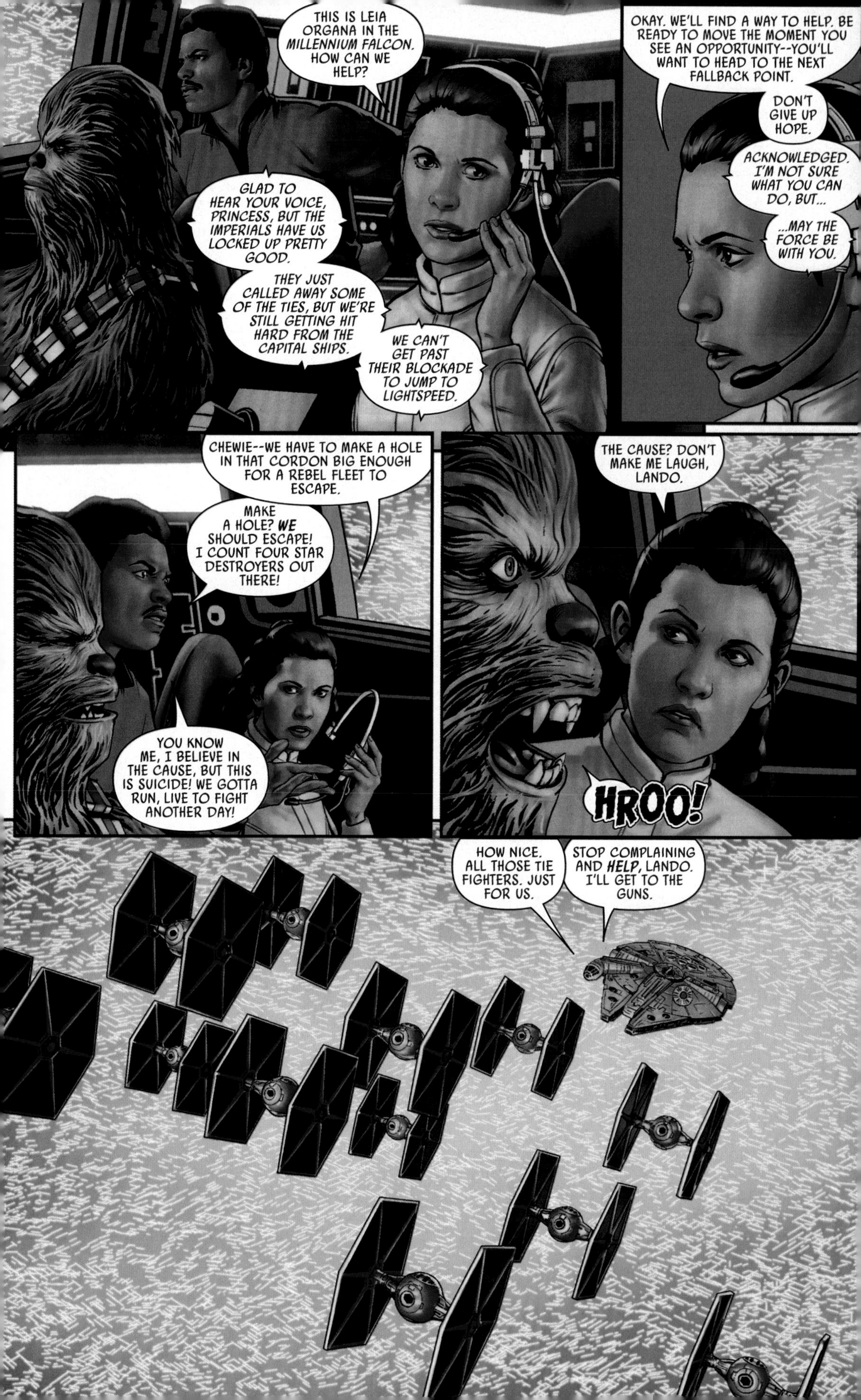
THIS IS LEIA ORGANA IN THE MILLENNIUM FALCON. HOW CAN WE HELP?
GLAD TO HEAR YOUR VOICE, PRINCESS, BUT THE IMPERIALS HAVE US LOCKED UP PRETTY GOOD.
THEY JUST CALLED AWAY SOME OF THE TIES, BUT WE'RE STILL GETTING HIT HARD FROM THE CAPITAL SHIPS.
WE CAN'T GET PAST THEIR BLOCKADE TO JUMP TO LIGHTSPEED.
OKAY. WE'LL FIND A WAY TO HELP. BE READY TO MOVE THE MOMENT YOU SEE AN OPPORTUNITY--YOU'LL WANT TO HEAD TO THE NEXT FALLBACK POINT.
DON'T GIVE UP HOPE.
ACKNOWLEDGED. I'M NOT SURE WHAT YOU CAN DO, BUT...
...MAY THE FORCE BE WITH YOU.
CHEWIE--WE HAVE TO MAKE A HOLE IN THAT CORDON BIG ENOUGH FOR A REBEL FLEET TO ESCAPE.
MAKE A HOLE? WE SHOULD ESCAPE! I COUNT FOUR STAR DESTROYERS OUT THERE!
YOU KNOW ME, I BELIEVE IN THE CAUSE, BUT THIS IS SUICIDE! WE GOTTA RUN, LIVE TO FIGHT ANOTHER DAY!
THE CAUSE? DON'T MAKE ME LAUGH, LANDO.
HROO!
HOW NICE. ALL THOSE TIE FIGHTERS. JUST FOR US.
STOP COMPLAINING AND HELP, LANDO. I'LL GET TO THE GUNS.

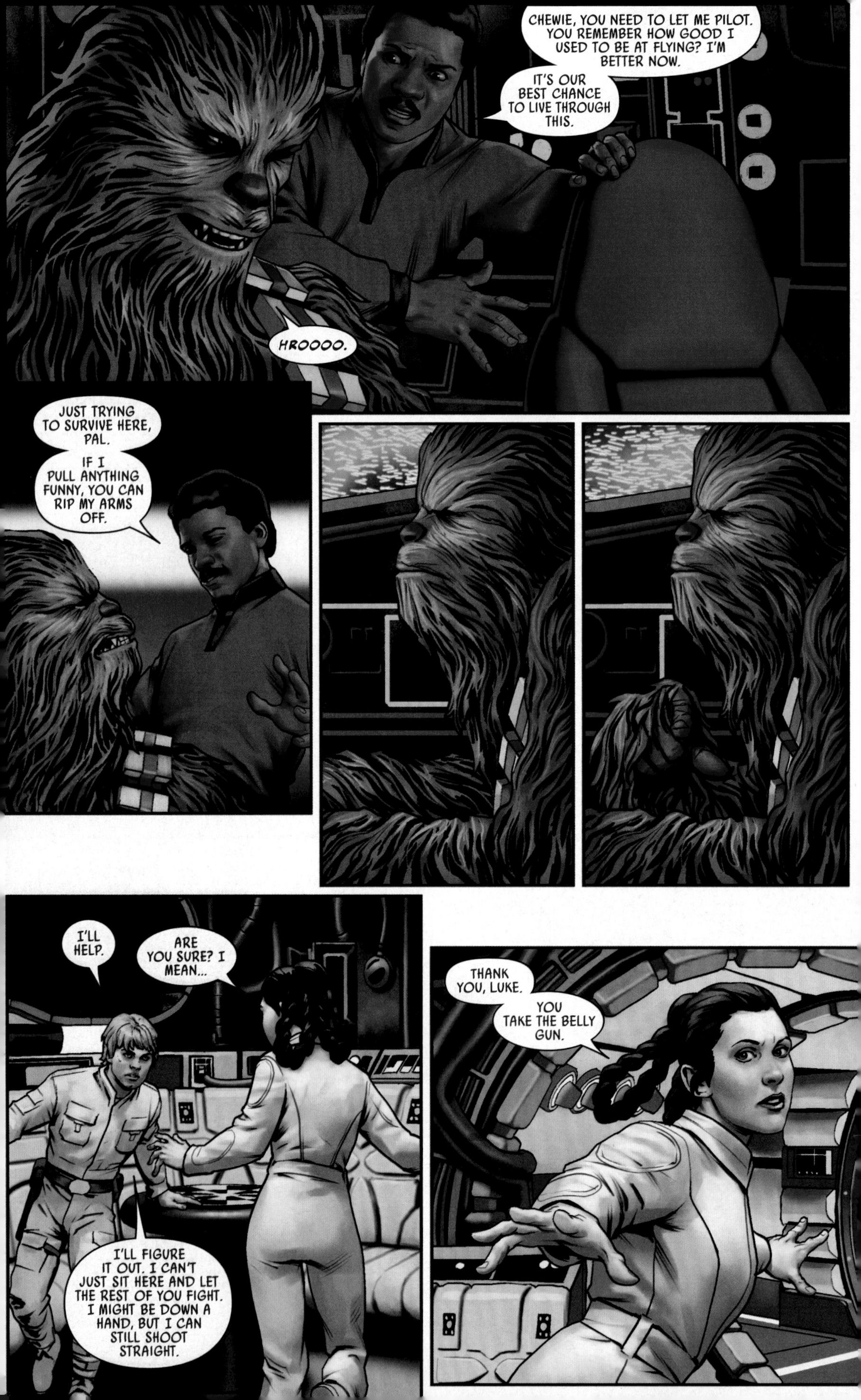
CHEWIE, YOU NEED TO LET ME PILOT. YOU REMEMBER HOW GOOD I USED TO BE AT FLYING? I'M BETTER NOW.
IT'S OUR BEST CHANCE TO LIVE THROUGH THIS.
HROOOO.
JUST TRYING TO SURVIVE HERE, PAL.
IF I PULL ANYTHING FUNNY, YOU CAN RIP MY ARMS OFF.
I'LL HELP.
ARE YOU SURE? I MEAN...
I'LL FIGURE IT OUT. I CAN'T JUST SIT HERE AND LET THE REST OF YOU FIGHT. I MIGHT BE DOWN A HAND, BUT I CAN STILL SHOOT STRAIGHT.
THANK YOU, LUKE.
YOU TAKE THE BELLY GUN.

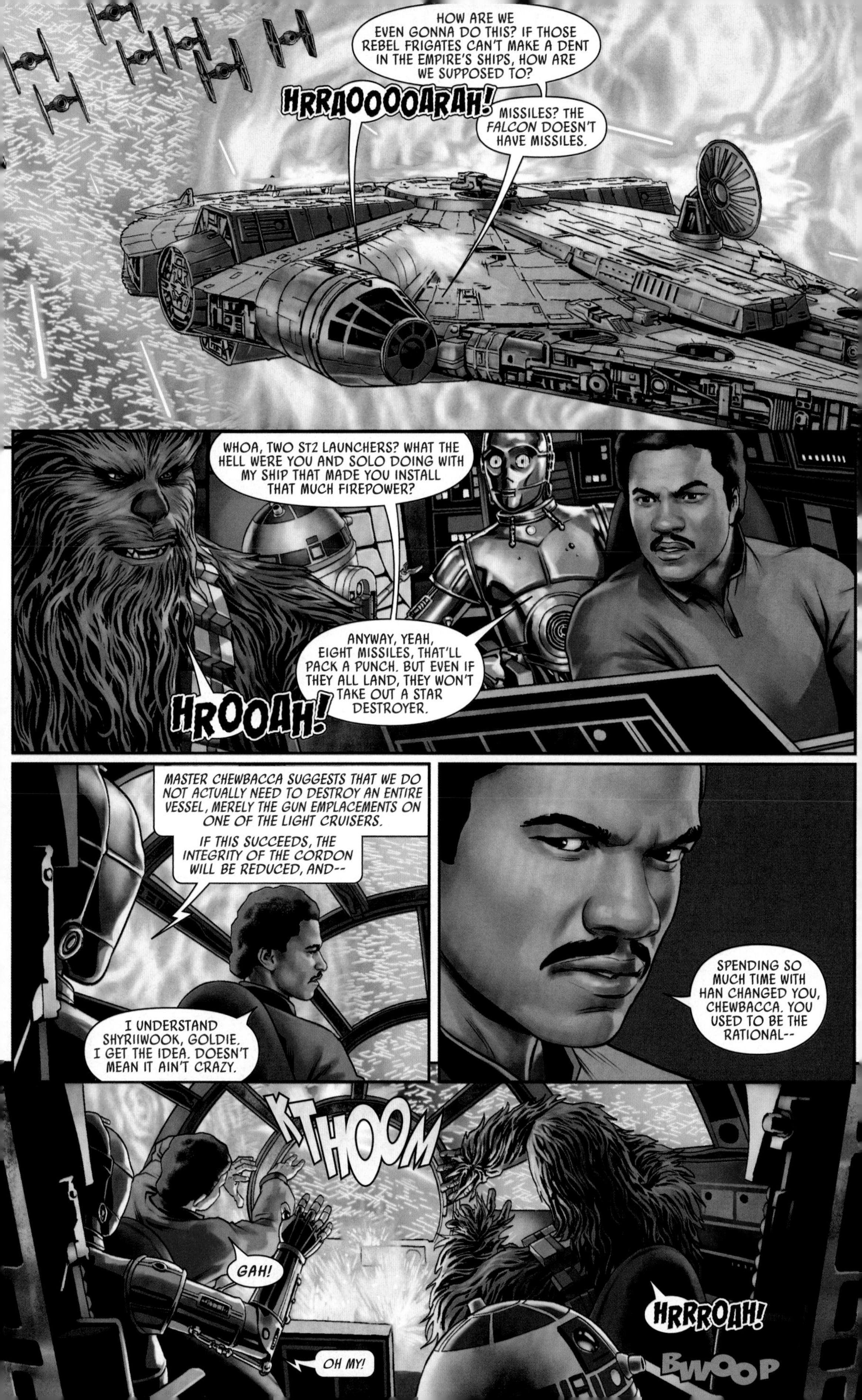
HOW ARE WE EVEN GONNA DO THIS? IF THOSE REBEL FRIGATES CAN'T MAKE A DENT IN THE EMPIRE'S SHIPS, HOW ARE WE SUPPOSED TO?
HRRAOOOOARAH!
MISSILES? THE *FALCON* DOESN'T HAVE MISSILES.
WHOA, TWO ST2 LAUNCHERS? WHAT THE HELL WERE YOU AND SOLO DOING WITH MY SHIP THAT MADE YOU INSTALL THAT MUCH FIREPOWER?
HROOAH!
ANYWAY, YEAH, EIGHT MISSILES, THAT'LL PACK A PUNCH. BUT EVEN IF THEY ALL LAND, THEY WON'T TAKE OUT A STAR DESTROYER.
MASTER CHEWBACCA SUGGESTS THAT WE DO NOT ACTUALLY NEED TO DESTROY AN ENTIRE VESSEL, MERELY THE GUN EMPLACEMENTS ON ONE OF THE LIGHT CRUISERS.
IF THIS SUCCEEDS, THE INTEGRITY OF THE CORDON WILL BE REDUCED, AND--
I UNDERSTAND SHYRIIWOOK, GOLDIE. I GET THE IDEA. DOESN'T MEAN IT AIN'T CRAZY.
SPENDING SO MUCH TIME WITH HAN CHANGED YOU, CHEWBACCA. YOU USED TO BE THE RATIONAL--
KTHOOM
GAH!
HRRROAH!
OH MY!
BWOOP

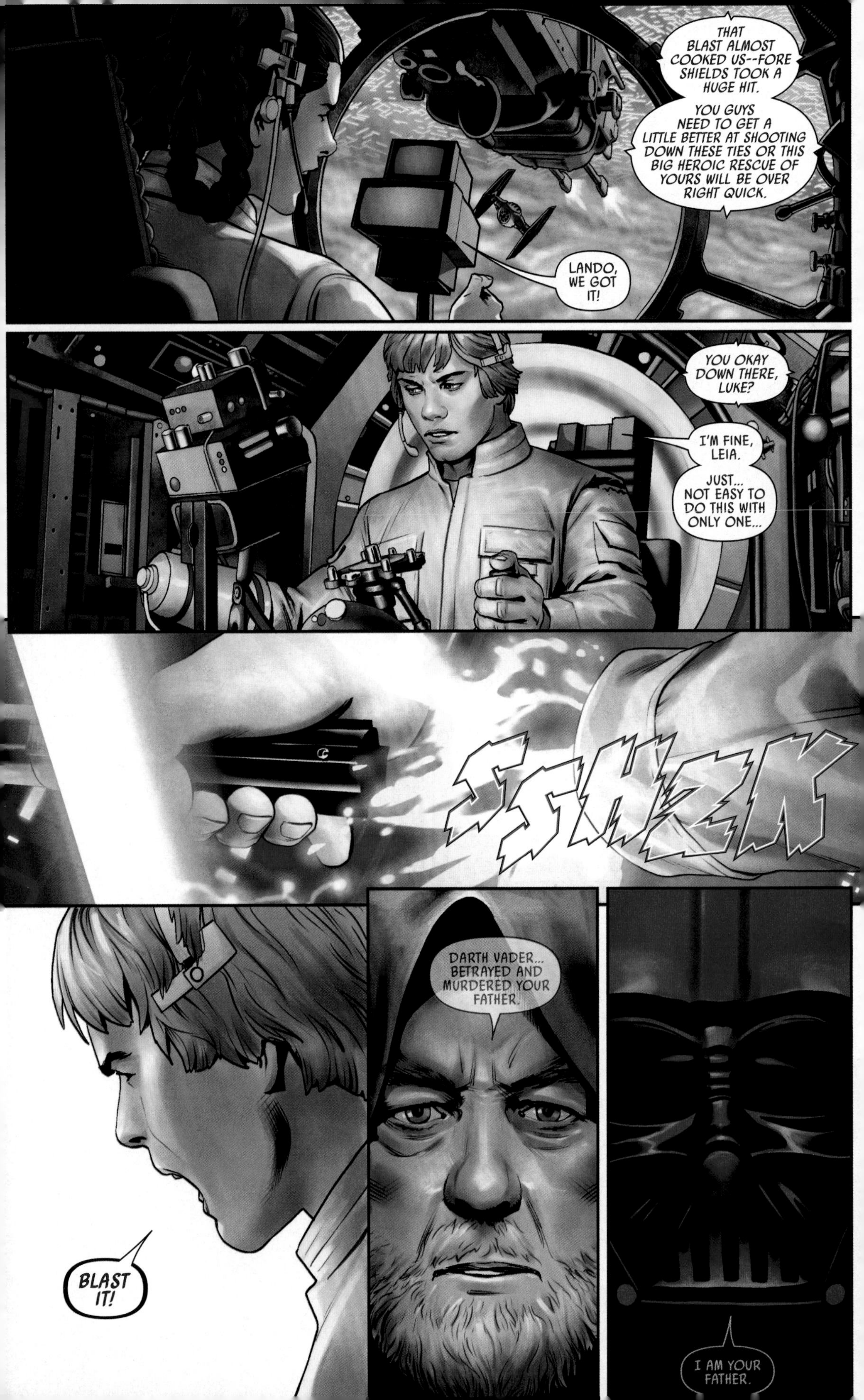
THAT BLAST ALMOST COOKED US--FORE SHIELDS TOOK A HUGE HIT.
YOU GUYS NEED TO GET A LITTLE BETTER AT SHOOTING DOWN THESE TIES OR THIS BIG HEROIC RESCUE OF YOURS WILL BE OVER RIGHT QUICK.
LANDO, WE GOT IT!
YOU OKAY DOWN THERE, LUKE?
I'M FINE, LEIA.
JUST... NOT EASY TO DO THIS WITH ONLY ONE...
SSHZK
BLAST IT!
DARTH VADER... BETRAYED AND MURDERED YOUR FATHER.
I AM YOUR FATHER.

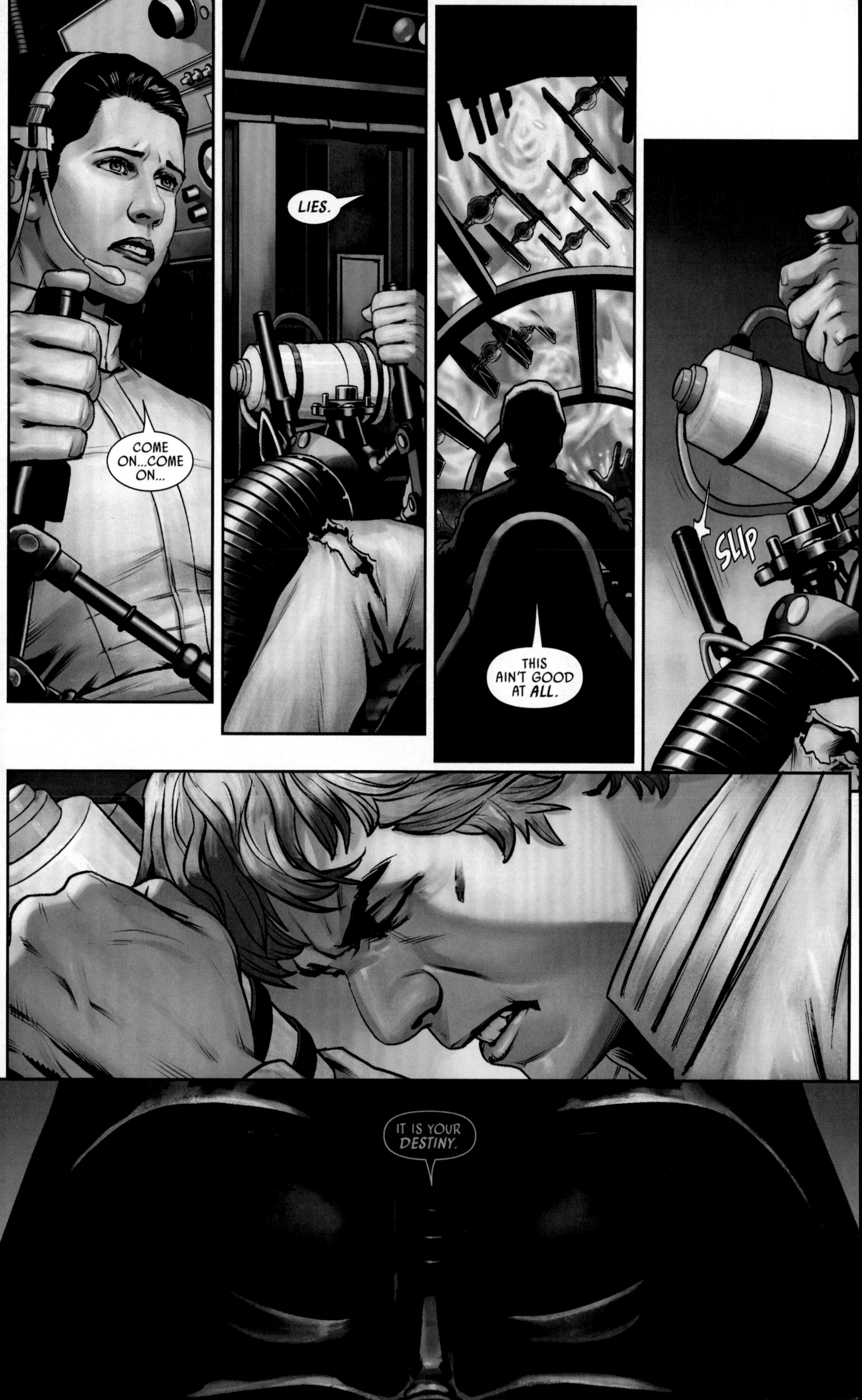
COME ON...COME ON...
LIES.
THIS AIN'T GOOD AT ALL.
SLIP
IT IS YOUR DESTINY.

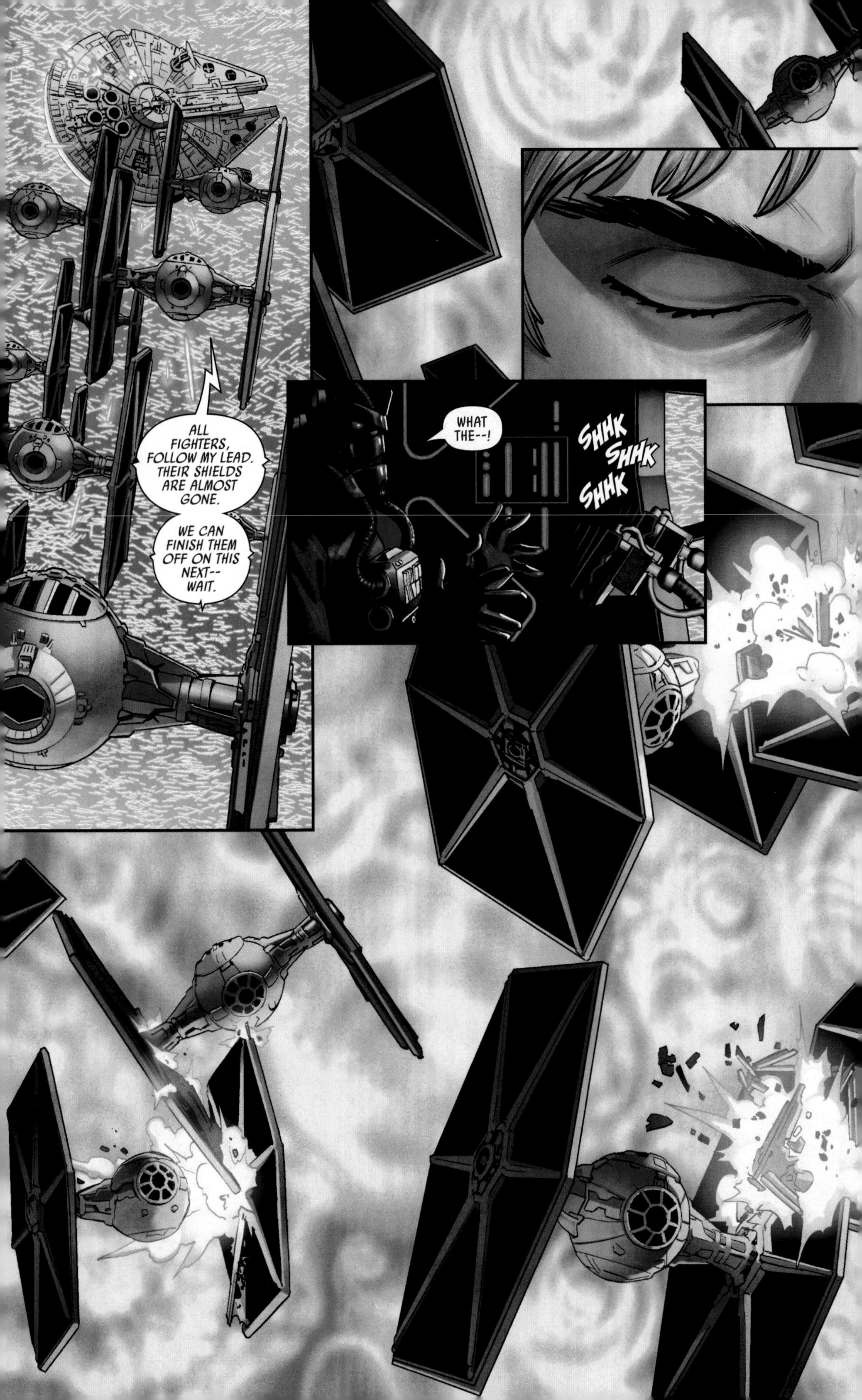
ALL FIGHTERS, FOLLOW MY LEAD. THEIR SHIELDS ARE ALMOST GONE.
WE CAN FINISH THEM OFF ON THIS NEXT-- WAIT.
WHAT THE--!
SHHK SHHK SHHK

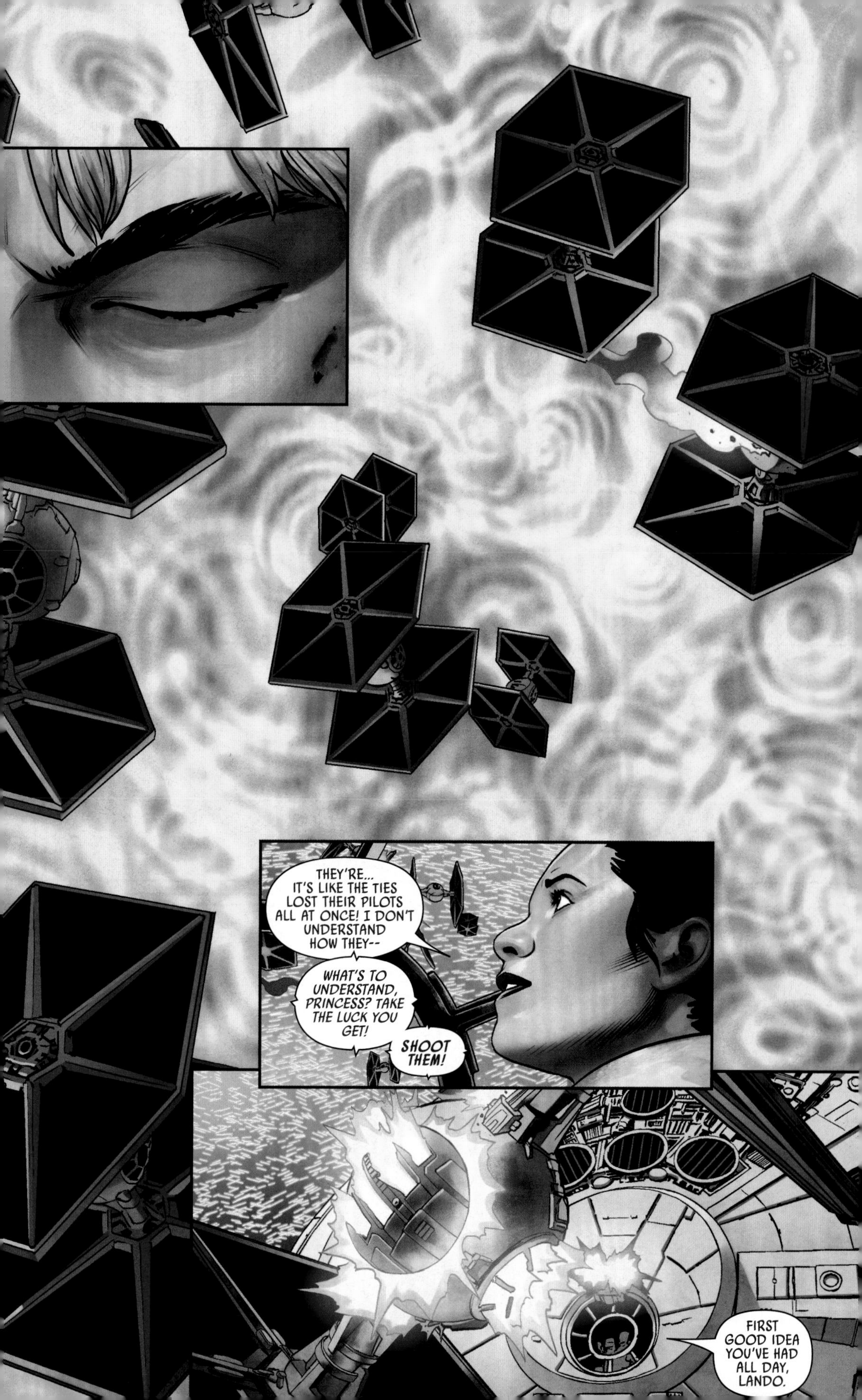
THEY'RE... IT'S LIKE THE TIES LOST THEIR PILOTS ALL AT ONCE! I DON'T UNDERSTAND HOW THEY--
WHAT'S TO UNDERSTAND, PRINCESS? TAKE THE LUCK YOU GET!
SHOOT THEM!
FIRST GOOD IDEA YOU'VE HAD ALL DAY, LANDO.

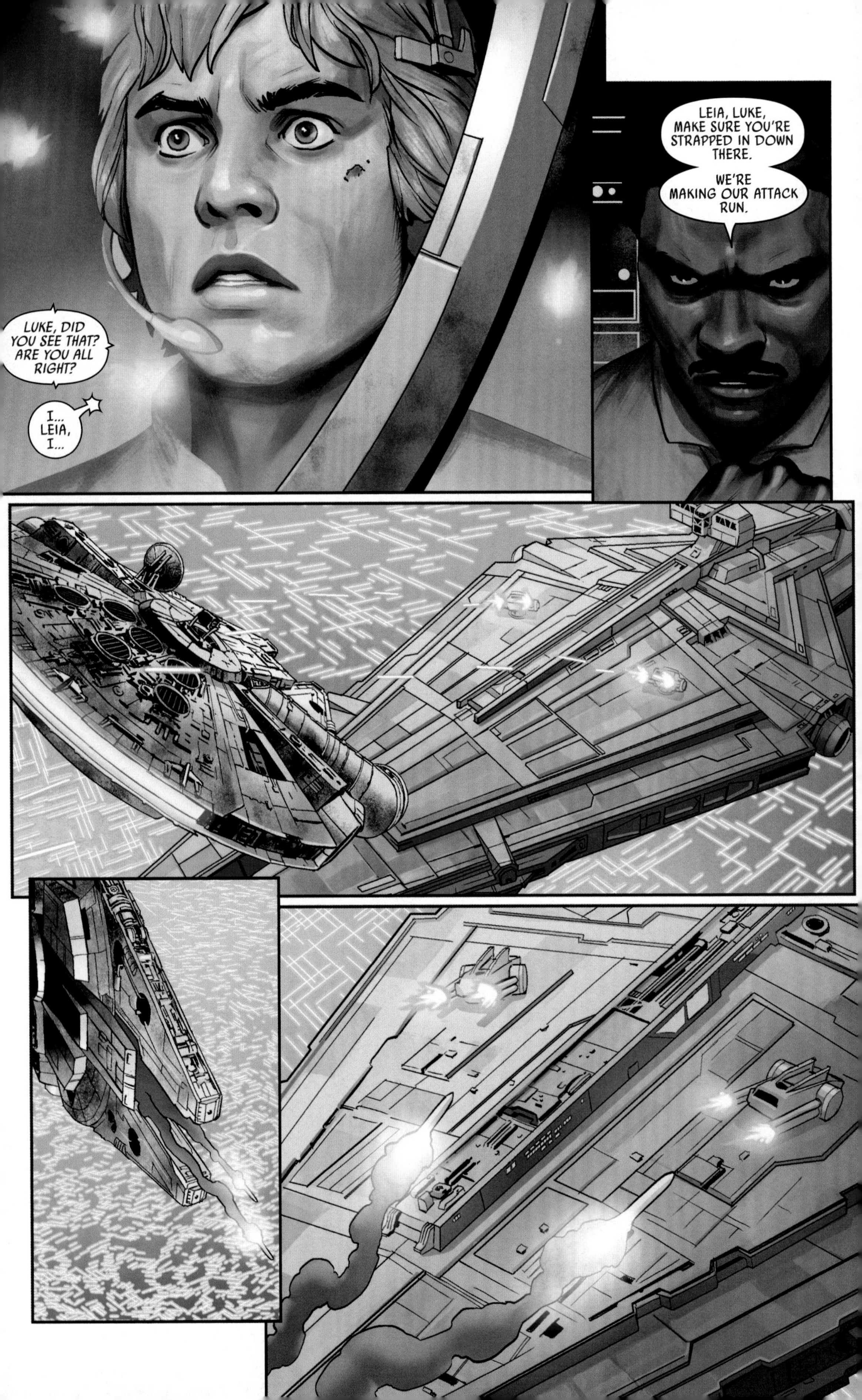
LUKE, DID YOU SEE THAT? ARE YOU ALL RIGHT?
I... LEIA, I...
LEIA, LUKE, MAKE SURE YOU'RE STRAPPED IN DOWN THERE.
WE'RE MAKING OUR ATTACK RUN.

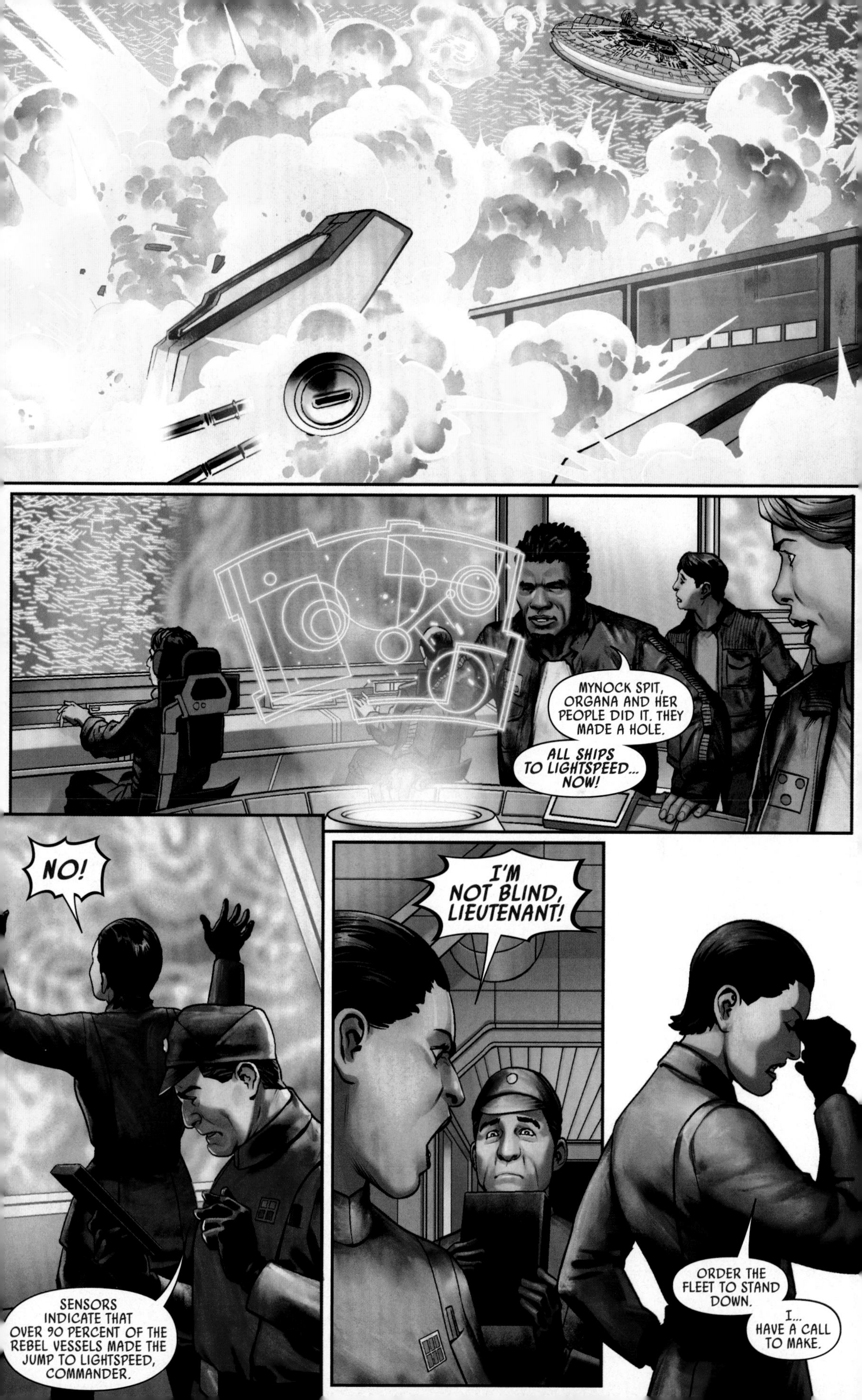

MYNOCK SPIT, ORGANA AND HER PEOPLE DID IT. THEY MADE A HOLE.
ALL SHIPS TO LIGHTSPEED... NOW!
NO!
SENSORS INDICATE THAT OVER 90 PERCENT OF THE REBEL VESSELS MADE THE JUMP TO LIGHTSPEED, COMMANDER.
I'M NOT BLIND, LIEUTENANT!
ORDER THE FLEET TO STAND DOWN.
I... HAVE A CALL TO MAKE.

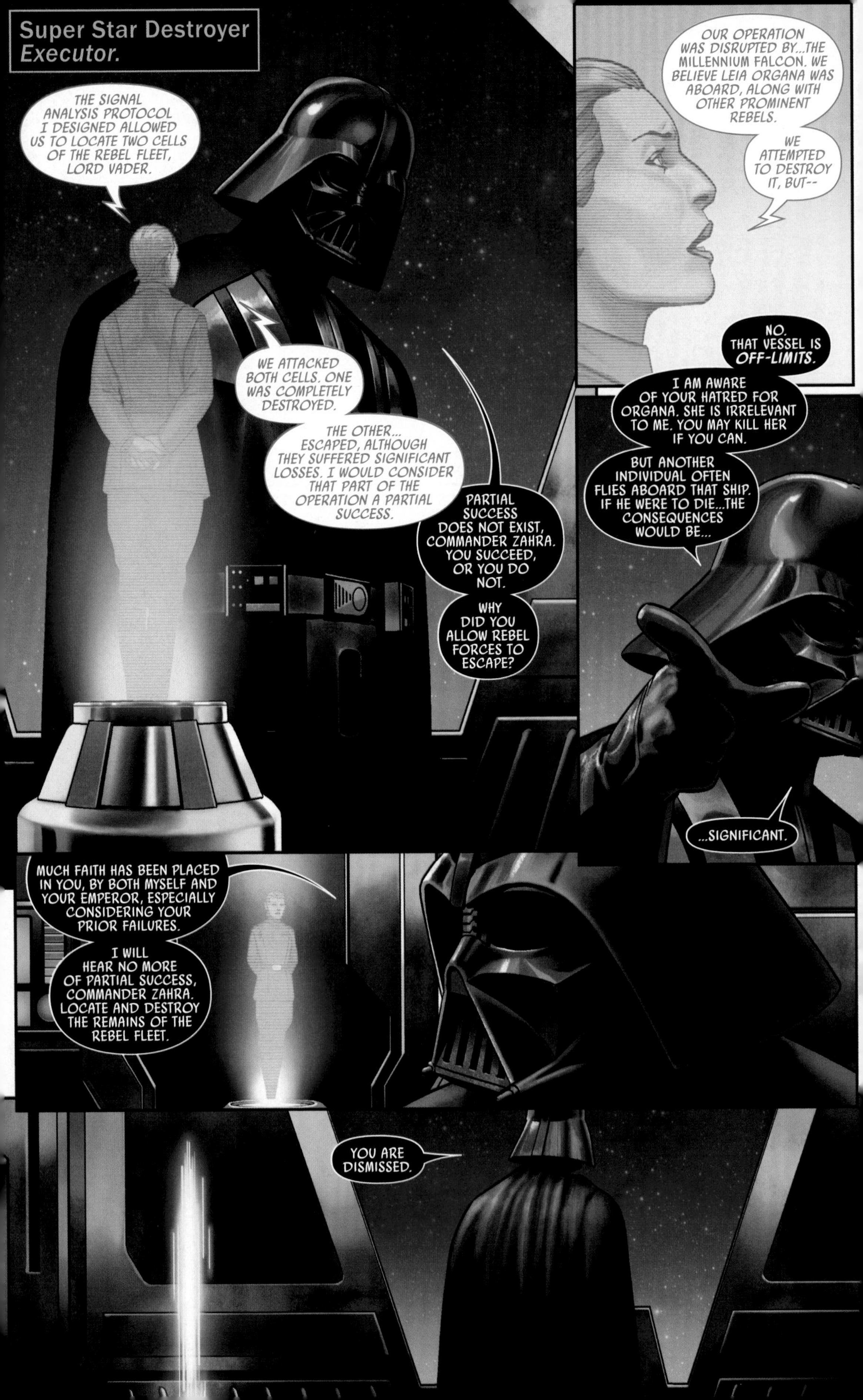
Super Star Destroyer
Executor.
THE SIGNAL ANALYSIS PROTOCOL I DESIGNED ALLOWED US TO LOCATE TWO CELLS OF THE REBEL FLEET, LORD VADER.
WE ATTACKED BOTH CELLS. ONE WAS COMPLETELY DESTROYED.
THE OTHER... ESCAPED, ALTHOUGH THEY SUFFERED SIGNIFICANT LOSSES. I WOULD CONSIDER THAT PART OF THE OPERATION A PARTIAL SUCCESS.
PARTIAL SUCCESS DOES NOT EXIST, COMMANDER ZAHRA. YOU SUCCEED, OR YOU DO NOT.
WHY DID YOU ALLOW REBEL FORCES TO ESCAPE?
OUR OPERATION WAS DISRUPTED BY...THE MILLENNIUM FALCON. WE BELIEVE LEIA ORGANA WAS ABOARD, ALONG WITH OTHER PROMINENT REBELS.
WE ATTEMPTED TO DESTROY IT, BUT--
NO. THAT VESSEL IS *OFF-LIMITS.*
I AM AWARE OF YOUR HATRED FOR ORGANA. SHE IS IRRELEVANT TO ME. YOU MAY KILL HER IF YOU CAN.
BUT ANOTHER INDIVIDUAL OFTEN FLIES ABOARD THAT SHIP. IF HE WERE TO DIE...THE CONSEQUENCES WOULD BE...
...SIGNIFICANT.
MUCH FAITH HAS BEEN PLACED IN YOU, BY BOTH MYSELF AND YOUR EMPEROR, ESPECIALLY CONSIDERING YOUR PRIOR FAILURES.
I WILL HEAR NO MORE OF PARTIAL SUCCESS, COMMANDER ZAHRA. LOCATE AND DESTROY THE REMAINS OF THE REBEL FLEET.
YOU ARE DISMISSED.

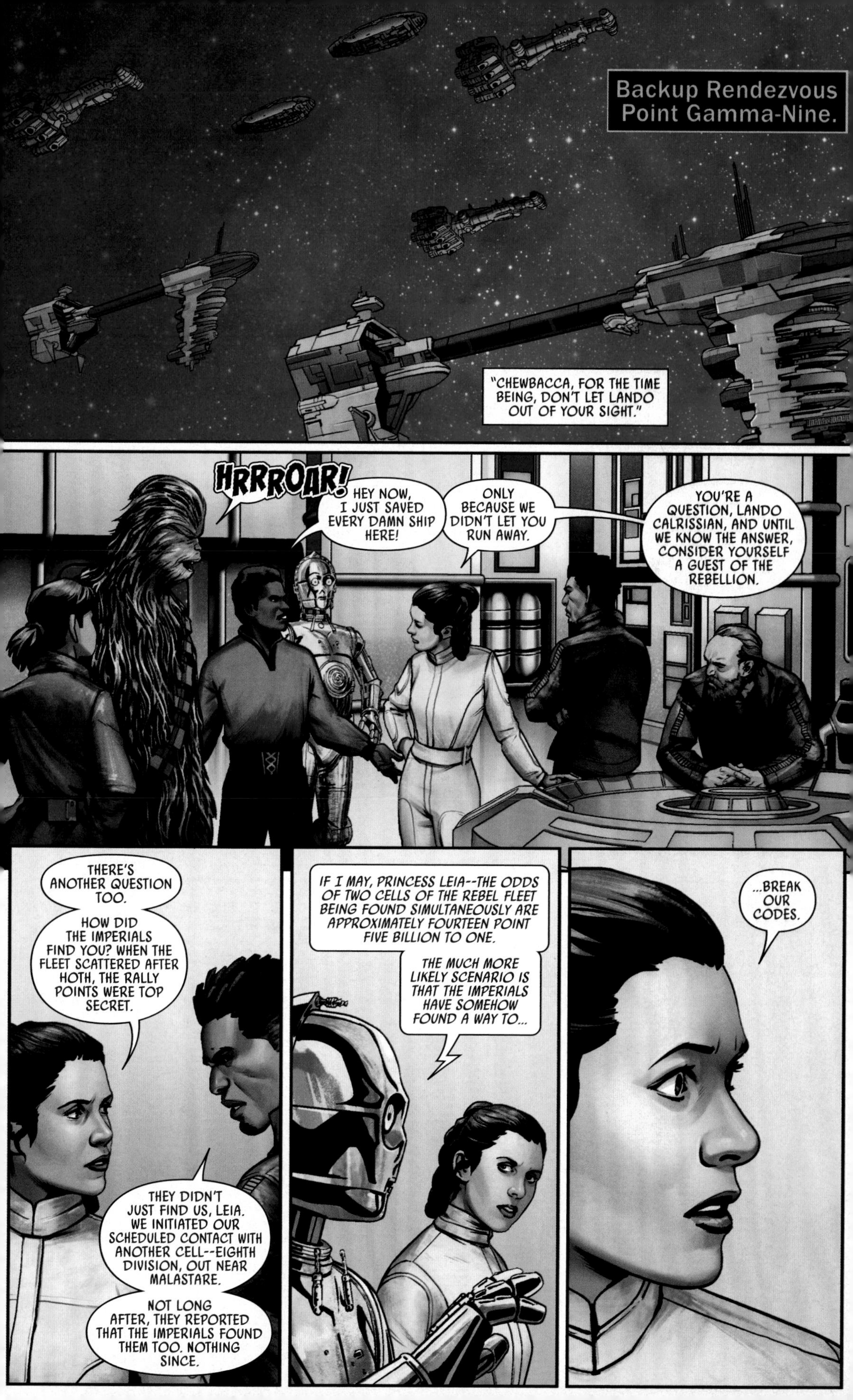
Backup Rendezvous Point Gamma-Nine.
"CHEWBACCA, FOR THE TIME BEING, DON'T LET LANDO OUT OF YOUR SIGHT."
HRRROAR!
HEY NOW, I JUST SAVED EVERY DAMN SHIP HERE!
ONLY BECAUSE WE DIDN'T LET YOU RUN AWAY.
YOU'RE A QUESTION, LANDO CALRISSIAN, AND UNTIL WE KNOW THE ANSWER, CONSIDER YOURSELF A GUEST OF THE REBELLION.
THERE'S ANOTHER QUESTION TOO.
HOW DID THE IMPERIALS FIND YOU? WHEN THE FLEET SCATTERED AFTER HOTH, THE RALLY POINTS WERE TOP SECRET.
THEY DIDN'T JUST FIND US, LEIA. WE INITIATED OUR SCHEDULED CONTACT WITH ANOTHER CELL--EIGHTH DIVISION, OUT NEAR MALASTARE.
NOT LONG AFTER, THEY REPORTED THAT THE IMPERIALS FOUND THEM TOO. NOTHING SINCE.
IF I MAY, PRINCESS LEIA--THE ODDS OF TWO CELLS OF THE REBEL FLEET BEING FOUND SIMULTANEOUSLY ARE APPROXIMATELY FOURTEEN POINT FIVE BILLION TO ONE.
THE MUCH MORE LIKELY SCENARIO IS THAT THE IMPERIALS HAVE SOMEHOW FOUND A WAY TO...
...BREAK OUR CODES.

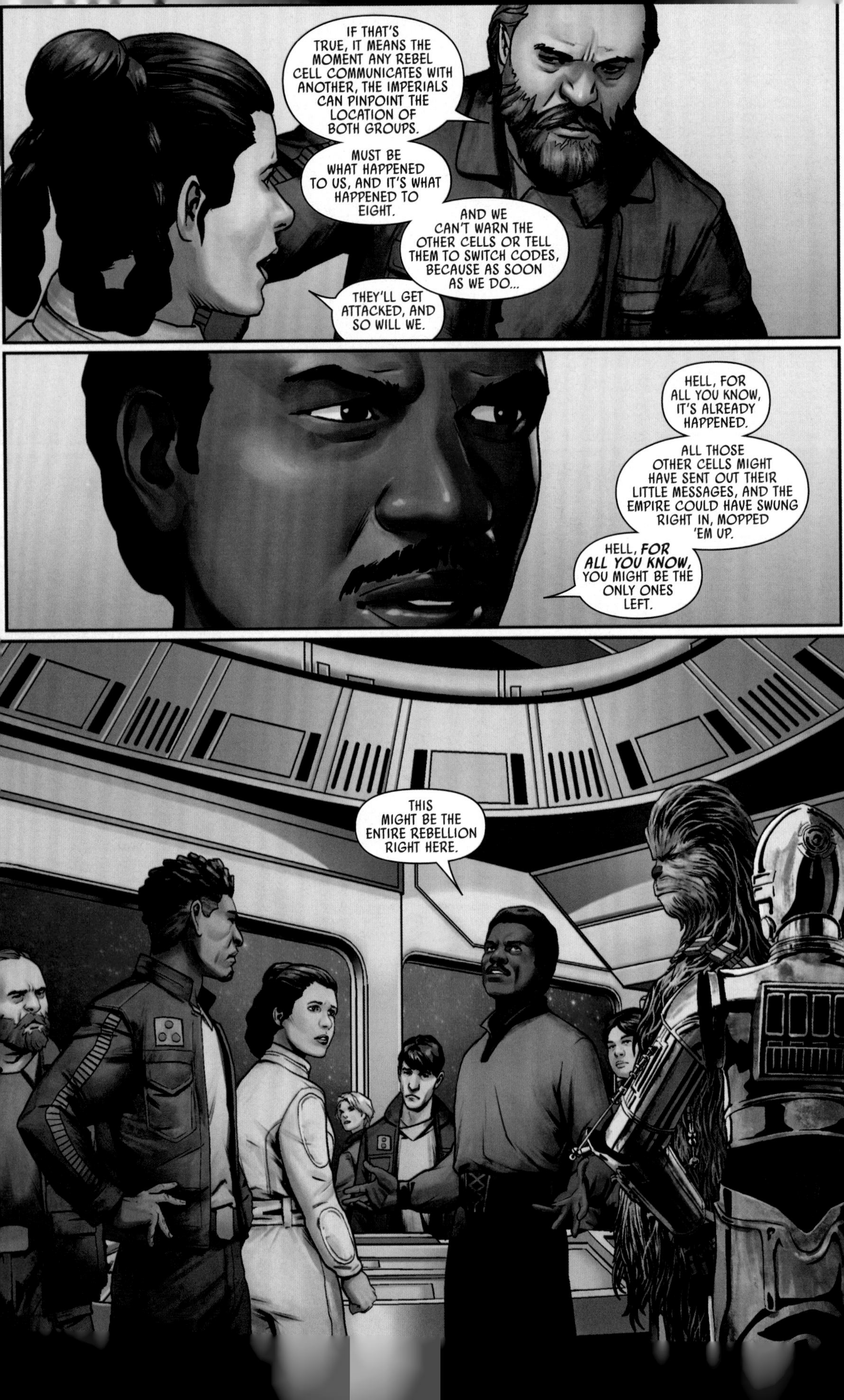
IF THAT'S TRUE, IT MEANS THE MOMENT ANY REBEL CELL COMMUNICATES WITH ANOTHER, THE IMPERIALS CAN PINPOINT THE LOCATION OF BOTH GROUPS.
MUST BE WHAT HAPPENED TO US, AND IT'S WHAT HAPPENED TO EIGHT.
AND WE CAN'T WARN THE OTHER CELLS OR TELL THEM TO SWITCH CODES, BECAUSE AS SOON AS WE DO...
THEY'LL GET ATTACKED, AND SO WILL WE.
HELL, FOR ALL YOU KNOW, IT'S ALREADY HAPPENED.
ALL THOSE OTHER CELLS MIGHT HAVE SENT OUT THEIR LITTLE MESSAGES, AND THE EMPIRE COULD HAVE SWUNG RIGHT IN, MOPPED 'EM UP.
HELL, ***FOR ALL YOU KNOW***, YOU MIGHT BE THE ONLY ONES LEFT.
THIS MIGHT BE THE ENTIRE REBELLION RIGHT HERE.

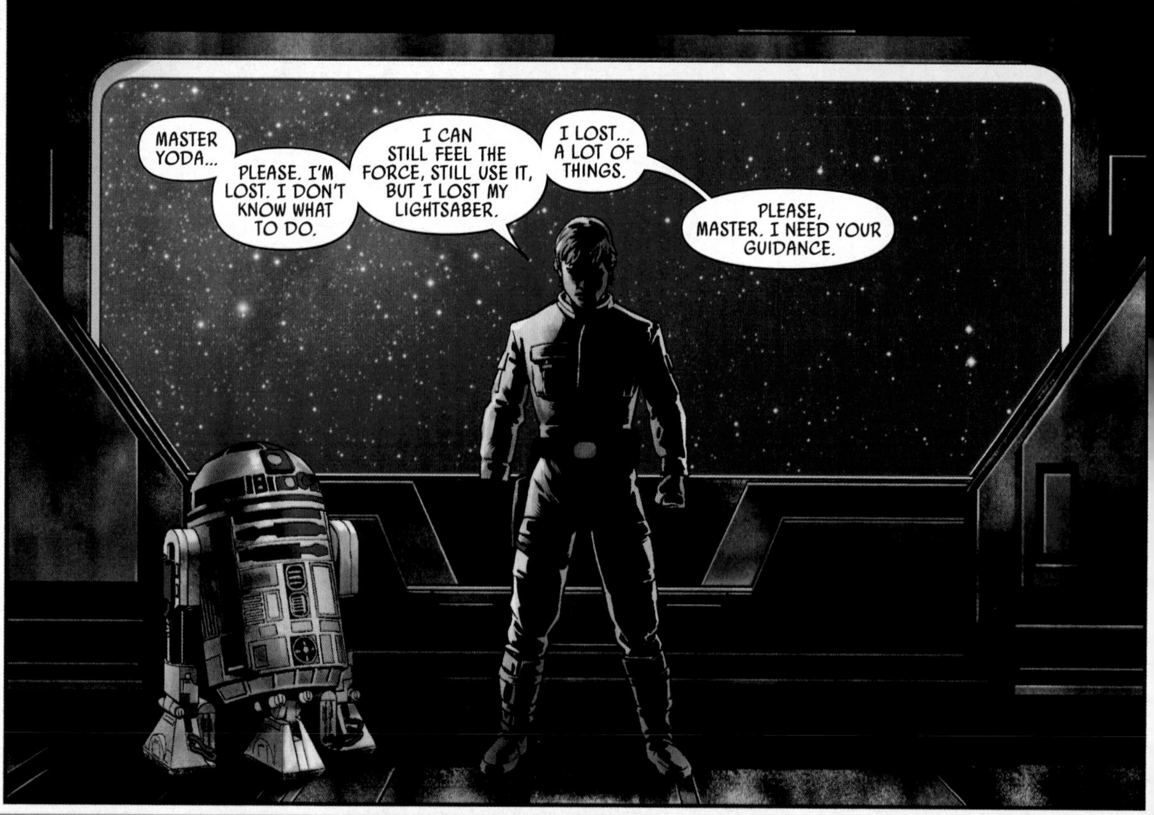
MASTER YODA...
PLEASE. I'M LOST. I DON'T KNOW WHAT TO DO.
I CAN STILL FEEL THE FORCE, STILL USE IT, BUT I LOST MY LIGHTSABER.
I LOST... A LOT OF THINGS.
PLEASE, MASTER. I NEED YOUR GUIDANCE.

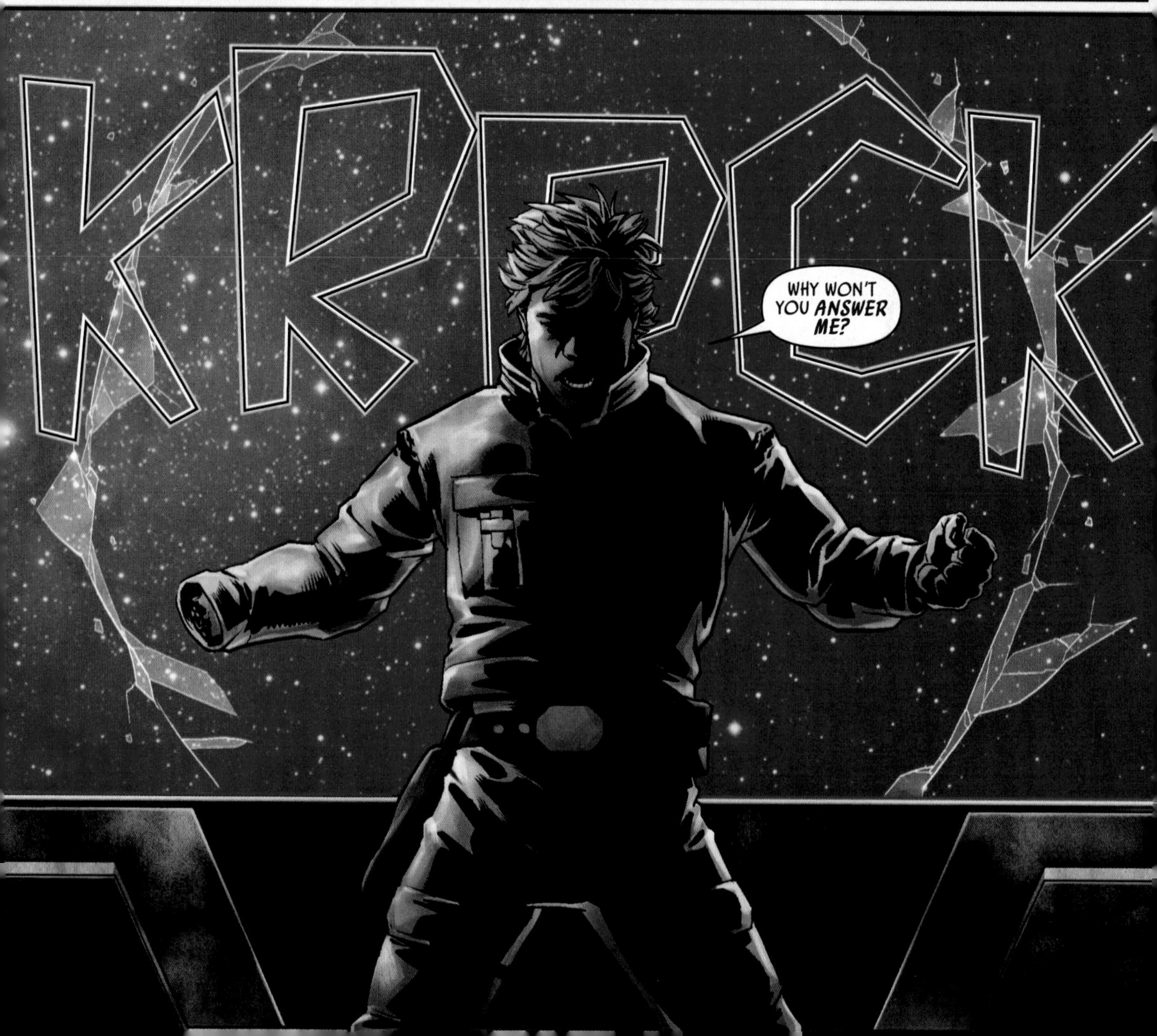
KRRCK
WHY WON'T YOU ANSWER ME?

BDEEP BEEP

YOU'RE RIGHT, ARTOO. I'M...I'M SORRY. I'M JUST...

IT'S NOT EASY RIGHT NOW.

I THOUGHT I WAS GOING TO BE A JEDI, BUT I'M NOT SURE BEN AND YODA WANT ME ANYMORE.

AND VADER TOLD ME SOMETHING ON CLOUD CITY.

IF IT'S TRUE, MAYBE I *SHOULDN'T* BE A JEDI.

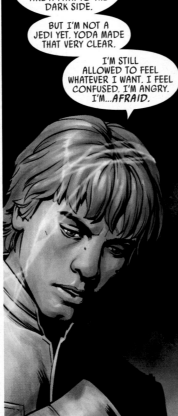

I KNOW JEDI AREN'T SUPPOSED TO FEEL THIS WAY. MASTER YODA TOLD ME THESE EMOTIONS ARE A PATH TO THE DARK SIDE.

BUT I'M NOT A JEDI YET. YODA MADE THAT VERY CLEAR.

I'M STILL ALLOWED TO FEEL WHATEVER I WANT. I FEEL CONFUSED. I'M ANGRY. I'M...*AFRAID.*

IF VADER IS MY FATHER, THERE'S NO WAY YODA COULDN'T HAVE KNOWN. BEN TOO. THEY LIED TO ME.

THAT'S BAD ENOUGH. BUT THE BIGGEST THING I'M WORRIED ABOUT...

...IF I'M NOT GOING TO BE A JEDI...

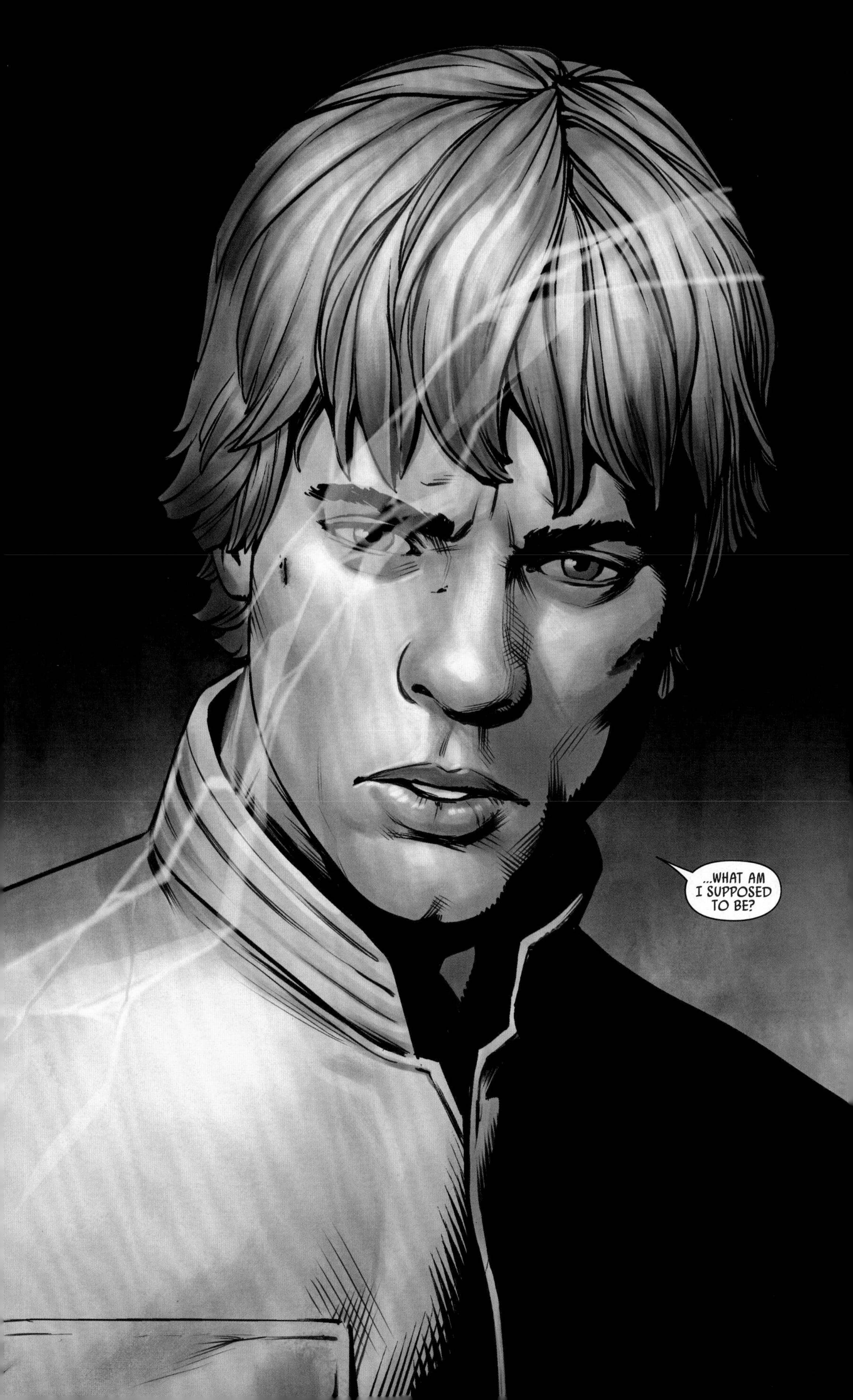
...WHAT AM I SUPPOSED TO BE?

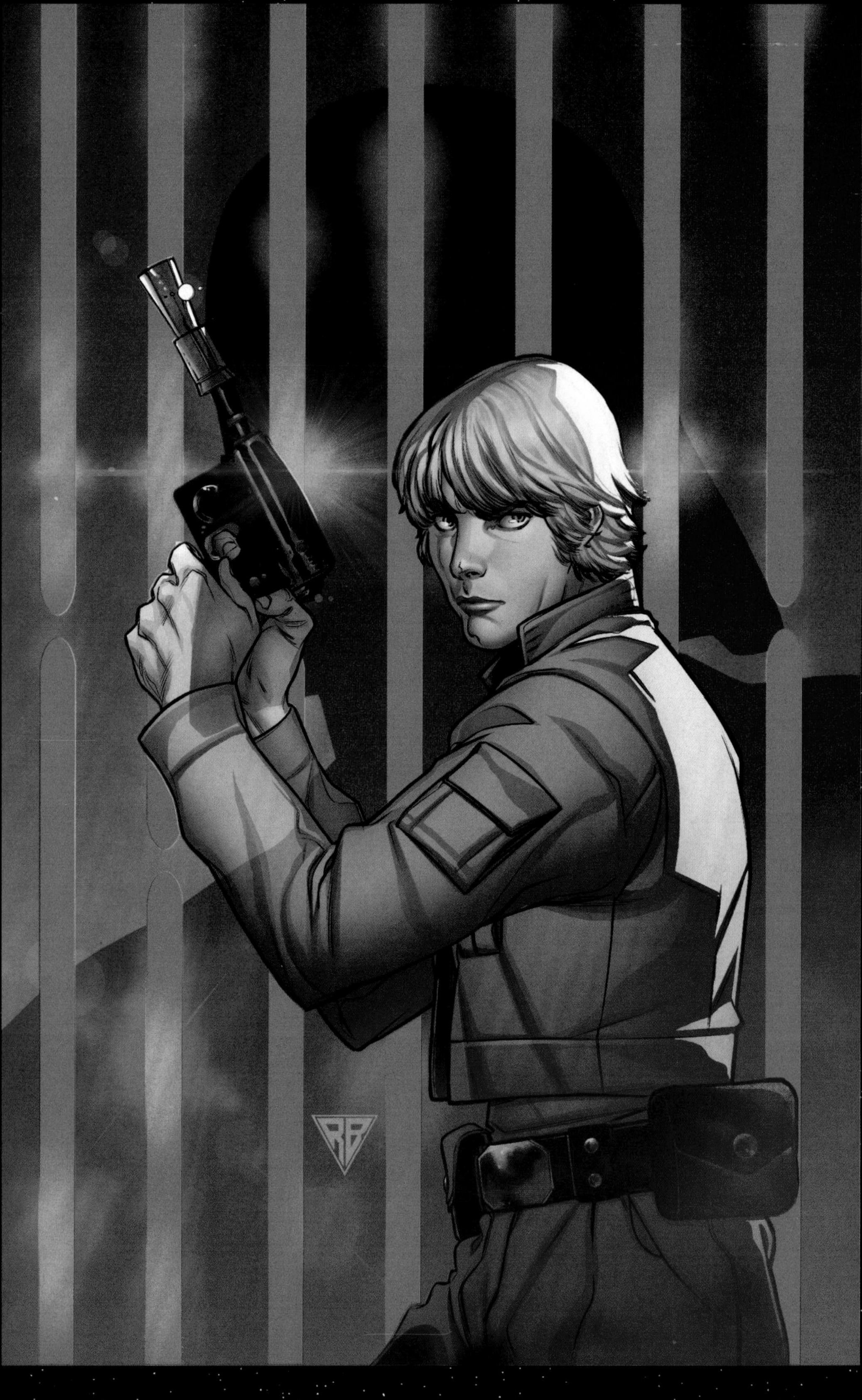

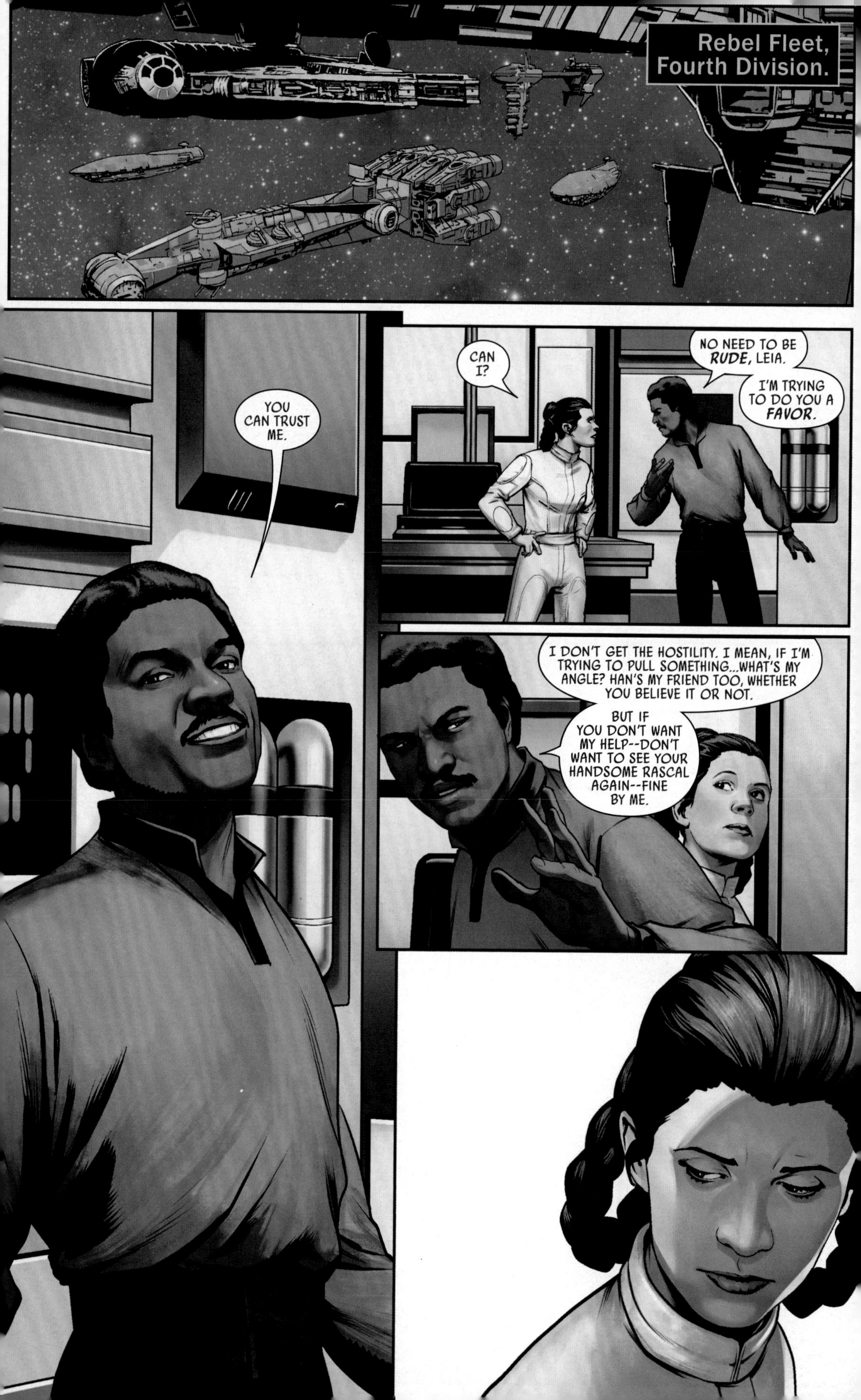
Rebel Fleet, Fourth Division.
YOU CAN TRUST ME.
CAN I?
NO NEED TO BE *RUDE,* LEIA.
I'M TRYING TO DO YOU A *FAVOR.*
I DON'T GET THE HOSTILITY. I MEAN, IF I'M TRYING TO PULL SOMETHING...WHAT'S MY ANGLE? HAN'S MY FRIEND TOO, WHETHER YOU BELIEVE IT OR NOT.
BUT IF YOU DON'T WANT MY HELP--DON'T WANT TO SEE YOUR HANDSOME RASCAL AGAIN--FINE BY ME.

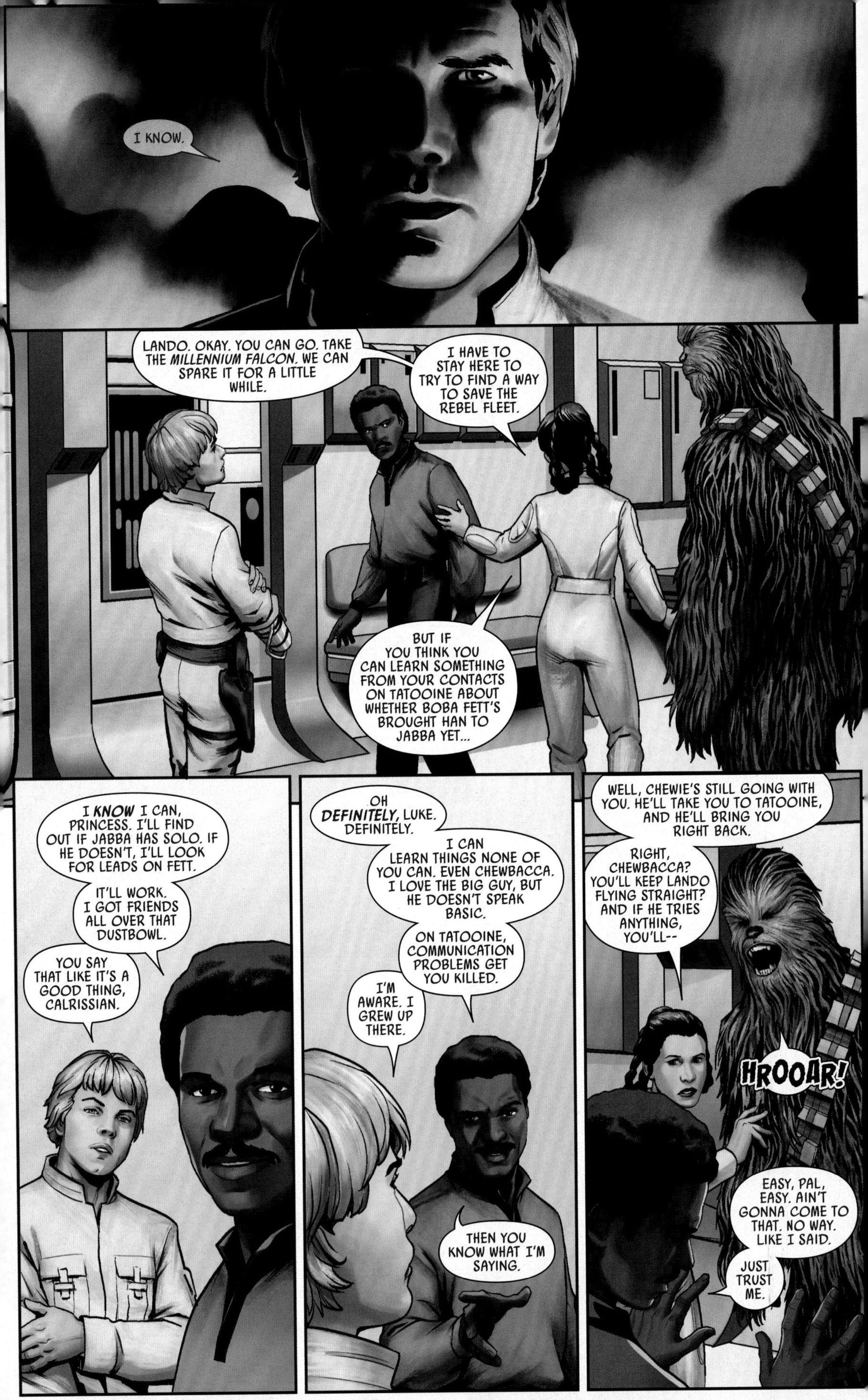
I KNOW.
LANDO. OKAY. YOU CAN GO. TAKE THE *MILLENNIUM FALCON*. WE CAN SPARE IT FOR A LITTLE WHILE.
I HAVE TO STAY HERE TO TRY TO FIND A WAY TO SAVE THE REBEL FLEET.
BUT IF YOU THINK YOU CAN LEARN SOMETHING FROM YOUR CONTACTS ON TATOOINE ABOUT WHETHER BOBA FETT'S BROUGHT HAN TO JABBA YET...
I ***KNOW*** I CAN, PRINCESS. I'LL FIND OUT IF JABBA HAS SOLO. IF HE DOESN'T, I'LL LOOK FOR LEADS ON FETT.
IT'LL WORK. I GOT FRIENDS ALL OVER THAT DUSTBOWL.
YOU SAY THAT LIKE IT'S A GOOD THING, CALRISSIAN.
OH ***DEFINITELY***, LUKE. DEFINITELY.
I CAN LEARN THINGS NONE OF YOU CAN. EVEN CHEWBACCA. I LOVE THE BIG GUY, BUT HE DOESN'T SPEAK BASIC.
ON TATOOINE, COMMUNICATION PROBLEMS GET YOU KILLED.
I'M AWARE. I GREW UP THERE.
THEN YOU KNOW WHAT I'M SAYING.
WELL, CHEWIE'S STILL GOING WITH YOU. HE'LL TAKE YOU TO TATOOINE, AND HE'LL BRING YOU RIGHT BACK.
RIGHT, CHEWBACCA? YOU'LL KEEP LANDO FLYING STRAIGHT? AND IF HE TRIES ANYTHING, YOU'LL--
HROOAR!
EASY, PAL, EASY. AIN'T GONNA COME TO THAT. NO WAY. LIKE I SAID.
JUST TRUST ME.

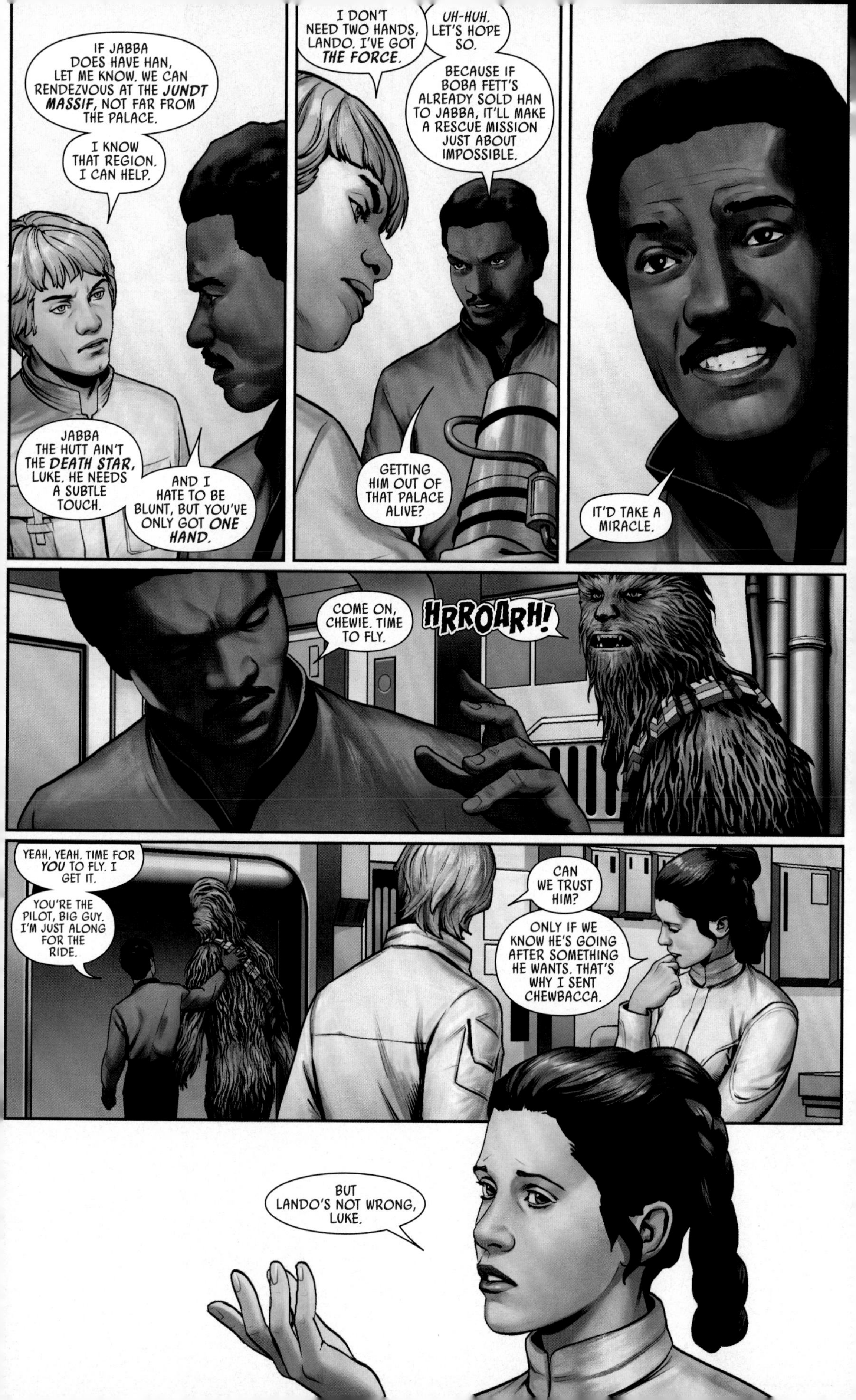
IF JABBA DOES HAVE HAN, LET ME KNOW. WE CAN RENDEZVOUS AT THE JUNDT MASSIF, NOT FAR FROM THE PALACE.
I KNOW THAT REGION. I CAN HELP.
JABBA THE HUTT AIN'T THE DEATH STAR, LUKE. HE NEEDS A SUBTLE TOUCH.
AND I HATE TO BE BLUNT, BUT YOU'VE ONLY GOT ONE HAND.
I DON'T NEED TWO HANDS, LANDO. I'VE GOT THE FORCE.
UH-HUH. LET'S HOPE SO.
BECAUSE IF BOBA FETT'S ALREADY SOLD HAN TO JABBA, IT'LL MAKE A RESCUE MISSION JUST ABOUT IMPOSSIBLE.
GETTING HIM OUT OF THAT PALACE ALIVE?
IT'D TAKE A MIRACLE.
COME ON, CHEWIE. TIME TO FLY.
HRROARH!
YEAH, YEAH. TIME FOR YOU TO FLY. I GET IT.
YOU'RE THE PILOT, BIG GUY. I'M JUST ALONG FOR THE RIDE.
CAN WE TRUST HIM?
ONLY IF WE KNOW HE'S GOING AFTER SOMETHING HE WANTS. THAT'S WHY I SENT CHEWBACCA.
BUT LANDO'S NOT WRONG, LUKE.

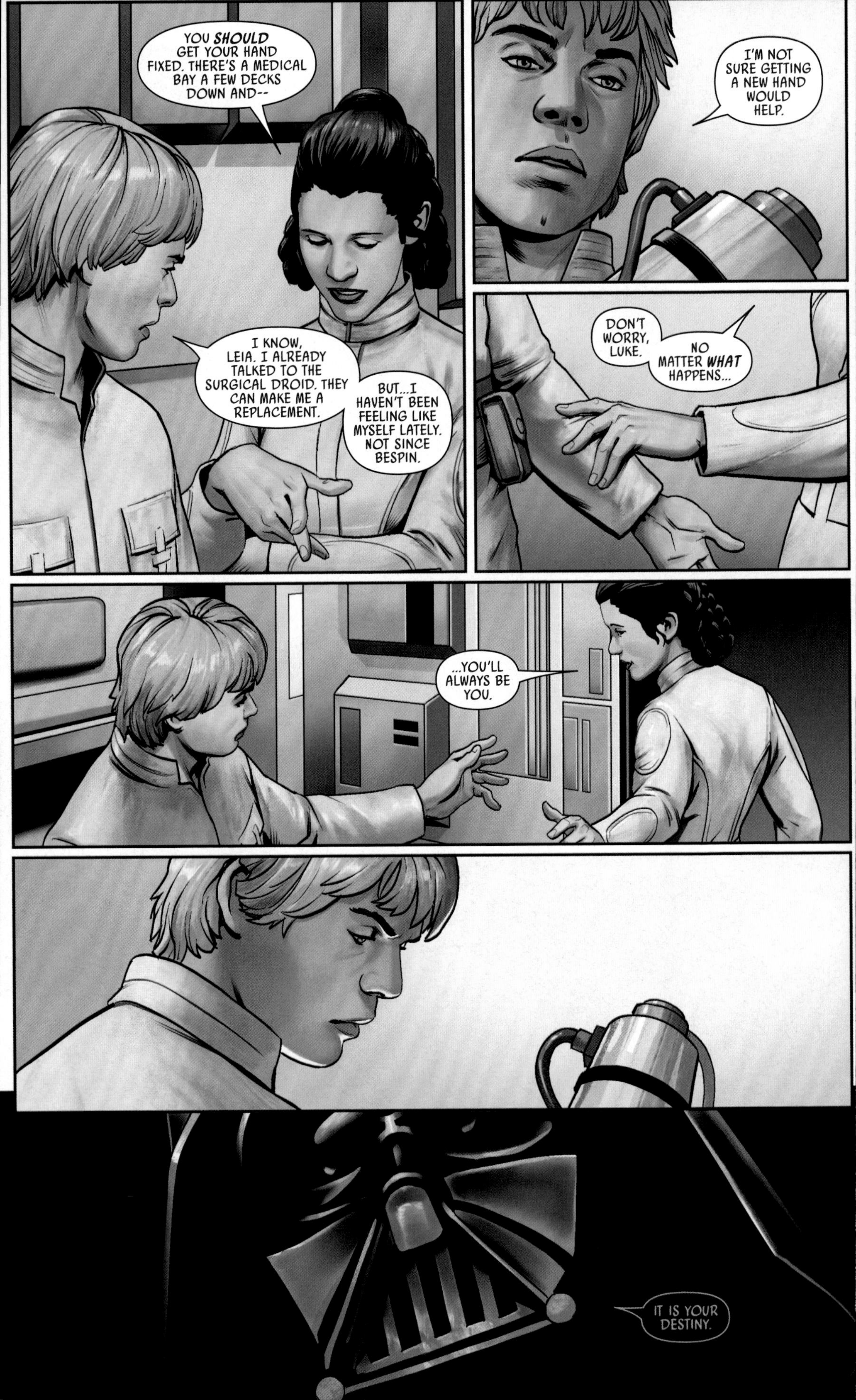
YOU SHOULD GET YOUR HAND FIXED. THERE'S A MEDICAL BAY A FEW DECKS DOWN AND--
I KNOW, LEIA. I ALREADY TALKED TO THE SURGICAL DROID. THEY CAN MAKE ME A REPLACEMENT.
BUT...I HAVEN'T BEEN FEELING LIKE MYSELF LATELY. NOT SINCE BESPIN.
I'M NOT SURE GETTING A NEW HAND WOULD HELP.
DON'T WORRY, LUKE.
NO MATTER WHAT HAPPENS...
...YOU'LL ALWAYS BE YOU.
IT IS YOUR DESTINY.

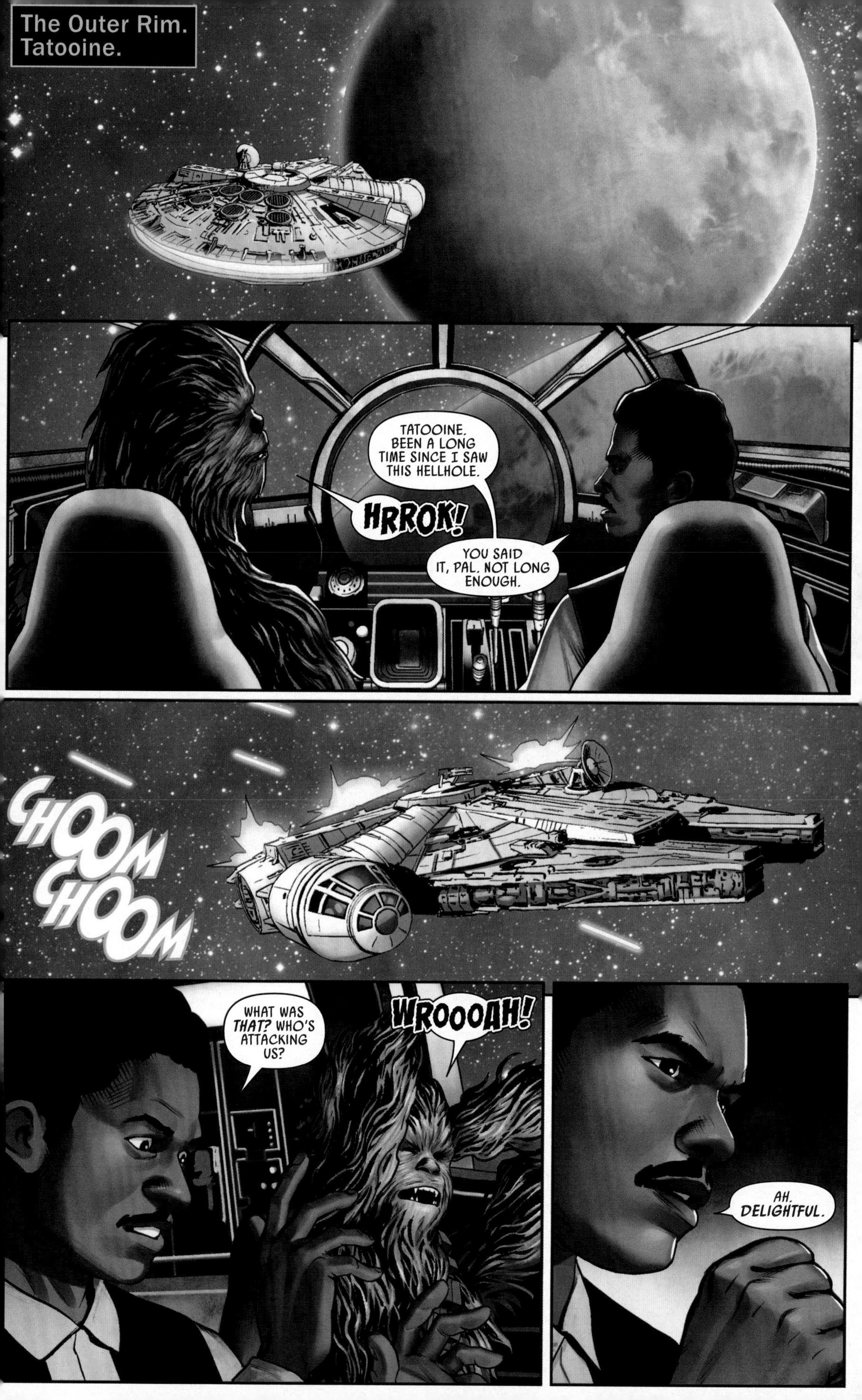
The Outer Rim.
Tatooine.
TATOOINE. BEEN A LONG TIME SINCE I SAW THIS HELLHOLE.
HRROK!
YOU SAID IT, PAL. NOT LONG ENOUGH.
CHOOM CHOOM
WHAT WAS *THAT?* WHO'S ATTACKING US?
WROOOAH!
AH. DELIGHTFUL.

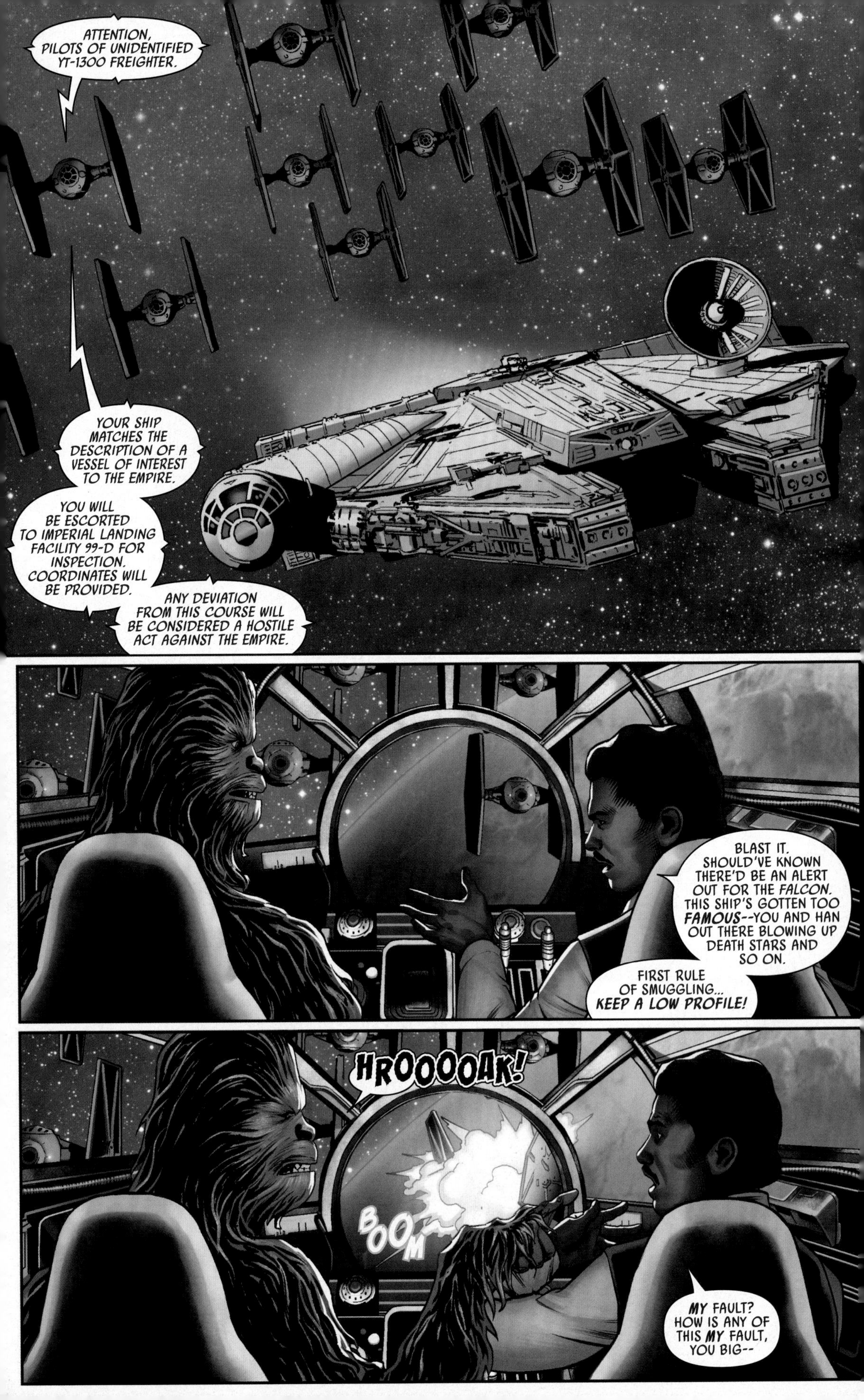
ATTENTION, PILOTS OF UNIDENTIFIED YT-1300 FREIGHTER.
YOUR SHIP MATCHES THE DESCRIPTION OF A VESSEL OF INTEREST TO THE EMPIRE.
YOU WILL BE ESCORTED TO IMPERIAL LANDING FACILITY 99-D FOR INSPECTION. COORDINATES WILL BE PROVIDED.
ANY DEVIATION FROM THIS COURSE WILL BE CONSIDERED A HOSTILE ACT AGAINST THE EMPIRE.
BLAST IT. SHOULD'VE KNOWN THERE'D BE AN ALERT OUT FOR THE *FALCON.* THIS SHIP'S GOTTEN TOO ***FAMOUS***--YOU AND HAN OUT THERE BLOWING UP DEATH STARS AND SO ON.
FIRST RULE OF SMUGGLING... **KEEP A LOW PROFILE!**
HROOOOAK!
BOOM
MY FAULT? HOW IS ANY OF THIS ***MY*** FAULT, YOU BIG--

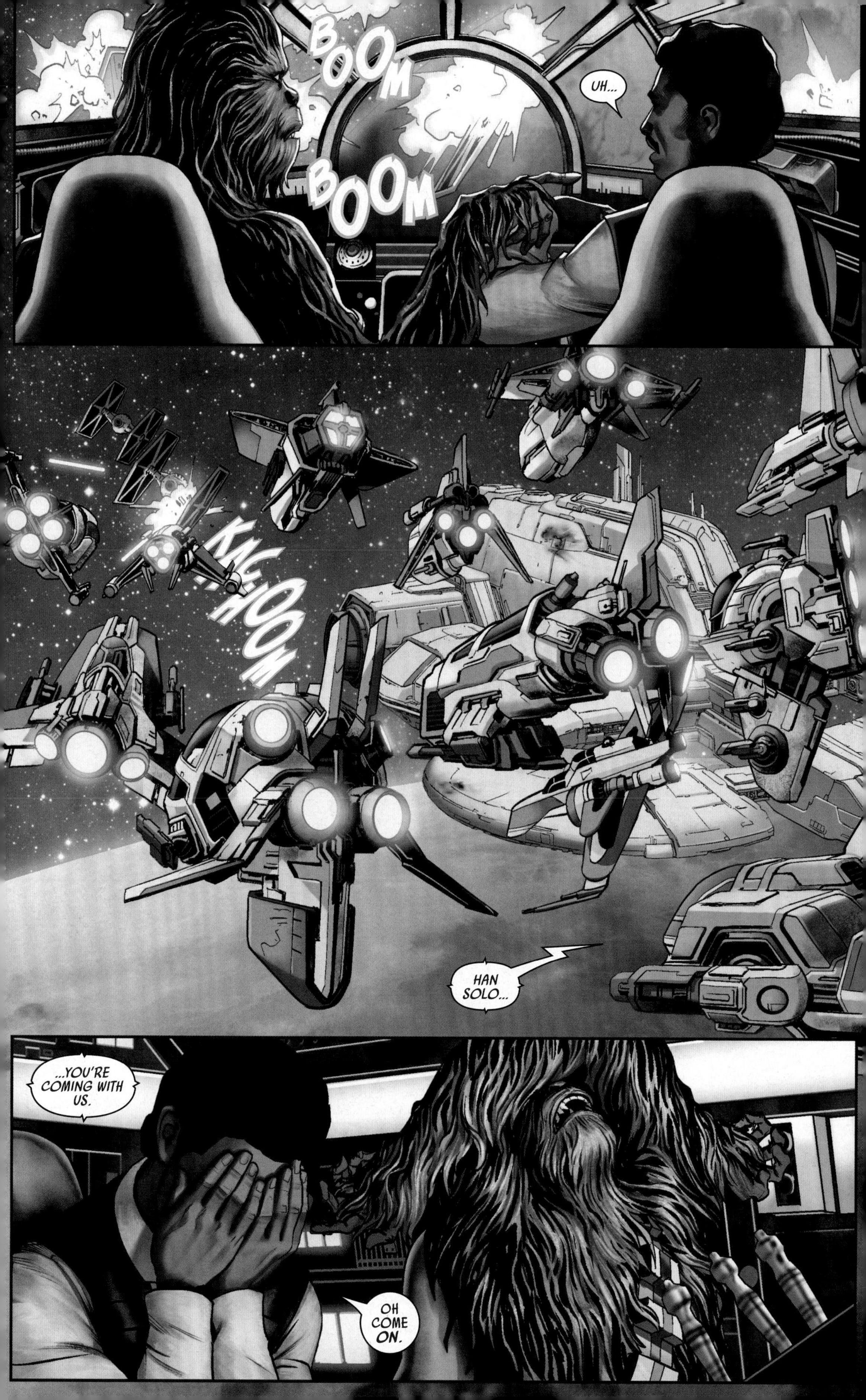
BOOM
UH...
BOOM
KA-KOOOM
HAN SOLO...
...YOU'RE COMING WITH US.
OH COME ON.

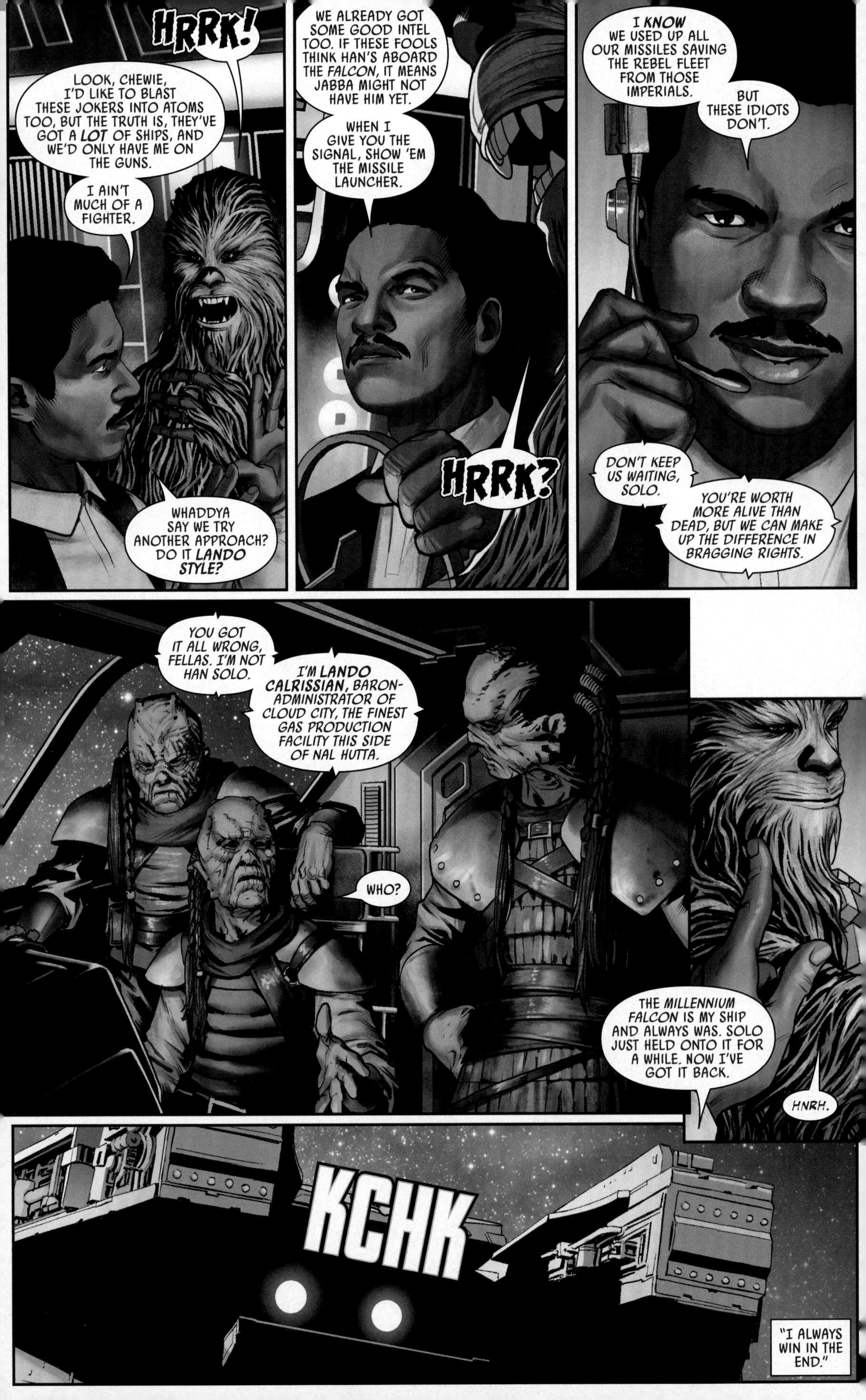
HRRK!
LOOK, CHEWIE, I'D LIKE TO BLAST THESE JOKERS INTO ATOMS TOO, BUT THE TRUTH IS, THEY'VE GOT A LOT OF SHIPS, AND WE'D ONLY HAVE ME ON THE GUNS.
I AIN'T MUCH OF A FIGHTER.
WHADDYA SAY WE TRY ANOTHER APPROACH? DO IT LANDO STYLE?
WE ALREADY GOT SOME GOOD INTEL TOO. IF THESE FOOLS THINK HAN'S ABOARD THE FALCON, IT MEANS JABBA MIGHT NOT HAVE HIM YET.
WHEN I GIVE YOU THE SIGNAL, SHOW 'EM THE MISSILE LAUNCHER.
HRRK?
I KNOW WE USED UP ALL OUR MISSILES SAVING THE REBEL FLEET FROM THOSE IMPERIALS.
BUT THESE IDIOTS DON'T.
DON'T KEEP US WAITING, SOLO.
YOU'RE WORTH MORE ALIVE THAN DEAD, BUT WE CAN MAKE UP THE DIFFERENCE IN BRAGGING RIGHTS.
YOU GOT IT ALL WRONG, FELLAS. I'M NOT HAN SOLO.
I'M LANDO CALRISSIAN, BARON-ADMINISTRATOR OF CLOUD CITY, THE FINEST GAS PRODUCTION FACILITY THIS SIDE OF NAL HUTTA.
WHO?
THE MILLENNIUM FALCON IS MY SHIP AND ALWAYS WAS. SOLO JUST HELD ONTO IT FOR A WHILE. NOW I'VE GOT IT BACK.
HNRH.
KCHK
"I ALWAYS WIN IN THE END."

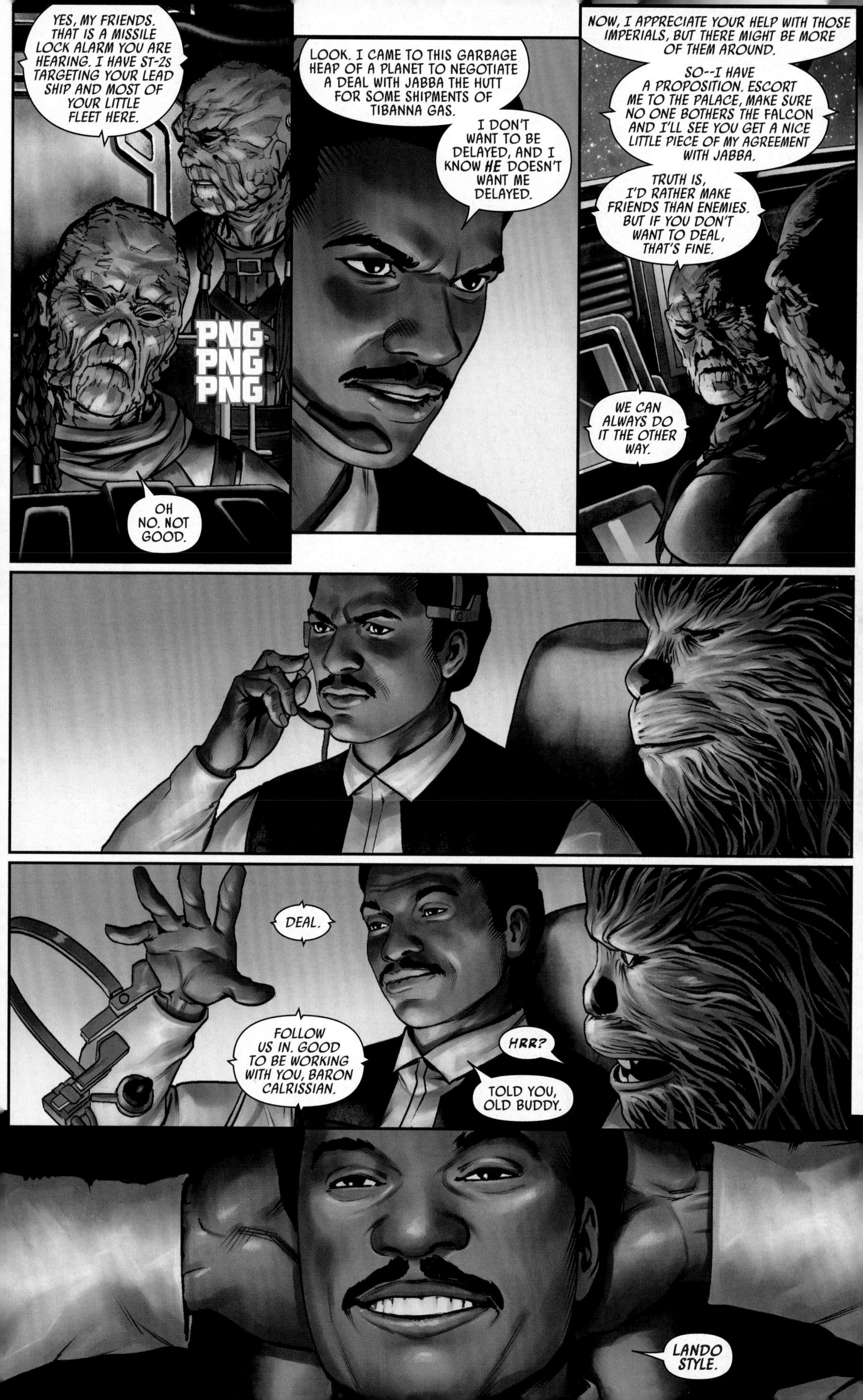
YES, MY FRIENDS. THAT IS A MISSILE LOCK ALARM YOU ARE HEARING. I HAVE ST-2s TARGETING YOUR LEAD SHIP AND MOST OF YOUR LITTLE FLEET HERE.
PNG PNG PNG
OH NO. NOT GOOD.
LOOK. I CAME TO THIS GARBAGE HEAP OF A PLANET TO NEGOTIATE A DEAL WITH JABBA THE HUTT FOR SOME SHIPMENTS OF TIBANNA GAS.
I DON'T WANT TO BE DELAYED, AND I KNOW HE DOESN'T WANT ME DELAYED.
NOW, I APPRECIATE YOUR HELP WITH THOSE IMPERIALS, BUT THERE MIGHT BE MORE OF THEM AROUND.
SO--I HAVE A PROPOSITION. ESCORT ME TO THE PALACE, MAKE SURE NO ONE BOTHERS THE FALCON AND I'LL SEE YOU GET A NICE LITTLE PIECE OF MY AGREEMENT WITH JABBA.
TRUTH IS, I'D RATHER MAKE FRIENDS THAN ENEMIES. BUT IF YOU DON'T WANT TO DEAL, THAT'S FINE.
WE CAN ALWAYS DO IT THE OTHER WAY.
DEAL.
FOLLOW US IN. GOOD TO BE WORKING WITH YOU, BARON CALRISSIAN.
HRR?
TOLD YOU, OLD BUDDY.
LANDO STYLE.

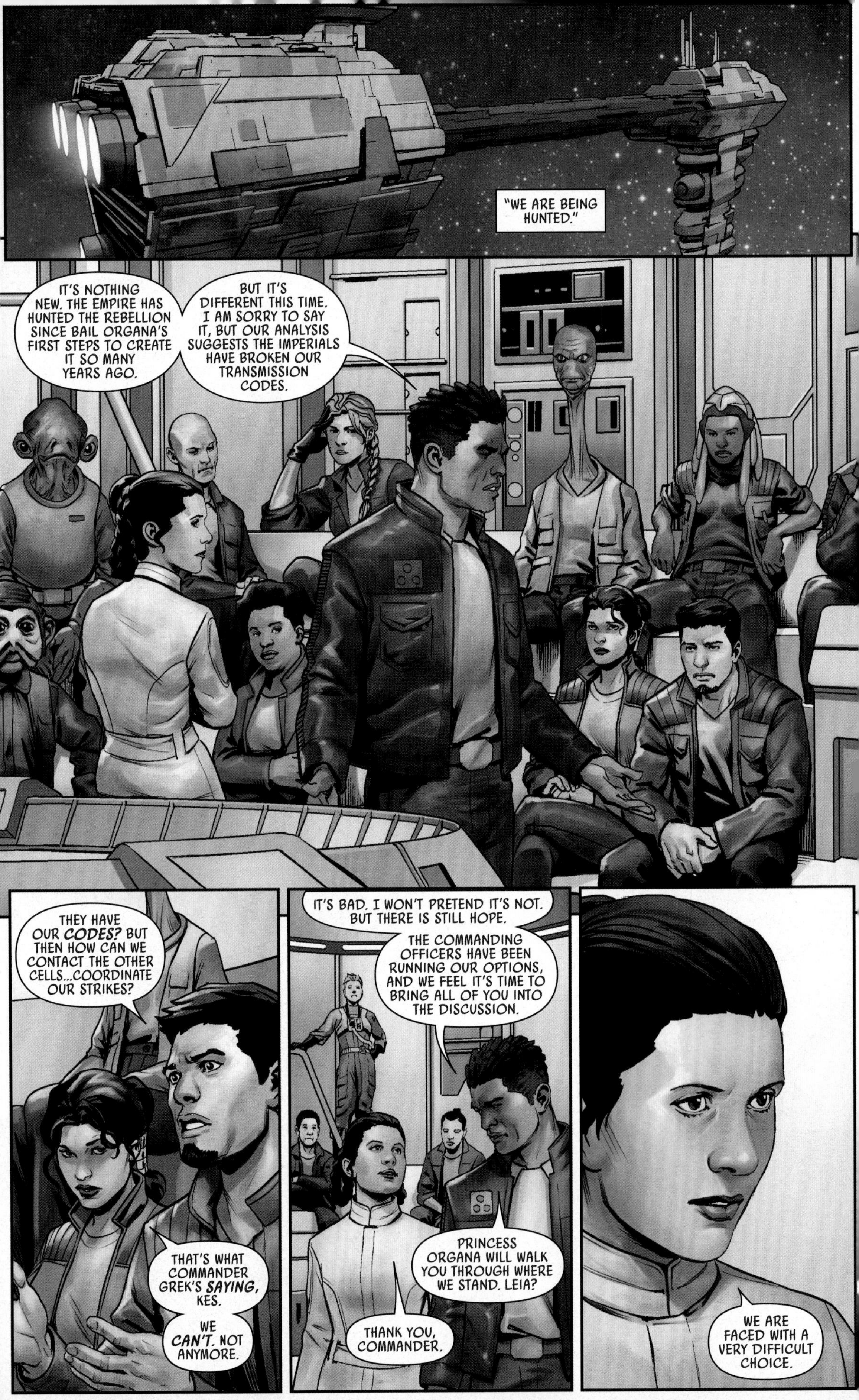
"WE ARE BEING HUNTED."
IT'S NOTHING NEW. THE EMPIRE HAS HUNTED THE REBELLION SINCE BAIL ORGANA'S FIRST STEPS TO CREATE IT SO MANY YEARS AGO.
BUT IT'S DIFFERENT THIS TIME. I AM SORRY TO SAY IT, BUT OUR ANALYSIS SUGGESTS THE IMPERIALS HAVE BROKEN OUR TRANSMISSION CODES.
THEY HAVE OUR *CODES?* BUT THEN HOW CAN WE CONTACT THE OTHER CELLS...COORDINATE OUR STRIKES?
THAT'S WHAT COMMANDER GREK'S *SAYING*, KES.
WE *CAN'T*. NOT ANYMORE.
IT'S BAD. I WON'T PRETEND IT'S NOT. BUT THERE IS STILL HOPE.
THE COMMANDING OFFICERS HAVE BEEN RUNNING OUR OPTIONS, AND WE FEEL IT'S TIME TO BRING ALL OF YOU INTO THE DISCUSSION.
PRINCESS ORGANA WILL WALK YOU THROUGH WHERE WE STAND. LEIA?
THANK YOU, COMMANDER.
WE ARE FACED WITH A VERY DIFFICULT CHOICE.

OUR FLEET DISPERSED INTO THE GALAXY AFTER HOTH. SMALL GROUPS, EACH TO ITS ASSIGNED RALLY POINT, NONE KNOWING THE LOCATION OF ANY OTHER CELL.

THIS WAS DONE TO MAKE IT HARDER FOR THE EMPIRE TO TRACK DOWN THE ENTIRE FLEET. EVEN IF THEY FOUND ONE CELL, THEY COULDN'T FIND US ALL.

THE ORIGINAL PLAN WAS TO SEND CODED COMMUNICATIONS AT SET INTERVALS TO OTHER CELLS AND SLOWLY PULL THE FLEET BACK TOGETHER.

WE CAN NO LONGER DO THAT.

EVERY TIME ONE CELL COMMUNICATES WITH ANOTHER, THE EMPIRE WILL INTERCEPT THE SIGNAL AND SEND FLEETS TO ERADICATE BOTH.

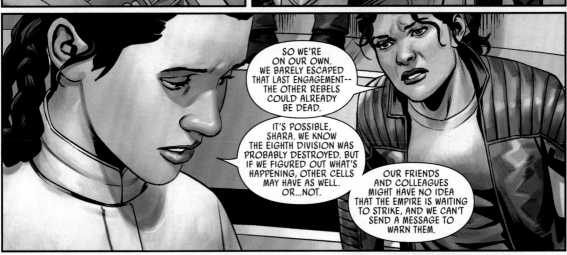

SO WE'RE ON OUR OWN. WE BARELY ESCAPED THAT LAST ENGAGEMENT-- THE OTHER REBELS COULD ALREADY BE DEAD.

IT'S POSSIBLE, SHARA. WE KNOW THE EIGHTH DIVISION WAS PROBABLY DESTROYED. BUT IF WE FIGURED OUT WHAT'S HAPPENING, OTHER CELLS MAY HAVE AS WELL. OR...NOT.

OUR FRIENDS AND COLLEAGUES MIGHT HAVE NO IDEA THAT THE EMPIRE IS WAITING TO STRIKE, AND WE CAN'T SEND A MESSAGE TO WARN THEM.

SO, THE CHOICE.

DO WE HIDE AND WAIT AND HOPE MON MOTHMA OR ACKBAR OR THE OTHER REBEL LEADERS HAVE SURVIVED AND WILL FIND A WAY TO CONTACT US WITH INSTRUCTIONS...

...OR DO WE GET OUT THERE AND SOLVE THIS *OURSELVES?*

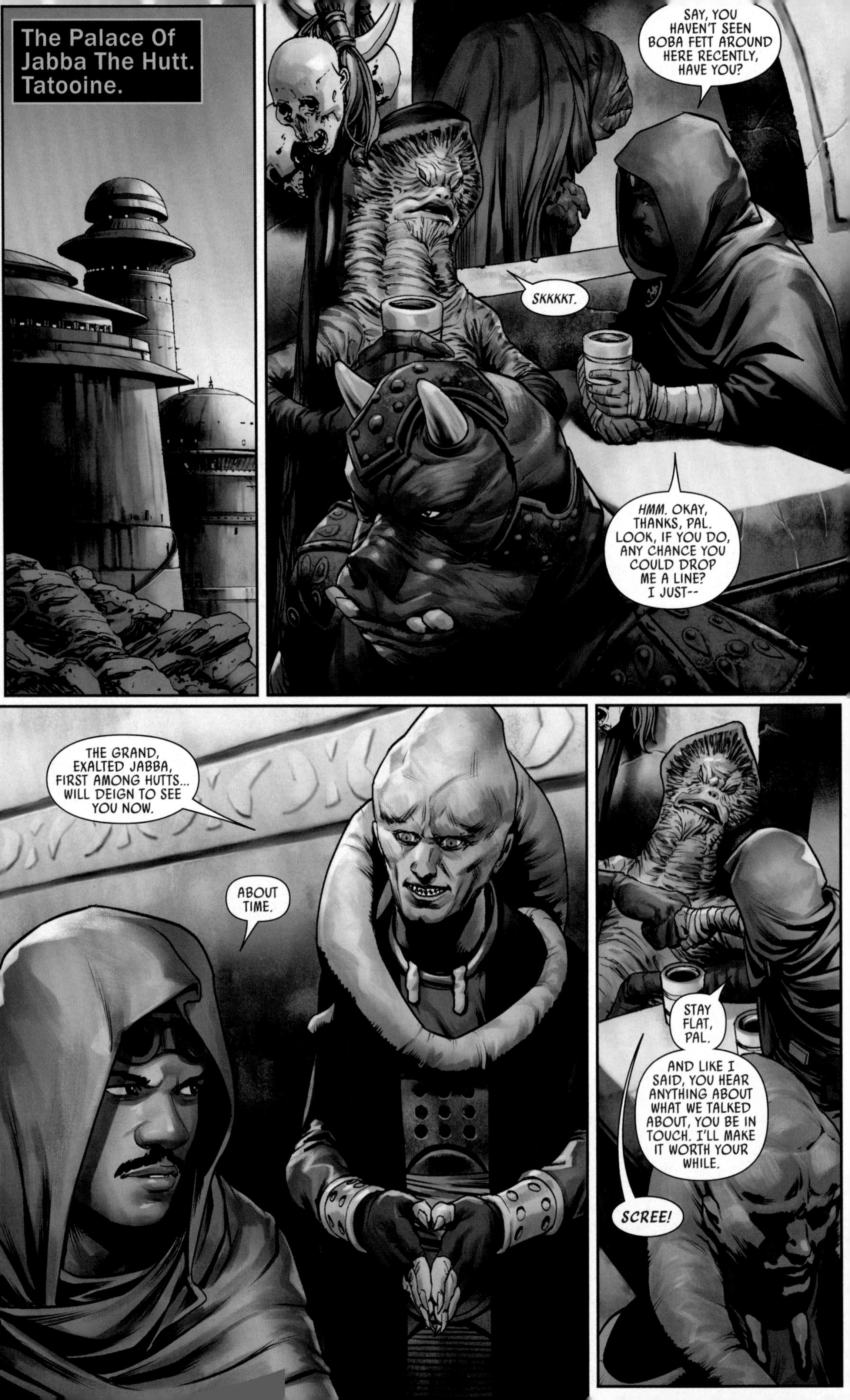
The Palace Of Jabba The Hutt. Tatooine.
SAY, YOU HAVEN'T SEEN BOBA FETT AROUND HERE RECENTLY, HAVE YOU?
SKKKKT.
HMM. OKAY, THANKS, PAL. LOOK, IF YOU DO, ANY CHANCE YOU COULD DROP ME A LINE? I JUST--
THE GRAND, EXALTED JABBA, FIRST AMONG HUTTS... WILL DEIGN TO SEE YOU NOW.
ABOUT TIME.
STAY FLAT, PAL.
AND LIKE I SAID, YOU HEAR ANYTHING ABOUT WHAT WE TALKED ABOUT, YOU BE IN TOUCH. I'LL MAKE IT WORTH YOUR WHILE.
SCREE!

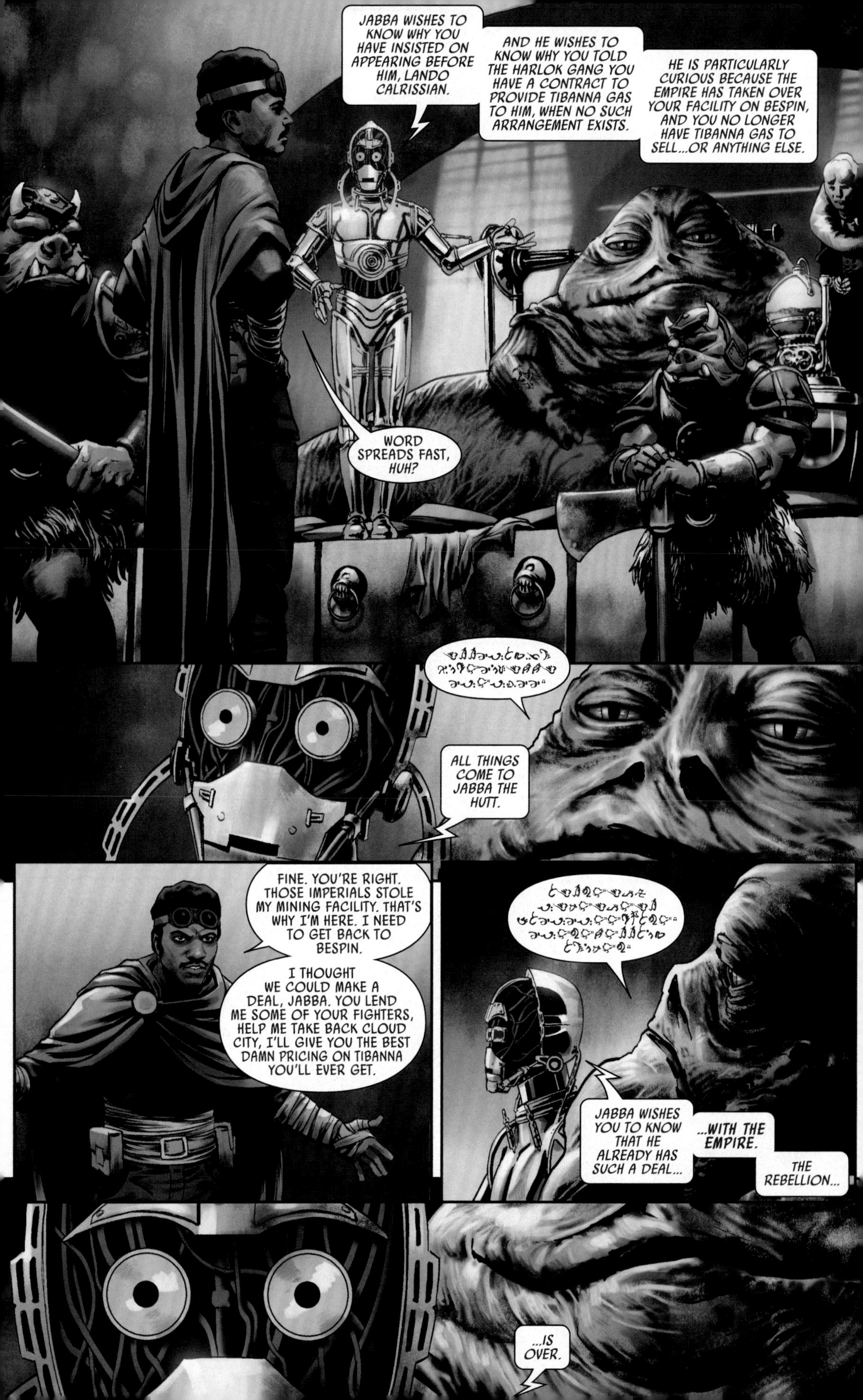
JABBA WISHES TO KNOW WHY YOU HAVE INSISTED ON APPEARING BEFORE HIM, LANDO CALRISSIAN.
AND HE WISHES TO KNOW WHY YOU TOLD THE HARLOK GANG YOU HAVE A CONTRACT TO PROVIDE TIBANNA GAS TO HIM, WHEN NO SUCH ARRANGEMENT EXISTS.
HE IS PARTICULARLY CURIOUS BECAUSE THE EMPIRE HAS TAKEN OVER YOUR FACILITY ON BESPIN, AND YOU NO LONGER HAVE TIBANNA GAS TO SELL...OR ANYTHING ELSE.
WORD SPREADS FAST, HUH?
ALL THINGS COME TO JABBA THE HUTT.
FINE. YOU'RE RIGHT. THOSE IMPERIALS STOLE MY MINING FACILITY. THAT'S WHY I'M HERE. I NEED TO GET BACK TO BESPIN.
I THOUGHT WE COULD MAKE A DEAL, JABBA. YOU LEND ME SOME OF YOUR FIGHTERS, HELP ME TAKE BACK CLOUD CITY, I'LL GIVE YOU THE BEST DAMN PRICING ON TIBANNA YOU'LL EVER GET.
JABBA WISHES YOU TO KNOW THAT HE ALREADY HAS SUCH A DEAL...
...WITH THE EMPIRE.
THE REBELLION...
...IS OVER.

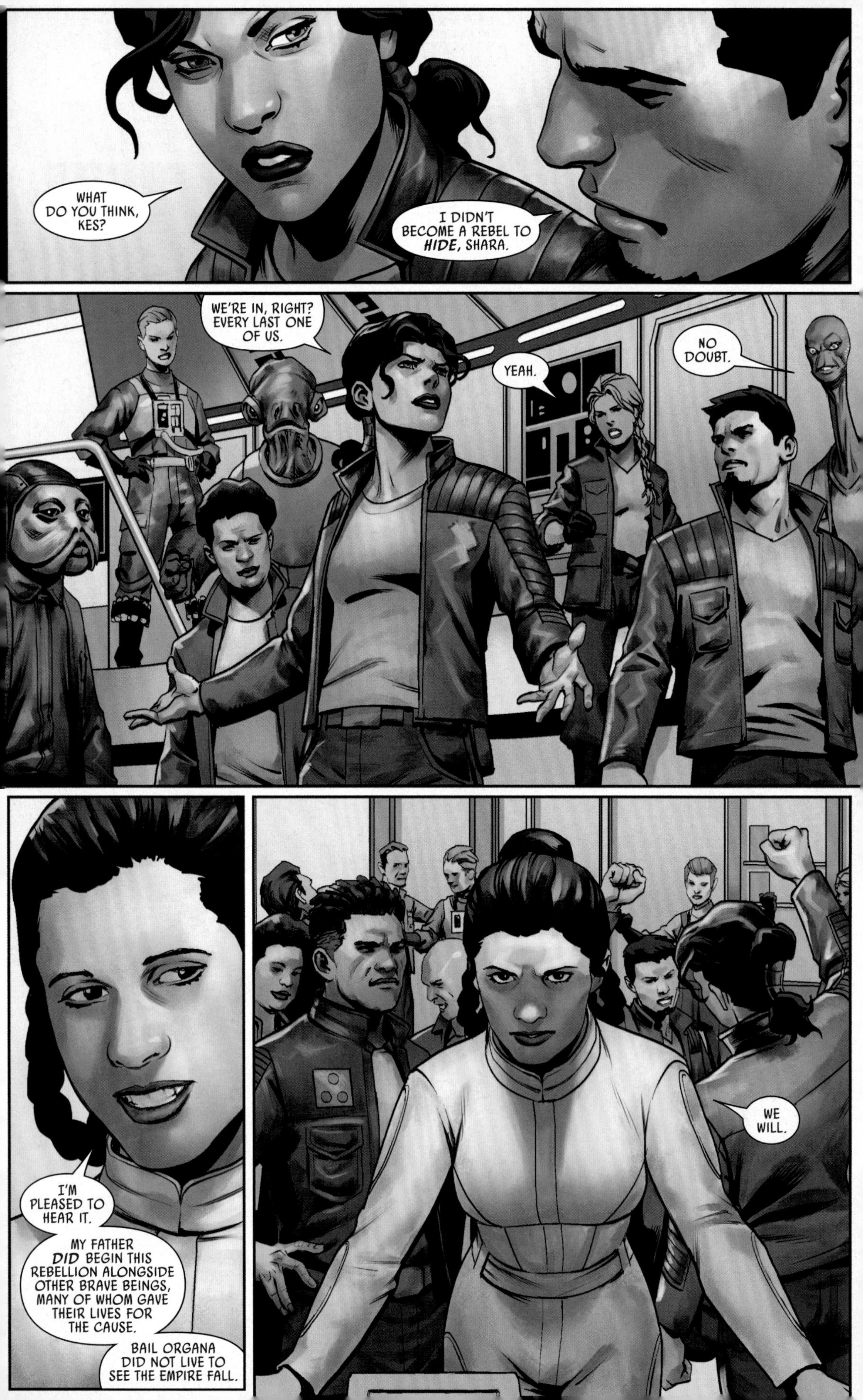
WHAT DO YOU THINK, KES?
I DIDN'T BECOME A REBEL TO *HIDE*, SHARA.
WE'RE IN, RIGHT? EVERY LAST ONE OF US.
YEAH.
NO DOUBT.
WE WILL.
I'M PLEASED TO HEAR IT.
MY FATHER *DID* BEGIN THIS REBELLION ALONGSIDE OTHER BRAVE BEINGS, MANY OF WHOM GAVE THEIR LIVES FOR THE CAUSE.
BAIL ORGANA DID NOT LIVE TO SEE THE EMPIRE FALL.

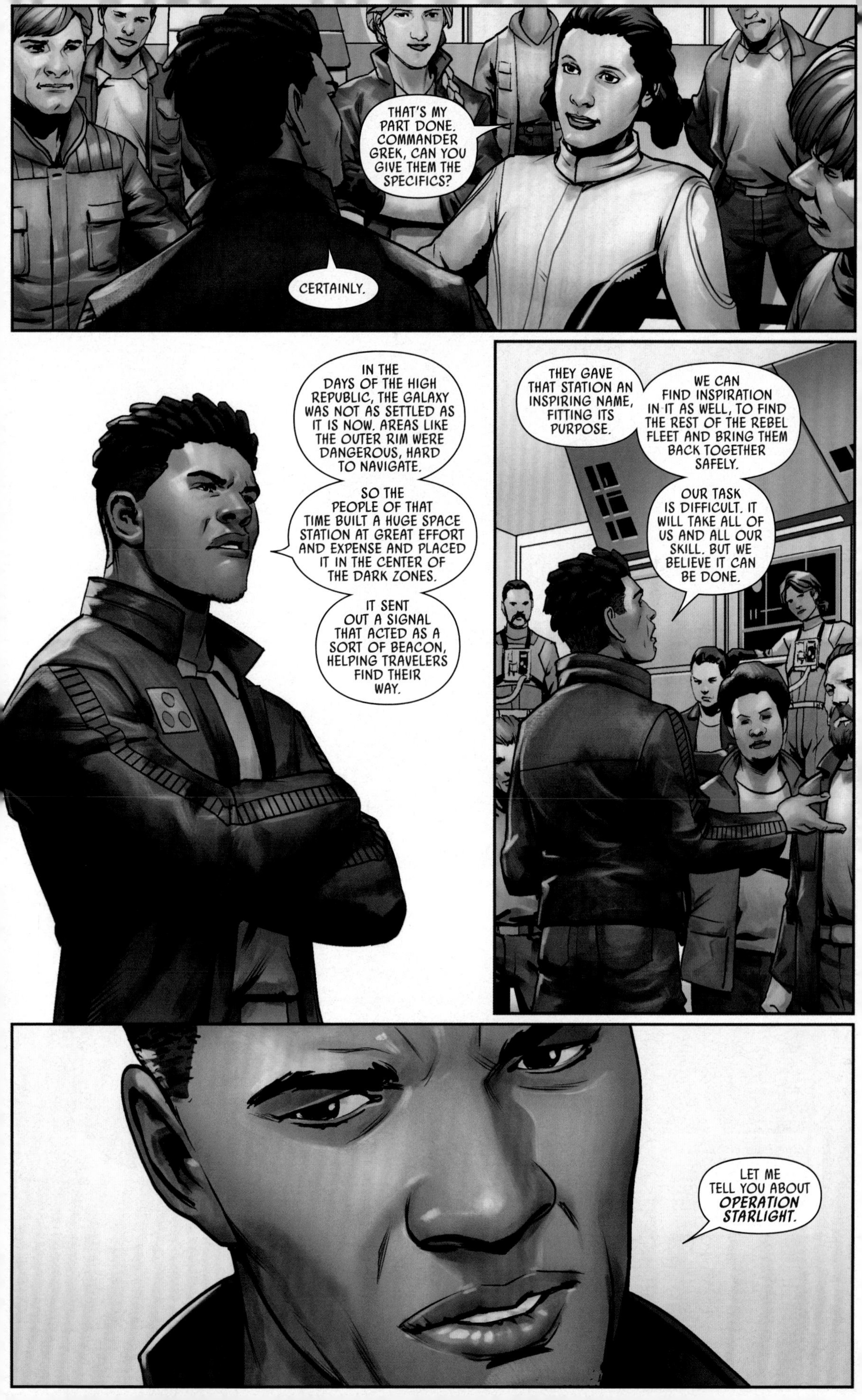
THAT'S MY PART DONE. COMMANDER GREK, CAN YOU GIVE THEM THE SPECIFICS?
CERTAINLY.
IN THE DAYS OF THE HIGH REPUBLIC, THE GALAXY WAS NOT AS SETTLED AS IT IS NOW. AREAS LIKE THE OUTER RIM WERE DANGEROUS, HARD TO NAVIGATE.
SO THE PEOPLE OF THAT TIME BUILT A HUGE SPACE STATION AT GREAT EFFORT AND EXPENSE AND PLACED IT IN THE CENTER OF THE DARK ZONES.
IT SENT OUT A SIGNAL THAT ACTED AS A SORT OF BEACON, HELPING TRAVELERS FIND THEIR WAY.
THEY GAVE THAT STATION AN INSPIRING NAME, FITTING ITS PURPOSE.
WE CAN FIND INSPIRATION IN IT AS WELL, TO FIND THE REST OF THE REBEL FLEET AND BRING THEM BACK TOGETHER SAFELY.
OUR TASK IS DIFFICULT. IT WILL TAKE ALL OF US AND ALL OUR SKILL. BUT WE BELIEVE IT CAN BE DONE.
LET ME TELL YOU ABOUT *OPERATION STARLIGHT.*

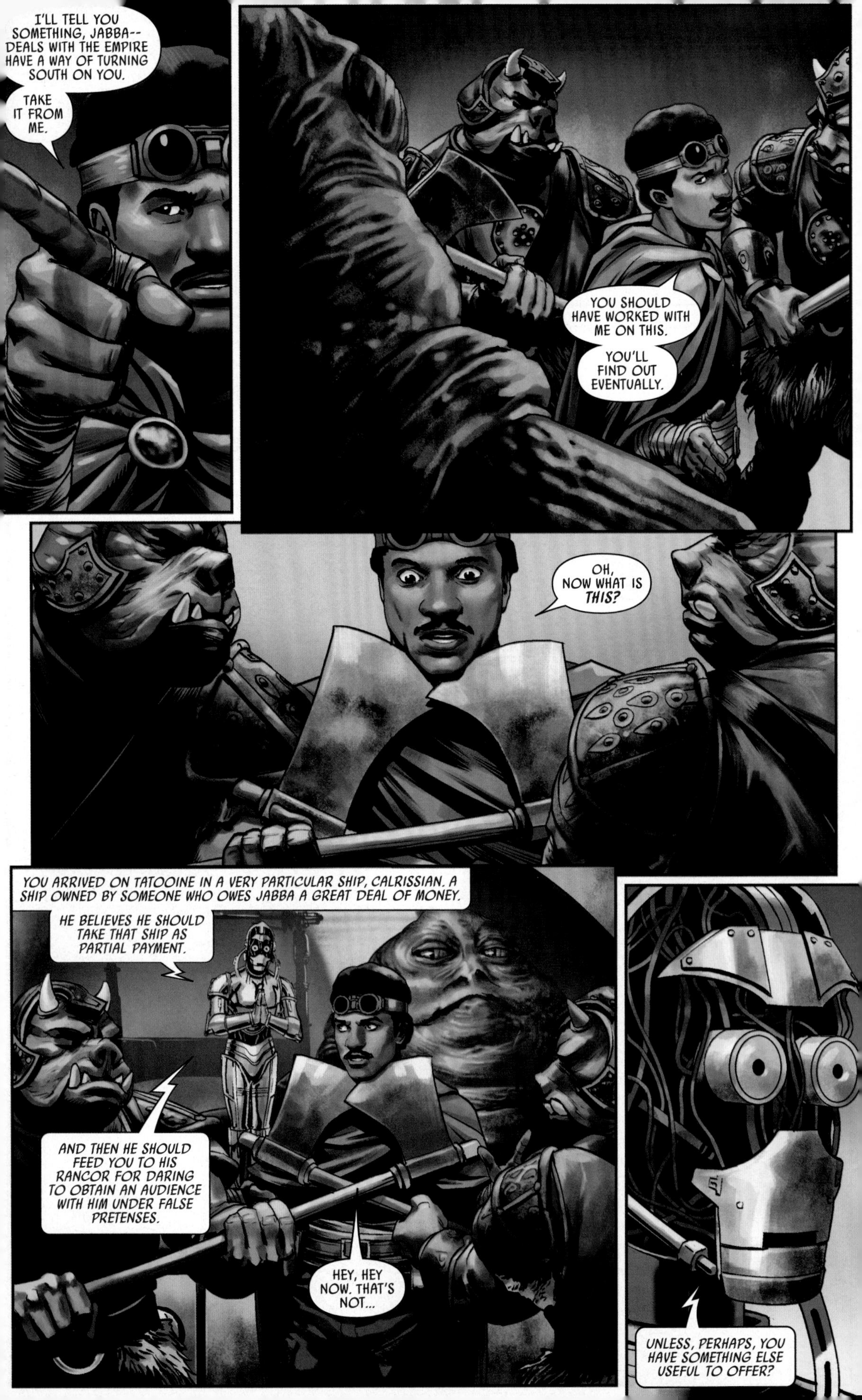
I'LL TELL YOU SOMETHING, JABBA-- DEALS WITH THE EMPIRE HAVE A WAY OF TURNING SOUTH ON YOU.
TAKE IT FROM ME.
YOU SHOULD HAVE WORKED WITH ME ON THIS.
YOU'LL FIND OUT EVENTUALLY.
OH, NOW WHAT IS THIS?
YOU ARRIVED ON TATOOINE IN A VERY PARTICULAR SHIP, CALRISSIAN. A SHIP OWNED BY SOMEONE WHO OWES JABBA A GREAT DEAL OF MONEY.
HE BELIEVES HE SHOULD TAKE THAT SHIP AS PARTIAL PAYMENT.
AND THEN HE SHOULD FEED YOU TO HIS RANCOR FOR DARING TO OBTAIN AN AUDIENCE WITH HIM UNDER FALSE PRETENSES.
HEY, HEY NOW. THAT'S NOT...
UNLESS, PERHAPS, YOU HAVE SOMETHING ELSE USEFUL TO OFFER?

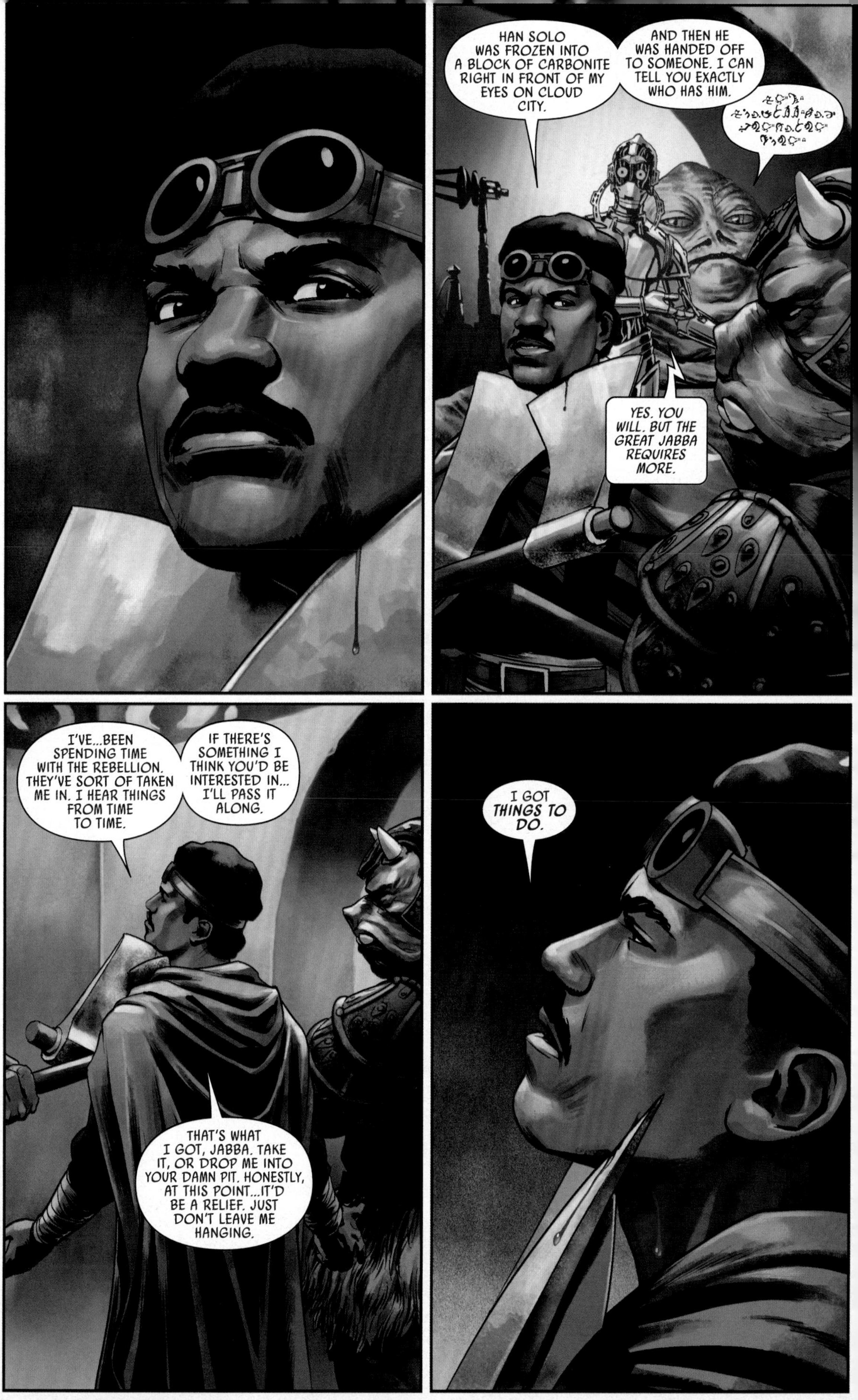
HAN SOLO WAS FROZEN INTO A BLOCK OF CARBONITE RIGHT IN FRONT OF MY EYES ON CLOUD CITY.
AND THEN HE WAS HANDED OFF TO SOMEONE. I CAN TELL YOU EXACTLY WHO HAS HIM.
YES. YOU WILL. BUT THE GREAT JABBA REQUIRES MORE.
I'VE...BEEN SPENDING TIME WITH THE REBELLION. THEY'VE SORT OF TAKEN ME IN. I HEAR THINGS FROM TIME TO TIME.
IF THERE'S SOMETHING I THINK YOU'D BE INTERESTED IN... I'LL PASS IT ALONG.
THAT'S WHAT I GOT, JABBA. TAKE IT, OR DROP ME INTO YOUR DAMN PIT. HONESTLY, AT THIS POINT...IT'D BE A RELIEF. JUST DON'T LEAVE ME HANGING.
I GOT *THINGS TO DO.*

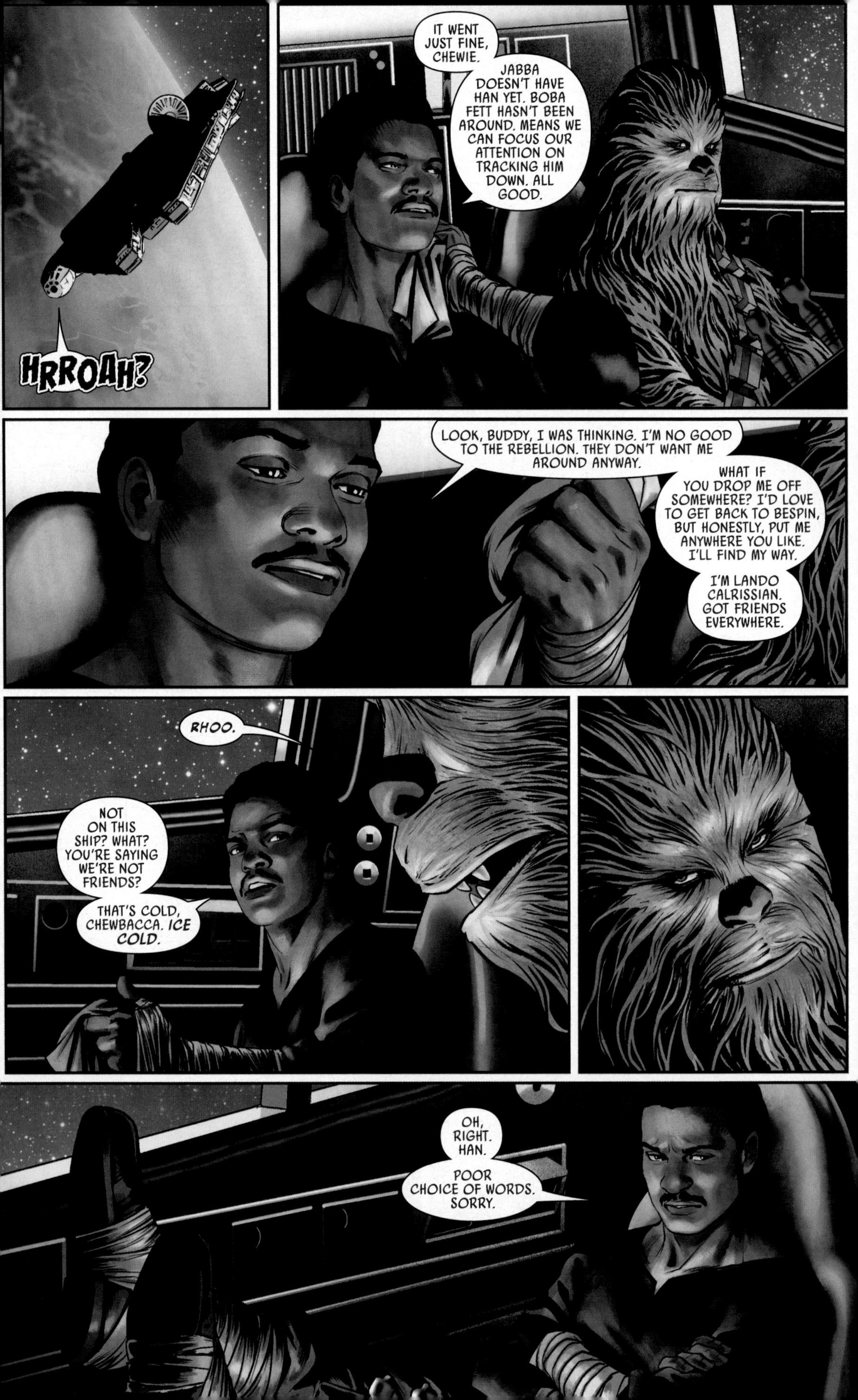
HRROAH?
IT WENT JUST FINE, CHEWIE.
JABBA DOESN'T HAVE HAN YET. BOBA FETT HASN'T BEEN AROUND. MEANS WE CAN FOCUS OUR ATTENTION ON TRACKING HIM DOWN. ALL GOOD.
LOOK, BUDDY, I WAS THINKING. I'M NO GOOD TO THE REBELLION. THEY DON'T WANT ME AROUND ANYWAY.
WHAT IF YOU DROP ME OFF SOMEWHERE? I'D LOVE TO GET BACK TO BESPIN, BUT HONESTLY, PUT ME ANYWHERE YOU LIKE. I'LL FIND MY WAY.
I'M LANDO CALRISSIAN. GOT FRIENDS EVERYWHERE.
RHOO.
NOT ON THIS SHIP? WHAT? YOU'RE SAYING WE'RE NOT FRIENDS?
THAT'S COLD, CHEWBACCA. *ICE COLD.*
OH, RIGHT. HAN.
POOR CHOICE OF WORDS. SORRY.

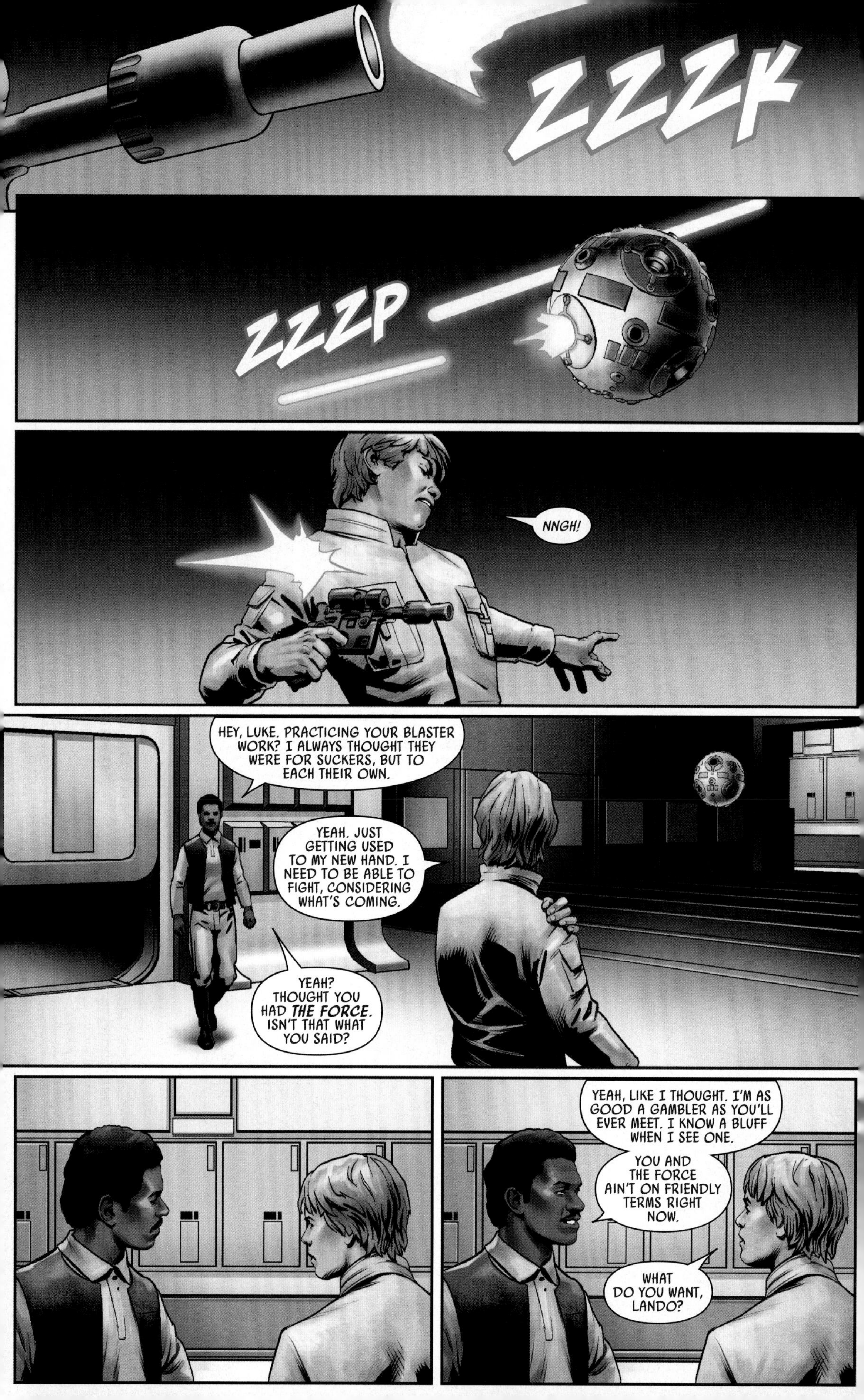
ZZZK
ZZZP
NNGH!
HEY, LUKE. PRACTICING YOUR BLASTER WORK? I ALWAYS THOUGHT THEY WERE FOR SUCKERS, BUT TO EACH THEIR OWN.
YEAH. JUST GETTING USED TO MY NEW HAND. I NEED TO BE ABLE TO FIGHT, CONSIDERING WHAT'S COMING.
YEAH? THOUGHT YOU HAD *THE FORCE.* ISN'T THAT WHAT YOU SAID?
YEAH, LIKE I THOUGHT. I'M AS GOOD A GAMBLER AS YOU'LL EVER MEET. I KNOW A BLUFF WHEN I SEE ONE.
YOU AND THE FORCE AIN'T ON FRIENDLY TERMS RIGHT NOW.
WHAT DO YOU WANT, LANDO?

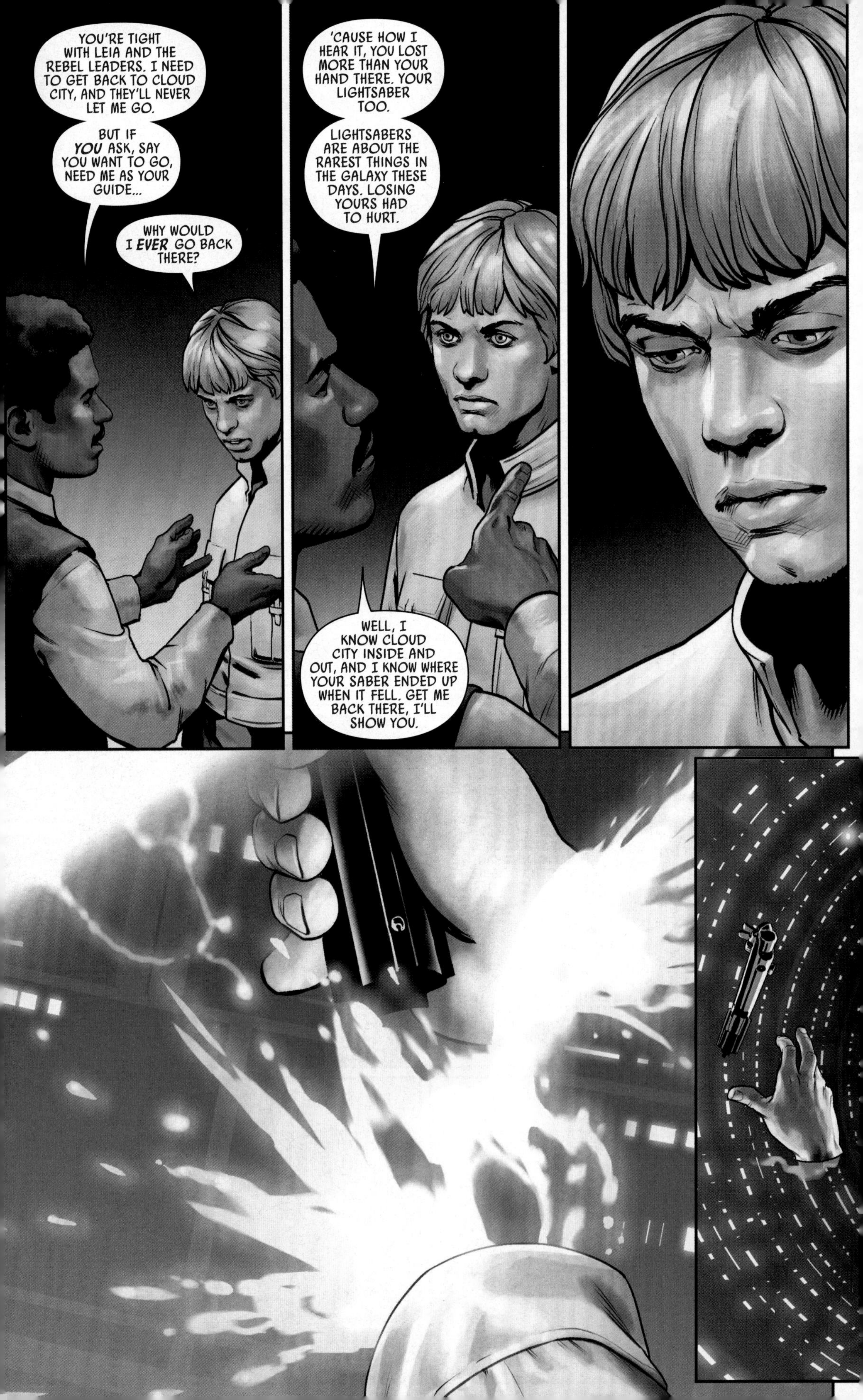
YOU'RE TIGHT WITH LEIA AND THE REBEL LEADERS. I NEED TO GET BACK TO CLOUD CITY, AND THEY'LL NEVER LET ME GO.
BUT IF *YOU* ASK, SAY YOU WANT TO GO, NEED ME AS YOUR GUIDE...
WHY WOULD I *EVER* GO BACK THERE?
'CAUSE HOW I HEAR IT, YOU LOST MORE THAN YOUR HAND THERE. YOUR LIGHTSABER TOO.
LIGHTSABERS ARE ABOUT THE RAREST THINGS IN THE GALAXY THESE DAYS. LOSING YOURS HAD TO HURT.
WELL, I KNOW CLOUD CITY INSIDE AND OUT, AND I KNOW WHERE YOUR SABER ENDED UP WHEN IT FELL. GET ME BACK THERE, I'LL SHOW YOU.

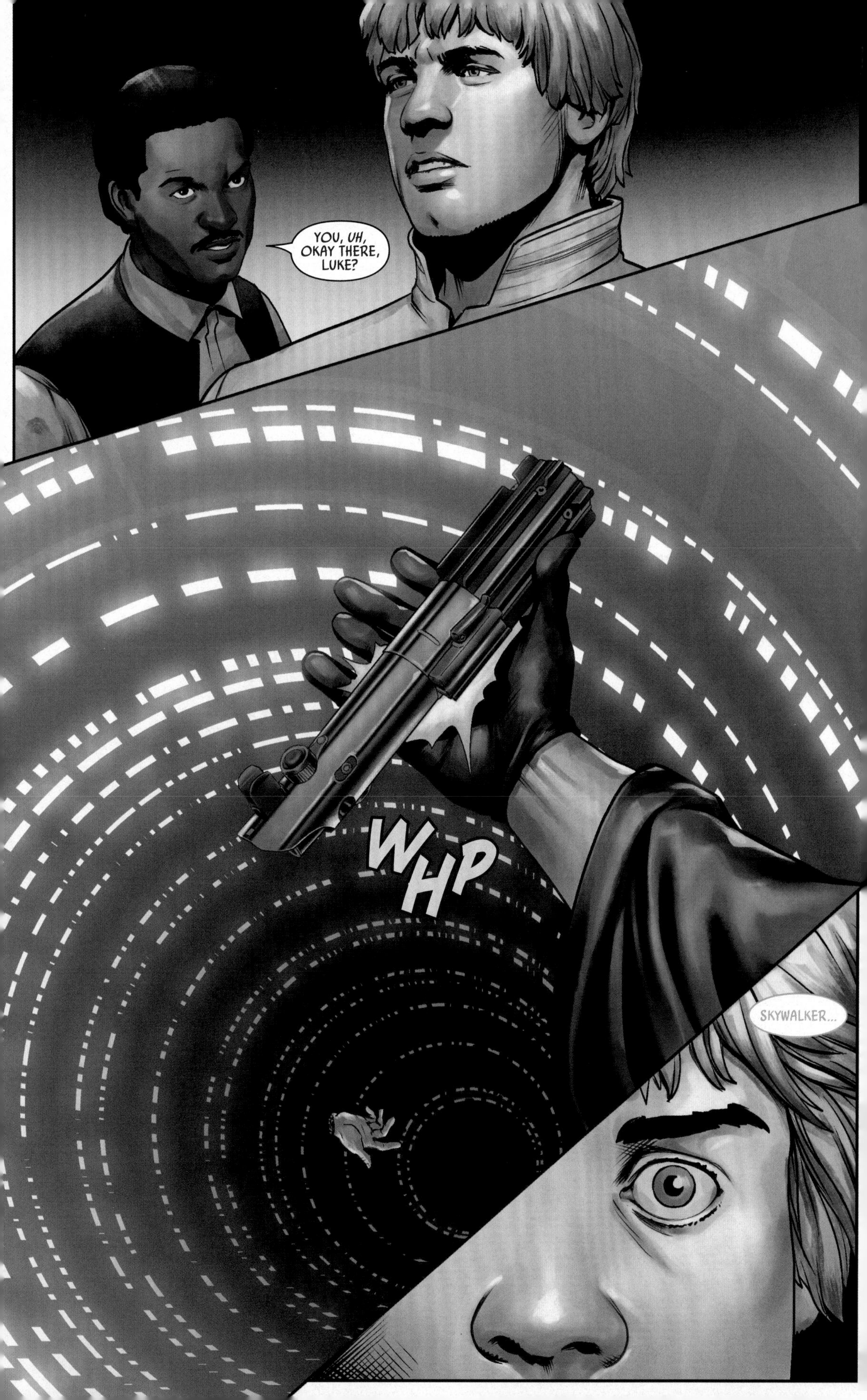
YOU, UH, OKAY THERE, LUKE?
WHP
SKYWALKER...

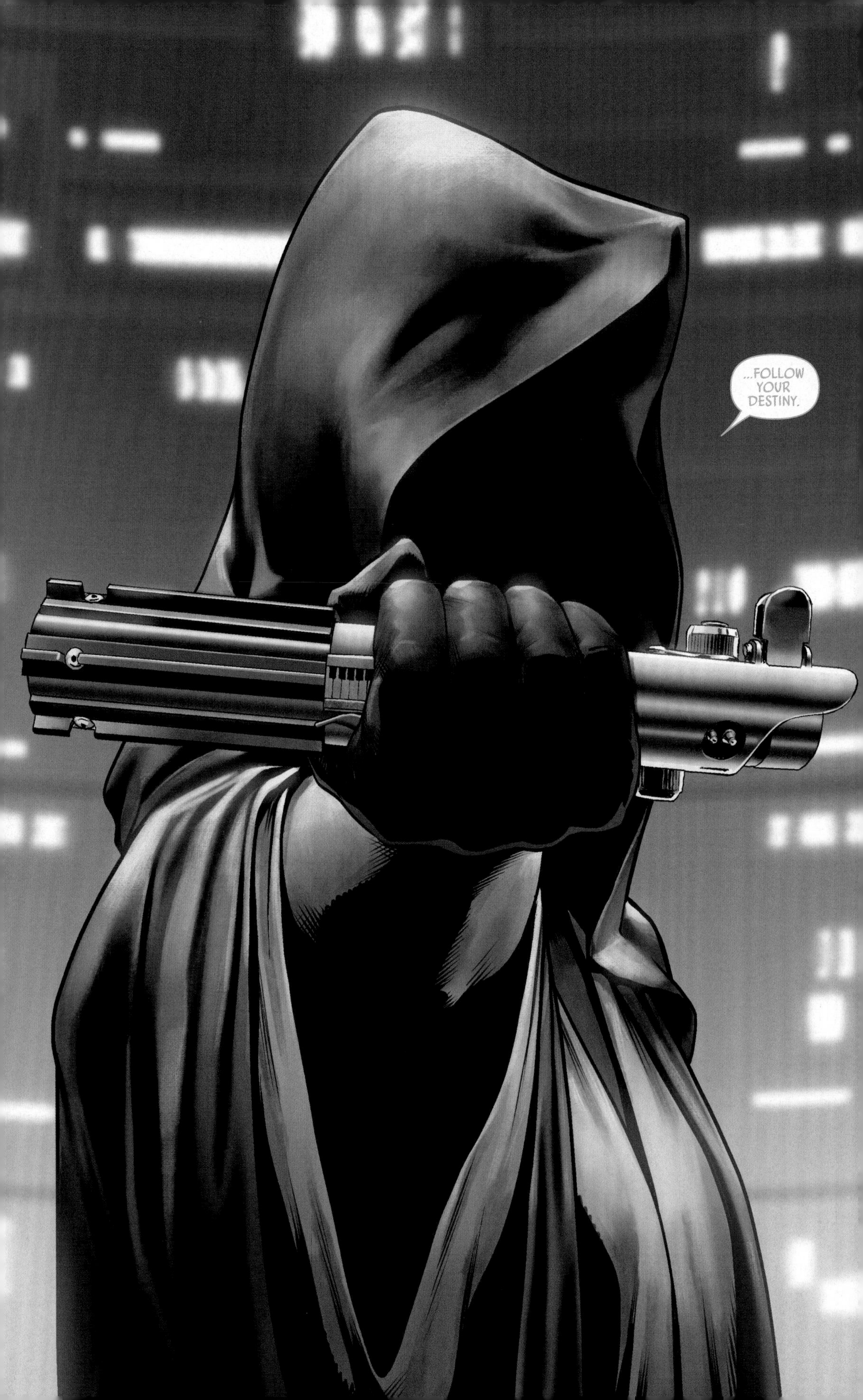
...FOLLOW YOUR DESTINY.

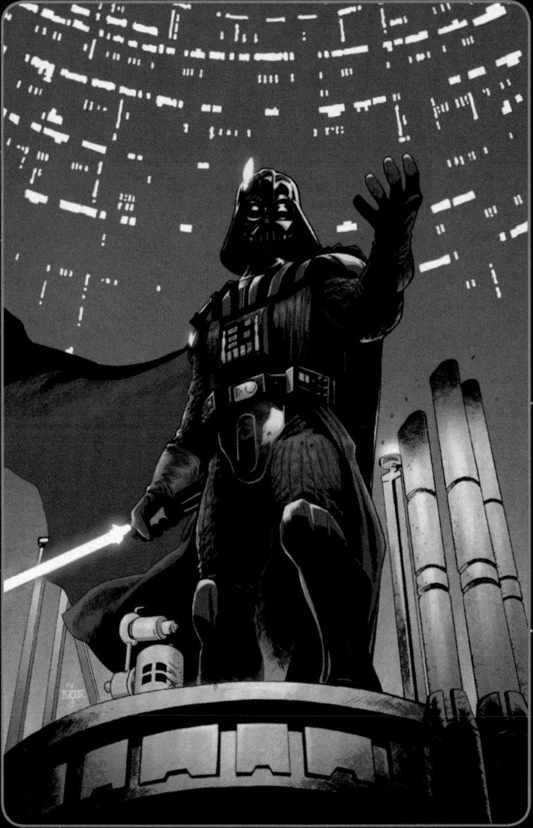

#1 Variant by
MAHMUD ASRAR & MATTHEW WILSON

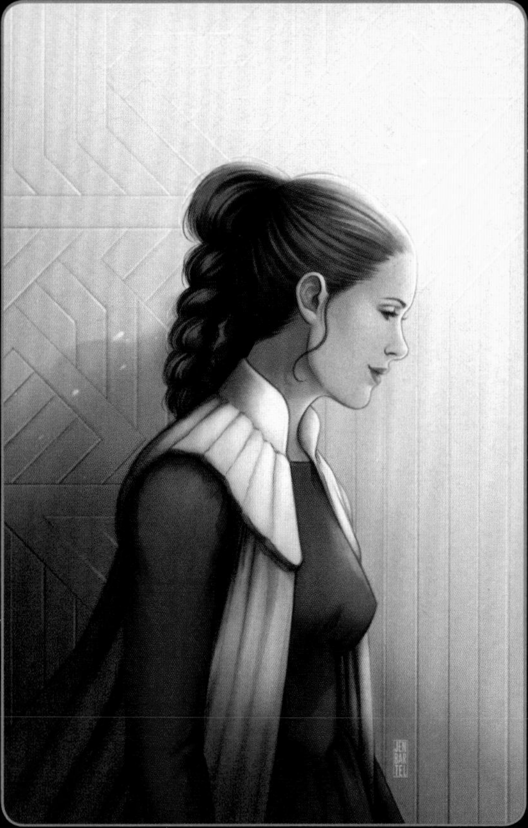

#1 Variant by
JEN BARTEL

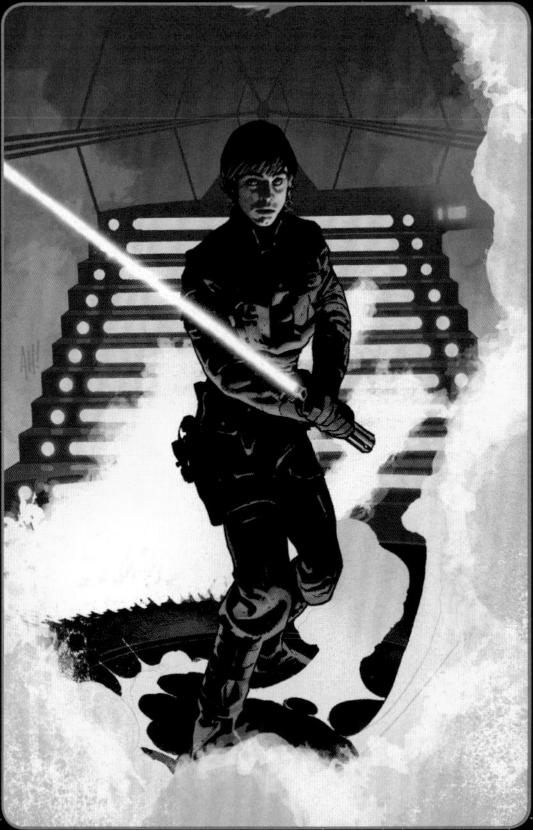

#1 Variant by
ADAM HUGHES

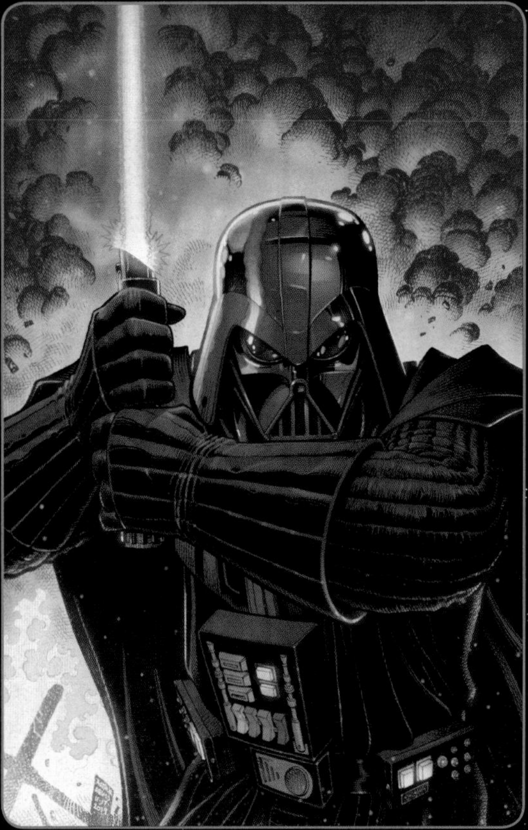

#1 Variant by
ARTHUR ADAMS & JESUS ABURTOV

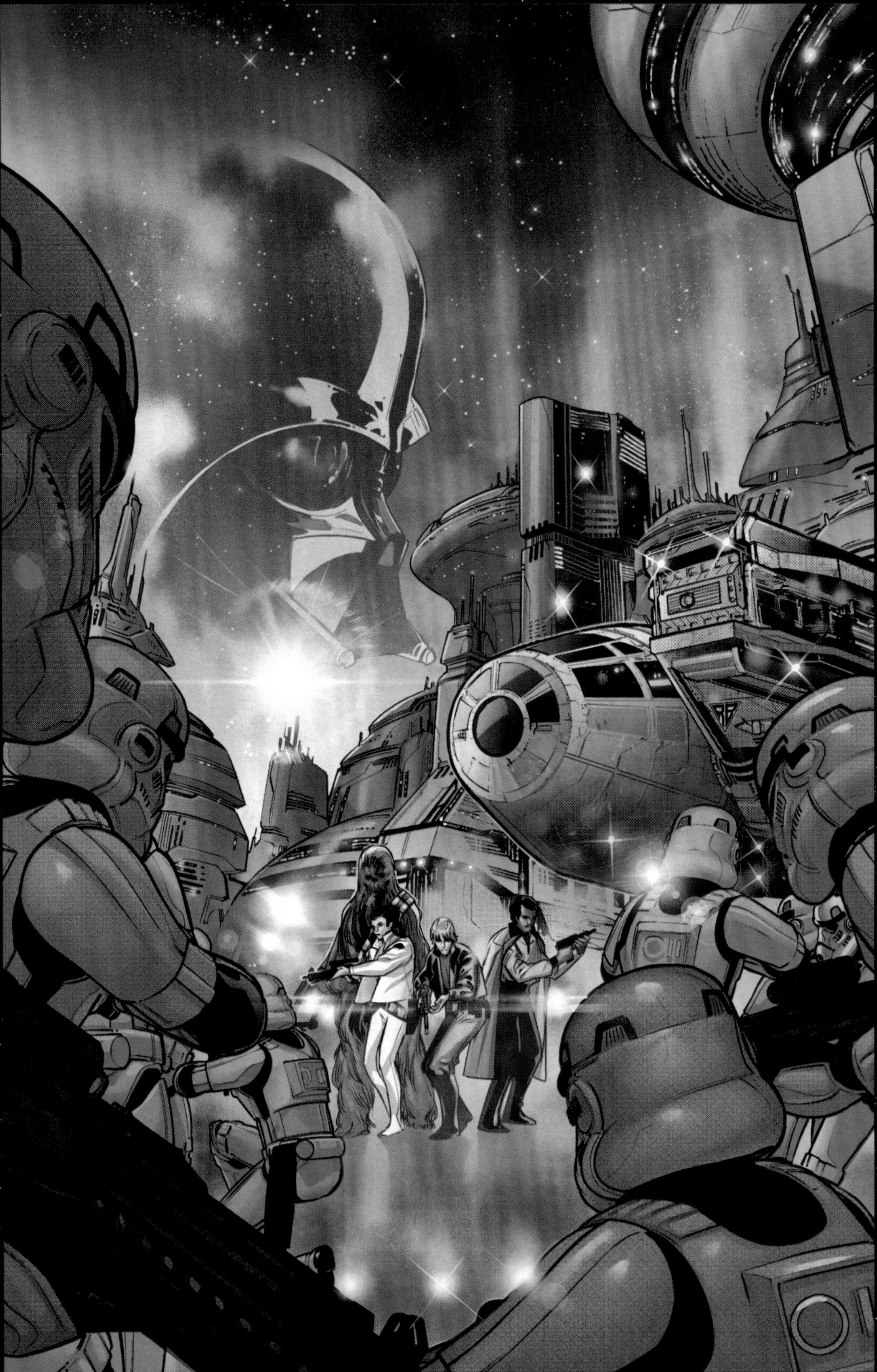

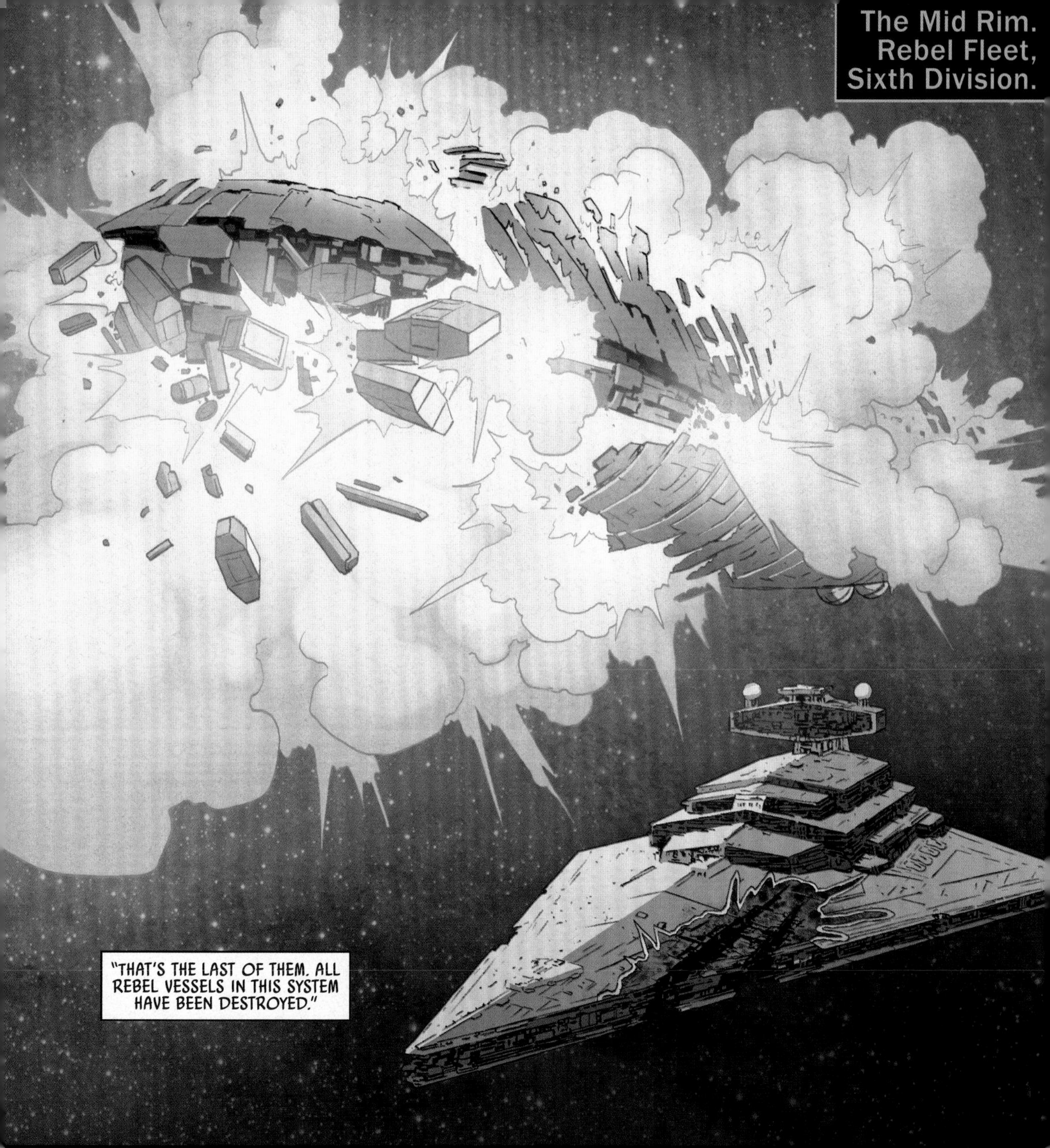
The Mid Rim. Rebel Fleet, Sixth Division.
"THAT'S THE LAST OF THEM. ALL REBEL VESSELS IN THIS SYSTEM HAVE BEEN DESTROYED."

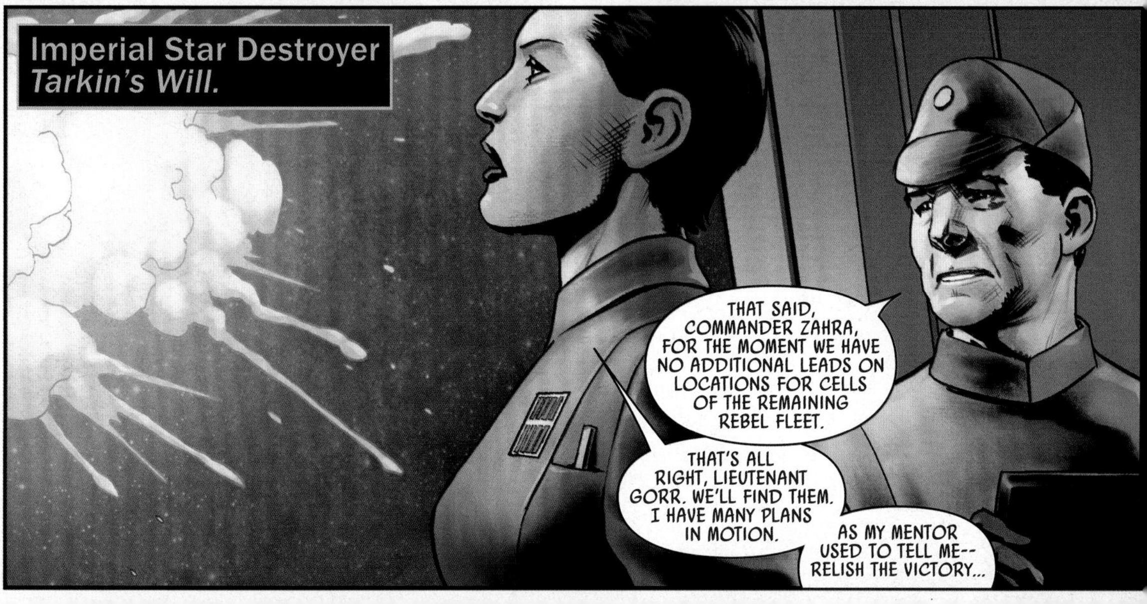
Imperial Star Destroyer *Tarkin's Will.*
THAT SAID, COMMANDER ZAHRA, FOR THE MOMENT WE HAVE NO ADDITIONAL LEADS ON LOCATIONS FOR CELLS OF THE REMAINING REBEL FLEET.
THAT'S ALL RIGHT, LIEUTENANT GORR. WE'LL FIND THEM. I HAVE MANY PLANS IN MOTION.
AS MY MENTOR USED TO TELL ME--RELISH THE VICTORY...

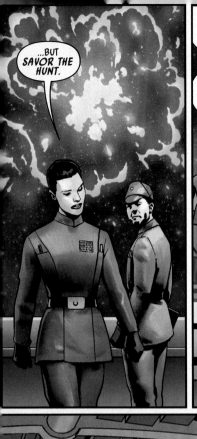

...BUT *SAVOR THE HUNT.*

COMMANDER, IF I MAY--WHILE WE ARE AWAITING OUR NEXT ENGAGEMENT, I THOUGHT THIS COULD BE A GOOD OPPORTUNITY TO EXECUTE REPAIRS ON THE SHIP'S HULL.

I'VE TAKEN THE LIBERTY OF DRAWING UP A DUTY ROSTER, AND I BELIEVE THAT WE COULD HAVE THE DAMAGE LARGELY REPAIRED WITHIN--

LIEUTENANT GORR, WHY WOULD YOU DO SOMETHING SO FOOLISH?

DON'T YOU KNOW WHAT THIS SHIP *REPRESENTS?*

NOT JUST TO ME...

...BUT TO EVERY SOUL ABOARD?

I APOLOGIZE IF I HAVE OFFENDED YOU IN ANY WAY, COMMANDER, BUT I WAS ASSIGNED TO THE *TARKIN'S WILL* AS YOUR SECOND ONLY DAYS BEFORE WE EMBARKED.

I WASN'T BRIEFED, AND...

THIS VESSEL IS A MEMORIAL TO THE GREAT TRAGEDY OF THE *DEATH STAR.*

AND AN INSTRUMENT OF VENGEANCE FOR EVERYONE WHO DIED WITH IT.

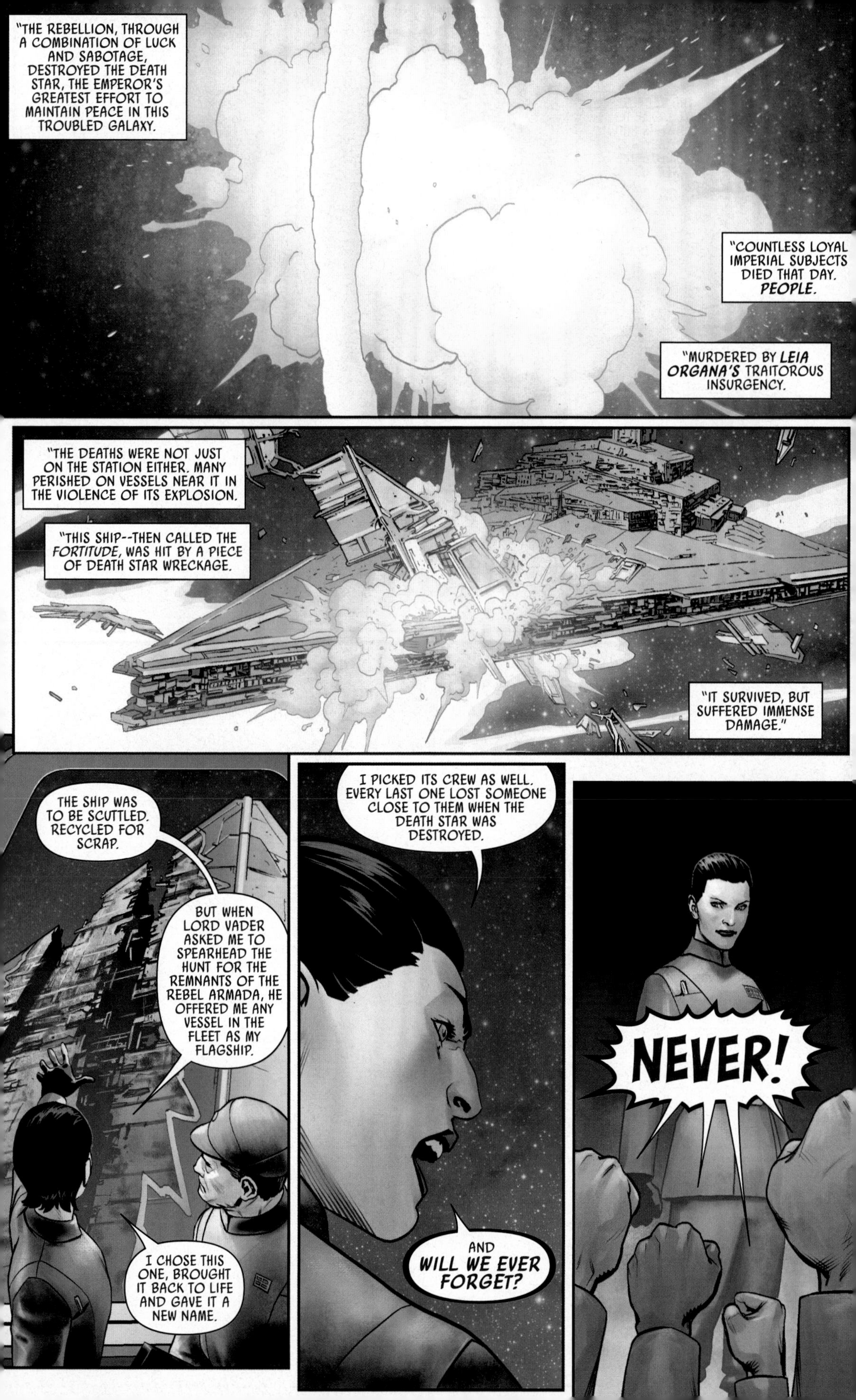
"THE REBELLION, THROUGH A COMBINATION OF LUCK AND SABOTAGE, DESTROYED THE DEATH STAR, THE EMPEROR'S GREATEST EFFORT TO MAINTAIN PEACE IN THIS TROUBLED GALAXY.
"COUNTLESS LOYAL IMPERIAL SUBJECTS DIED THAT DAY. PEOPLE.
"MURDERED BY LEIA ORGANA'S TRAITOROUS INSURGENCY.
"THE DEATHS WERE NOT JUST ON THE STATION EITHER. MANY PERISHED ON VESSELS NEAR IT IN THE VIOLENCE OF ITS EXPLOSION.
"THIS SHIP--THEN CALLED THE FORTITUDE, WAS HIT BY A PIECE OF DEATH STAR WRECKAGE.
"IT SURVIVED, BUT SUFFERED IMMENSE DAMAGE."
THE SHIP WAS TO BE SCUTTLED. RECYCLED FOR SCRAP.
BUT WHEN LORD VADER ASKED ME TO SPEARHEAD THE HUNT FOR THE REMNANTS OF THE REBEL ARMADA, HE OFFERED ME ANY VESSEL IN THE FLEET AS MY FLAGSHIP.
I CHOSE THIS ONE, BROUGHT IT BACK TO LIFE AND GAVE IT A NEW NAME.
I PICKED ITS CREW AS WELL. EVERY LAST ONE LOST SOMEONE CLOSE TO THEM WHEN THE DEATH STAR WAS DESTROYED.
AND WILL WE EVER FORGET?
NEVER!

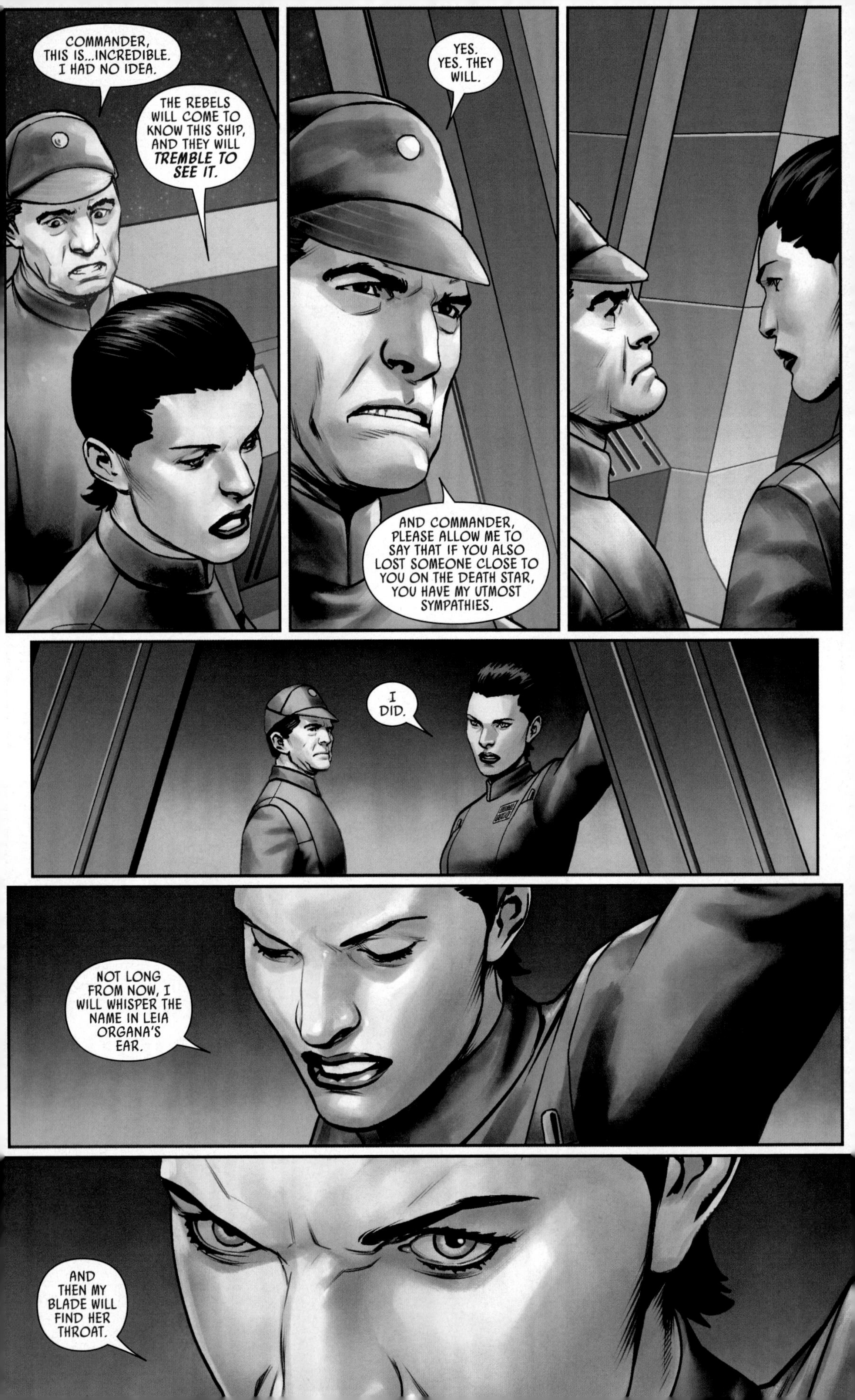

COMMANDER, THIS IS...INCREDIBLE. I HAD NO IDEA.
THE REBELS WILL COME TO KNOW THIS SHIP, AND THEY WILL *TREMBLE TO SEE IT.*
YES. YES. THEY WILL.
AND COMMANDER, PLEASE ALLOW ME TO SAY THAT IF YOU ALSO LOST SOMEONE CLOSE TO YOU ON THE DEATH STAR, YOU HAVE MY UTMOST SYMPATHIES.
I DID.
NOT LONG FROM NOW, I WILL WHISPER THE NAME IN LEIA ORGANA'S EAR.
AND THEN MY BLADE WILL FIND HER THROAT.

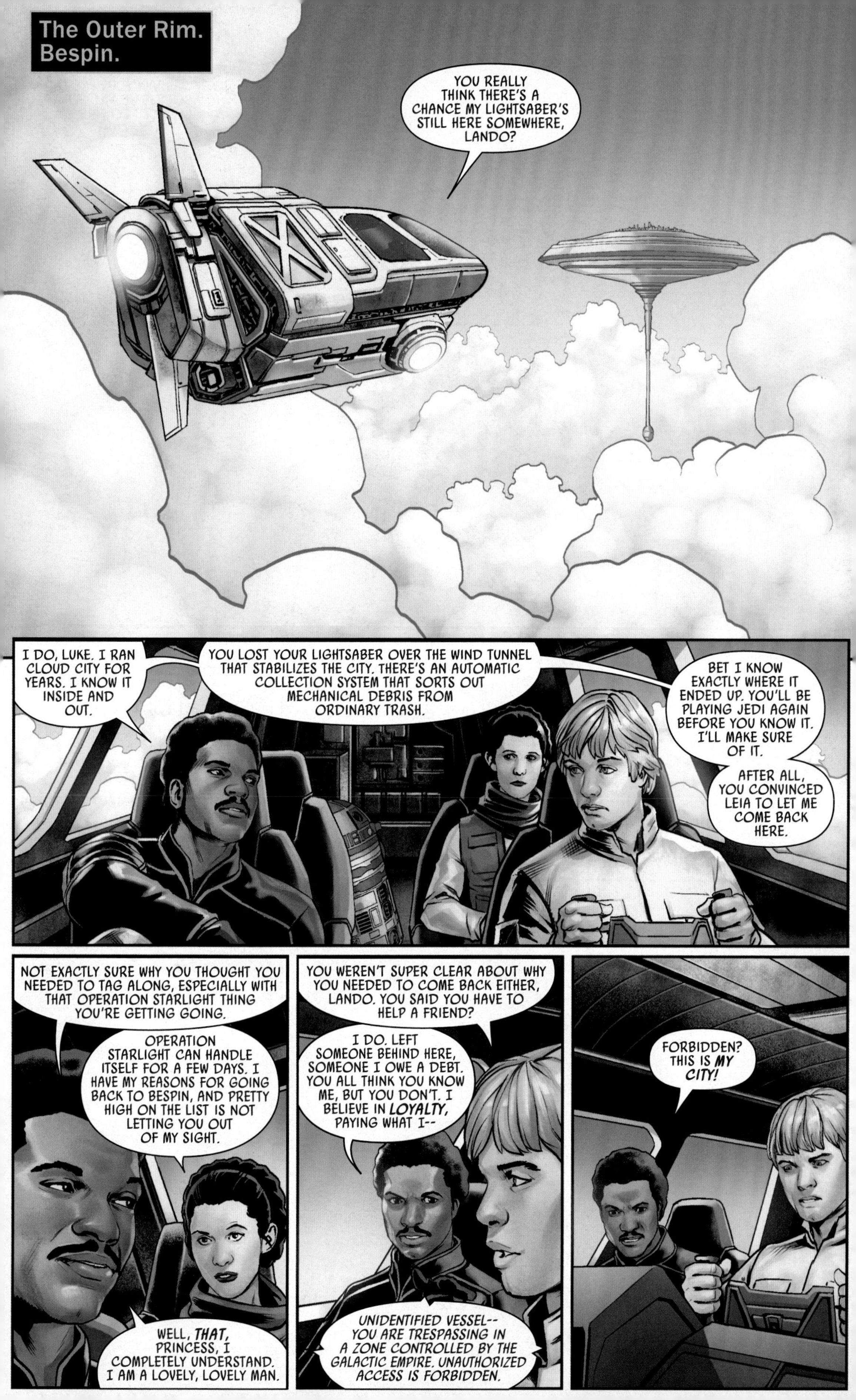
The Outer Rim.
Bespin.
YOU REALLY THINK THERE'S A CHANCE MY LIGHTSABER'S STILL HERE SOMEWHERE, LANDO?
I DO, LUKE. I RAN CLOUD CITY FOR YEARS. I KNOW IT INSIDE AND OUT.
YOU LOST YOUR LIGHTSABER OVER THE WIND TUNNEL THAT STABILIZES THE CITY. THERE'S AN AUTOMATIC COLLECTION SYSTEM THAT SORTS OUT MECHANICAL DEBRIS FROM ORDINARY TRASH.
BET I KNOW EXACTLY WHERE IT ENDED UP. YOU'LL BE PLAYING JEDI AGAIN BEFORE YOU KNOW IT. I'LL MAKE SURE OF IT.
AFTER ALL, YOU CONVINCED LEIA TO LET ME COME BACK HERE.
NOT EXACTLY SURE WHY YOU THOUGHT YOU NEEDED TO TAG ALONG, ESPECIALLY WITH THAT OPERATION STARLIGHT THING YOU'RE GETTING GOING.
OPERATION STARLIGHT CAN HANDLE ITSELF FOR A FEW DAYS. I HAVE MY REASONS FOR GOING BACK TO BESPIN, AND PRETTY HIGH ON THE LIST IS NOT LETTING YOU OUT OF MY SIGHT.
WELL, *THAT*, PRINCESS, I COMPLETELY UNDERSTAND. I AM A LOVELY, LOVELY MAN.
YOU WEREN'T SUPER CLEAR ABOUT WHY YOU NEEDED TO COME BACK EITHER, LANDO. YOU SAID YOU HAVE TO HELP A FRIEND?
I DO. LEFT SOMEONE BEHIND HERE, SOMEONE I OWE A DEBT. YOU ALL THINK YOU KNOW ME, BUT YOU DON'T. I BELIEVE IN *LOYALTY*, PAYING WHAT I--
UNIDENTIFIED VESSEL-- YOU ARE TRESPASSING IN A ZONE CONTROLLED BY THE GALACTIC EMPIRE. UNAUTHORIZED ACCESS IS FORBIDDEN.
FORBIDDEN? THIS IS *MY CITY!*

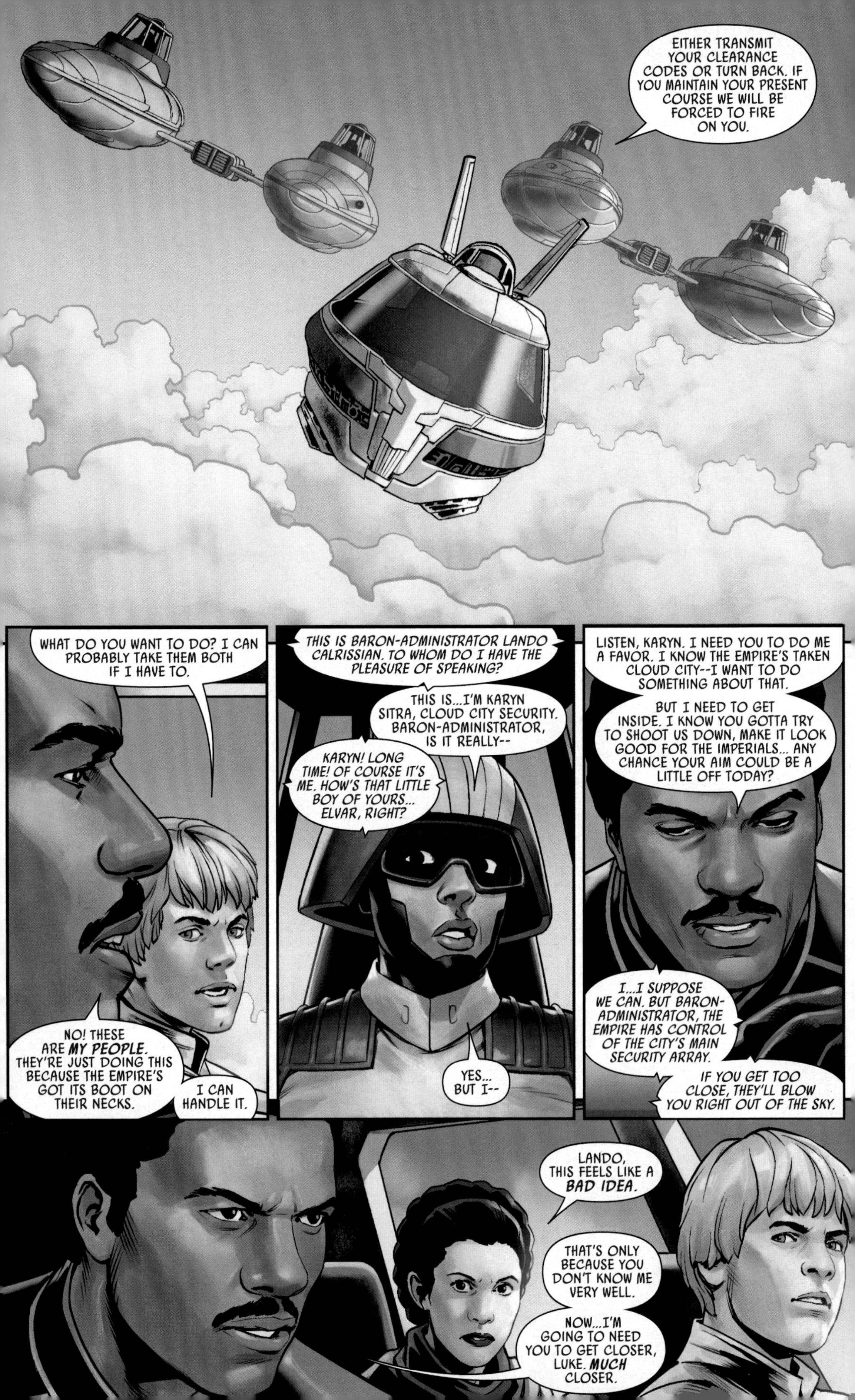
EITHER TRANSMIT YOUR CLEARANCE CODES OR TURN BACK. IF YOU MAINTAIN YOUR PRESENT COURSE WE WILL BE FORCED TO FIRE ON YOU.
WHAT DO YOU WANT TO DO? I CAN PROBABLY TAKE THEM BOTH IF I HAVE TO.
NO! THESE ARE *MY PEOPLE.* THEY'RE JUST DOING THIS BECAUSE THE EMPIRE'S GOT ITS BOOT ON THEIR NECKS.
I CAN HANDLE IT.
THIS IS BARON-ADMINISTRATOR LANDO CALRISSIAN. TO WHOM DO I HAVE THE PLEASURE OF SPEAKING?
THIS IS...I'M KARYN SITRA, CLOUD CITY SECURITY. BARON-ADMINISTRATOR, IS IT REALLY--
KARYN! LONG TIME! OF COURSE IT'S ME. HOW'S THAT LITTLE BOY OF YOURS... ELVAR, RIGHT?
YES... BUT I--
LISTEN, KARYN. I NEED YOU TO DO ME A FAVOR. I KNOW THE EMPIRE'S TAKEN CLOUD CITY--I WANT TO DO SOMETHING ABOUT THAT.
BUT I NEED TO GET INSIDE. I KNOW YOU GOTTA TRY TO SHOOT US DOWN, MAKE IT LOOK GOOD FOR THE IMPERIALS... ANY CHANCE YOUR AIM COULD BE A LITTLE OFF TODAY?
I...I SUPPOSE WE CAN. BUT BARON-ADMINISTRATOR, THE EMPIRE HAS CONTROL OF THE CITY'S MAIN SECURITY ARRAY.
IF YOU GET TOO CLOSE, THEY'LL BLOW YOU RIGHT OUT OF THE SKY.
LANDO, THIS FEELS LIKE A *BAD IDEA.*
THAT'S ONLY BECAUSE YOU DON'T KNOW ME VERY WELL.
NOW...I'M GOING TO NEED YOU TO GET CLOSER, LUKE. *MUCH* CLOSER.

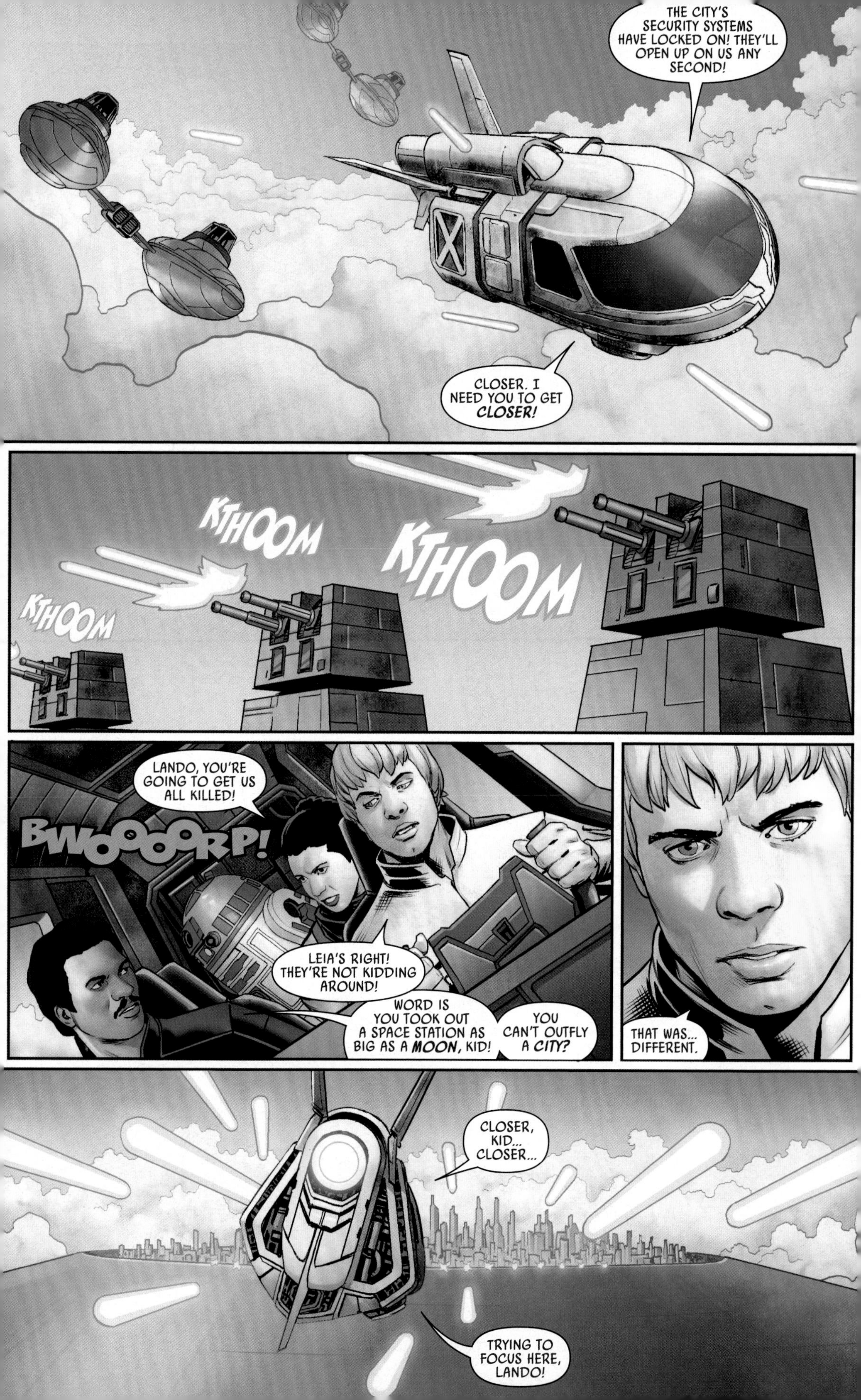
THE CITY'S SECURITY SYSTEMS HAVE LOCKED ON! THEY'LL OPEN UP ON US ANY SECOND!
CLOSER. I NEED YOU TO GET CLOSER!
KTHOOM
KTHOOM
KTHOOM
LANDO, YOU'RE GOING TO GET US ALL KILLED!
BWOOOORP!
LEIA'S RIGHT! THEY'RE NOT KIDDING AROUND!
WORD IS YOU TOOK OUT A SPACE STATION AS BIG AS A MOON, KID!
YOU CAN'T OUTFLY A CITY?
THAT WAS... DIFFERENT.
CLOSER, KID... CLOSER...
TRYING TO FOCUS HERE, LANDO!

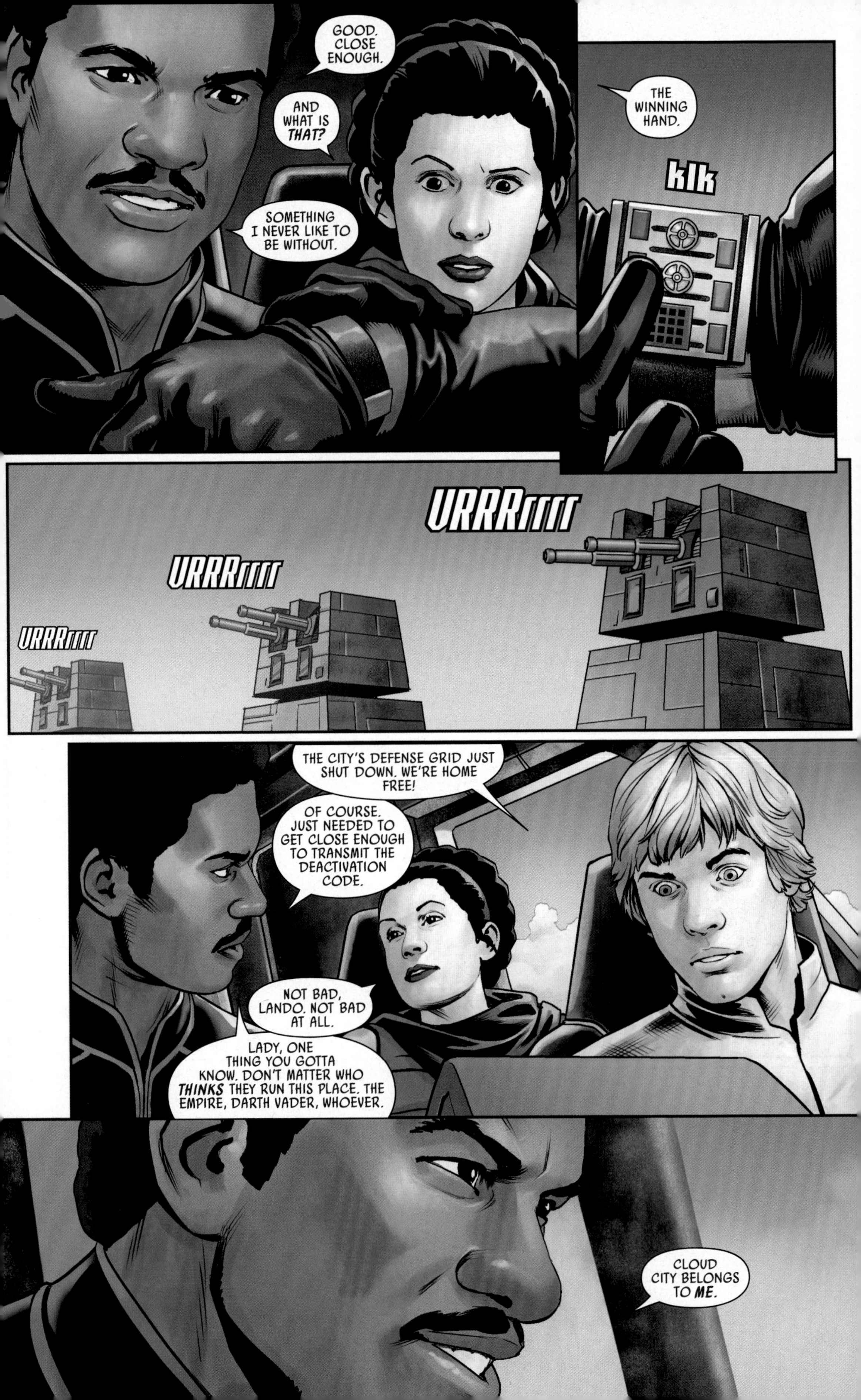
GOOD. CLOSE ENOUGH.
AND WHAT IS *THAT?*
SOMETHING I NEVER LIKE TO BE WITHOUT.
THE WINNING HAND.
klk
URRRrrrr
URRRrrrr
URRRrrrr
THE CITY'S DEFENSE GRID JUST SHUT DOWN. WE'RE HOME FREE!
OF COURSE. JUST NEEDED TO GET CLOSE ENOUGH TO TRANSMIT THE DEACTIVATION CODE.
NOT BAD, LANDO. NOT BAD AT ALL.
LADY, ONE THING YOU GOTTA KNOW. DON'T MATTER WHO ***THINKS*** THEY RUN THIS PLACE. THE EMPIRE, DARTH VADER, WHOEVER.
CLOUD CITY BELONGS TO ***ME.***

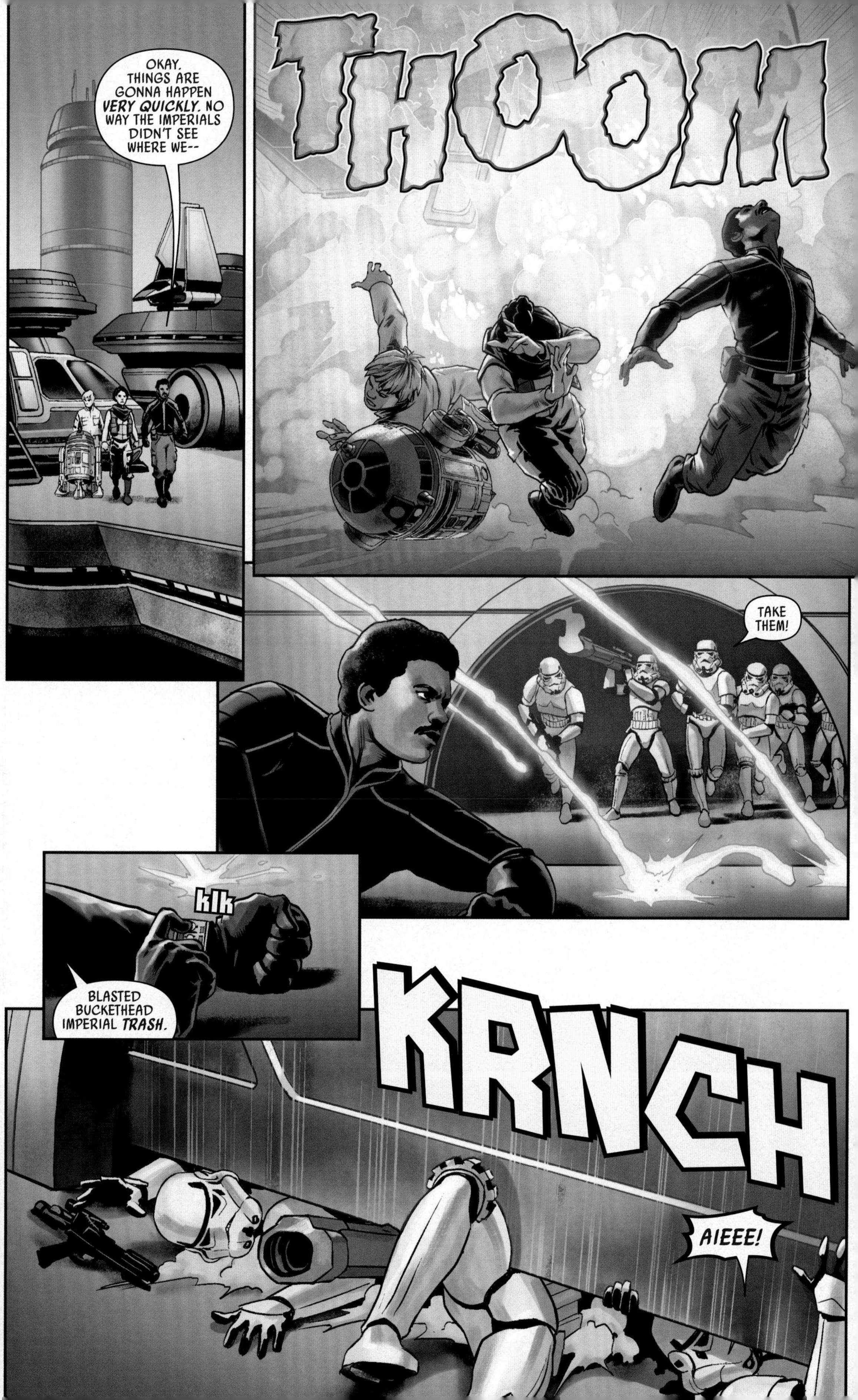
OKAY. THINGS ARE GONNA HAPPEN VERY QUICKLY. NO WAY THE IMPERIALS DIDN'T SEE WHERE WE--
THOOM
TAKE THEM!
klk
BLASTED BUCKETHEAD IMPERIAL TRASH.
KRNCH
AIEEE!

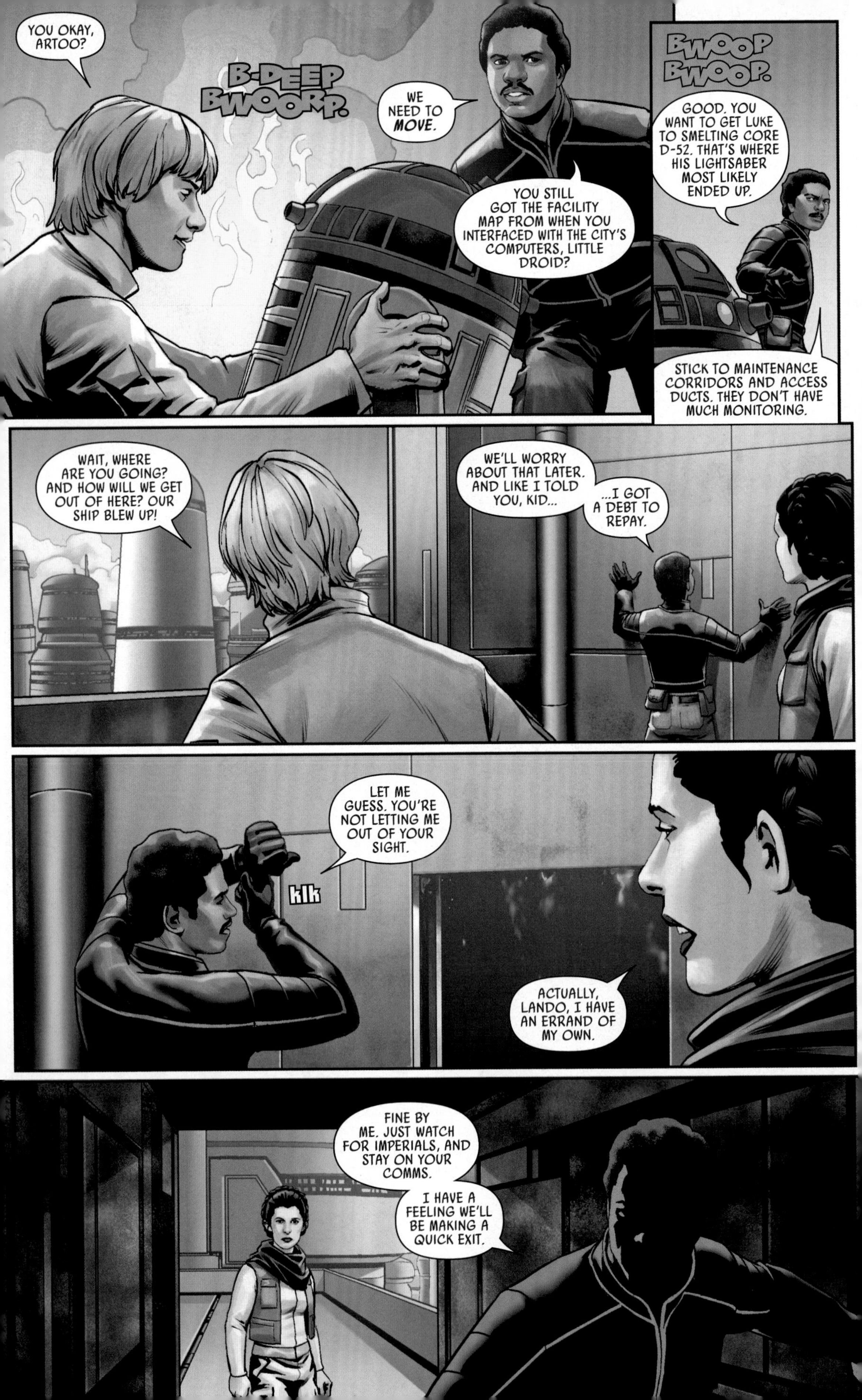
YOU OKAY, ARTOO?
B-DEEP BWOORP.
WE NEED TO MOVE.
YOU STILL GOT THE FACILITY MAP FROM WHEN YOU INTERFACED WITH THE CITY'S COMPUTERS, LITTLE DROID?
BWOOP BWOOP.
GOOD. YOU WANT TO GET LUKE TO SMELTING CORE D-52. THAT'S WHERE HIS LIGHTSABER MOST LIKELY ENDED UP.
STICK TO MAINTENANCE CORRIDORS AND ACCESS DUCTS. THEY DON'T HAVE MUCH MONITORING.
WAIT, WHERE ARE YOU GOING? AND HOW WILL WE GET OUT OF HERE? OUR SHIP BLEW UP!
WE'LL WORRY ABOUT THAT LATER. AND LIKE I TOLD YOU, KID...
...I GOT A DEBT TO REPAY.
LET ME GUESS. YOU'RE NOT LETTING ME OUT OF YOUR SIGHT.
klk
ACTUALLY, LANDO, I HAVE AN ERRAND OF MY OWN.
FINE BY ME. JUST WATCH FOR IMPERIALS, AND STAY ON YOUR COMMS.
I HAVE A FEELING WE'LL BE MAKING A QUICK EXIT.

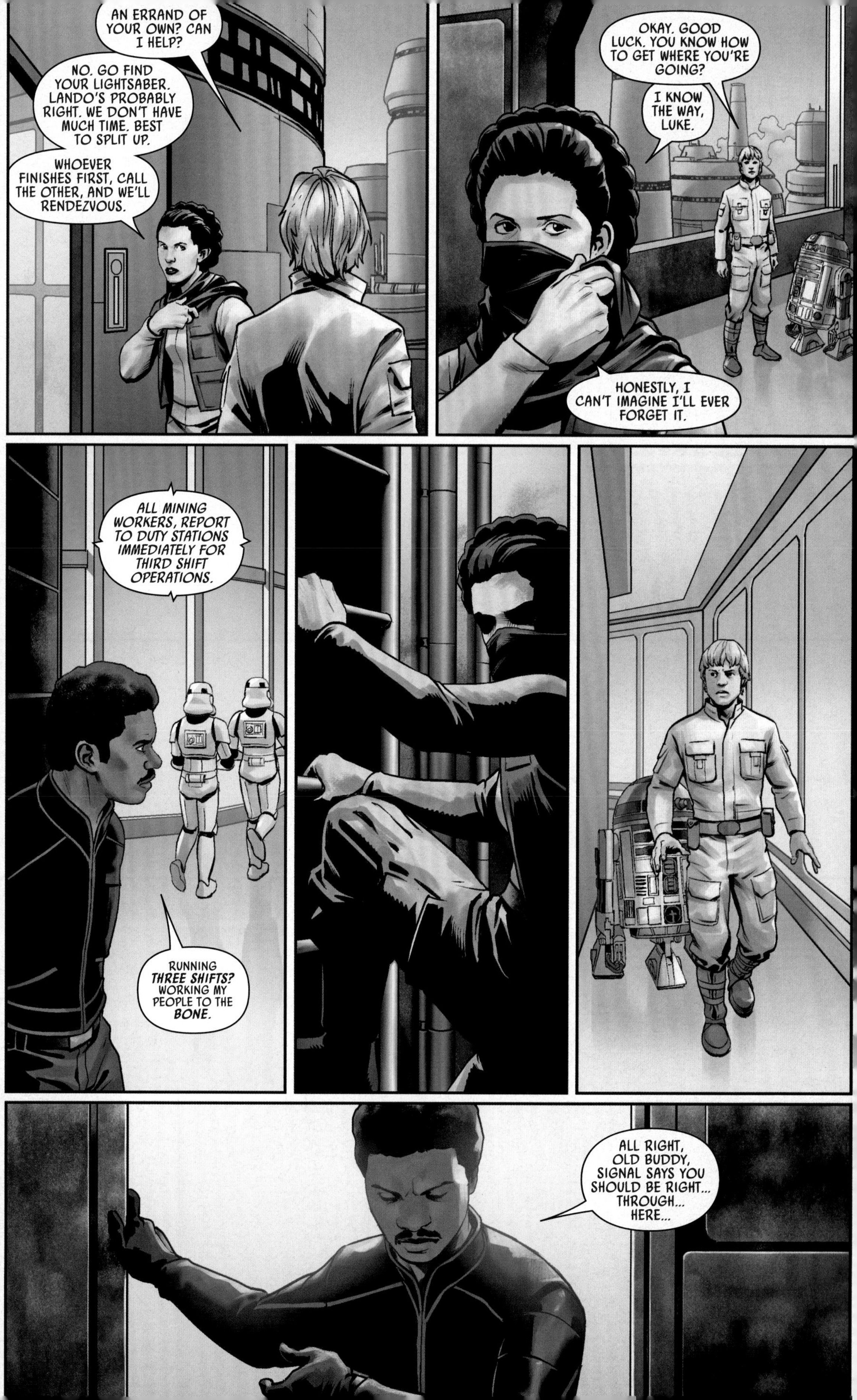
AN ERRAND OF YOUR OWN? CAN I HELP?
NO. GO FIND YOUR LIGHTSABER. LANDO'S PROBABLY RIGHT. WE DON'T HAVE MUCH TIME. BEST TO SPLIT UP.
WHOEVER FINISHES FIRST, CALL THE OTHER, AND WE'LL RENDEZVOUS.
OKAY. GOOD LUCK. YOU KNOW HOW TO GET WHERE YOU'RE GOING?
I KNOW THE WAY, LUKE.
HONESTLY, I CAN'T IMAGINE I'LL EVER FORGET IT.
ALL MINING WORKERS, REPORT TO DUTY STATIONS IMMEDIATELY FOR THIRD SHIFT OPERATIONS.
RUNNING *THREE SHIFTS?* WORKING MY PEOPLE TO THE *BONE.*
ALL RIGHT, OLD BUDDY, SIGNAL SAYS YOU SHOULD BE RIGHT... THROUGH... HERE...

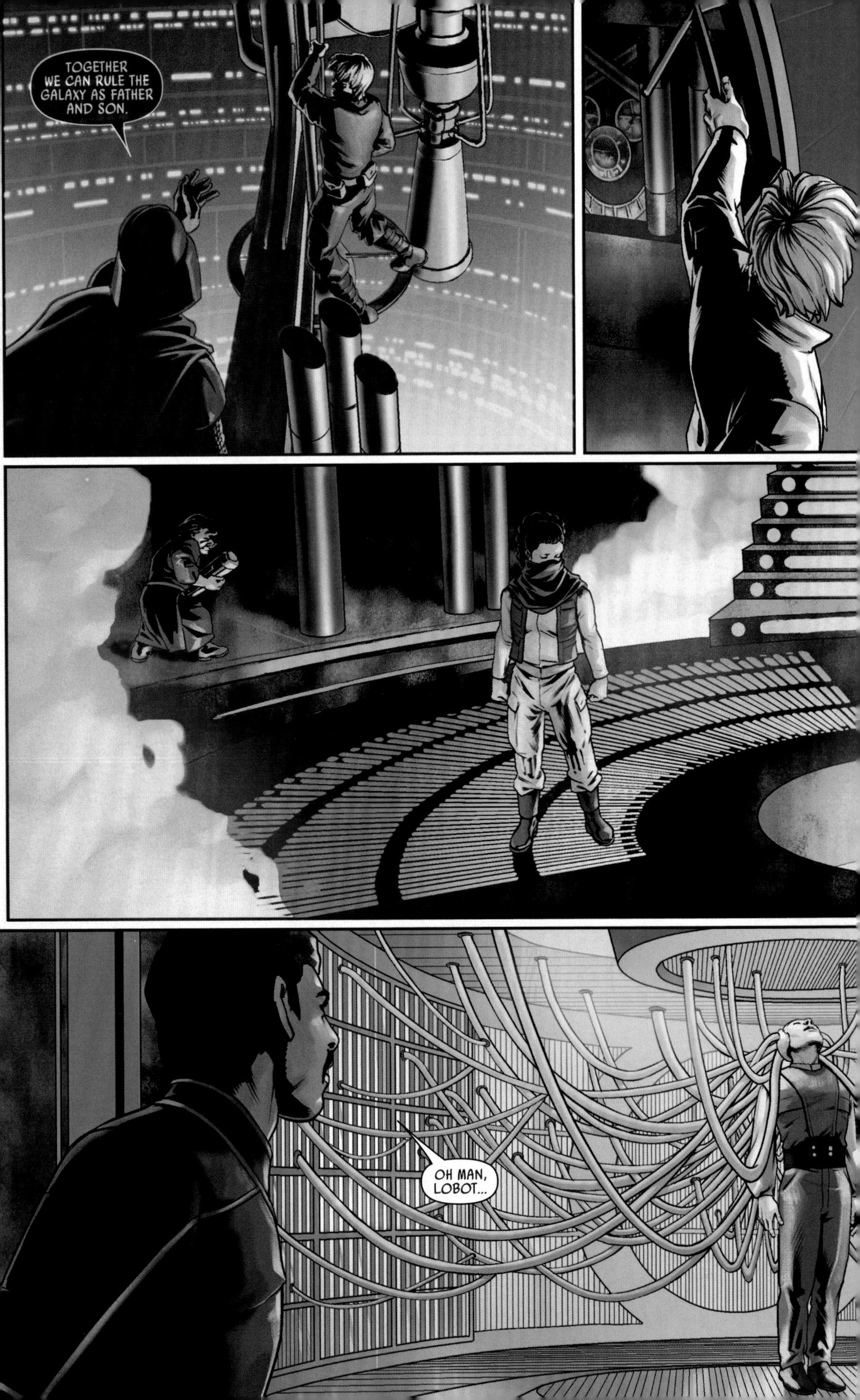
TOGETHER WE CAN RULE THE GALAXY AS FATHER AND SON.
OH MAN, LOBOT...

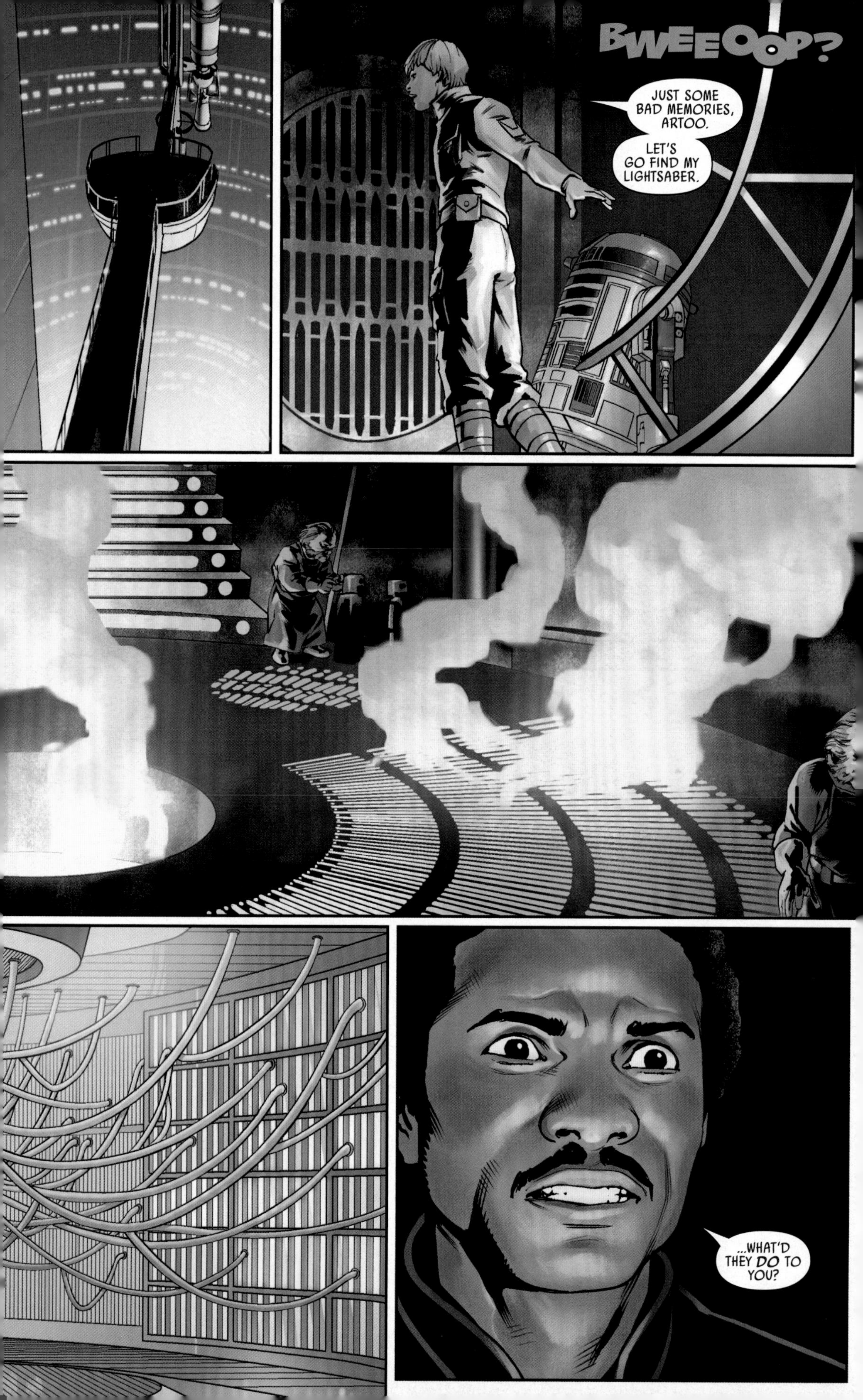
BWEEOOP?
JUST SOME BAD MEMORIES, ARTOO.
LET'S GO FIND MY LIGHTSABER.
...WHAT'D THEY DO TO YOU?

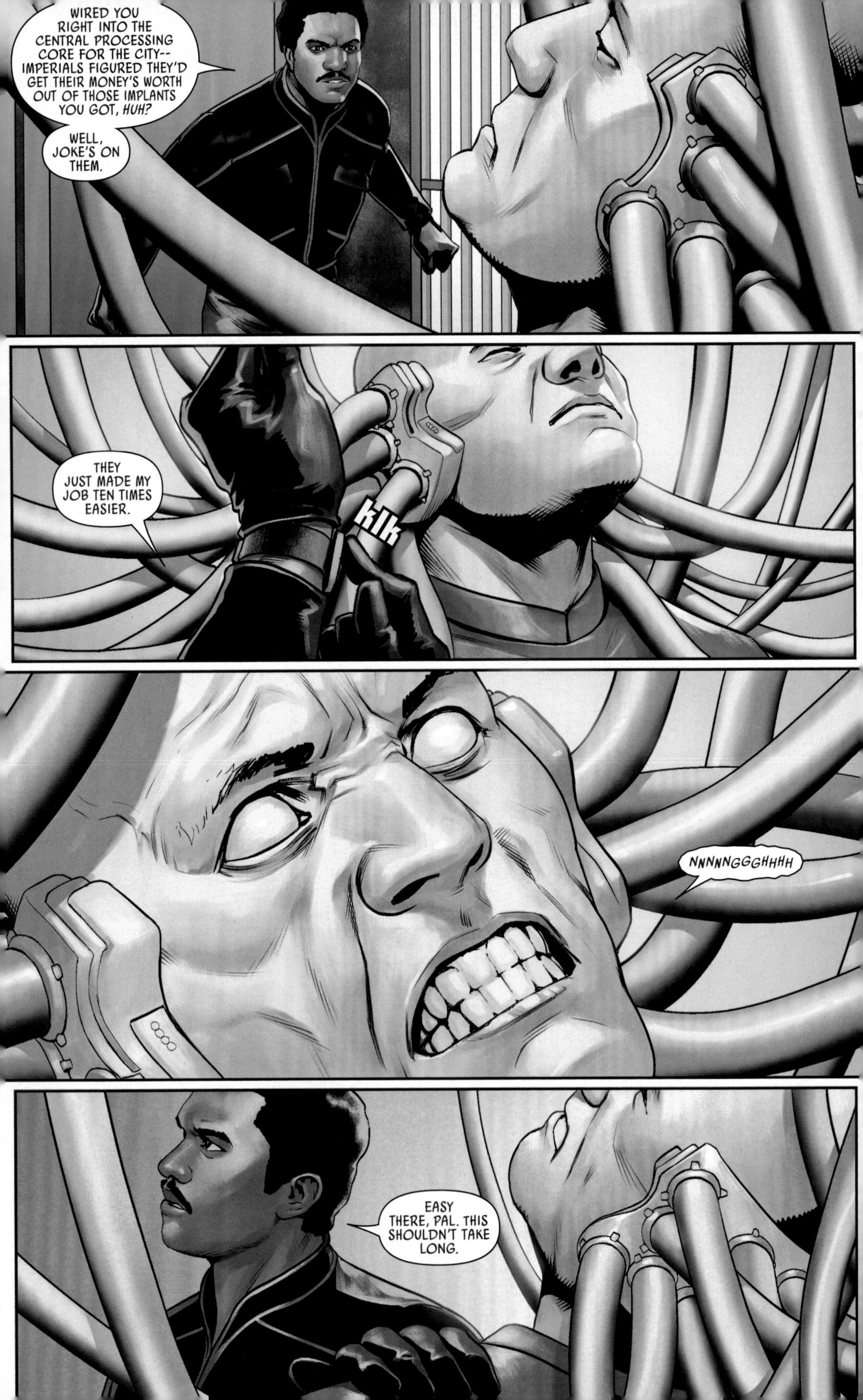
WIRED YOU RIGHT INTO THE CENTRAL PROCESSING CORE FOR THE CITY-- IMPERIALS FIGURED THEY'D GET THEIR MONEY'S WORTH OUT OF THOSE IMPLANTS YOU GOT, *HUH?*
WELL, JOKE'S ON THEM.
THEY JUST MADE MY JOB TEN TIMES EASIER.
klk
NNNNNGGGHHHH
EASY THERE, PAL. THIS SHOULDN'T TAKE LONG.

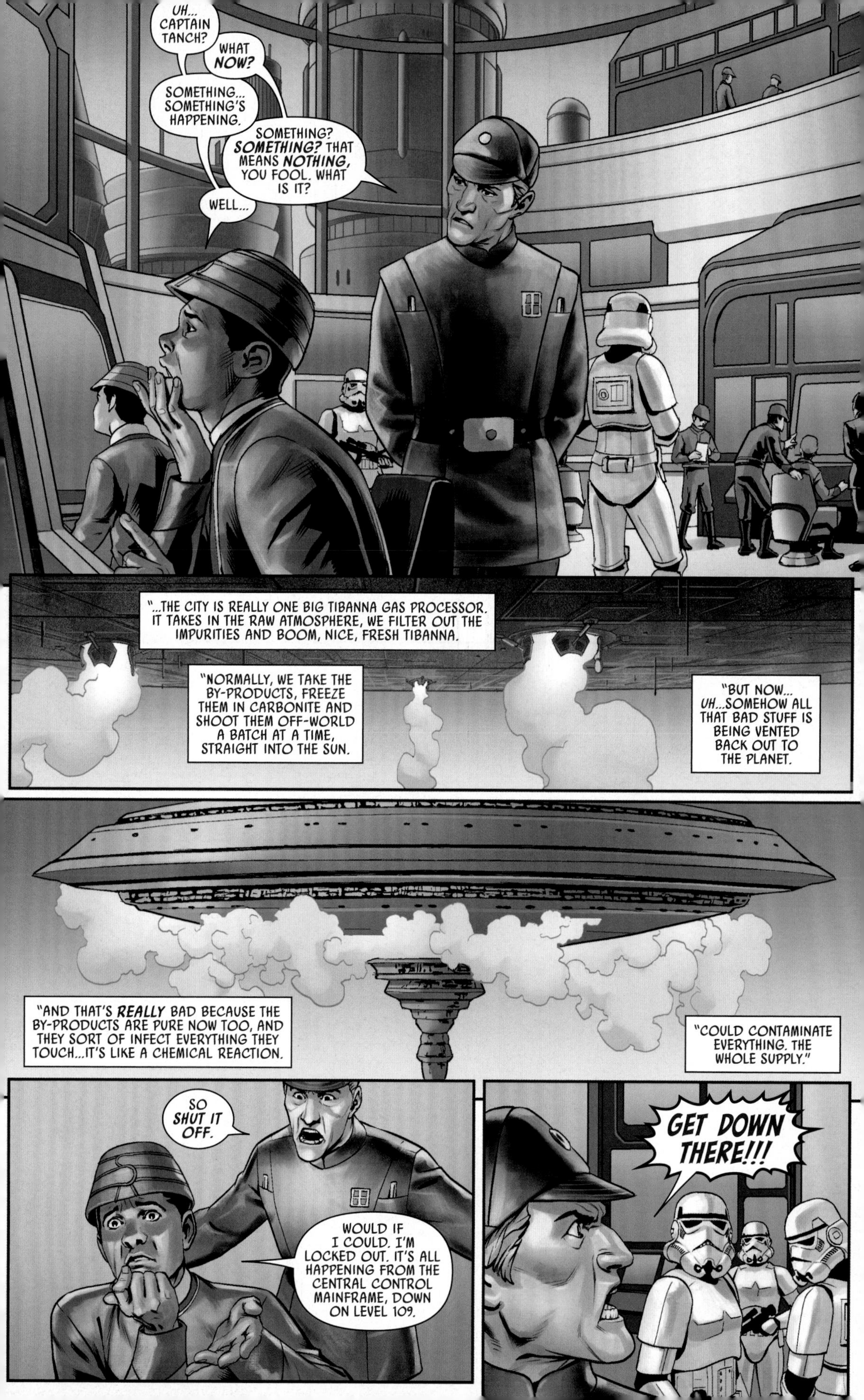
UH... CAPTAIN TANCH?
WHAT NOW?
SOMETHING... SOMETHING'S HAPPENING.
SOMETHING? SOMETHING? THAT MEANS NOTHING, YOU FOOL. WHAT IS IT?
WELL...
"...THE CITY IS REALLY ONE BIG TIBANNA GAS PROCESSOR. IT TAKES IN THE RAW ATMOSPHERE, WE FILTER OUT THE IMPURITIES AND BOOM, NICE, FRESH TIBANNA.
"NORMALLY, WE TAKE THE BY-PRODUCTS, FREEZE THEM IN CARBONITE AND SHOOT THEM OFF-WORLD A BATCH AT A TIME, STRAIGHT INTO THE SUN.
"BUT NOW... UH...SOMEHOW ALL THAT BAD STUFF IS BEING VENTED BACK OUT TO THE PLANET.
"AND THAT'S REALLY BAD BECAUSE THE BY-PRODUCTS ARE PURE NOW TOO, AND THEY SORT OF INFECT EVERYTHING THEY TOUCH...IT'S LIKE A CHEMICAL REACTION.
"COULD CONTAMINATE EVERYTHING. THE WHOLE SUPPLY."
SO SHUT IT OFF.
WOULD IF I COULD. I'M LOCKED OUT. IT'S ALL HAPPENING FROM THE CENTRAL CONTROL MAINFRAME, DOWN ON LEVEL 109.
GET DOWN THERE!!!

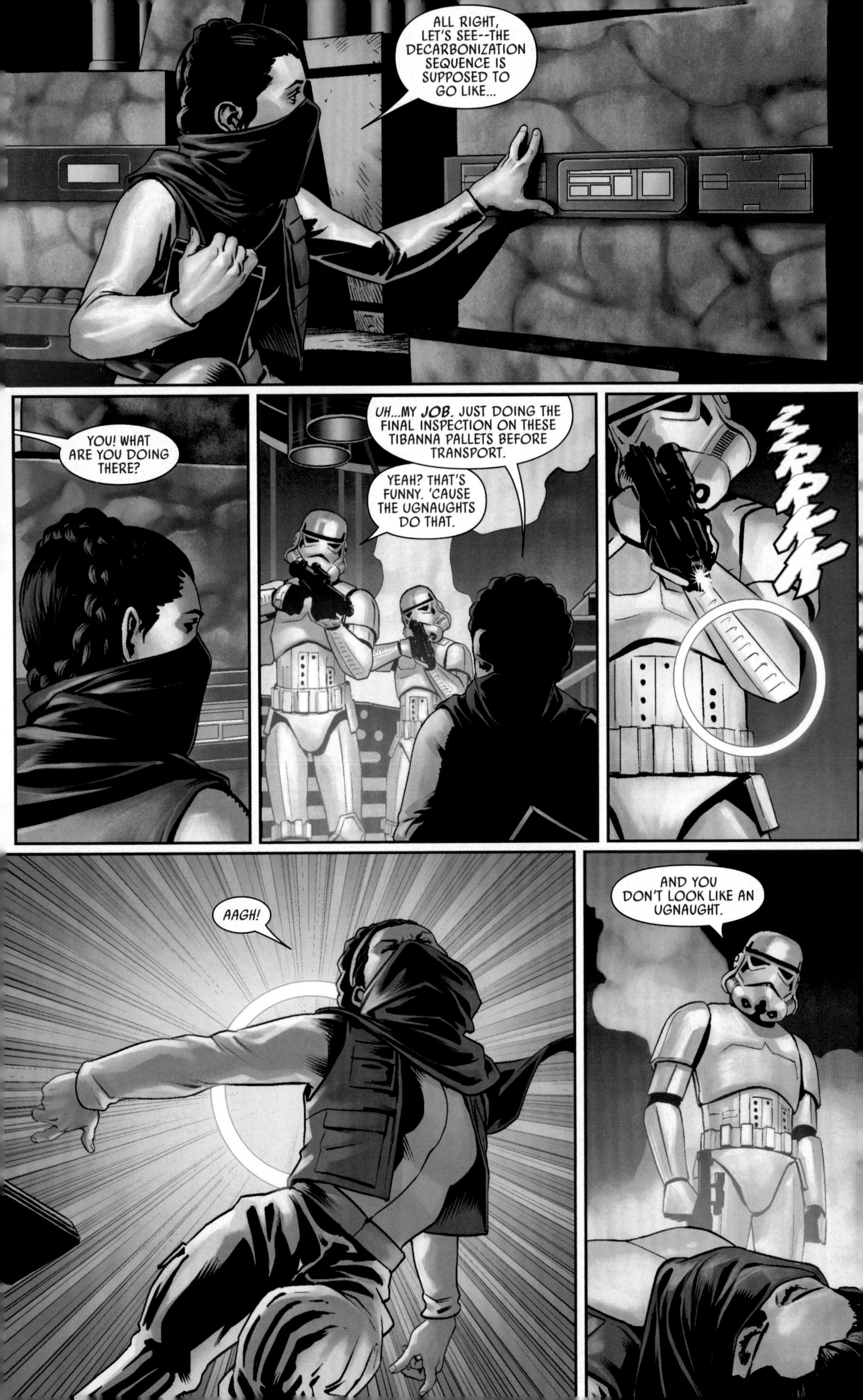
ALL RIGHT, LET'S SEE--THE DECARBONIZATION SEQUENCE IS SUPPOSED TO GO LIKE...
YOU! WHAT ARE YOU DOING THERE?
UH...MY JOB. JUST DOING THE FINAL INSPECTION ON THESE TIBANNA PALLETS BEFORE TRANSPORT.
YEAH? THAT'S FUNNY. 'CAUSE THE UGNAUGHTS DO THAT.
ZZRRKK
AAGH!
AND YOU DON'T LOOK LIKE AN UGNAUGHT.

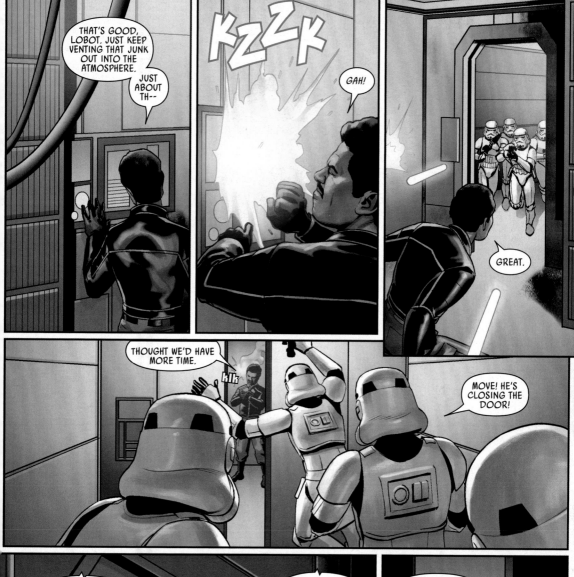

THAT'S GOOD, LOBOT. JUST KEEP VENTING THAT JUNK OUT INTO THE ATMOSPHERE.

JUST ABOUT TH--

KZZK

GAH!

GREAT.

THOUGHT WE'D HAVE MORE TIME.

klk

MOVE! HE'S CLOSING THE DOOR!

LUKE! GOT INTO A BIT OF, AH, TROUBLE UP HERE. CAN YOU GET TO LEVEL 109, TAKE SOME OF THE HEAT OFF?

IS THAT BLASTER FIRE IN THE BACKGROUND, LANDO?

YOU GONNA HELP OR NOT? YOU THINK YOU'LL EVER GET OFF THIS PLANET WITHOUT ME? FAT CHANCE!

TAKE IT EASY. OF COURSE I'LL HELP.

BUT ARTOO JUST GOT ME INTO THAT SMELTING CHAMBER WHERE MY LIGHTSABER SHOULD BE. LET ME GRAB IT, AND THEN I'LL BE RIGHT...UH...

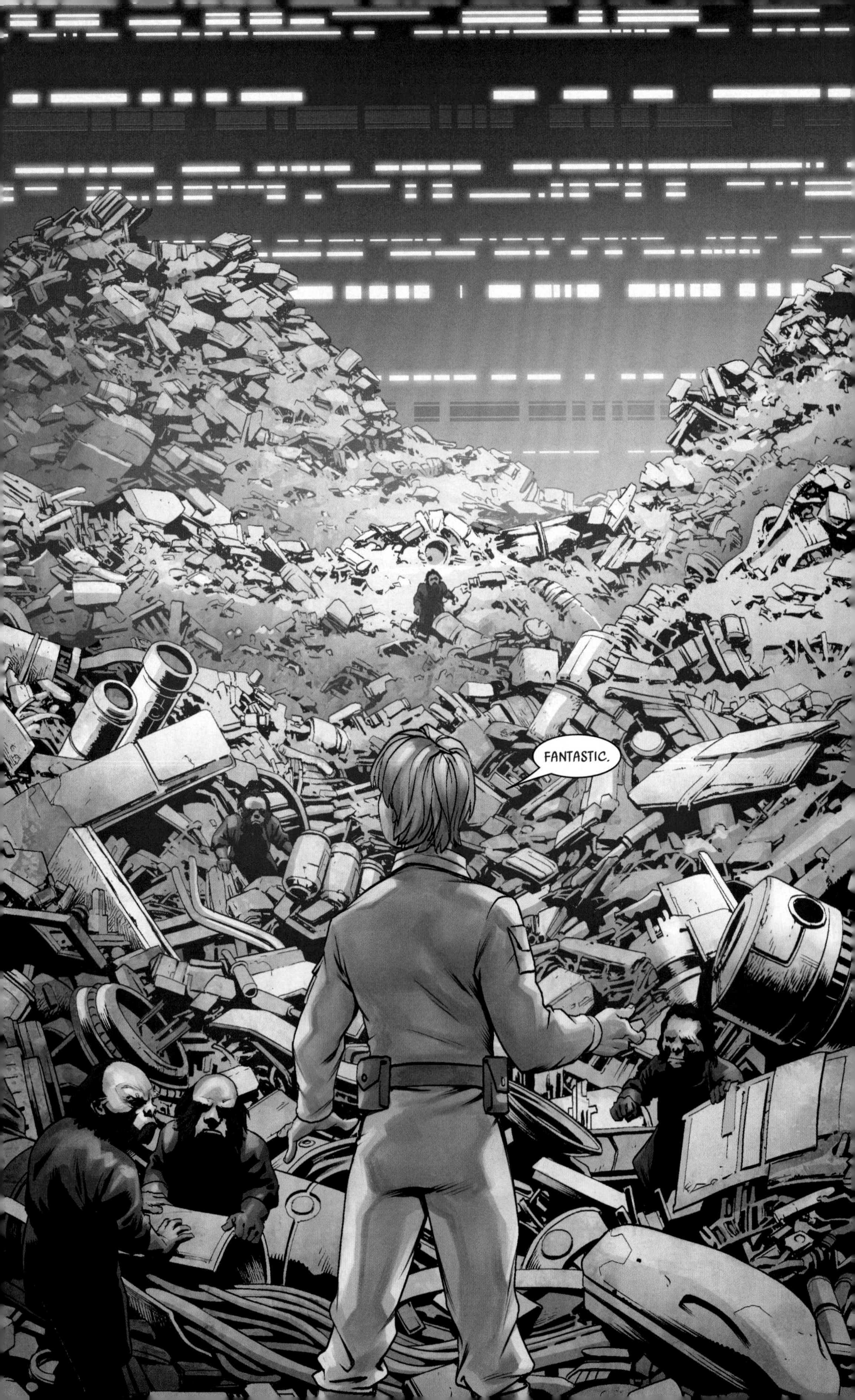
FANTASTIC.

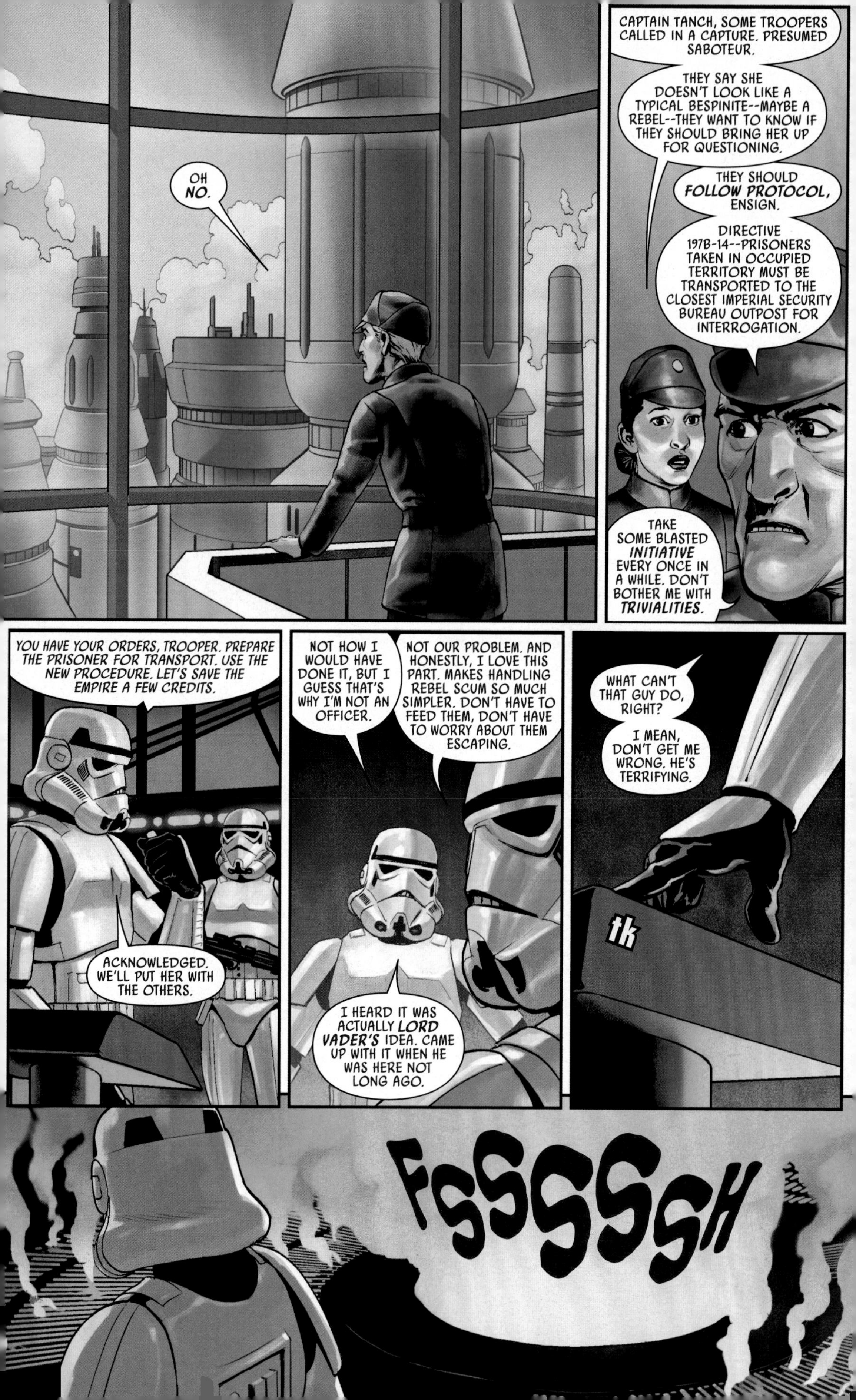
OH NO.
CAPTAIN TANCH, SOME TROOPERS CALLED IN A CAPTURE. PRESUMED SABOTEUR.
THEY SAY SHE DOESN'T LOOK LIKE A TYPICAL BESPINITE--MAYBE A REBEL--THEY WANT TO KNOW IF THEY SHOULD BRING HER UP FOR QUESTIONING.
THEY SHOULD FOLLOW PROTOCOL, ENSIGN.
DIRECTIVE 197B-14--PRISONERS TAKEN IN OCCUPIED TERRITORY MUST BE TRANSPORTED TO THE CLOSEST IMPERIAL SECURITY BUREAU OUTPOST FOR INTERROGATION.
TAKE SOME BLASTED INITIATIVE EVERY ONCE IN A WHILE. DON'T BOTHER ME WITH TRIVIALITIES.
YOU HAVE YOUR ORDERS, TROOPER. PREPARE THE PRISONER FOR TRANSPORT. USE THE NEW PROCEDURE. LET'S SAVE THE EMPIRE A FEW CREDITS.
ACKNOWLEDGED. WE'LL PUT HER WITH THE OTHERS.
NOT HOW I WOULD HAVE DONE IT, BUT I GUESS THAT'S WHY I'M NOT AN OFFICER.
NOT OUR PROBLEM. AND HONESTLY, I LOVE THIS PART. MAKES HANDLING REBEL SCUM SO MUCH SIMPLER. DON'T HAVE TO FEED THEM, DON'T HAVE TO WORRY ABOUT THEM ESCAPING.
I HEARD IT WAS ACTUALLY LORD VADER'S IDEA. CAME UP WITH IT WHEN HE WAS HERE NOT LONG AGO.
WHAT CAN'T THAT GUY DO, RIGHT?
I MEAN, DON'T GET ME WRONG. HE'S TERRIFYING.
tk
FSSSSSH

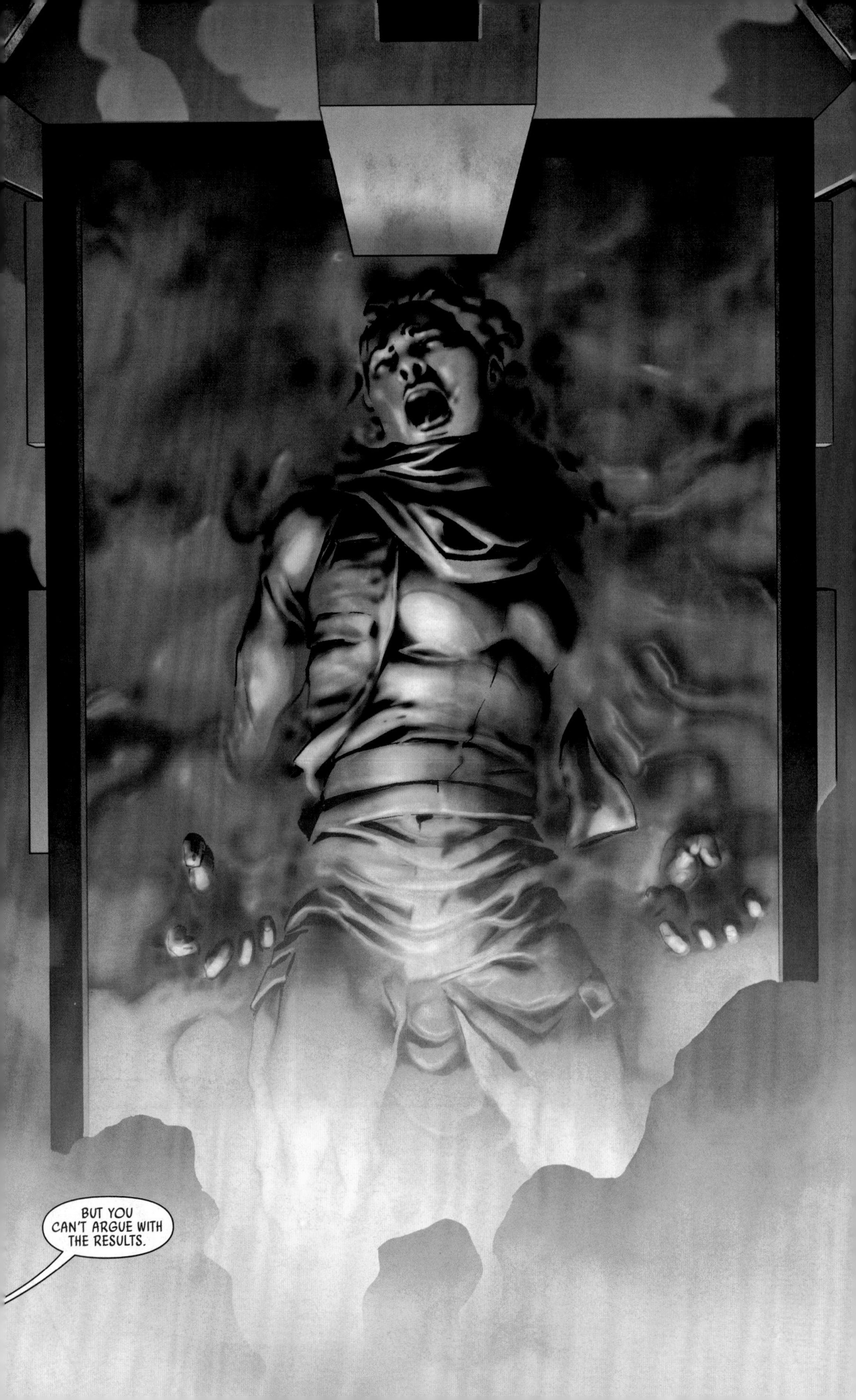
BUT YOU CAN'T ARGUE WITH THE RESULTS.

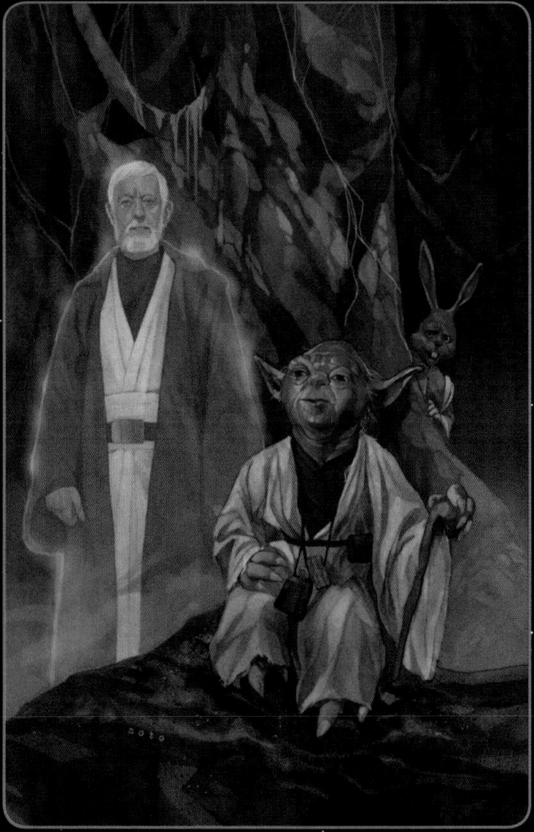

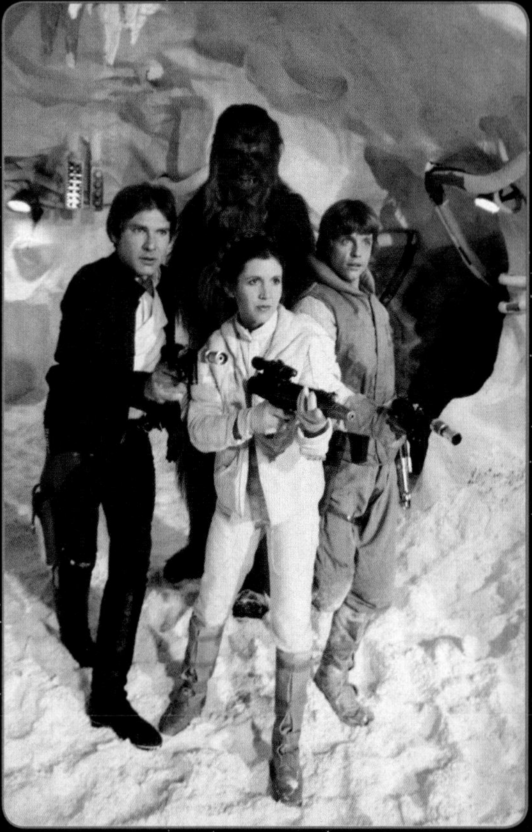

#1 Party Variant by
PHIL NOTO

#1 Movie Variant

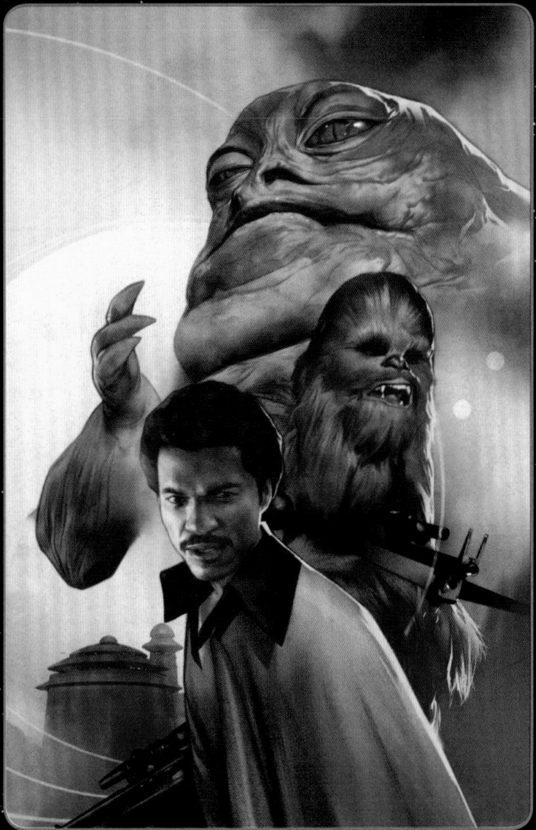

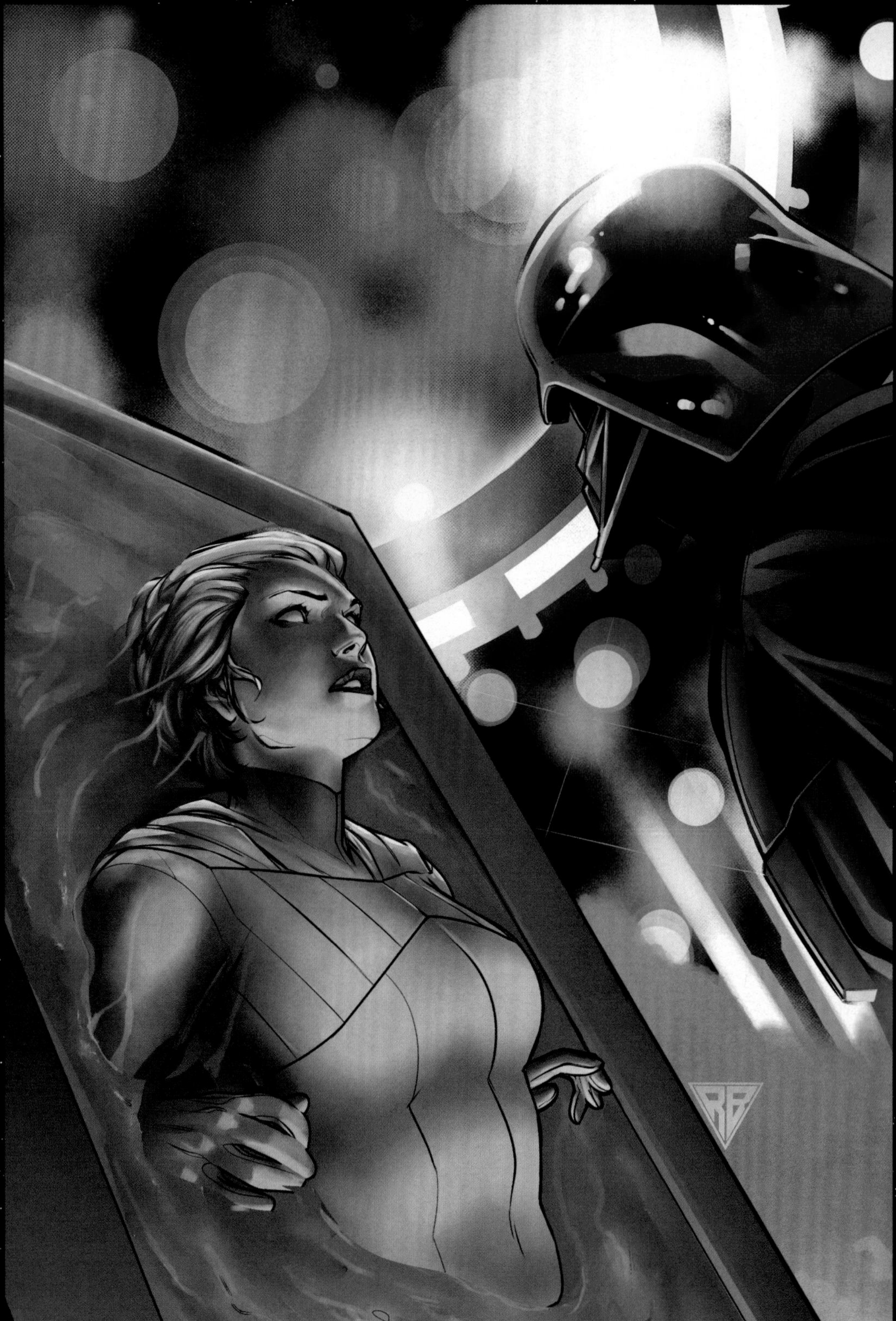

4

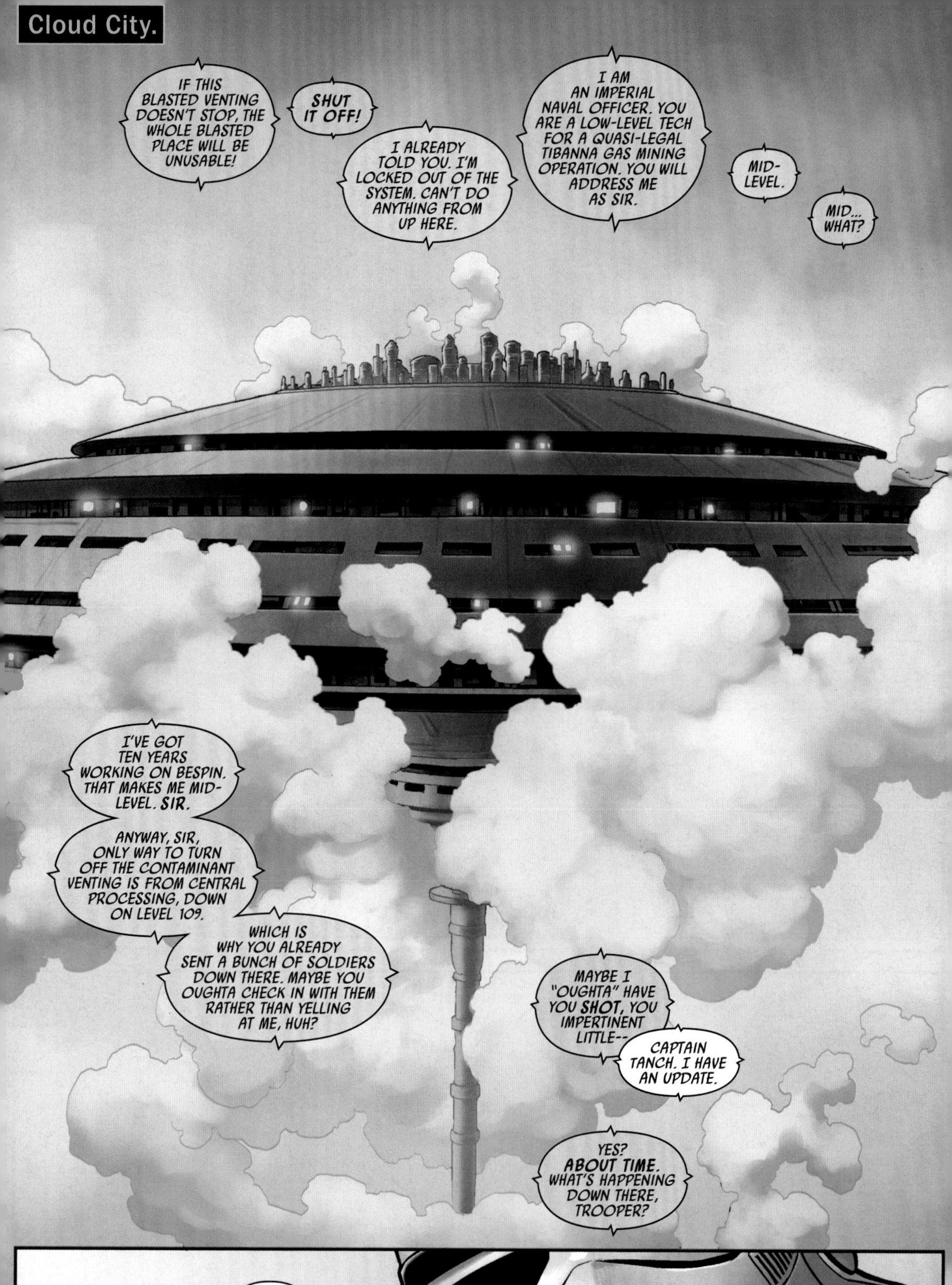
Cloud City.
IF THIS BLASTED VENTING DOESN'T STOP, THE WHOLE BLASTED PLACE WILL BE UNUSABLE!
SHUT IT OFF!
I ALREADY TOLD YOU. I'M LOCKED OUT OF THE SYSTEM. CAN'T DO ANYTHING FROM UP HERE.
I AM AN IMPERIAL NAVAL OFFICER. YOU ARE A LOW-LEVEL TECH FOR A QUASI-LEGAL TIBANNA GAS MINING OPERATION. YOU WILL ADDRESS ME AS SIR.
MID-LEVEL.
MID... WHAT?
I'VE GOT TEN YEARS WORKING ON BESPIN. THAT MAKES ME MID-LEVEL. SIR.
ANYWAY, SIR, ONLY WAY TO TURN OFF THE CONTAMINANT VENTING IS FROM CENTRAL PROCESSING, DOWN ON LEVEL 109.
WHICH IS WHY YOU ALREADY SENT A BUNCH OF SOLDIERS DOWN THERE. MAYBE YOU OUGHTA CHECK IN WITH THEM RATHER THAN YELLING AT ME, HUH?
MAYBE I "OUGHTA" HAVE YOU SHOT, YOU IMPERTINENT LITTLE--
CAPTAIN TANCH. I HAVE AN UPDATE.
YES? ABOUT TIME. WHAT'S HAPPENING DOWN THERE, TROOPER?
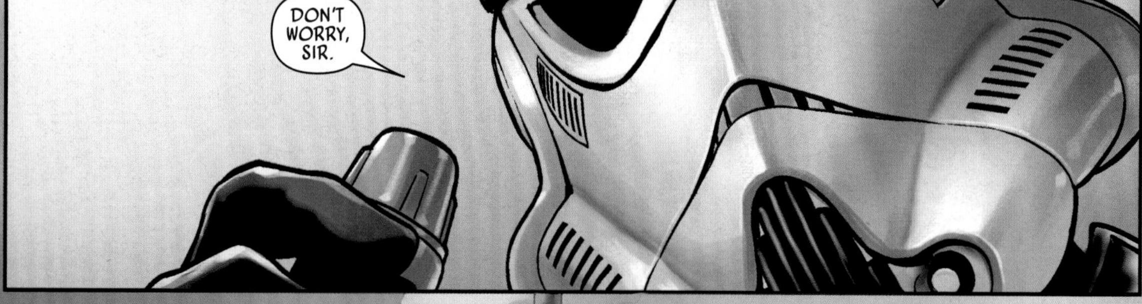
DON'T WORRY, SIR.

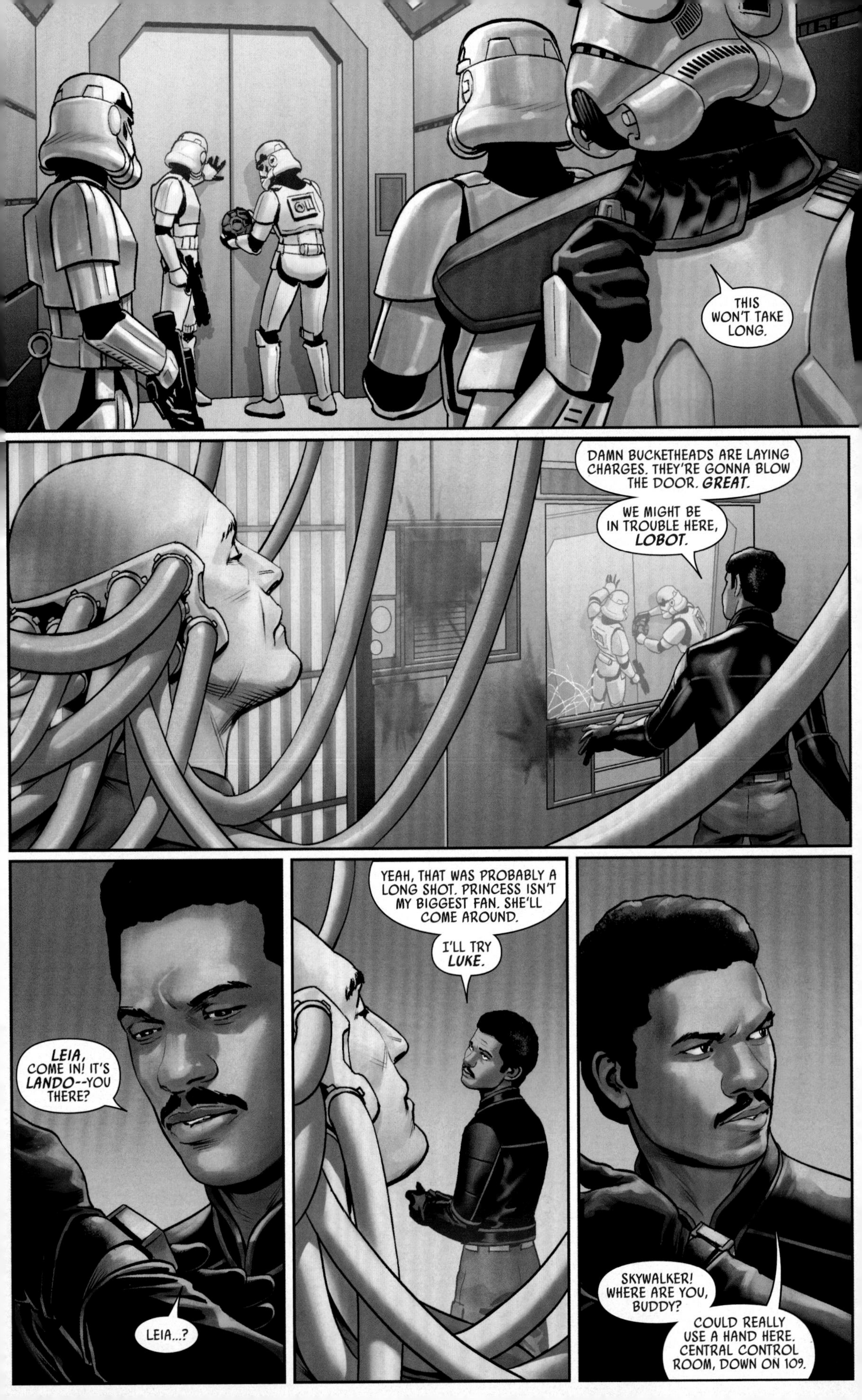
THIS WON'T TAKE LONG.
DAMN BUCKETHEADS ARE LAYING CHARGES. THEY'RE GONNA BLOW THE DOOR. GREAT.
WE MIGHT BE IN TROUBLE HERE, LOBOT.
LEIA, COME IN! IT'S LANDO--YOU THERE?
LEIA...?
YEAH, THAT WAS PROBABLY A LONG SHOT. PRINCESS ISN'T MY BIGGEST FAN. SHE'LL COME AROUND.
I'LL TRY LUKE.
SKYWALKER! WHERE ARE YOU, BUDDY?
COULD REALLY USE A HAND HERE. CENTRAL CONTROL ROOM, DOWN ON 109.

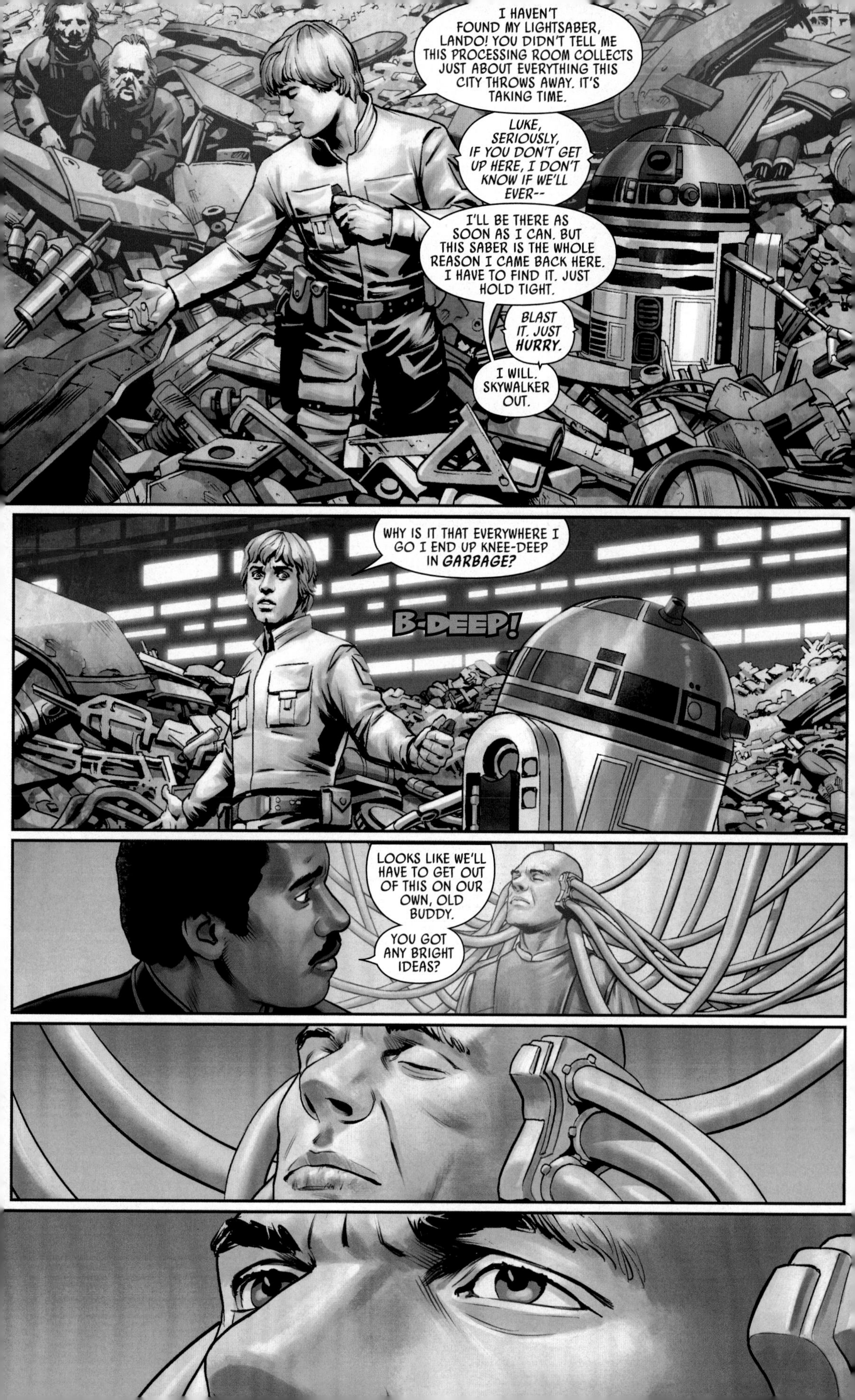
I HAVEN'T FOUND MY LIGHTSABER, LANDO! YOU DIDN'T TELL ME THIS PROCESSING ROOM COLLECTS JUST ABOUT EVERYTHING THIS CITY THROWS AWAY. IT'S TAKING TIME.
LUKE, SERIOUSLY, IF YOU DON'T GET UP HERE, I DON'T KNOW IF WE'LL EVER--
I'LL BE THERE AS SOON AS I CAN. BUT THIS SABER IS THE WHOLE REASON I CAME BACK HERE. I HAVE TO FIND IT. JUST HOLD TIGHT.
BLAST IT. JUST *HURRY.*
I WILL. SKYWALKER OUT.
WHY IS IT THAT EVERYWHERE I GO I END UP KNEE-DEEP IN *GARBAGE?*
B-DEEP!
LOOKS LIKE WE'LL HAVE TO GET OUT OF THIS ON OUR OWN, OLD BUDDY.
YOU GOT ANY BRIGHT IDEAS?

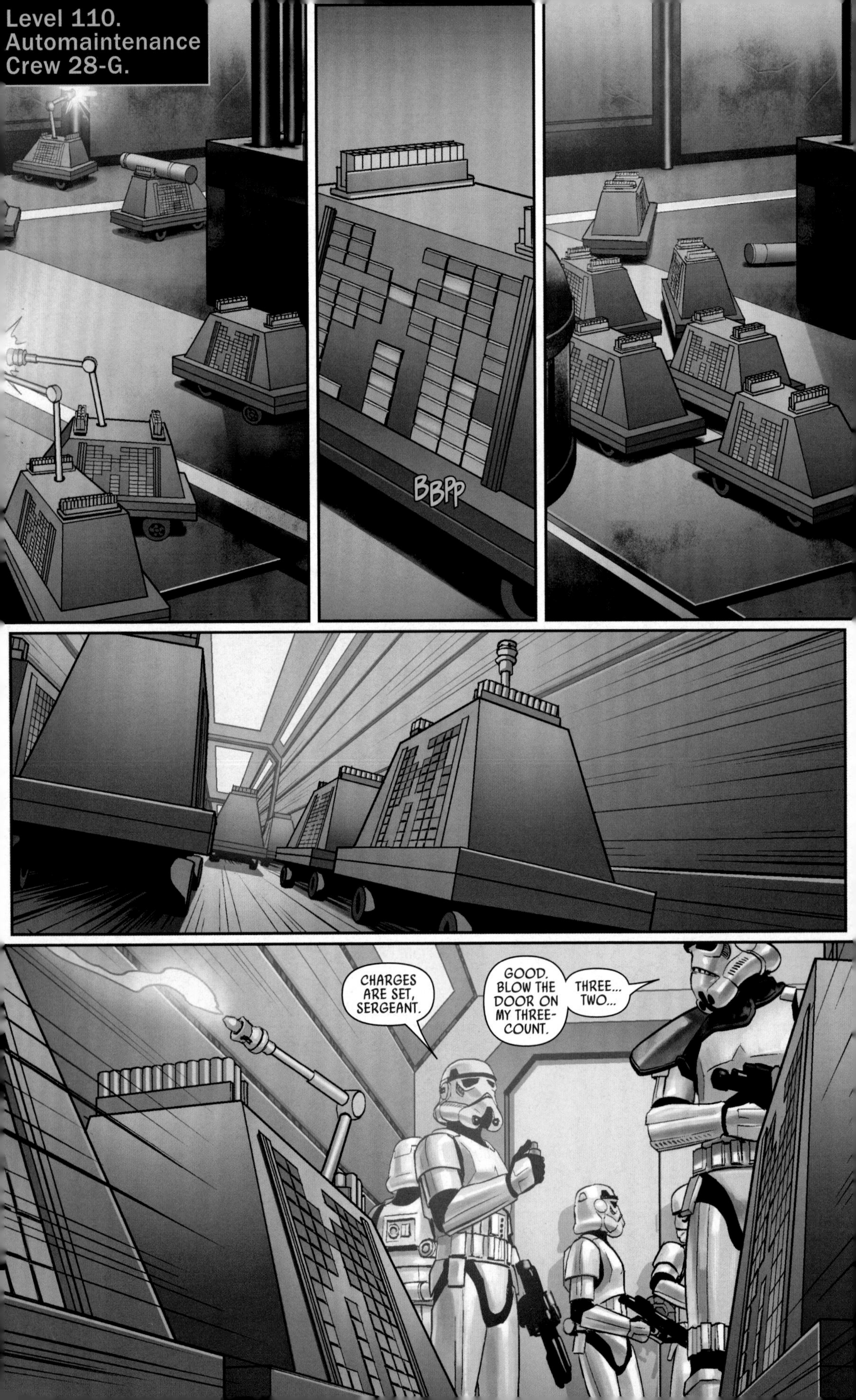
Level 110. Automaintenance Crew 28-G.
BBPP
CHARGES ARE SET, SERGEANT.
GOOD. BLOW THE DOOR ON MY THREE-COUNT.
THREE... TWO...

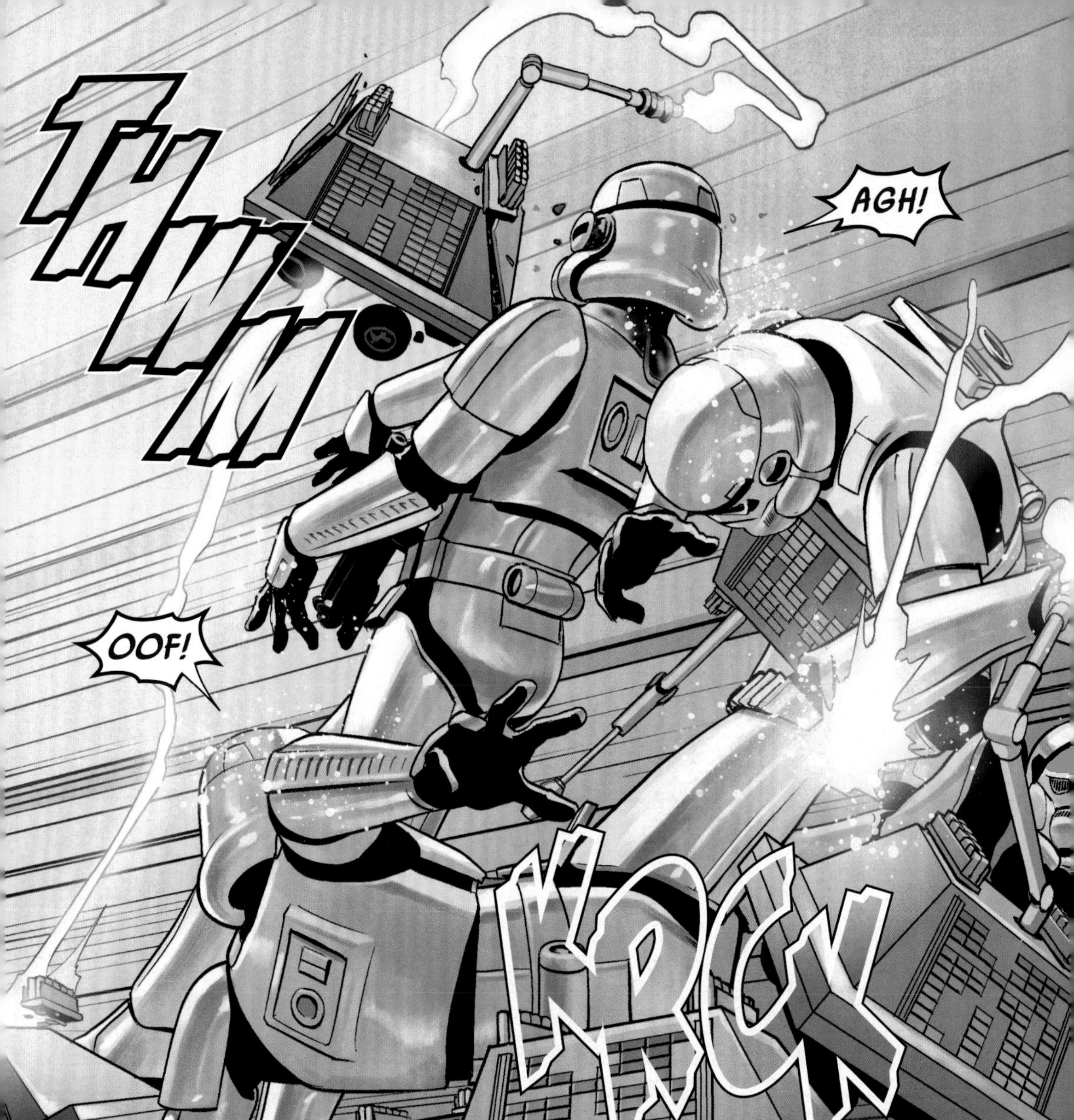
THWM
AGH!
OOF!
KRCK

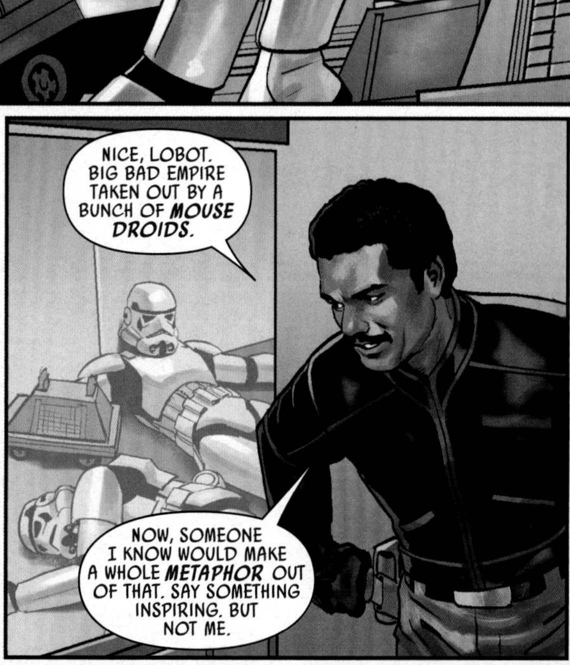
NICE, LOBOT. BIG BAD EMPIRE TAKEN OUT BY A BUNCH OF MOUSE DROIDS.
NOW, SOMEONE I KNOW WOULD MAKE A WHOLE METAPHOR OUT OF THAT. SAY SOMETHING INSPIRING. BUT NOT ME.

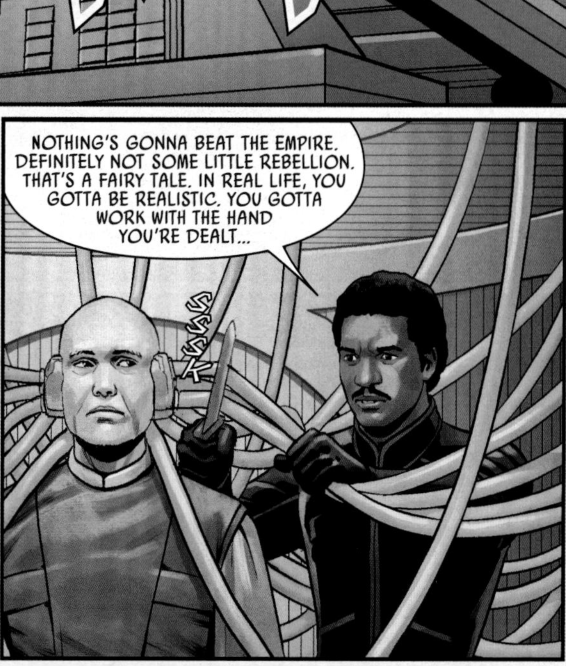
NOTHING'S GONNA BEAT THE EMPIRE. DEFINITELY NOT SOME LITTLE REBELLION. THAT'S A FAIRY TALE. IN REAL LIFE, YOU GOTTA BE REALISTIC. YOU GOTTA WORK WITH THE HAND YOU'RE DEALT...
SSSSK

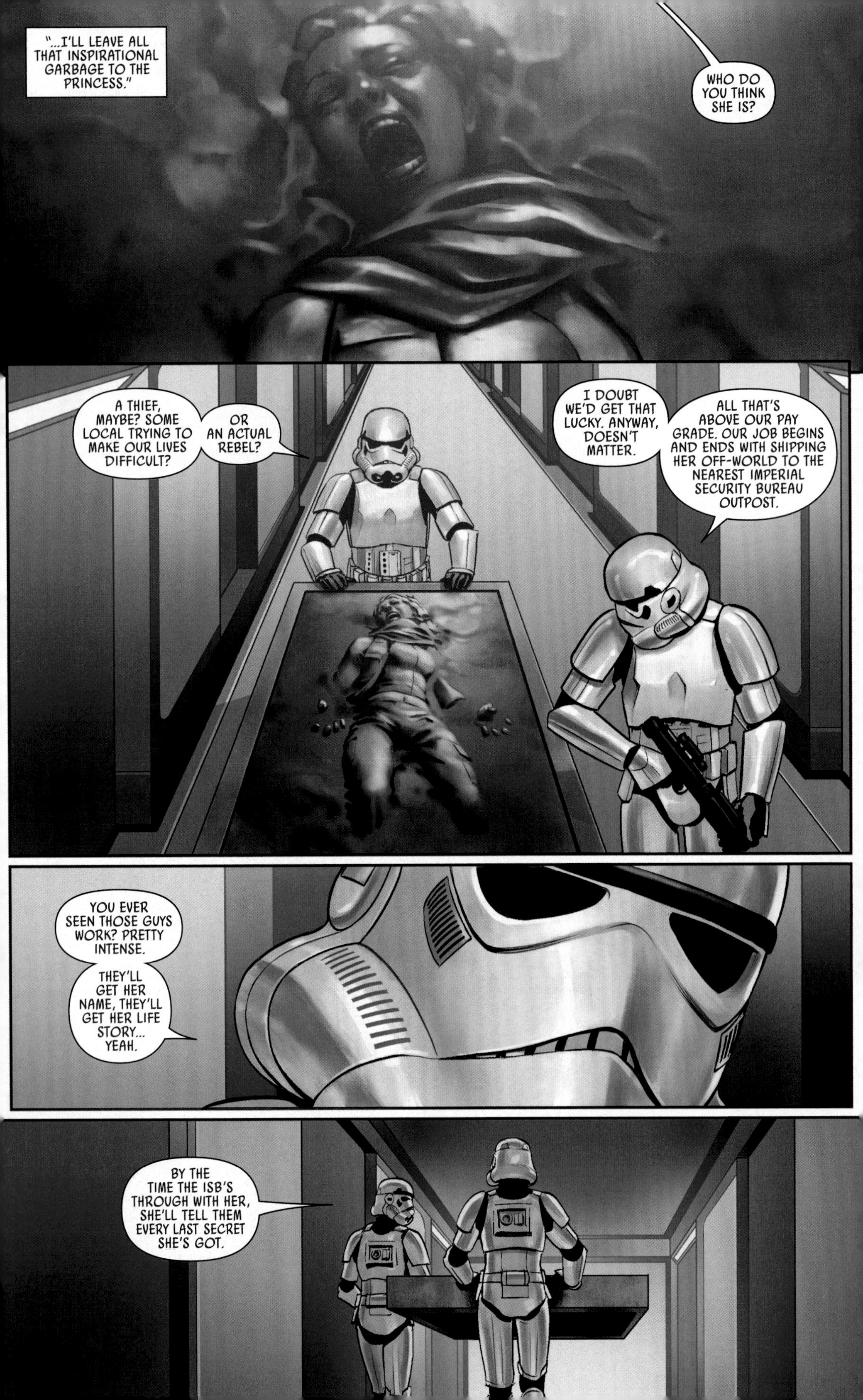
"...I'LL LEAVE ALL THAT INSPIRATIONAL GARBAGE TO THE PRINCESS."
WHO DO YOU THINK SHE IS?
A THIEF, MAYBE? SOME LOCAL TRYING TO MAKE OUR LIVES DIFFICULT?
OR AN ACTUAL REBEL?
I DOUBT WE'D GET THAT LUCKY. ANYWAY, DOESN'T MATTER.
ALL THAT'S ABOVE OUR PAY GRADE. OUR JOB BEGINS AND ENDS WITH SHIPPING HER OFF-WORLD TO THE NEAREST IMPERIAL SECURITY BUREAU OUTPOST.
YOU EVER SEEN THOSE GUYS WORK? PRETTY INTENSE.
THEY'LL GET HER NAME, THEY'LL GET HER LIFE STORY... YEAH.
BY THE TIME THE ISB'S THROUGH WITH HER, SHE'LL TELL THEM EVERY LAST SECRET SHE'S GOT.

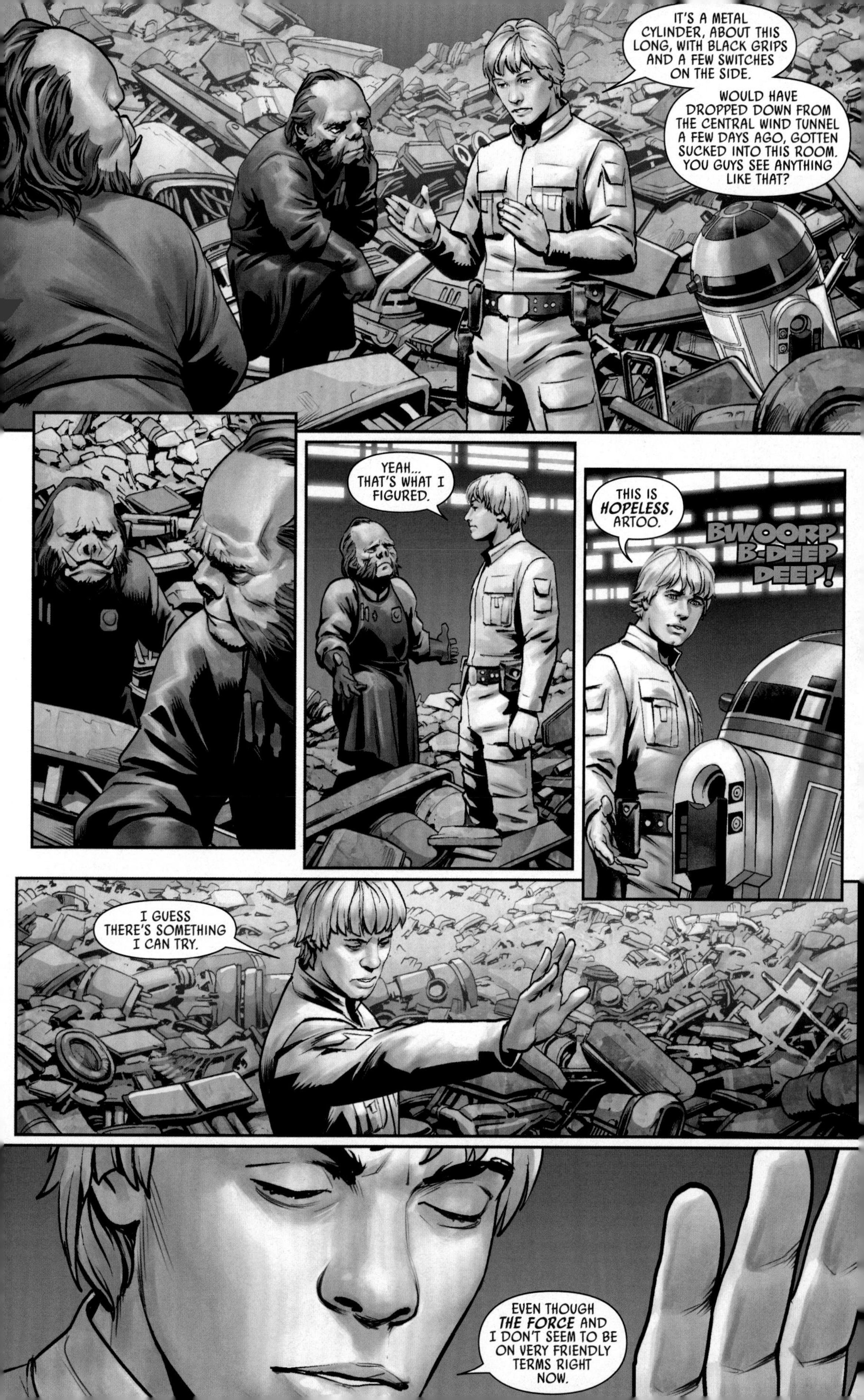
IT'S A METAL CYLINDER, ABOUT THIS LONG, WITH BLACK GRIPS AND A FEW SWITCHES ON THE SIDE.
WOULD HAVE DROPPED DOWN FROM THE CENTRAL WIND TUNNEL A FEW DAYS AGO, GOTTEN SUCKED INTO THIS ROOM. YOU GUYS SEE ANYTHING LIKE THAT?
YEAH... THAT'S WHAT I FIGURED.
THIS IS *HOPELESS*, ARTOO.
BWOORP B-DEEP DEEP!
I GUESS THERE'S SOMETHING I CAN TRY.
EVEN THOUGH *THE FORCE* AND I DON'T SEEM TO BE ON VERY FRIENDLY TERMS RIGHT NOW.

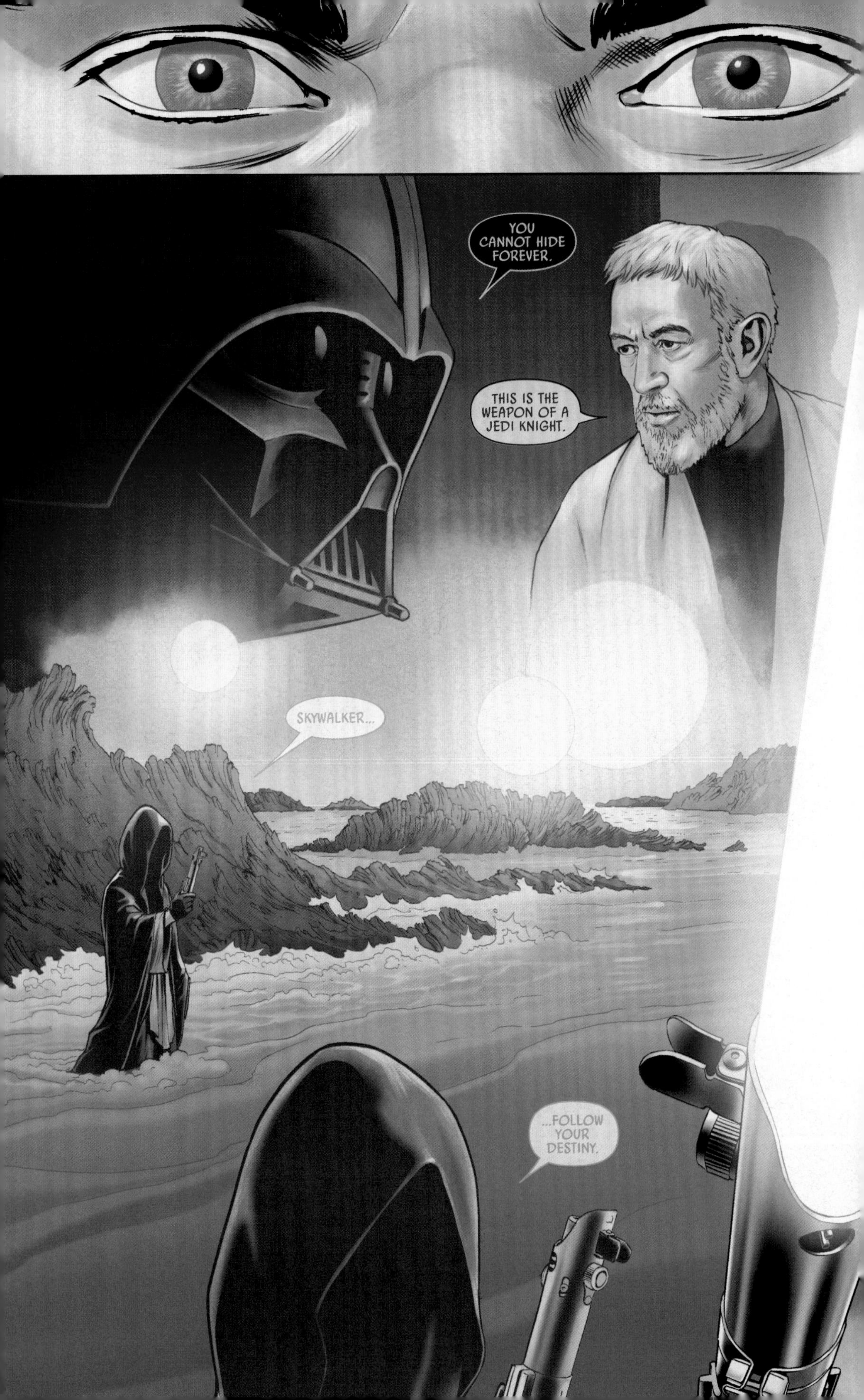
YOU CANNOT HIDE FOREVER.
THIS IS THE WEAPON OF A JEDI KNIGHT.
SKYWALKER...
...FOLLOW YOUR DESTINY.

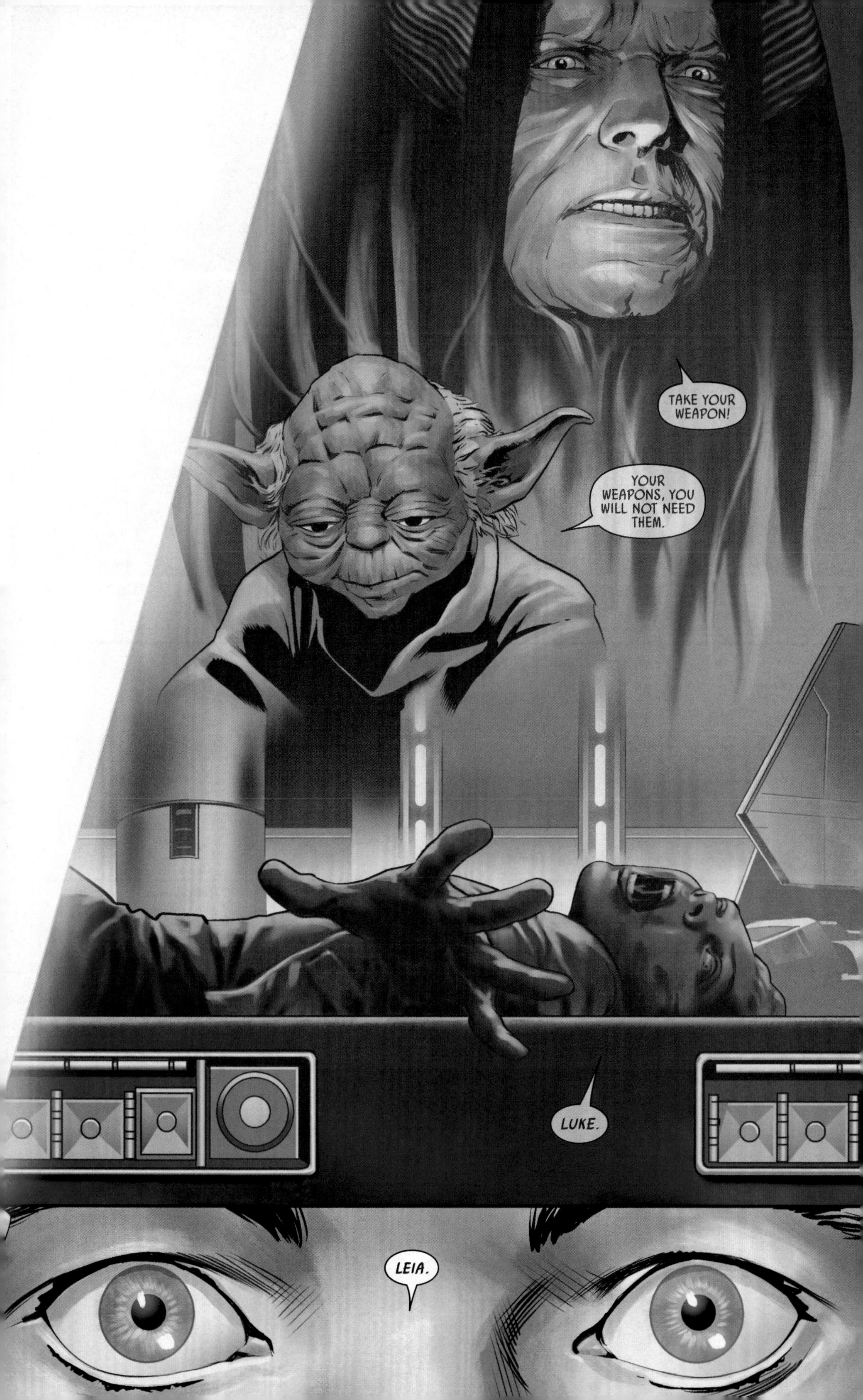
TAKE YOUR WEAPON!
YOUR WEAPONS, YOU WILL NOT NEED THEM.
LUKE.
LEIA.

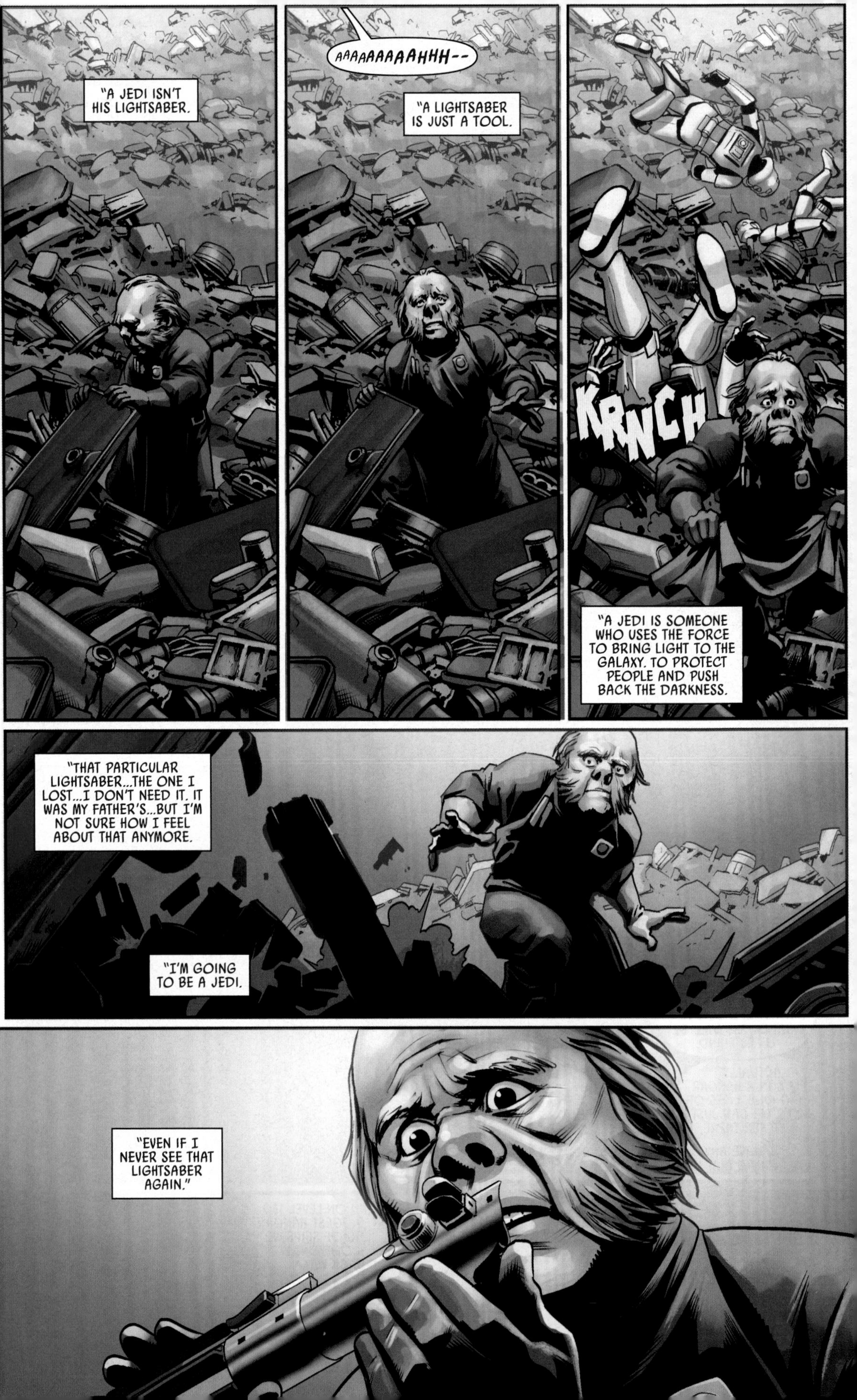
"A JEDI ISN'T HIS LIGHTSABER.
AAAAAAAAAHHH--
"A LIGHTSABER IS JUST A TOOL.
KRNCH
"A JEDI IS SOMEONE WHO USES THE FORCE TO BRING LIGHT TO THE GALAXY. TO PROTECT PEOPLE AND PUSH BACK THE DARKNESS.
"THAT PARTICULAR LIGHTSABER...THE ONE I LOST...I DON'T NEED IT. IT WAS MY FATHER'S...BUT I'M NOT SURE HOW I FEEL ABOUT THAT ANYMORE.
"I'M GOING TO BE A JEDI.
"EVEN IF I NEVER SEE THAT LIGHTSABER AGAIN."

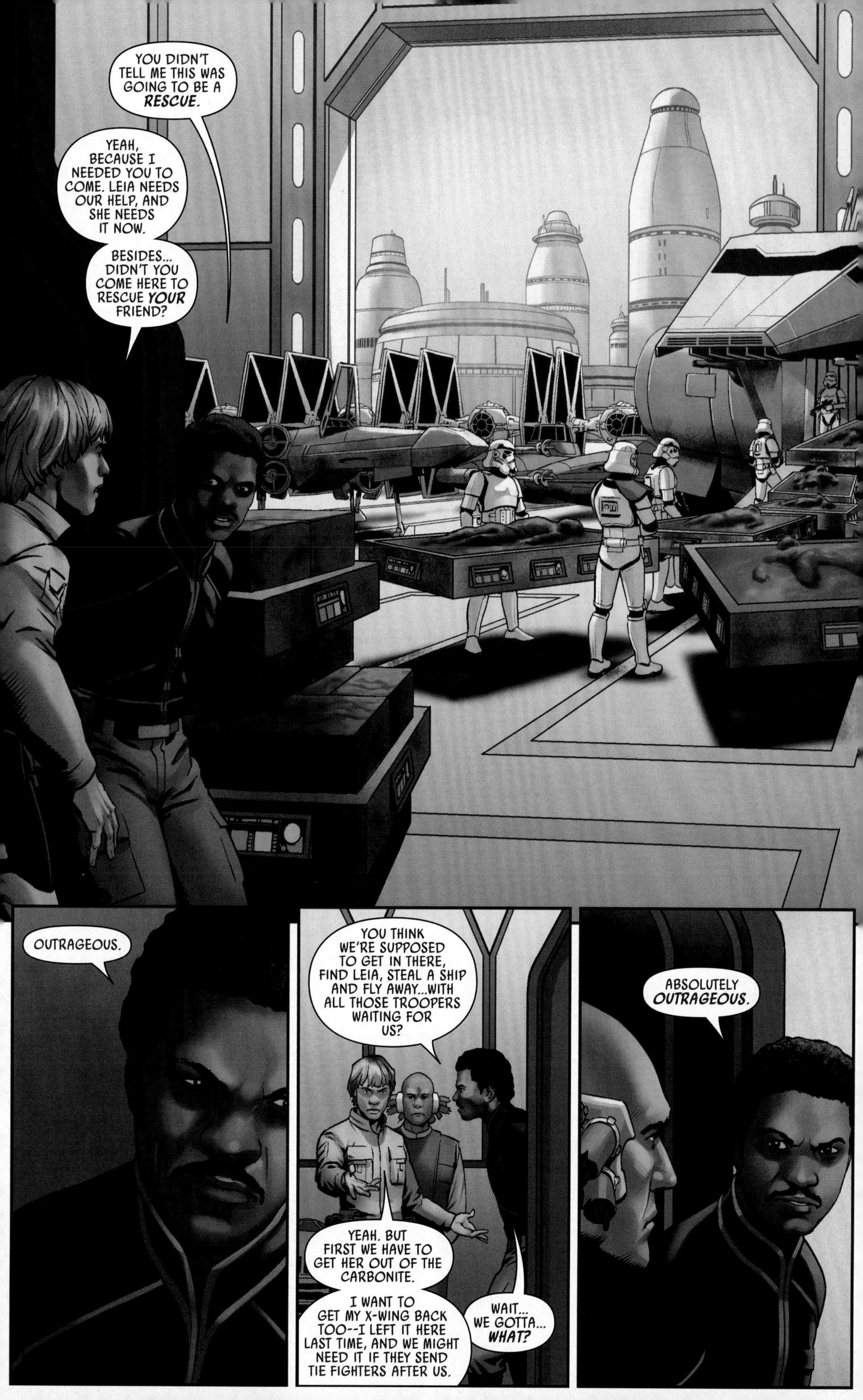
YOU DIDN'T TELL ME THIS WAS GOING TO BE A *RESCUE.*
YEAH, BECAUSE I NEEDED YOU TO COME. LEIA NEEDS OUR HELP, AND SHE NEEDS IT NOW.
BESIDES... DIDN'T YOU COME HERE TO RESCUE *YOUR* FRIEND?
OUTRAGEOUS.
YOU THINK WE'RE SUPPOSED TO GET IN THERE, FIND LEIA, STEAL A SHIP AND FLY AWAY...WITH ALL THOSE TROOPERS WAITING FOR US?
YEAH. BUT FIRST WE HAVE TO GET HER OUT OF THE CARBONITE.
I WANT TO GET MY X-WING BACK TOO--I LEFT IT HERE LAST TIME, AND WE MIGHT NEED IT IF THEY SEND TIE FIGHTERS AFTER US.
WAIT... WE GOTTA... *WHAT?*
ABSOLUTELY *OUTRAGEOUS.*

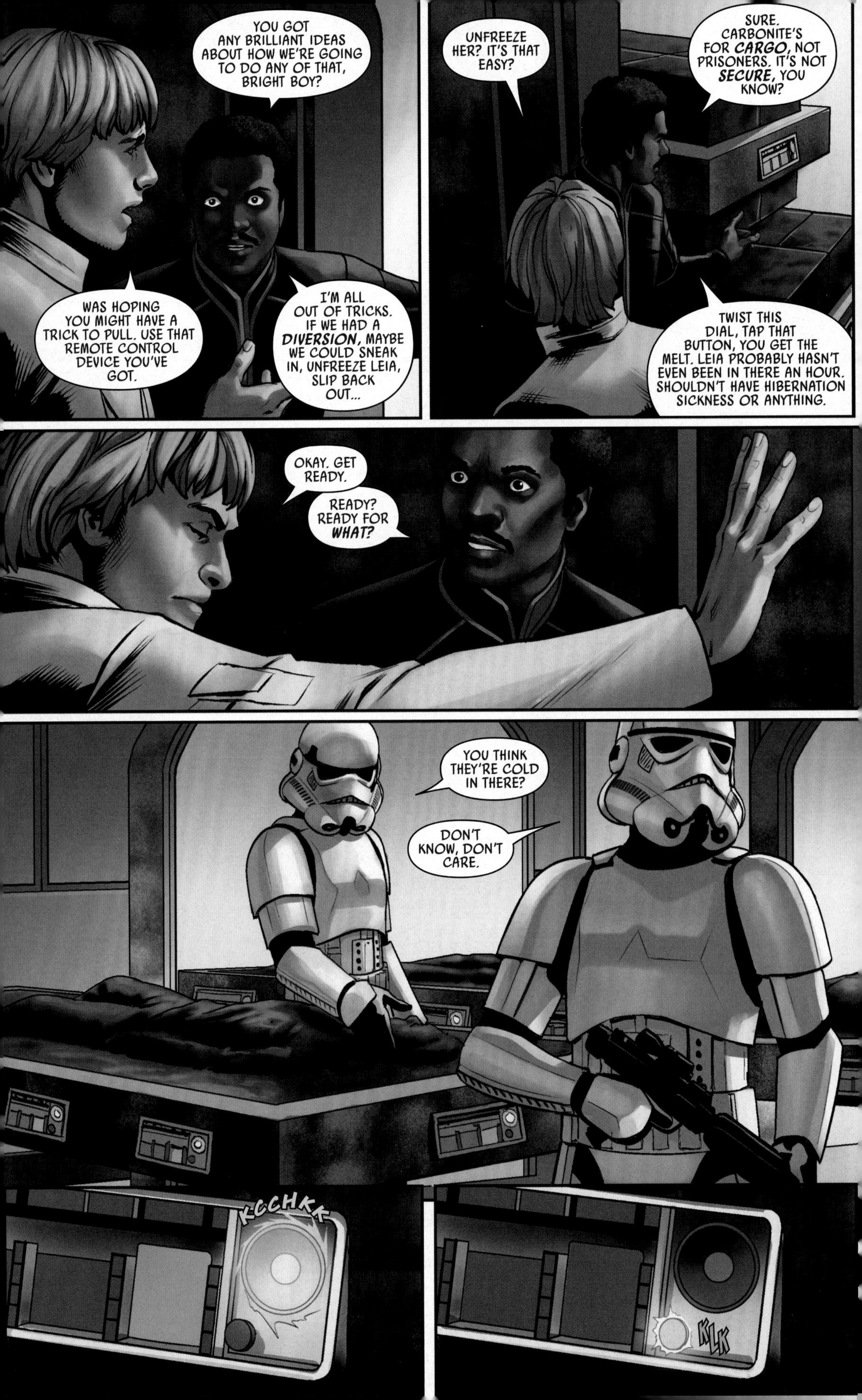
YOU GOT ANY BRILLIANT IDEAS ABOUT HOW WE'RE GOING TO DO ANY OF THAT, BRIGHT BOY?
WAS HOPING YOU MIGHT HAVE A TRICK TO PULL. USE THAT REMOTE CONTROL DEVICE YOU'VE GOT.
I'M ALL OUT OF TRICKS. IF WE HAD A DIVERSION, MAYBE WE COULD SNEAK IN, UNFREEZE LEIA, SLIP BACK OUT...
UNFREEZE HER? IT'S THAT EASY?
SURE. CARBONITE'S FOR CARGO, NOT PRISONERS. IT'S NOT SECURE, YOU KNOW?
TWIST THIS DIAL, TAP THAT BUTTON, YOU GET THE MELT. LEIA PROBABLY HASN'T EVEN BEEN IN THERE AN HOUR. SHOULDN'T HAVE HIBERNATION SICKNESS OR ANYTHING.
OKAY. GET READY.
READY? READY FOR WHAT?
YOU THINK THEY'RE COLD IN THERE?
DON'T KNOW, DON'T CARE.
KCCHKK
KLK

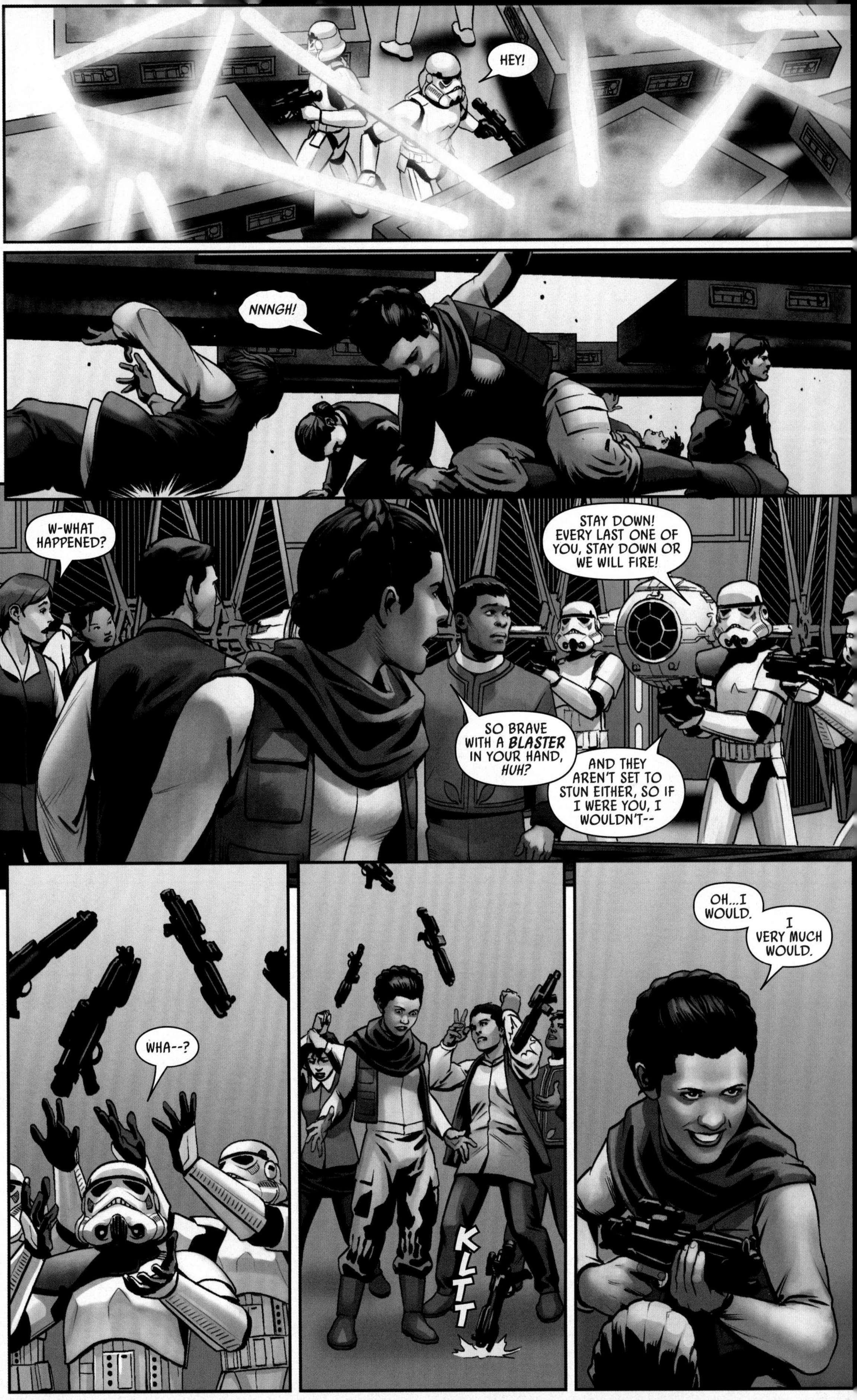
HEY!
NNNGH!
W-WHAT HAPPENED?
STAY DOWN! EVERY LAST ONE OF YOU, STAY DOWN OR WE WILL FIRE!
SO BRAVE WITH A BLASTER IN YOUR HAND, HUH?
AND THEY AREN'T SET TO STUN EITHER, SO IF I WERE YOU, I WOULDN'T--
WHA--?
KLTT
OH...I WOULD.
I VERY MUCH WOULD.

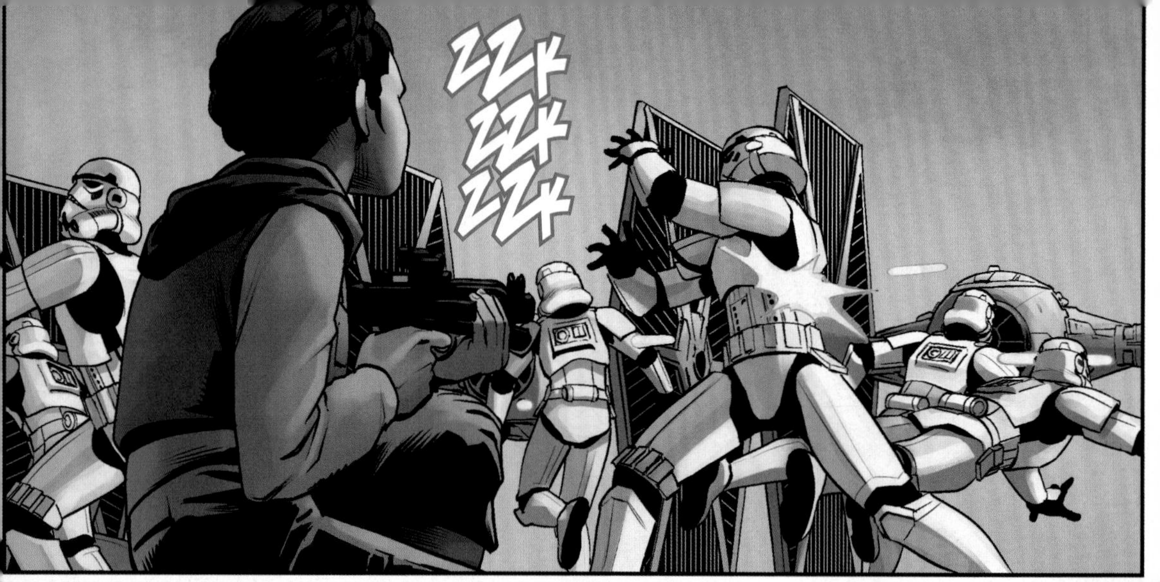
ZZK ZZK ZZK

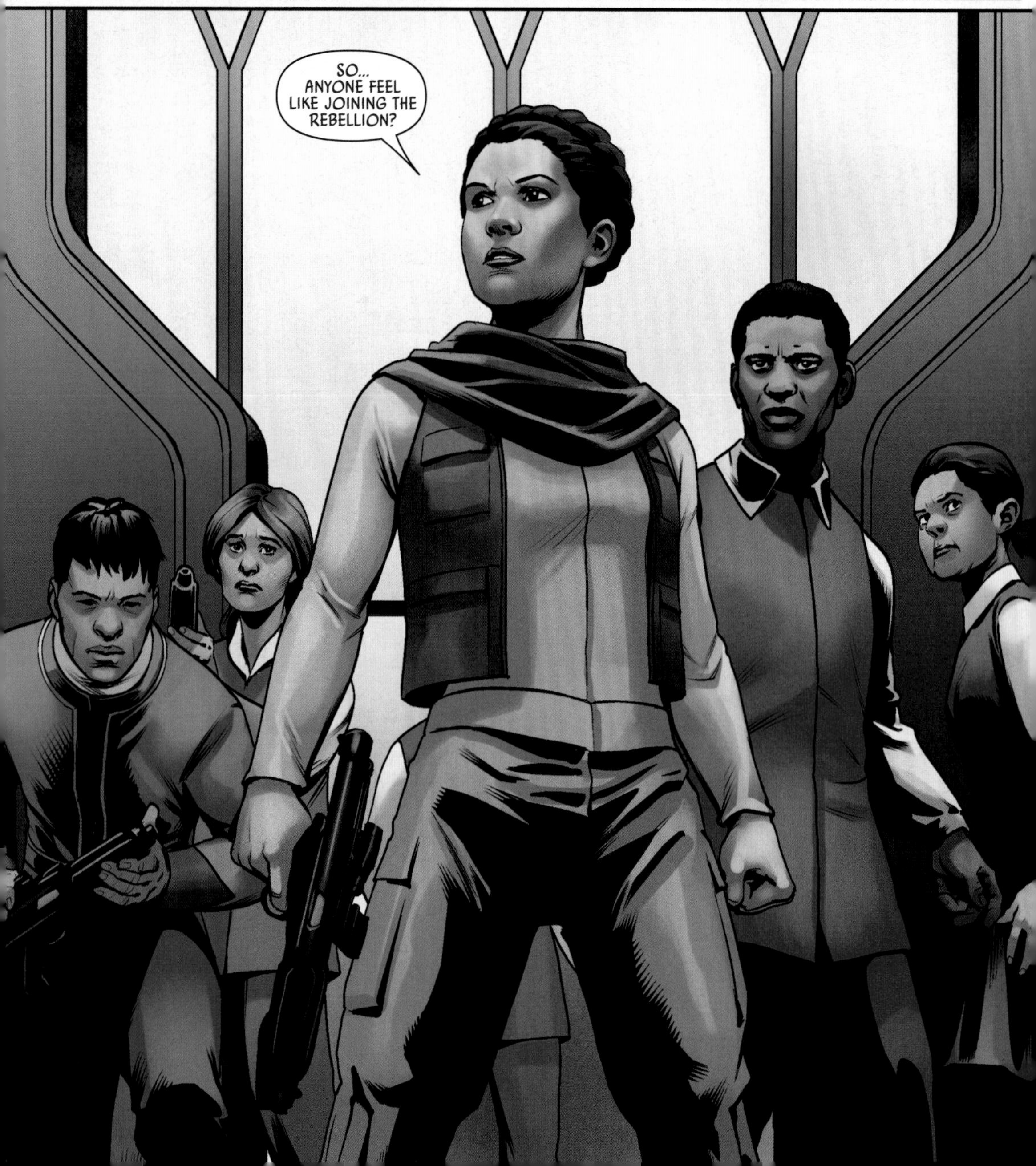
SO... ANYONE FEEL LIKE JOINING THE REBELLION?

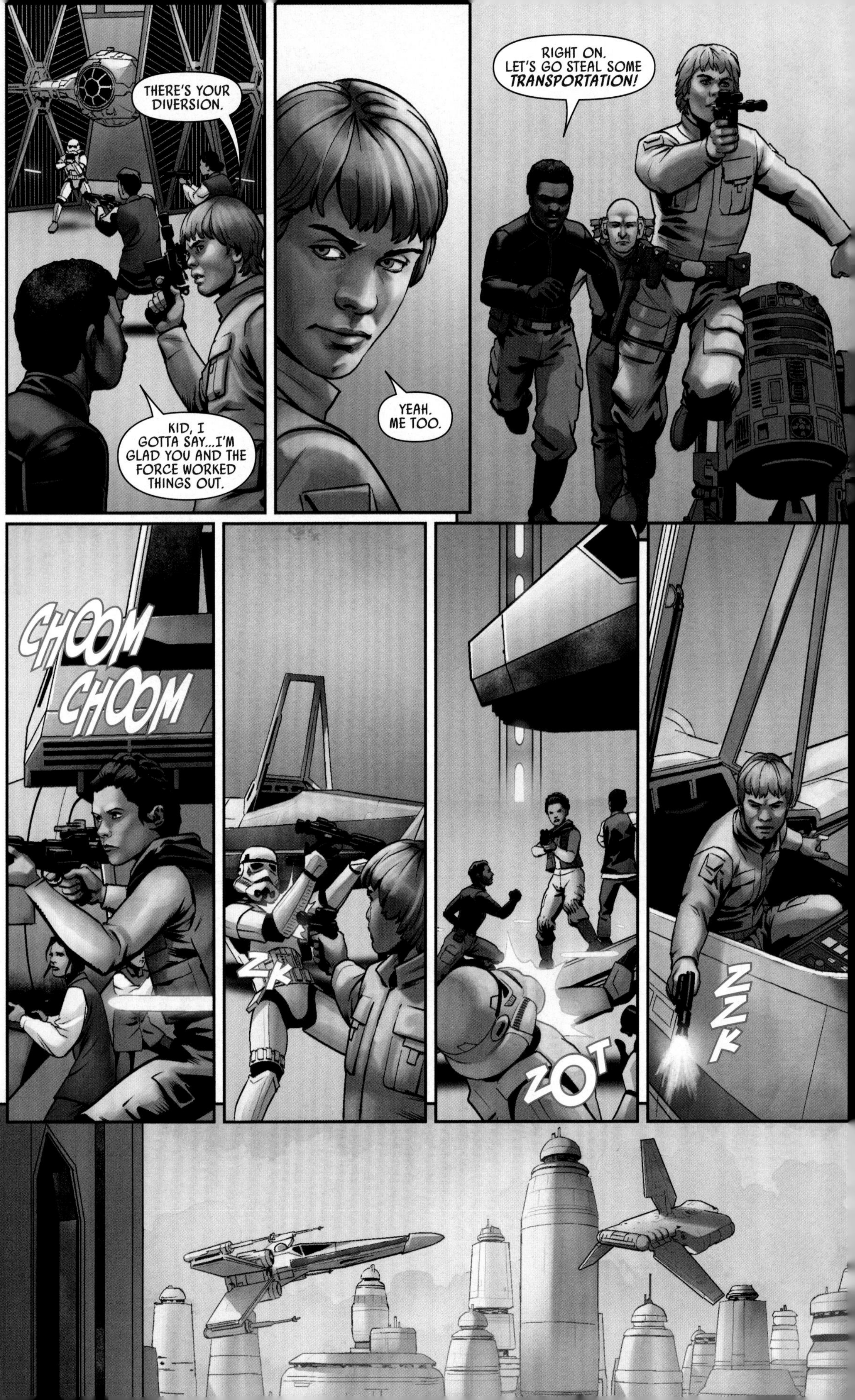
THERE'S YOUR DIVERSION.
KID, I GOTTA SAY...I'M GLAD YOU AND THE FORCE WORKED THINGS OUT.
YEAH. ME TOO.
RIGHT ON. LET'S GO STEAL SOME TRANSPORTATION!
CHOOM
CHOOM
ZK
ZOT
ZZK

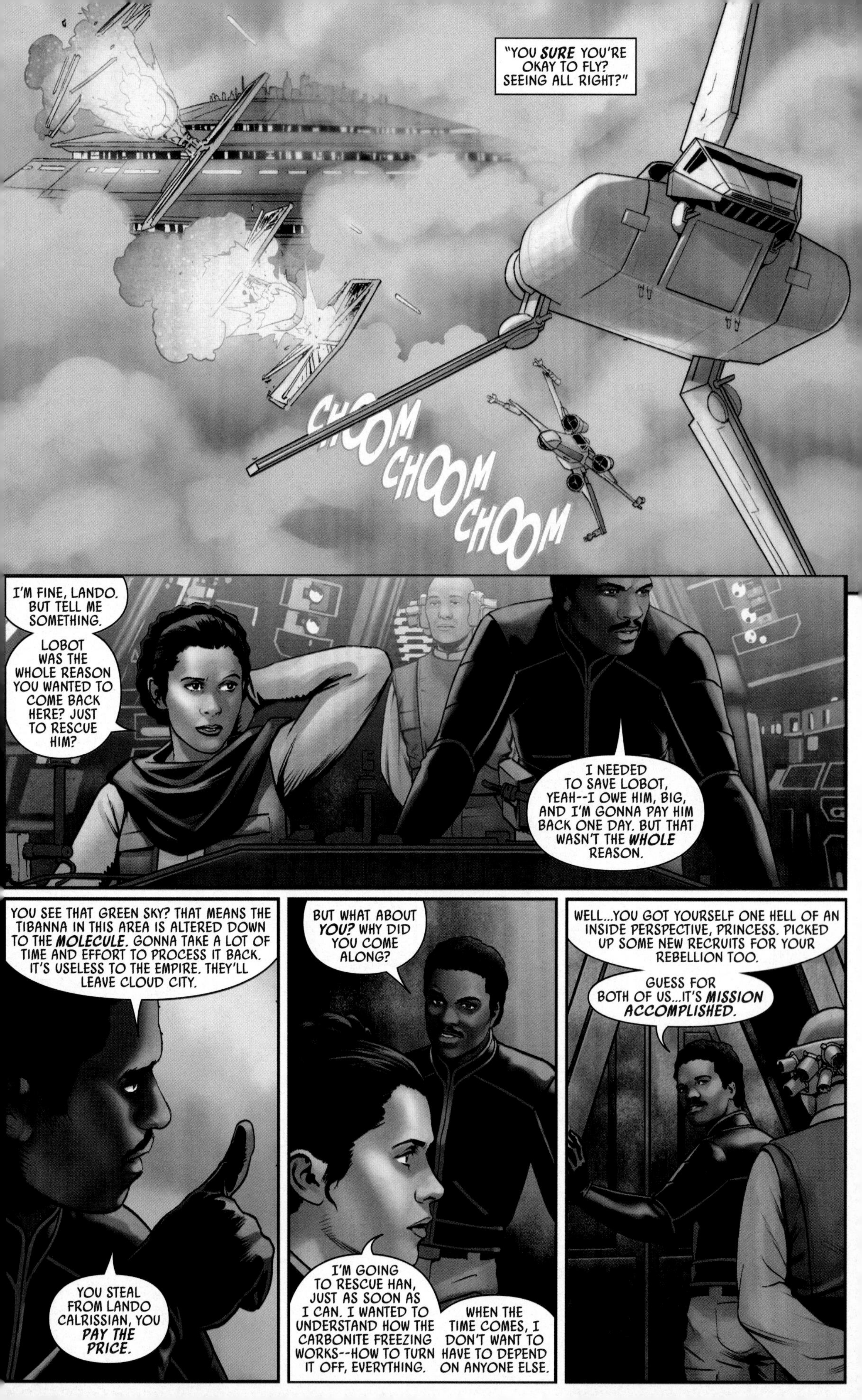

"YOU SURE YOU'RE OKAY TO FLY? SEEING ALL RIGHT?"
CHOOM CHOOM CHOOM
I'M FINE, LANDO. BUT TELL ME SOMETHING.
LOBOT WAS THE WHOLE REASON YOU WANTED TO COME BACK HERE? JUST TO RESCUE HIM?
I NEEDED TO SAVE LOBOT, YEAH--I OWE HIM, BIG, AND I'M GONNA PAY HIM BACK ONE DAY. BUT THAT WASN'T THE WHOLE REASON.
YOU SEE THAT GREEN SKY? THAT MEANS THE TIBANNA IN THIS AREA IS ALTERED DOWN TO THE MOLECULE. GONNA TAKE A LOT OF TIME AND EFFORT TO PROCESS IT BACK. IT'S USELESS TO THE EMPIRE. THEY'LL LEAVE CLOUD CITY.
YOU STEAL FROM LANDO CALRISSIAN, YOU PAY THE PRICE.
BUT WHAT ABOUT YOU? WHY DID YOU COME ALONG?
I'M GOING TO RESCUE HAN, JUST AS SOON AS I CAN. I WANTED TO UNDERSTAND HOW THE CARBONITE FREEZING WORKS--HOW TO TURN IT OFF, EVERYTHING.
WHEN THE TIME COMES, I DON'T WANT TO HAVE TO DEPEND ON ANYONE ELSE.
WELL...YOU GOT YOURSELF ONE HELL OF AN INSIDE PERSPECTIVE, PRINCESS. PICKED UP SOME NEW RECRUITS FOR YOUR REBELLION TOO.
GUESS FOR BOTH OF US...IT'S MISSION ACCOMPLISHED.

BARON-ADMINISTRATOR CALRISSIAN...WE ALL WANT TO THANK YOU. THANK YOU SO MUCH.

UH...SURE. OF COURSE. MY PLEASURE.

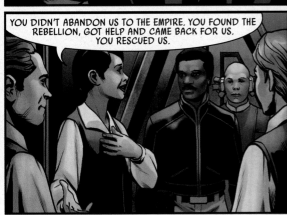

YOU DIDN'T ABANDON US TO THE EMPIRE. YOU FOUND THE REBELLION, GOT HELP AND CAME BACK FOR US. YOU RESCUED US.

YOU'RE A HERO.

I JUST DID WHAT I HAD TO. NO BIG DEAL.

NOW, THAT HAD TO BE A GRUELING EXPERIENCE. YOU ALL TRY TO GET SOME REST. WE'LL GET YOU MEDICAL ATTENTION BACK AT THE FLEET. THEY'VE GOT A WHOLE MEDICAL FRIGATE ACTUALLY.

THANK YOU, BARON-ADMINISTRATOR. THANK YOU.

HUH.

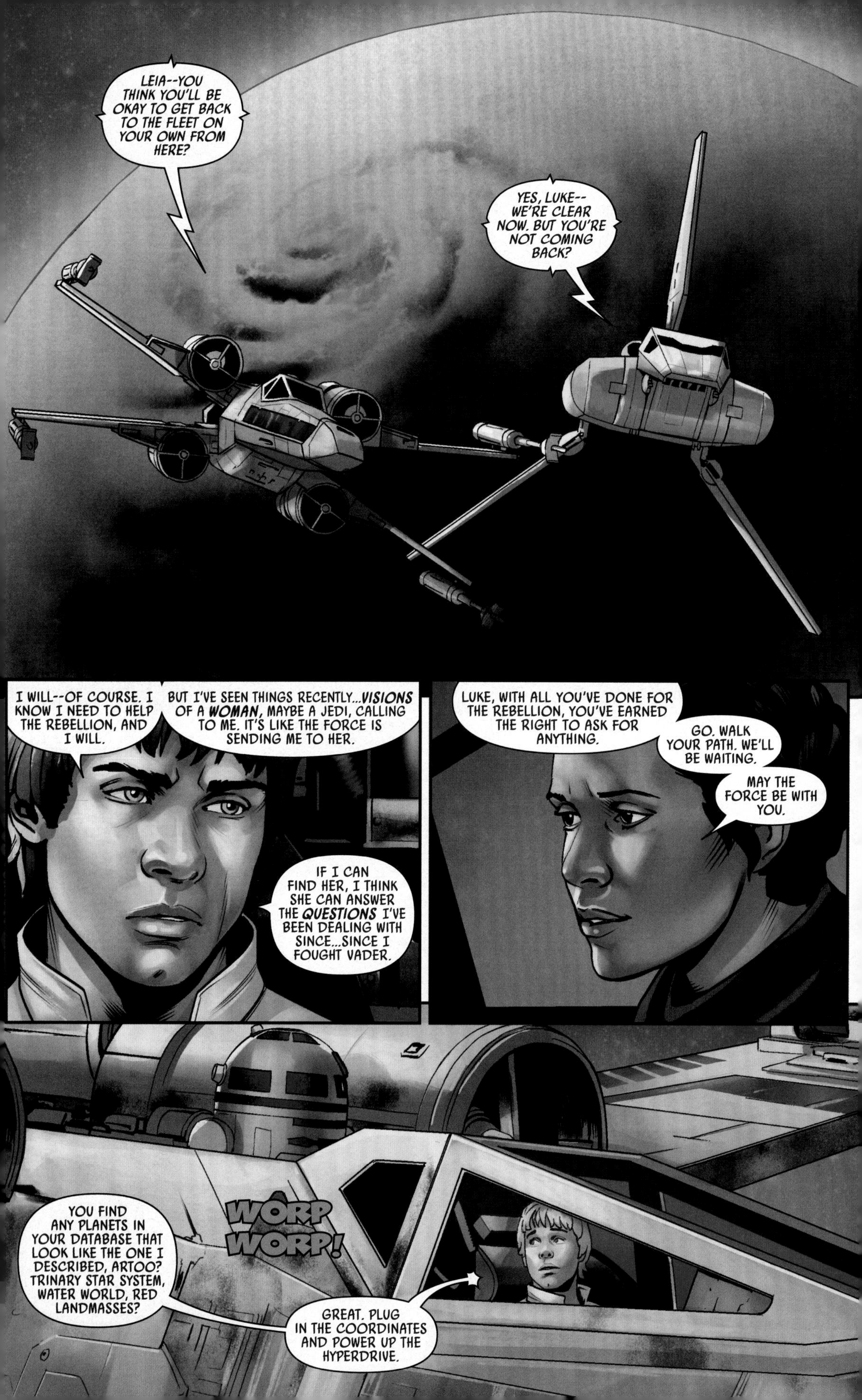
LEIA--YOU THINK YOU'LL BE OKAY TO GET BACK TO THE FLEET ON YOUR OWN FROM HERE?
YES, LUKE-- WE'RE CLEAR NOW. BUT YOU'RE NOT COMING BACK?
I WILL--OF COURSE. I KNOW I NEED TO HELP THE REBELLION, AND I WILL.
BUT I'VE SEEN THINGS RECENTLY...VISIONS OF A WOMAN, MAYBE A JEDI, CALLING TO ME. IT'S LIKE THE FORCE IS SENDING ME TO HER.
IF I CAN FIND HER, I THINK SHE CAN ANSWER THE QUESTIONS I'VE BEEN DEALING WITH SINCE...SINCE I FOUGHT VADER.
LUKE, WITH ALL YOU'VE DONE FOR THE REBELLION, YOU'VE EARNED THE RIGHT TO ASK FOR ANYTHING.
GO. WALK YOUR PATH. WE'LL BE WAITING.
MAY THE FORCE BE WITH YOU.
YOU FIND ANY PLANETS IN YOUR DATABASE THAT LOOK LIKE THE ONE I DESCRIBED, ARTOO? TRINARY STAR SYSTEM, WATER WORLD, RED LANDMASSES?
WORP WORP!
GREAT. PLUG IN THE COORDINATES AND POWER UP THE HYPERDRIVE.

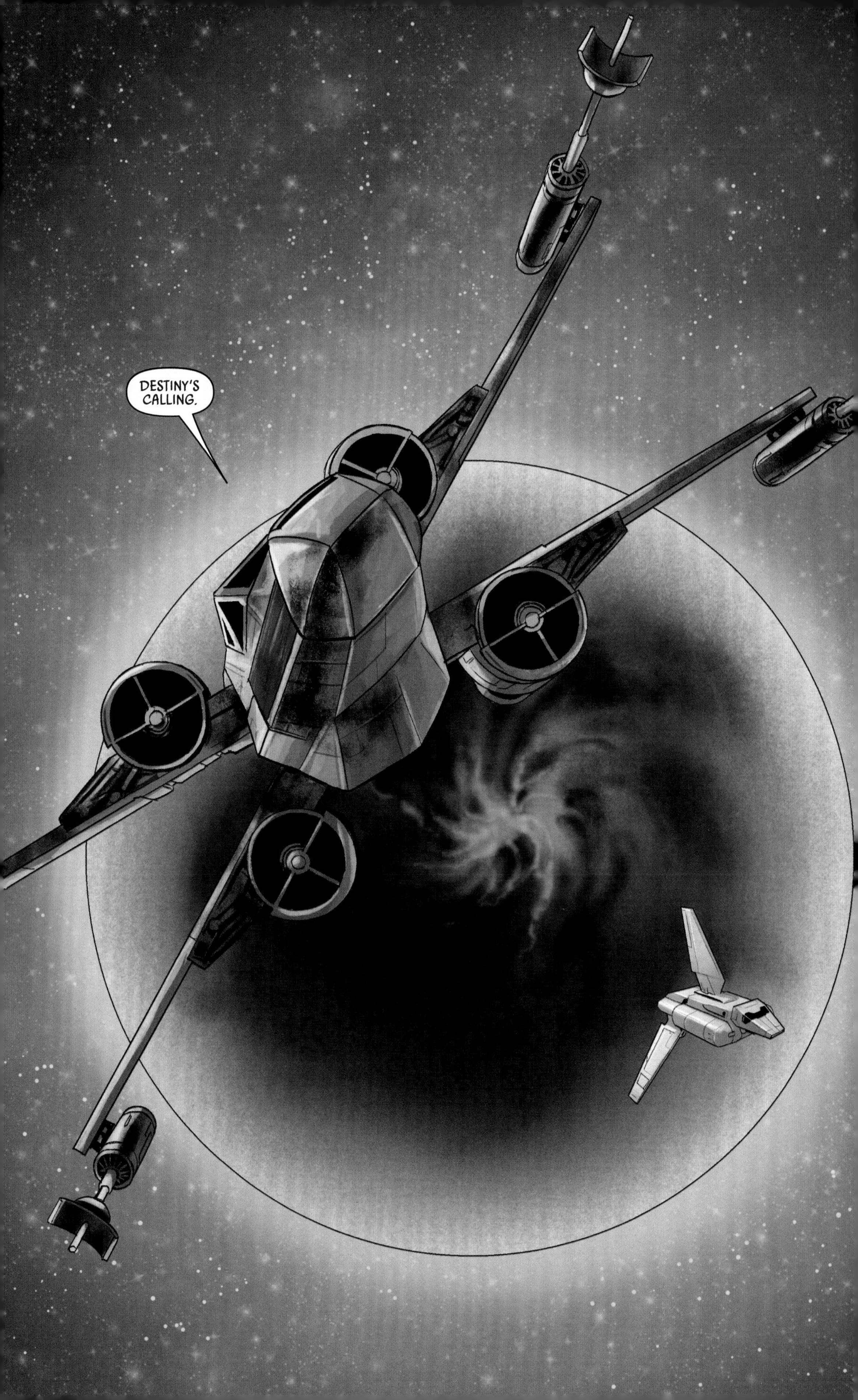
DESTINY'S CALLING.

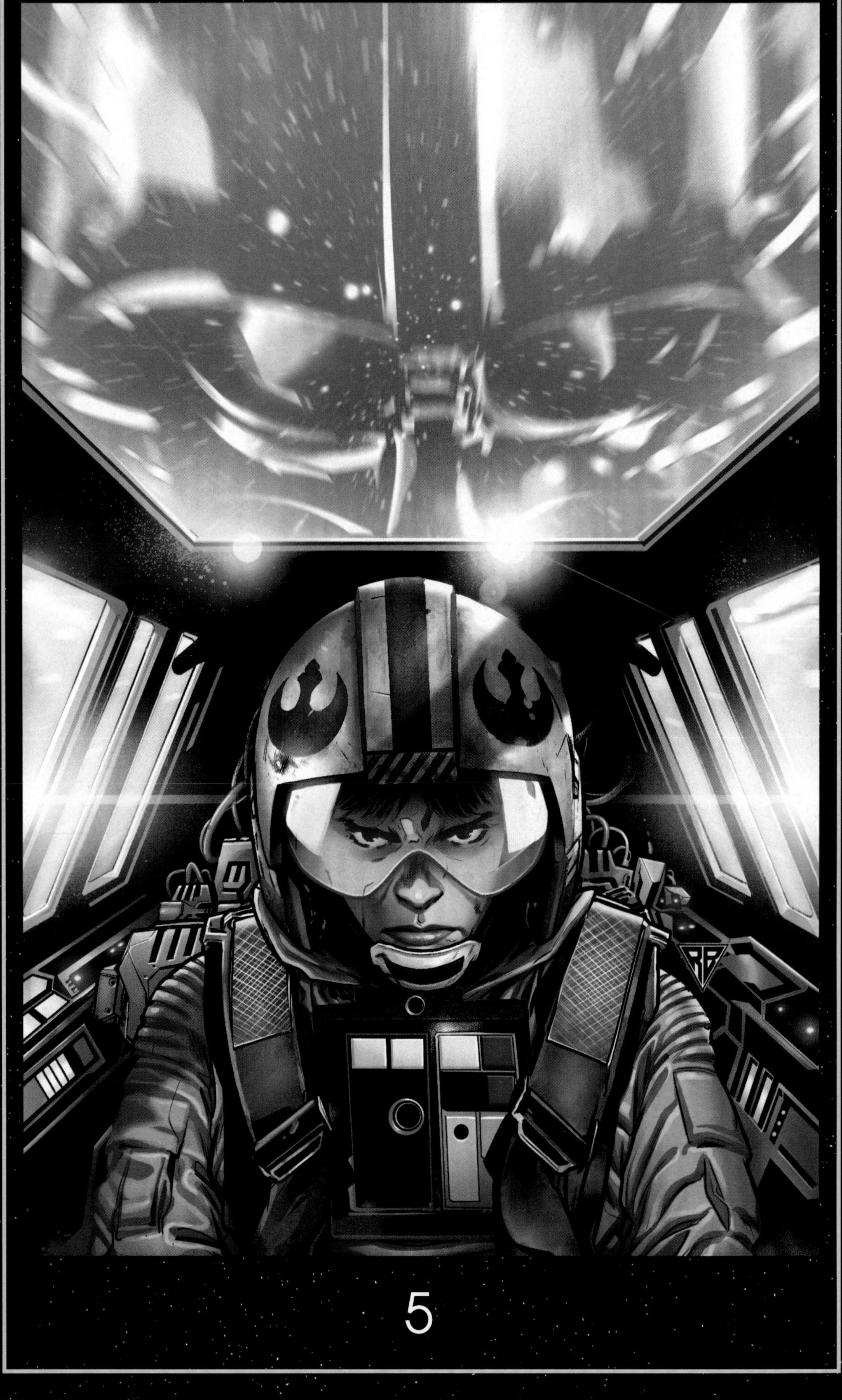

5

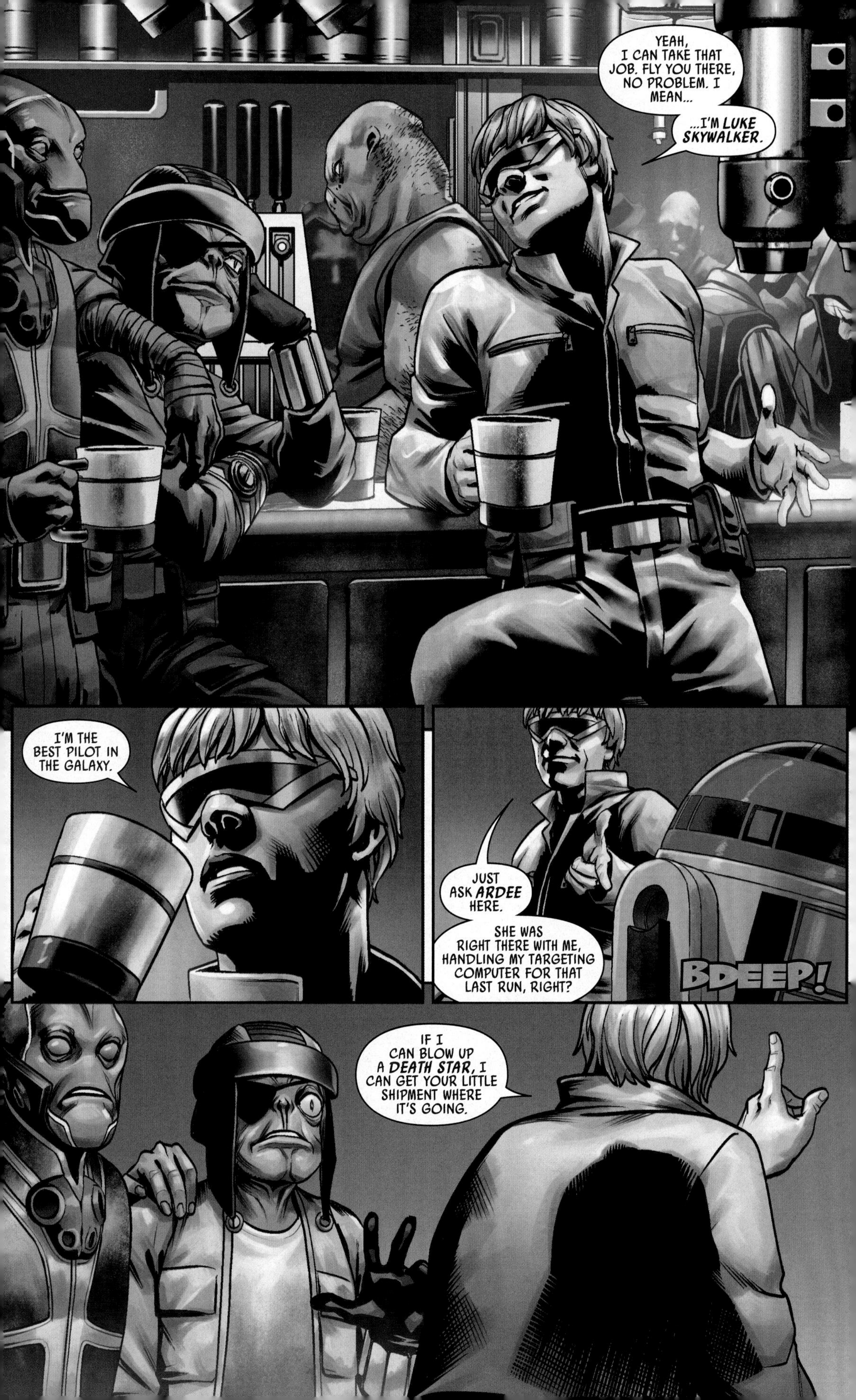

YEAH, I CAN TAKE THAT JOB. FLY YOU THERE, NO PROBLEM. I MEAN...
...I'M LUKE SKYWALKER.
I'M THE BEST PILOT IN THE GALAXY.
JUST ASK ARDEE HERE.
SHE WAS RIGHT THERE WITH ME, HANDLING MY TARGETING COMPUTER FOR THAT LAST RUN, RIGHT?
BDEEP!
IF I CAN BLOW UP A DEATH STAR, I CAN GET YOUR LITTLE SHIPMENT WHERE IT'S GOING.

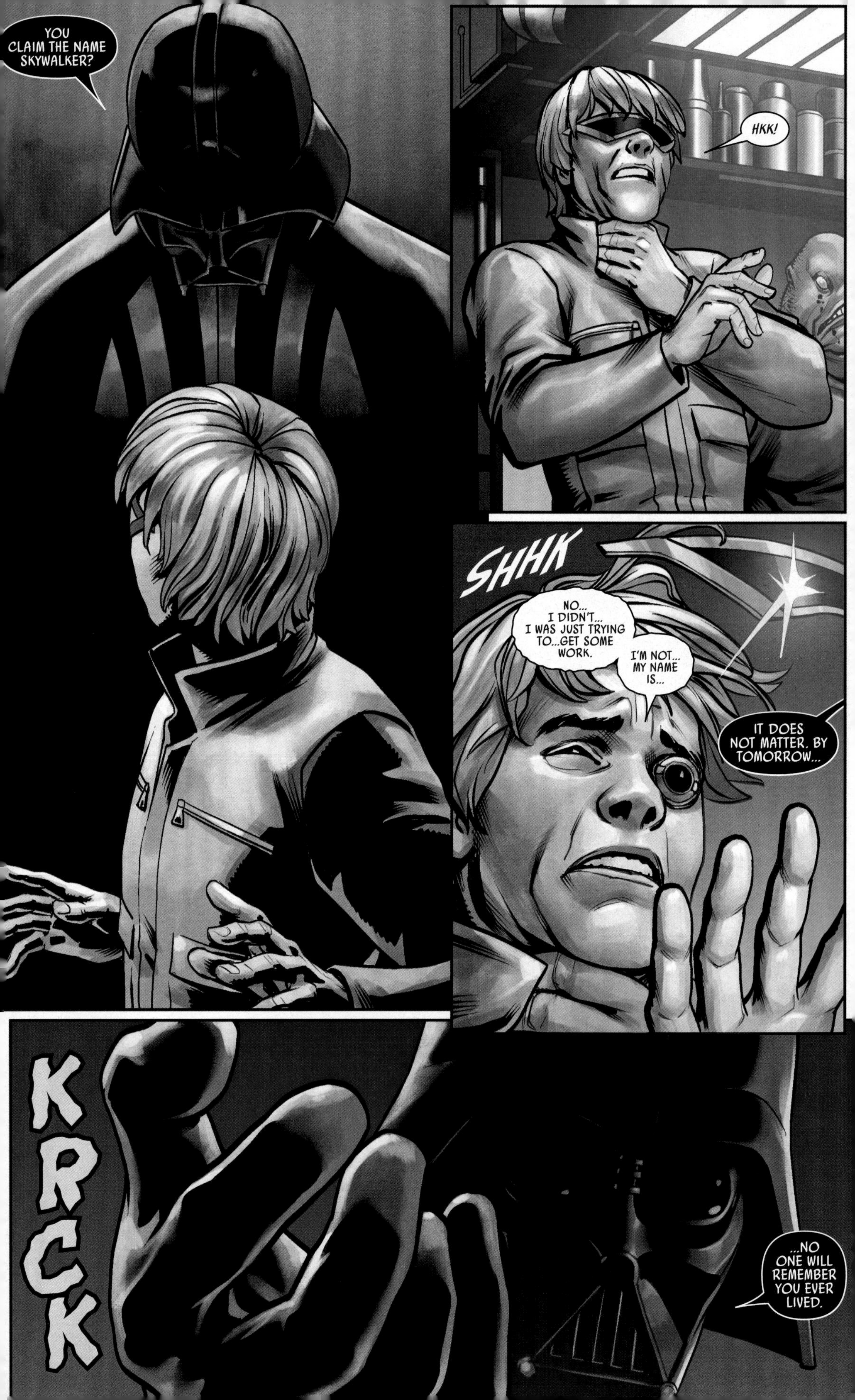
YOU CLAIM THE NAME SKYWALKER?
HKK!
SHHK
NO... I DIDN'T... I WAS JUST TRYING TO...GET SOME WORK.
I'M NOT... MY NAME IS...
IT DOES NOT MATTER. BY TOMORROW...
KRCK
...NO ONE WILL REMEMBER YOU EVER LIVED.

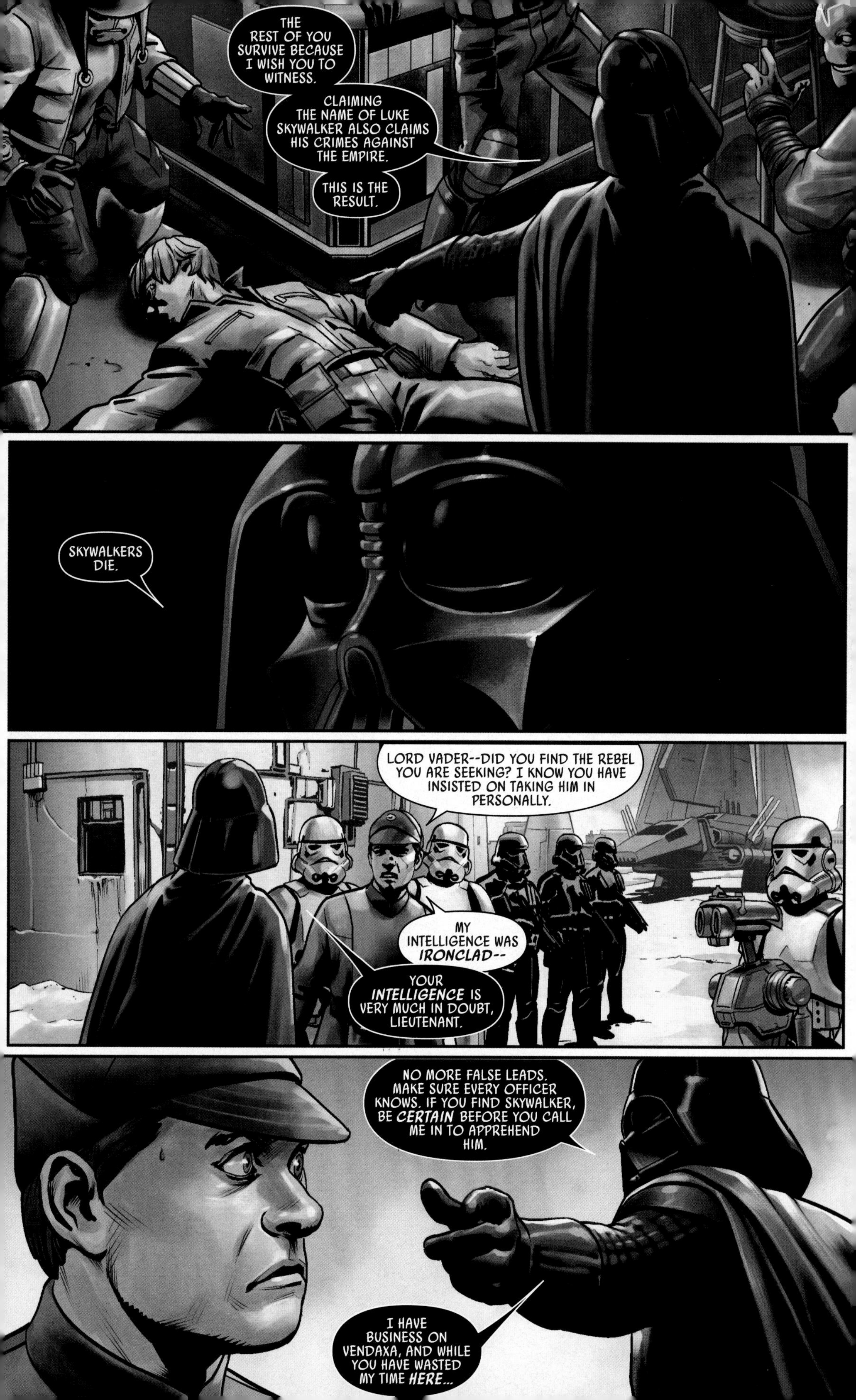
THE REST OF YOU SURVIVE BECAUSE I WISH YOU TO WITNESS.
CLAIMING THE NAME OF LUKE SKYWALKER ALSO CLAIMS HIS CRIMES AGAINST THE EMPIRE.
THIS IS THE RESULT.
SKYWALKERS DIE.
LORD VADER--DID YOU FIND THE REBEL YOU ARE SEEKING? I KNOW YOU HAVE INSISTED ON TAKING HIM IN PERSONALLY.
MY INTELLIGENCE WAS IRONCLAD--
YOUR INTELLIGENCE IS VERY MUCH IN DOUBT, LIEUTENANT.
NO MORE FALSE LEADS. MAKE SURE EVERY OFFICER KNOWS. IF YOU FIND SKYWALKER, BE CERTAIN BEFORE YOU CALL ME IN TO APPREHEND HIM.
I HAVE BUSINESS ON VENDAXA, AND WHILE YOU HAVE WASTED MY TIME HERE...

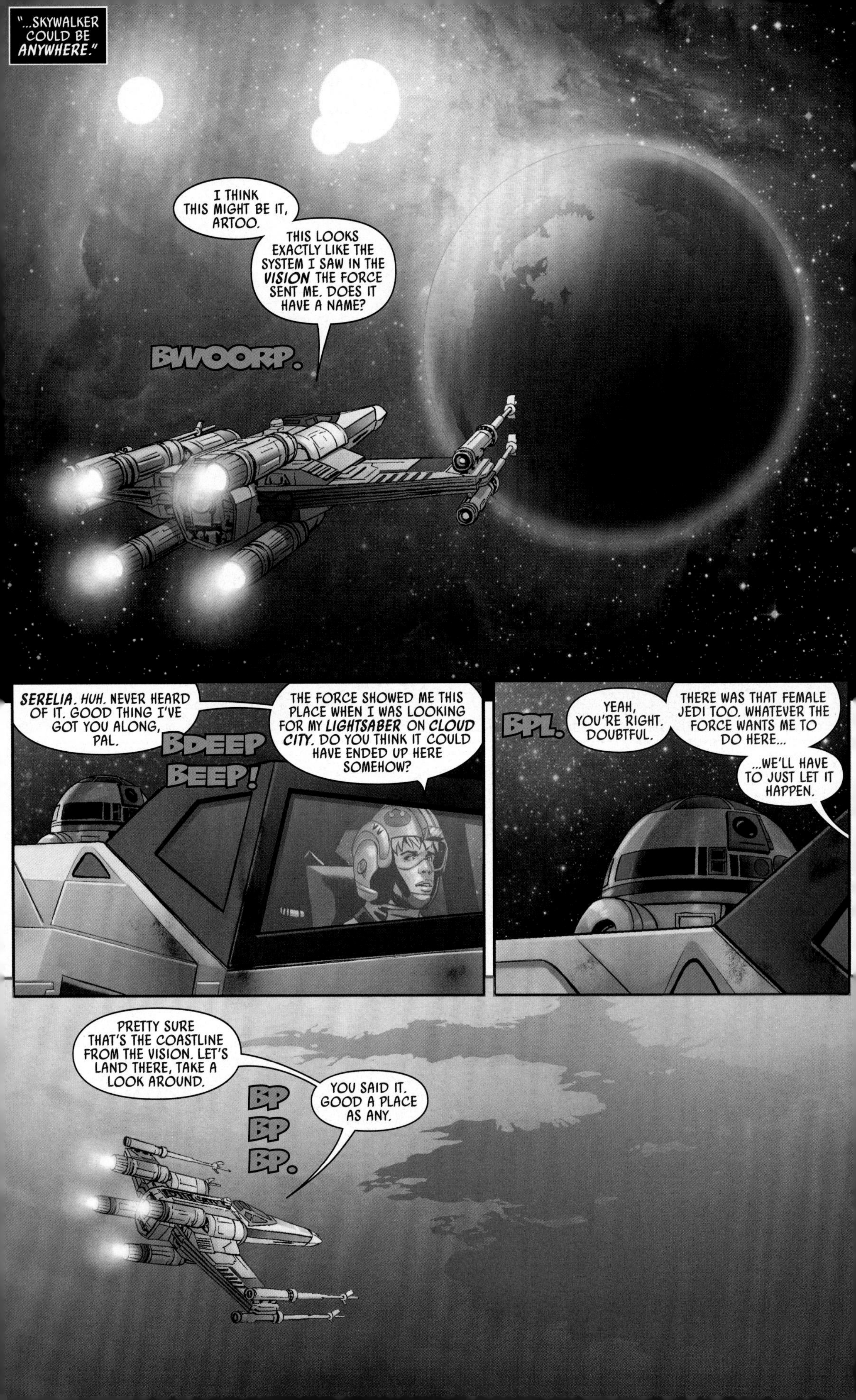
"...SKYWALKER COULD BE ANYWHERE."
I THINK THIS MIGHT BE IT, ARTOO.
THIS LOOKS EXACTLY LIKE THE SYSTEM I SAW IN THE VISION THE FORCE SENT ME. DOES IT HAVE A NAME?
BWOORP.
SERELIA. HUH. NEVER HEARD OF IT. GOOD THING I'VE GOT YOU ALONG, PAL.
BDEEP BEEP!
THE FORCE SHOWED ME THIS PLACE WHEN I WAS LOOKING FOR MY LIGHTSABER ON CLOUD CITY. DO YOU THINK IT COULD HAVE ENDED UP HERE SOMEHOW?
BPL.
YEAH, YOU'RE RIGHT. DOUBTFUL.
THERE WAS THAT FEMALE JEDI TOO. WHATEVER THE FORCE WANTS ME TO DO HERE...
...WE'LL HAVE TO JUST LET IT HAPPEN.
PRETTY SURE THAT'S THE COASTLINE FROM THE VISION. LET'S LAND THERE, TAKE A LOOK AROUND.
BP BP BP.
YOU SAID IT. GOOD A PLACE AS ANY.

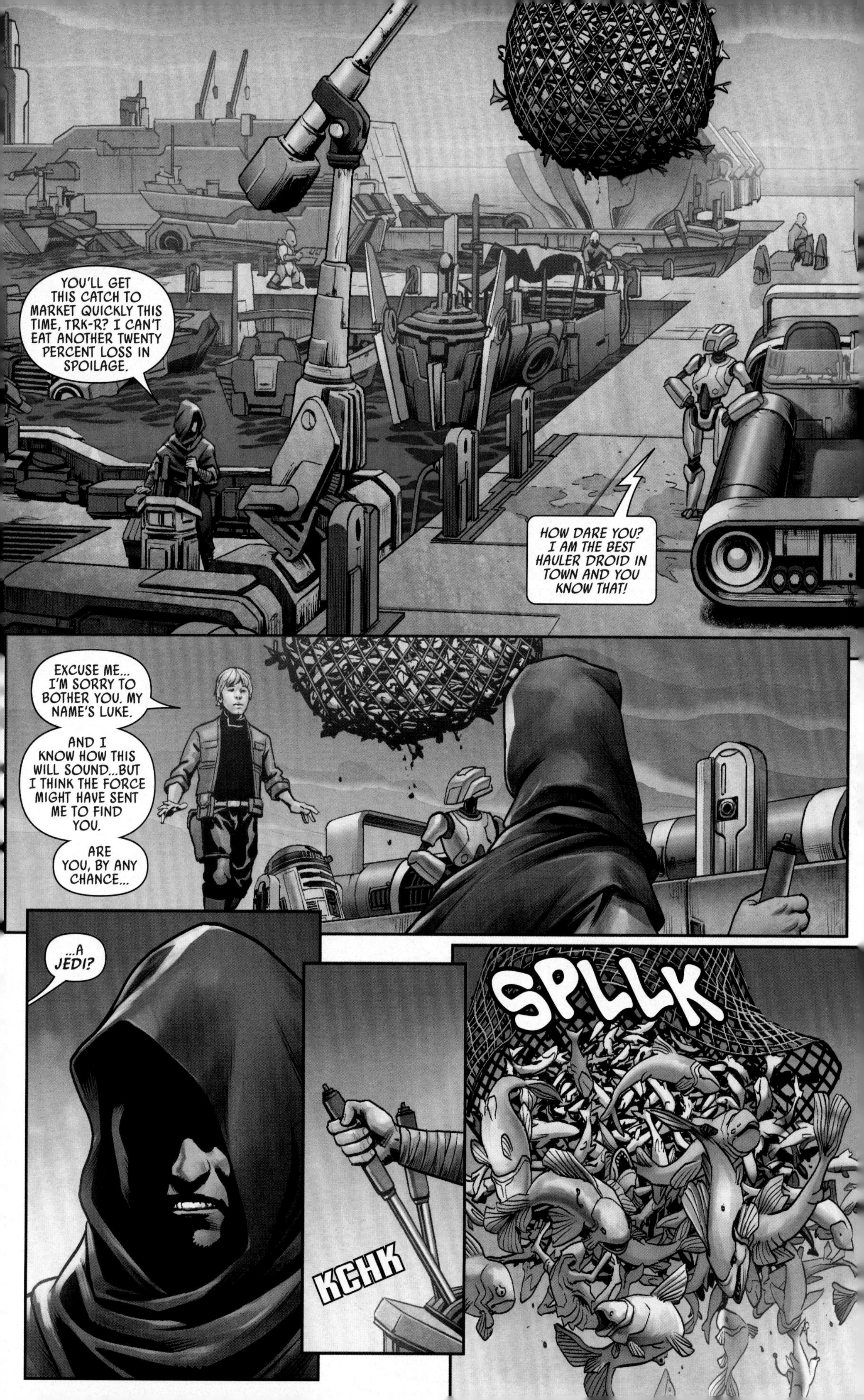
YOU'LL GET THIS CATCH TO MARKET QUICKLY THIS TIME, TRK-R? I CAN'T EAT ANOTHER TWENTY PERCENT LOSS IN SPOILAGE.
HOW DARE YOU? I AM THE BEST HAULER DROID IN TOWN AND YOU KNOW THAT!
EXCUSE ME... I'M SORRY TO BOTHER YOU. MY NAME'S LUKE.
AND I KNOW HOW THIS WILL SOUND...BUT I THINK THE FORCE MIGHT HAVE SENT ME TO FIND YOU.
ARE YOU, BY ANY CHANCE...
...A JEDI?
KCHK
SPLLK

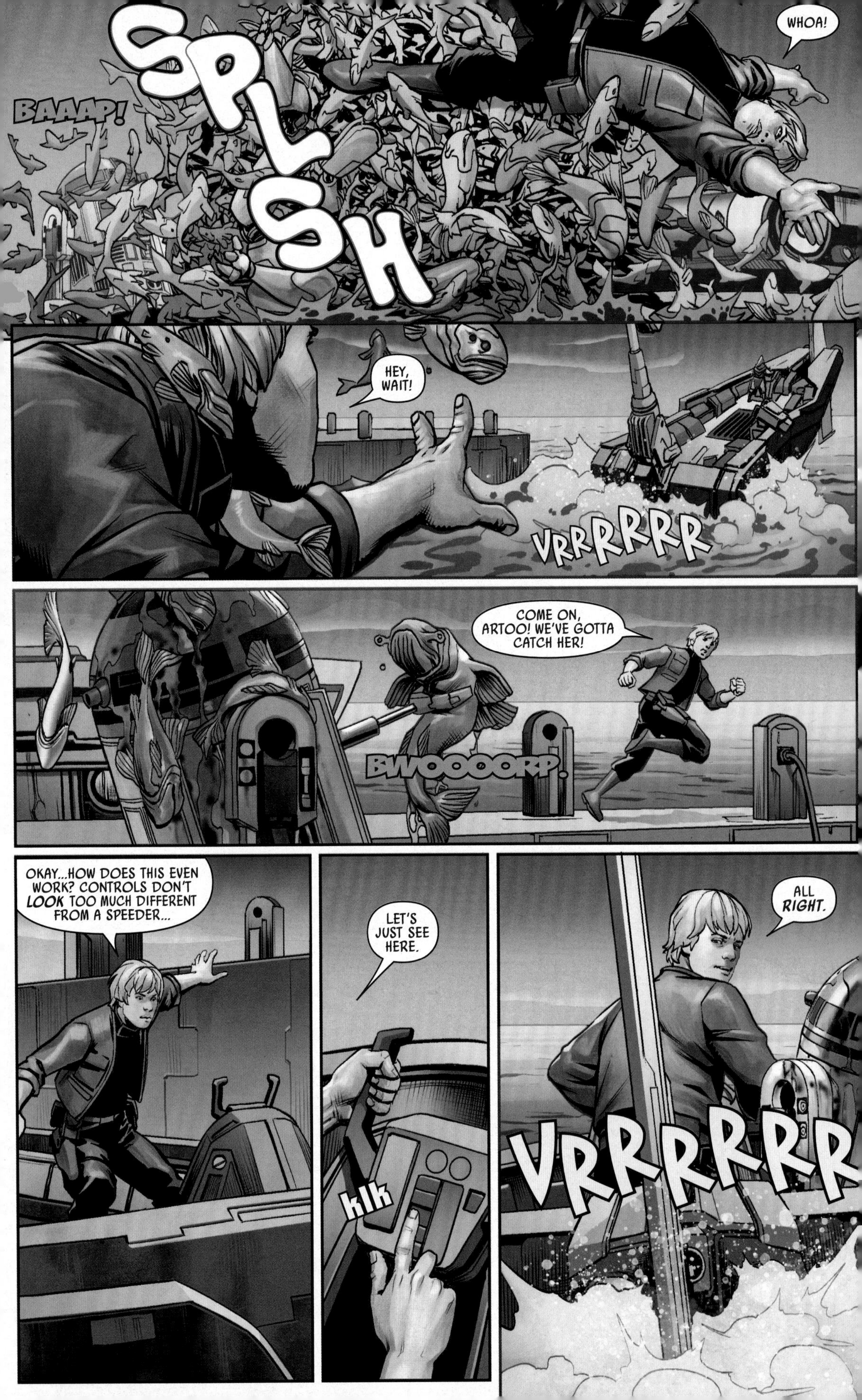
SPLSH
BAAAP!
WHOA!
HEY, WAIT!
VRRRRRR
COME ON, ARTOO! WE'VE GOTTA CATCH HER!
BWOOOOORP!
OKAY...HOW DOES THIS EVEN WORK? CONTROLS DON'T LOOK TOO MUCH DIFFERENT FROM A SPEEDER...
LET'S JUST SEE HERE.
klk
ALL RIGHT.
VRRRRRR

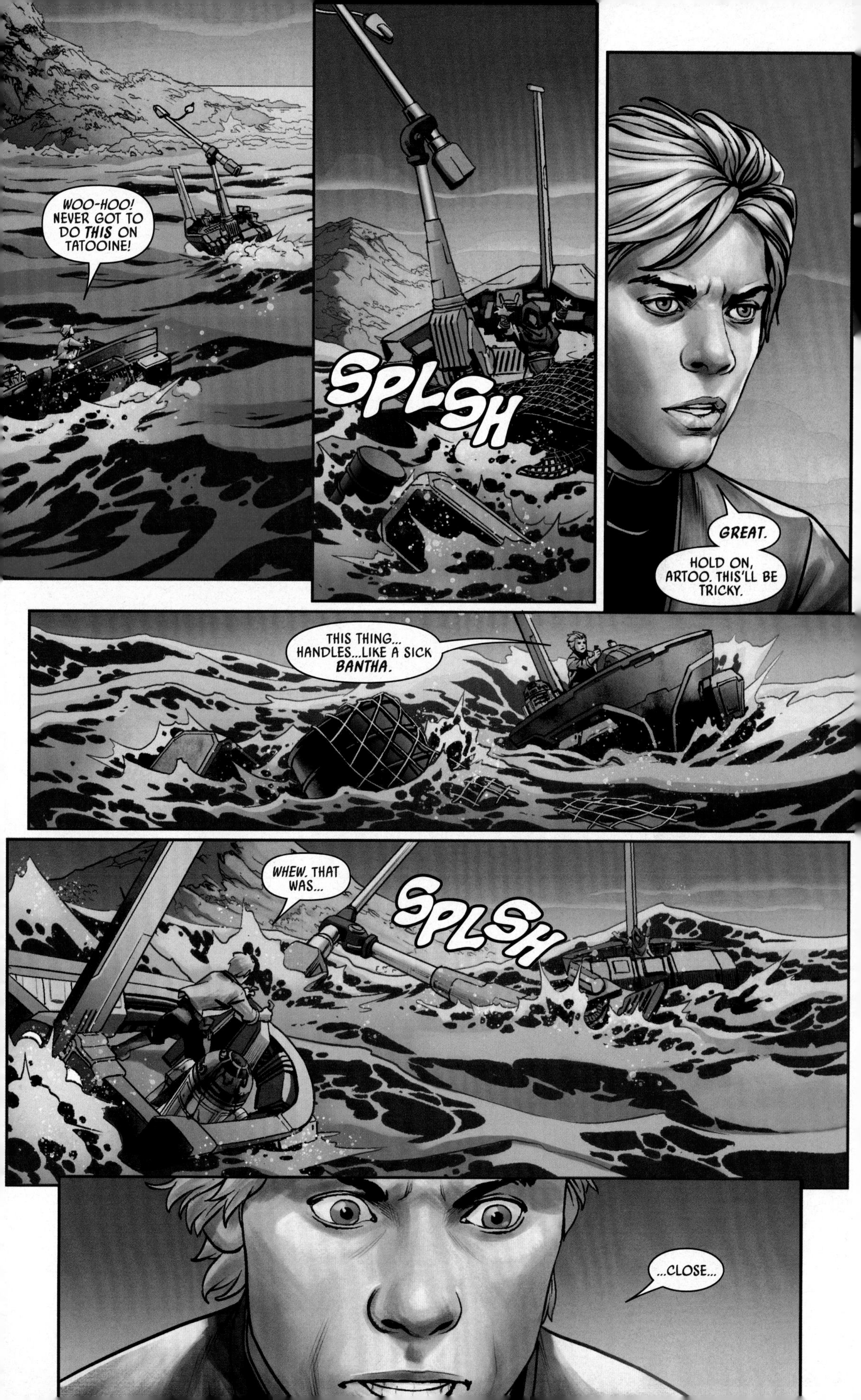
WOO-HOO! NEVER GOT TO DO THIS ON TATOOINE!
SPLSH
GREAT.
HOLD ON, ARTOO. THIS'LL BE TRICKY.
THIS THING... HANDLES...LIKE A SICK BANTHA.
WHEW. THAT WAS...
SPLSH
...CLOSE...

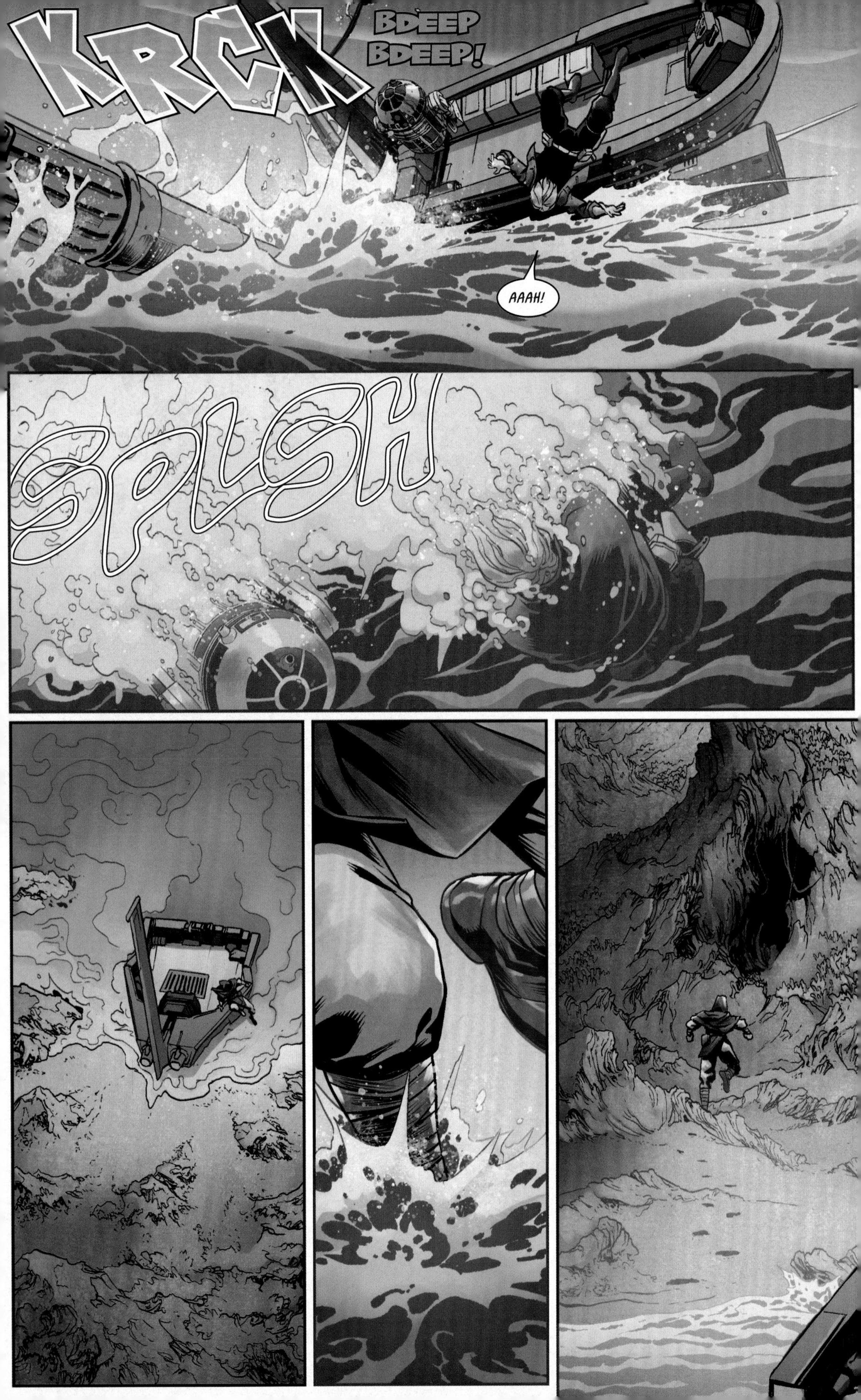
KRCK
BDEEP BDEEP!
AAAH!
SPLSH

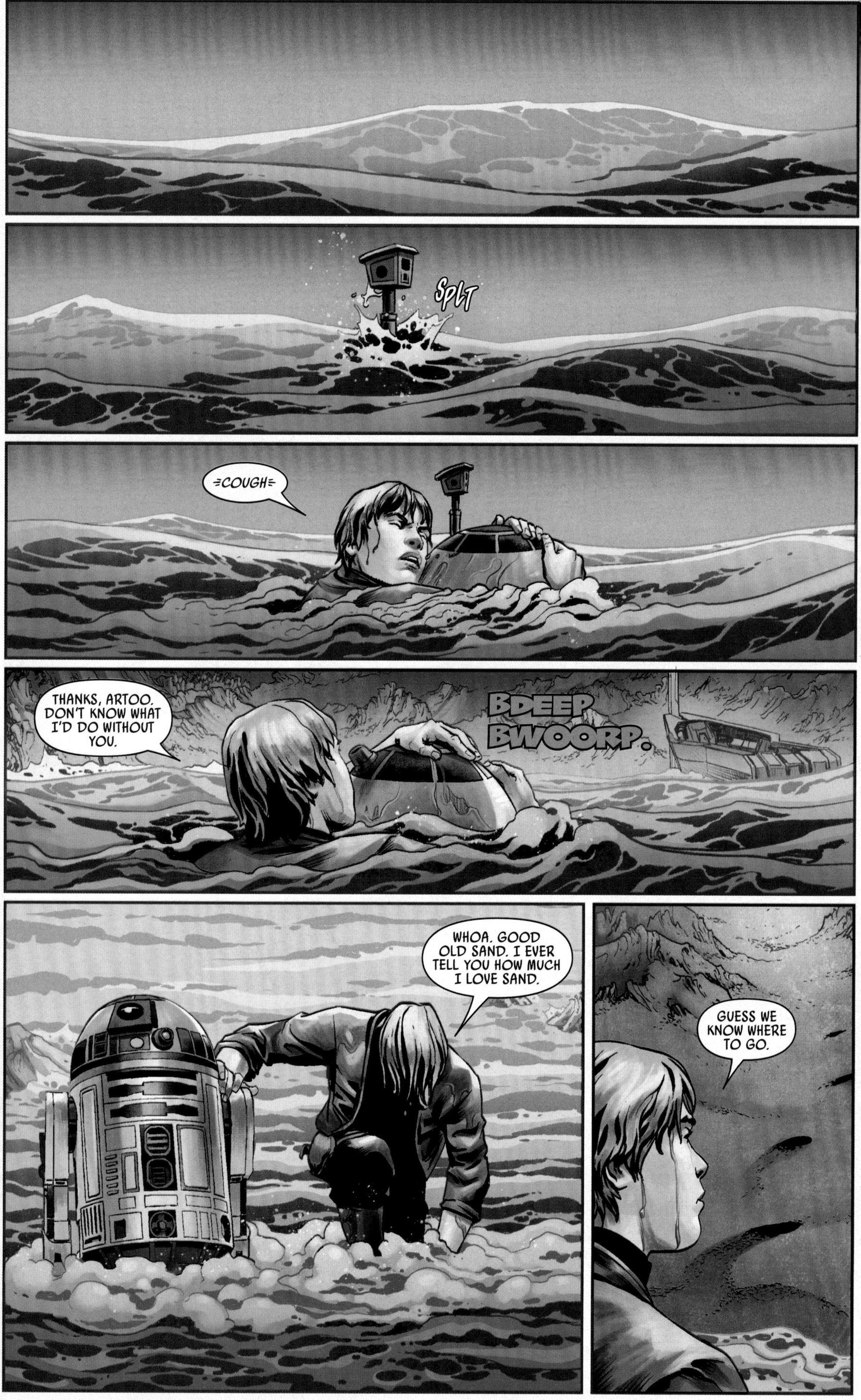
SPLT
=COUGH=
THANKS, ARTOO. DON'T KNOW WHAT I'D DO WITHOUT YOU.
BDEEP BWOORP.
WHOA. GOOD OLD SAND. I EVER TELL YOU HOW MUCH I LOVE SAND.
GUESS WE KNOW WHERE TO GO.

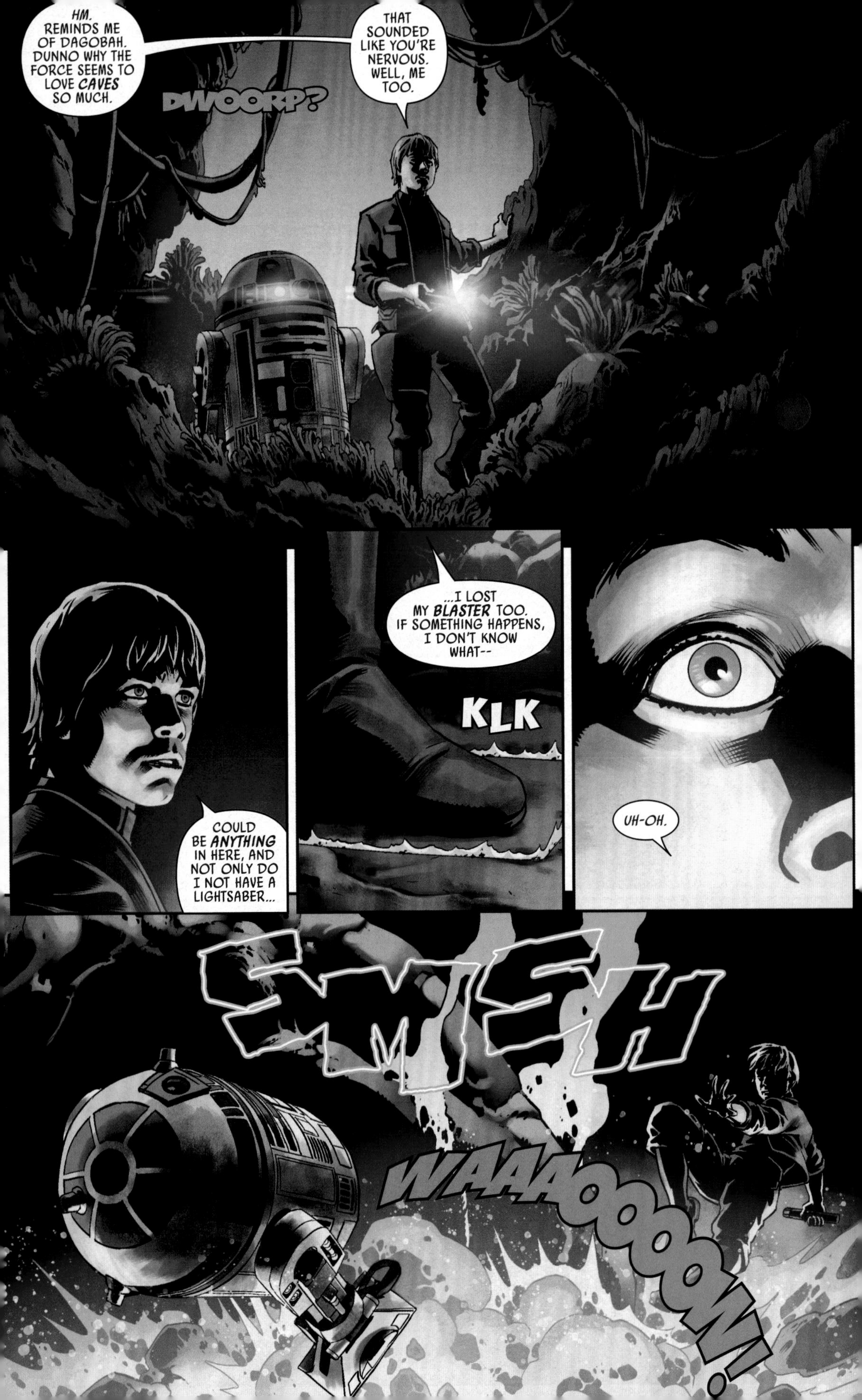
HM. REMINDS ME OF DAGOBAH. DUNNO WHY THE FORCE SEEMS TO LOVE CAVES SO MUCH.
DWOORP?
THAT SOUNDED LIKE YOU'RE NERVOUS. WELL, ME TOO.
COULD BE ANYTHING IN HERE, AND NOT ONLY DO I NOT HAVE A LIGHTSABER...
...I LOST MY BLASTER TOO. IF SOMETHING HAPPENS, I DON'T KNOW WHAT--
KLK
UH-OH.
SMSH
WAAAOOOOOW!

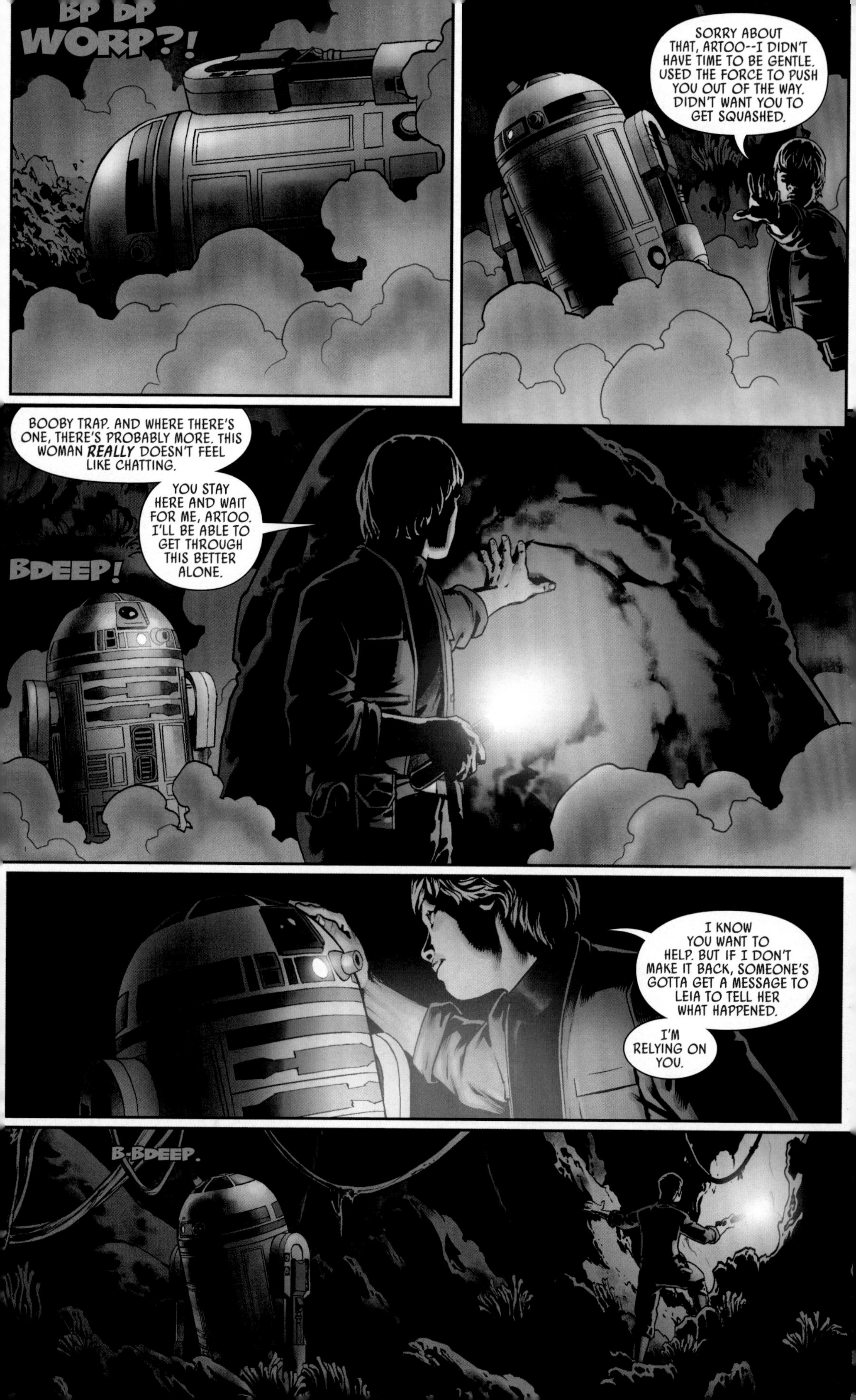
BP DP WORP?!
SORRY ABOUT THAT, ARTOO--I DIDN'T HAVE TIME TO BE GENTLE. USED THE FORCE TO PUSH YOU OUT OF THE WAY. DIDN'T WANT YOU TO GET SQUASHED.
BOOBY TRAP. AND WHERE THERE'S ONE, THERE'S PROBABLY MORE. THIS WOMAN REALLY DOESN'T FEEL LIKE CHATTING.
YOU STAY HERE AND WAIT FOR ME, ARTOO. I'LL BE ABLE TO GET THROUGH THIS BETTER ALONE.
BDEEP!
I KNOW YOU WANT TO HELP. BUT IF I DON'T MAKE IT BACK, SOMEONE'S GOTTA GET A MESSAGE TO LEIA TO TELL HER WHAT HAPPENED.
I'M RELYING ON YOU.
B-BDEEP.

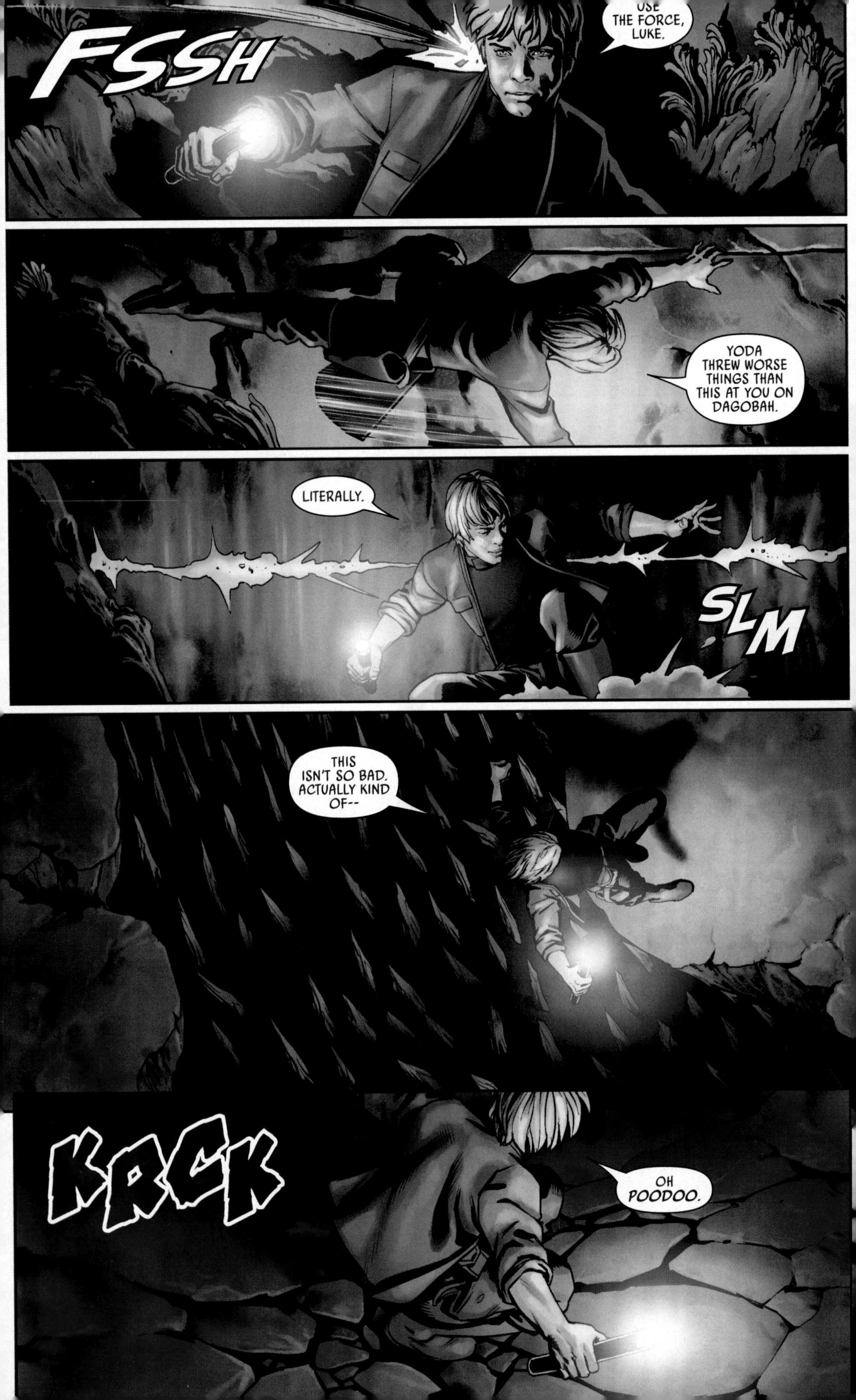
FSSH
USE THE FORCE, LUKE.
YODA THREW WORSE THINGS THAN THIS AT YOU ON DAGOBAH.
LITERALLY.
SLM
THIS ISN'T SO BAD. ACTUALLY KIND OF--
KRCK
OH POODOO.

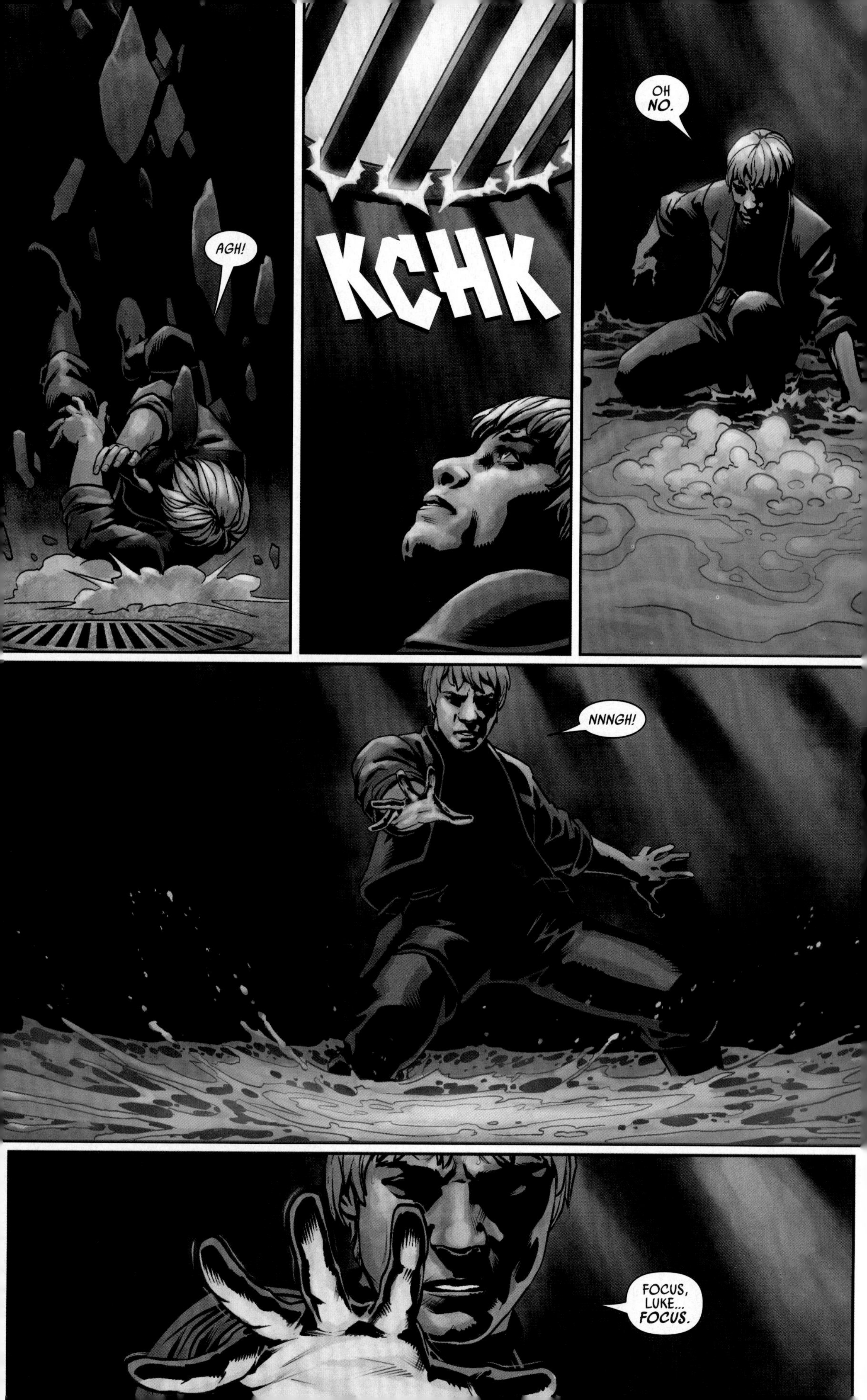
AGH!
KCHK
OH NO.
NNNGH!
FOCUS, LUKE... FOCUS.

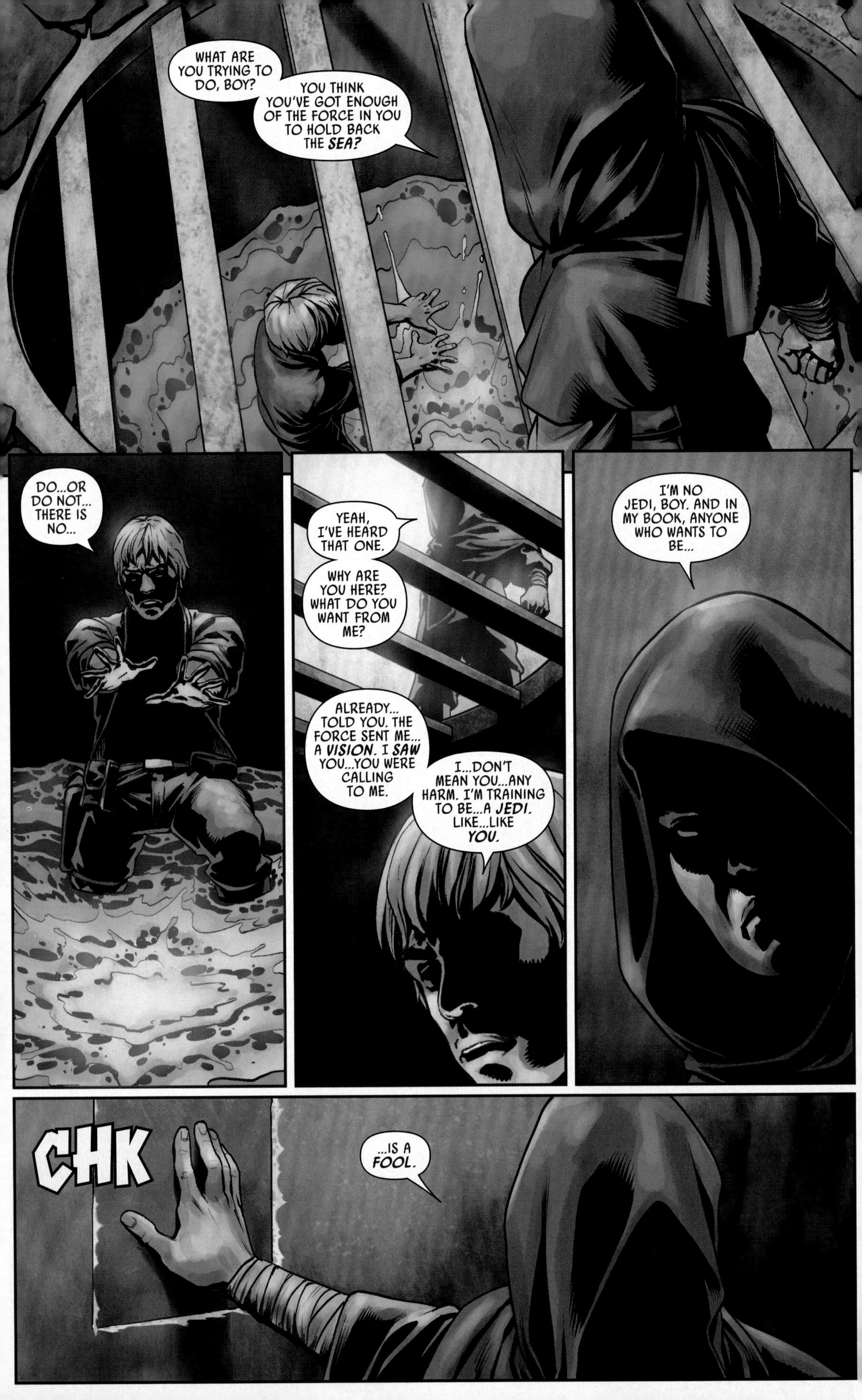
WHAT ARE YOU TRYING TO DO, BOY?
YOU THINK YOU'VE GOT ENOUGH OF THE FORCE IN YOU TO HOLD BACK THE SEA?
DO...OR DO NOT... THERE IS NO...
YEAH, I'VE HEARD THAT ONE.
WHY ARE YOU HERE? WHAT DO YOU WANT FROM ME?
ALREADY... TOLD YOU. THE FORCE SENT ME... A VISION. I SAW YOU...YOU WERE CALLING TO ME.
I...DON'T MEAN YOU...ANY HARM. I'M TRAINING TO BE...A JEDI. LIKE...LIKE YOU.
I'M NO JEDI, BOY. AND IN MY BOOK, ANYONE WHO WANTS TO BE...
CHK
...IS A FOOL.

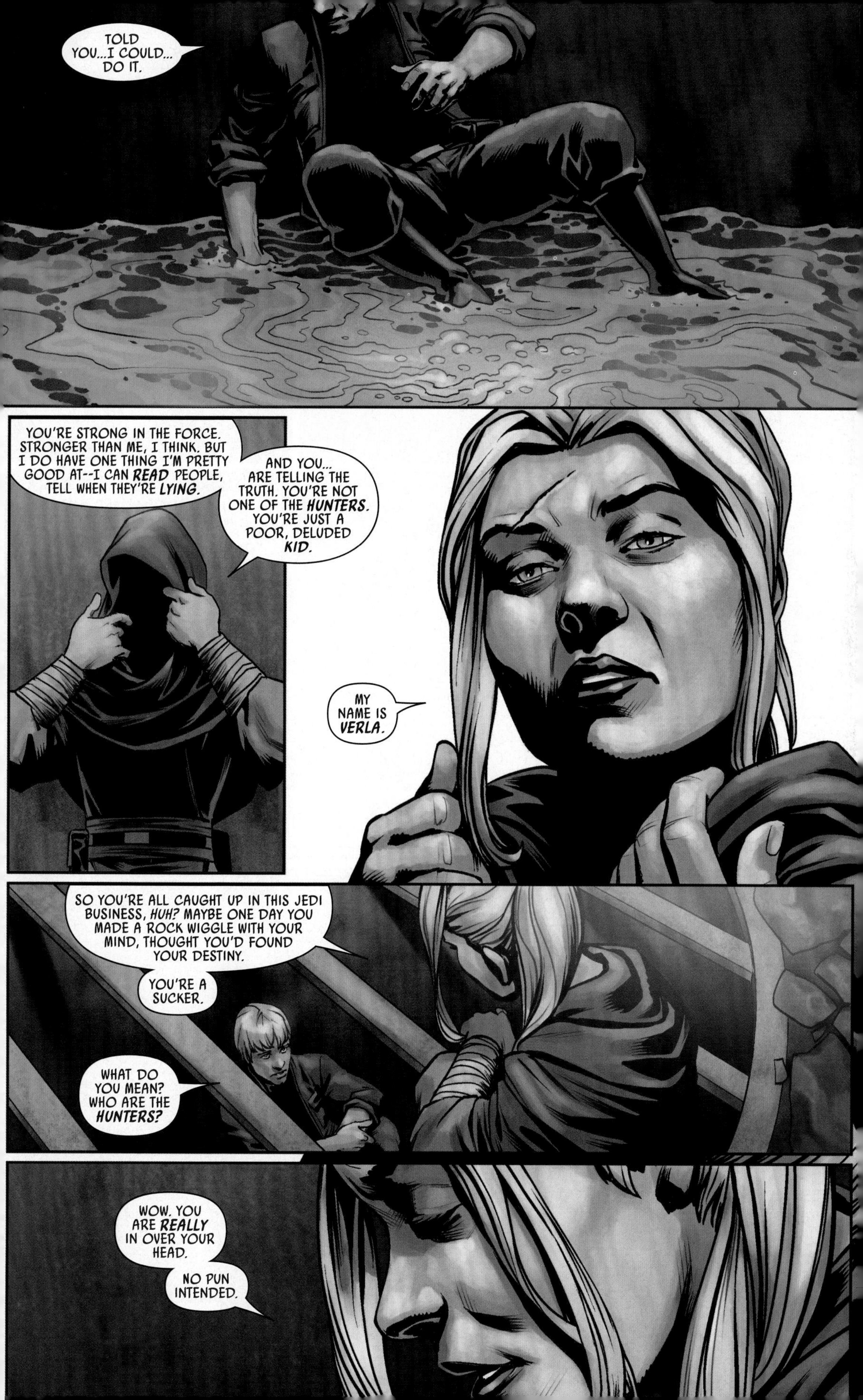

TOLD YOU...I COULD... DO IT.
YOU'RE STRONG IN THE FORCE. STRONGER THAN ME, I THINK. BUT I DO HAVE ONE THING I'M PRETTY GOOD AT--I CAN *READ* PEOPLE, TELL WHEN THEY'RE *LYING*.
AND YOU... ARE TELLING THE TRUTH. YOU'RE NOT ONE OF THE *HUNTERS*. YOU'RE JUST A POOR, DELUDED *KID*.
MY NAME IS *VERLA*.
SO YOU'RE ALL CAUGHT UP IN THIS JEDI BUSINESS, *HUH?* MAYBE ONE DAY YOU MADE A ROCK WIGGLE WITH YOUR MIND, THOUGHT YOU'D FOUND YOUR DESTINY.
YOU'RE A SUCKER.
WHAT DO YOU MEAN? WHO ARE THE *HUNTERS?*
WOW. YOU ARE *REALLY* IN OVER YOUR HEAD.
NO PUN INTENDED.

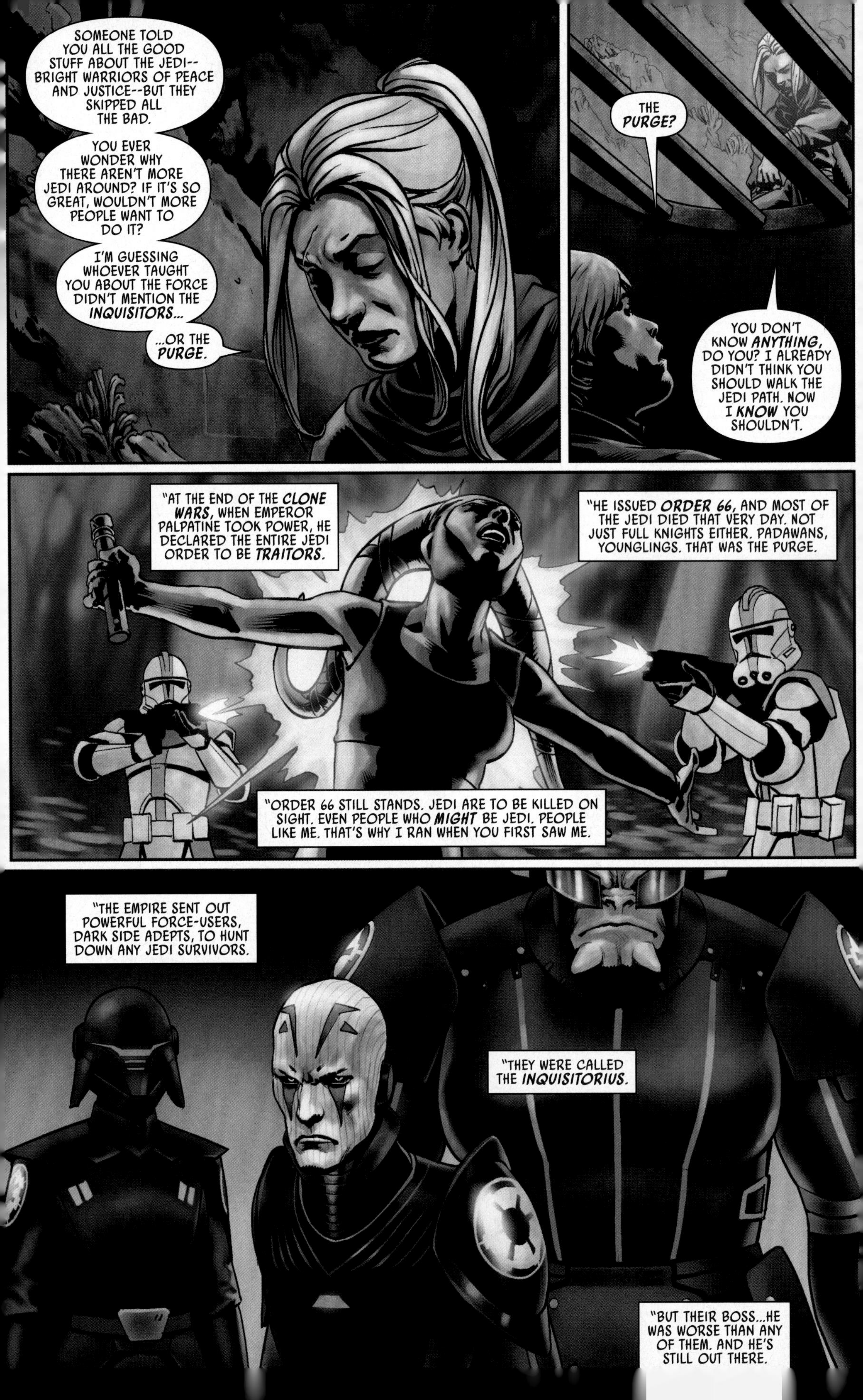
SOMEONE TOLD YOU ALL THE GOOD STUFF ABOUT THE JEDI--BRIGHT WARRIORS OF PEACE AND JUSTICE--BUT THEY SKIPPED ALL THE BAD.
YOU EVER WONDER WHY THERE AREN'T MORE JEDI AROUND? IF IT'S SO GREAT, WOULDN'T MORE PEOPLE WANT TO DO IT?
I'M GUESSING WHOEVER TAUGHT YOU ABOUT THE FORCE DIDN'T MENTION THE *INQUISITORS...*
...OR THE *PURGE.*
THE *PURGE?*
YOU DON'T KNOW *ANYTHING,* DO YOU? I ALREADY DIDN'T THINK YOU SHOULD WALK THE JEDI PATH. NOW I *KNOW* YOU SHOULDN'T.
"AT THE END OF THE *CLONE WARS,* WHEN EMPEROR PALPATINE TOOK POWER, HE DECLARED THE ENTIRE JEDI ORDER TO BE *TRAITORS.*
"HE ISSUED *ORDER 66,* AND MOST OF THE JEDI DIED THAT VERY DAY. NOT JUST FULL KNIGHTS EITHER. PADAWANS, YOUNGLINGS. THAT WAS THE PURGE.
"ORDER 66 STILL STANDS. JEDI ARE TO BE KILLED ON SIGHT. EVEN PEOPLE WHO *MIGHT* BE JEDI. PEOPLE LIKE ME. THAT'S WHY I RAN WHEN YOU FIRST SAW ME.
"THE EMPIRE SENT OUT POWERFUL FORCE-USERS, DARK SIDE ADEPTS, TO HUNT DOWN ANY JEDI SURVIVORS.
"THEY WERE CALLED THE *INQUISITORIUS.*
"BUT THEIR BOSS...HE WAS WORSE THAN ANY OF THEM. AND HE'S STILL OUT THERE.

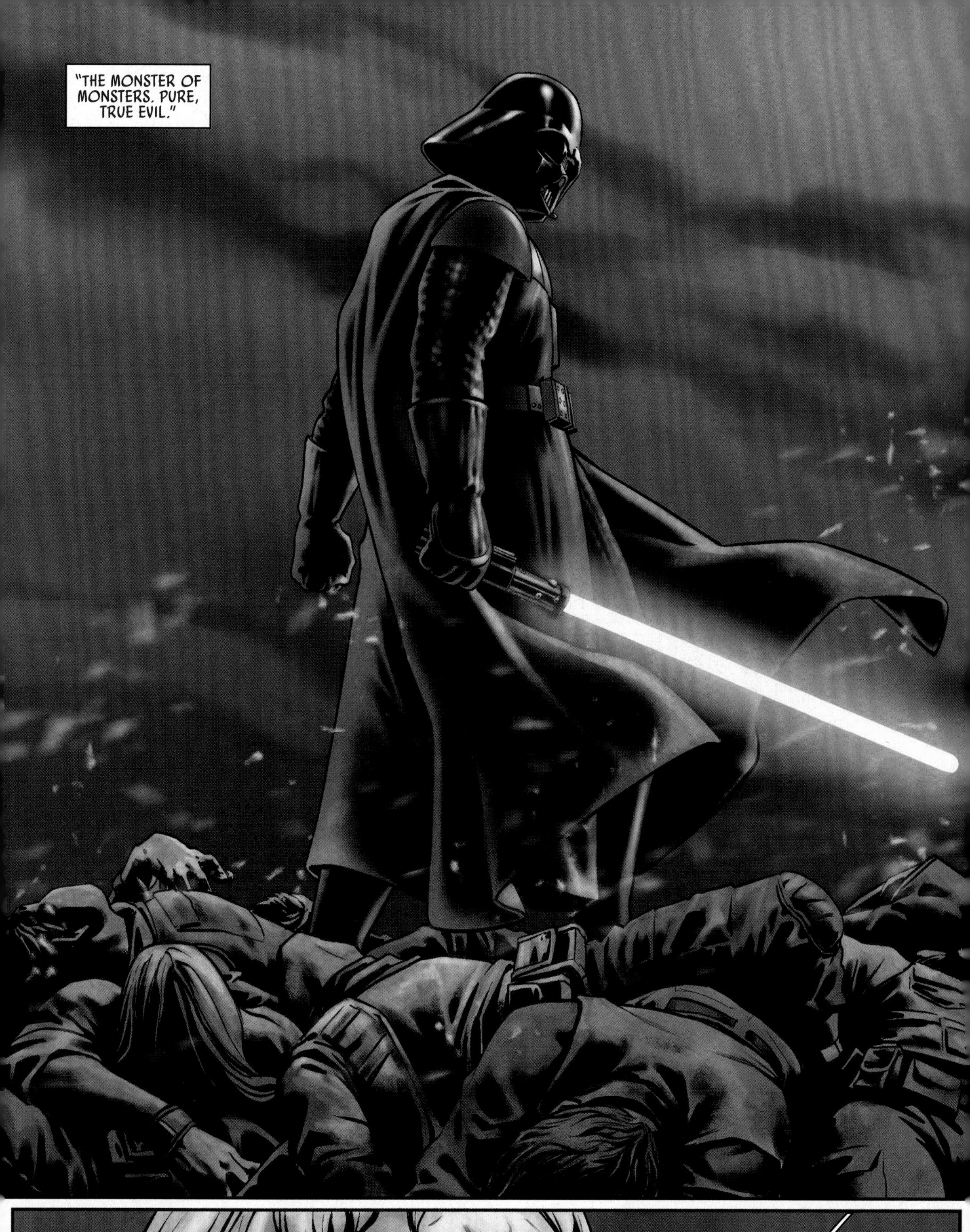
"THE MONSTER OF MONSTERS. PURE, TRUE EVIL."

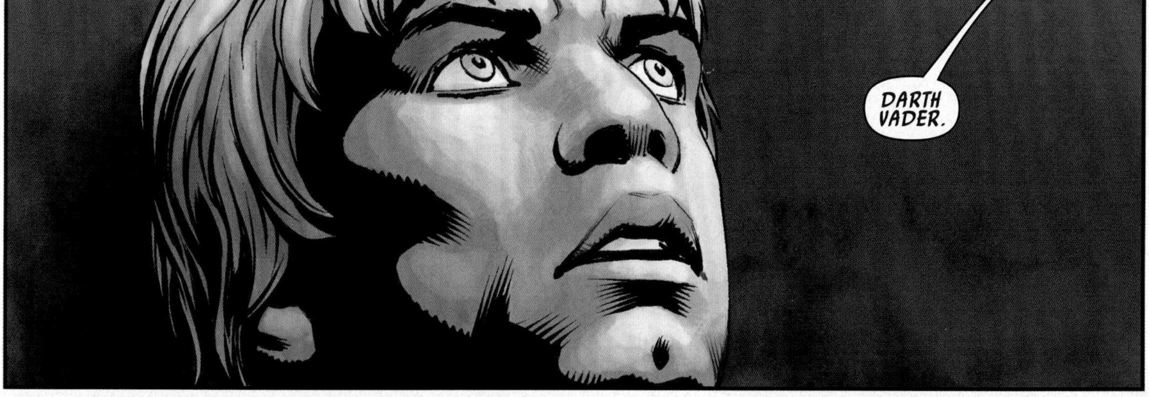
DARTH VADER.

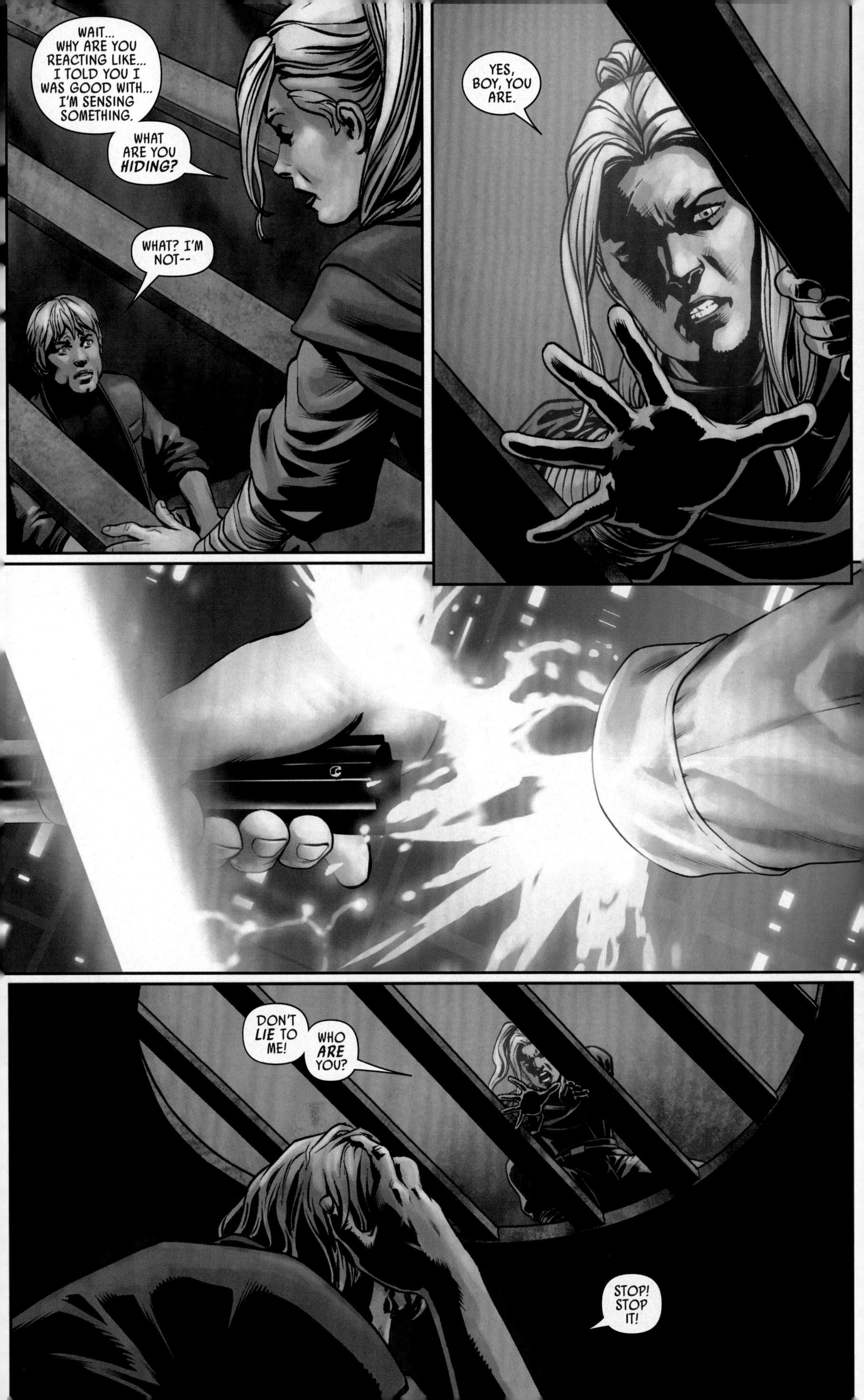
WAIT... WHY ARE YOU REACTING LIKE... I TOLD YOU I WAS GOOD WITH... I'M SENSING SOMETHING.
WHAT ARE YOU *HIDING?*
WHAT? I'M NOT--
YES, BOY, YOU ARE.
DON'T *LIE* TO ME!
WHO *ARE* YOU?
STOP! STOP IT!

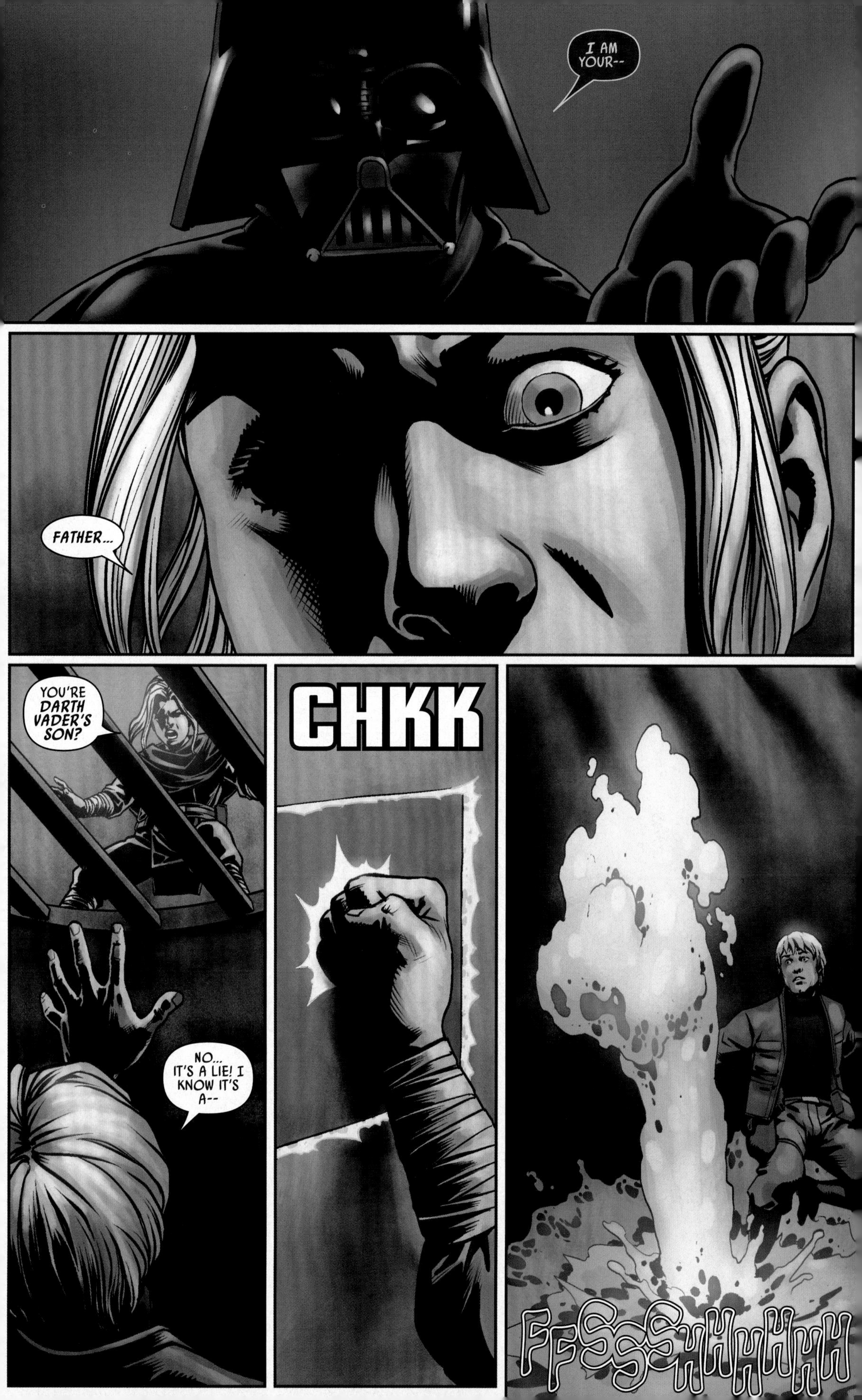
I AM YOUR--
FATHER...
YOU'RE DARTH VADER'S SON?
NO... IT'S A LIE! I KNOW IT'S A--
CHKK
FFSSSHHHHHH

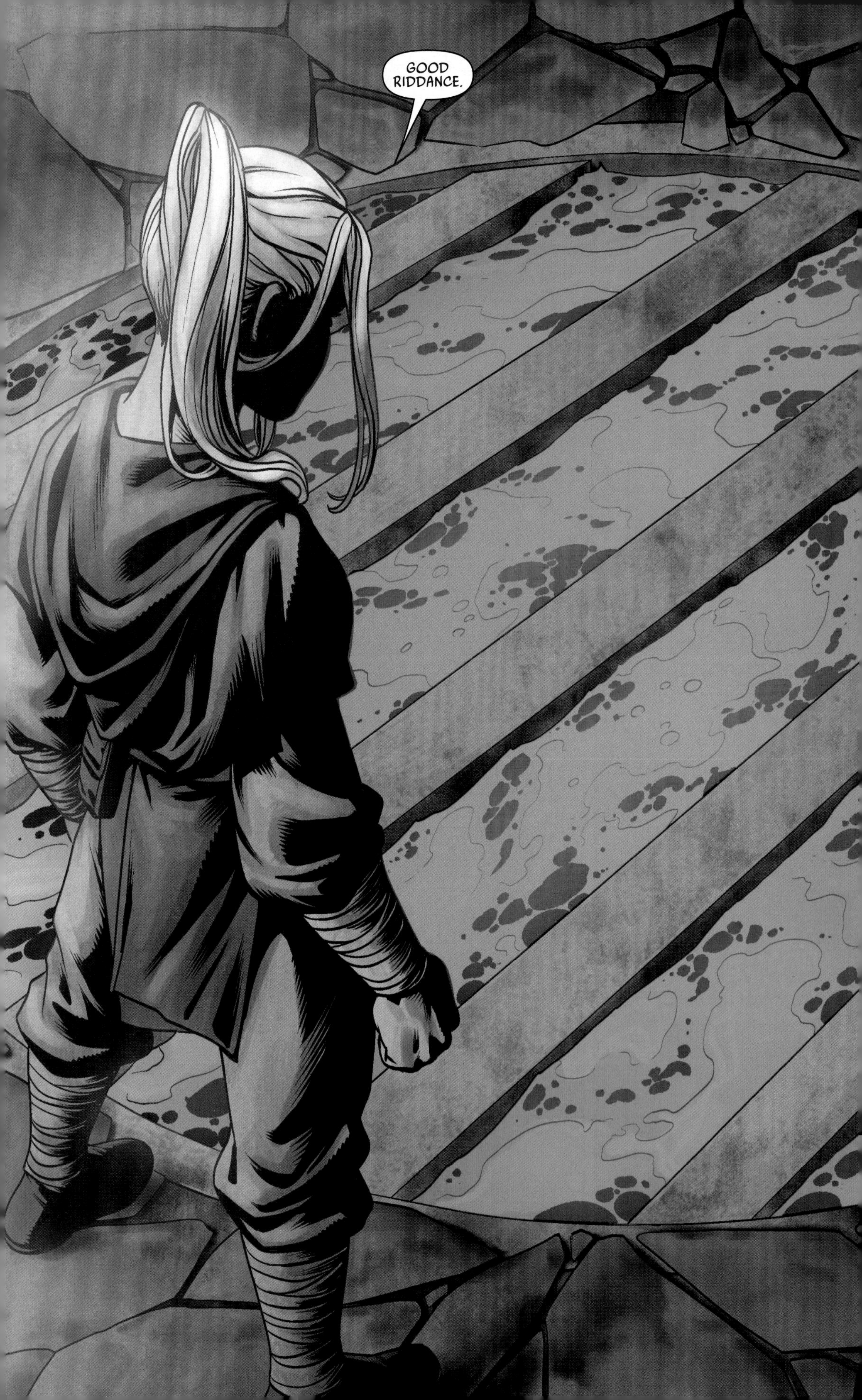
GOOD RIDDANCE.

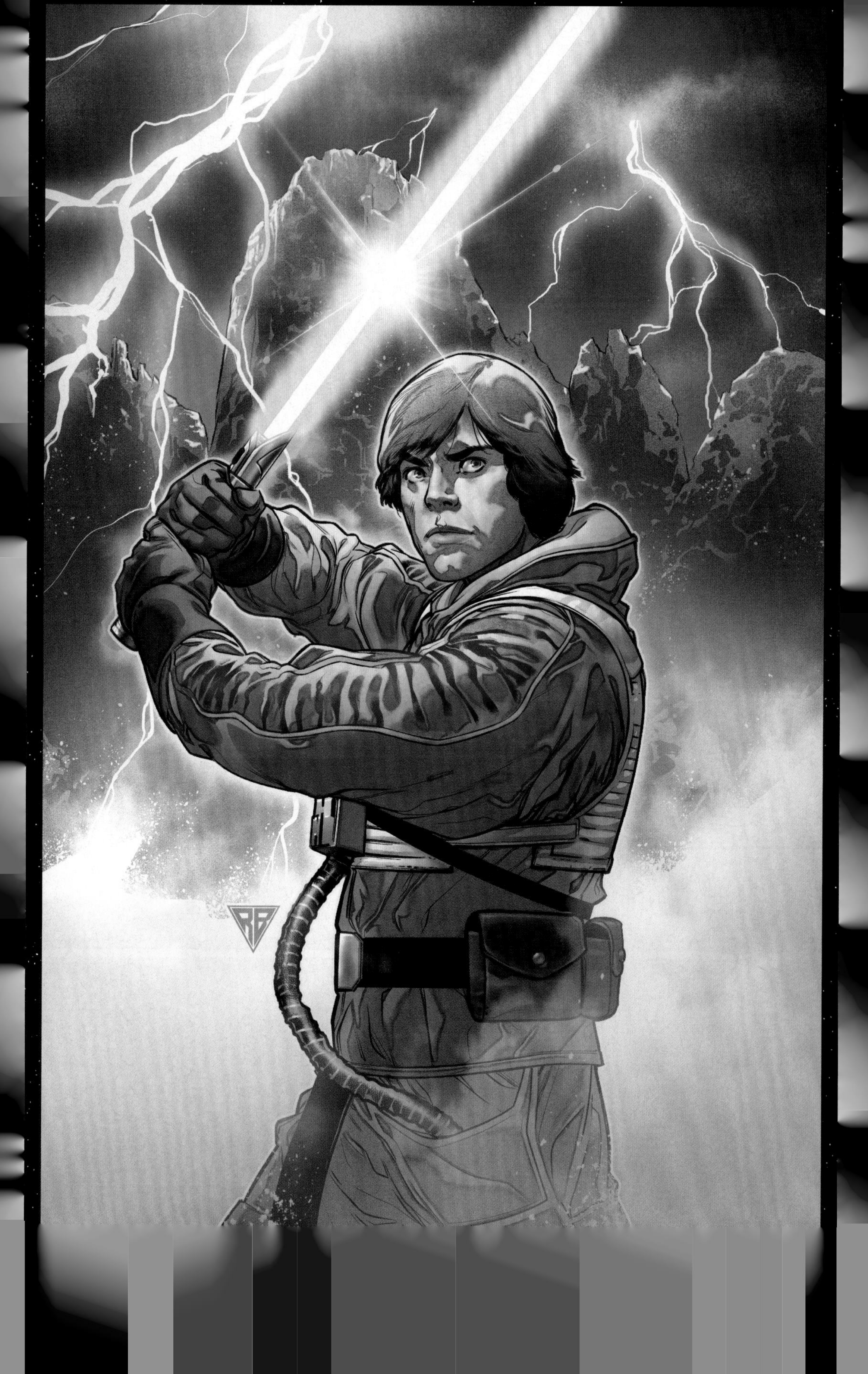

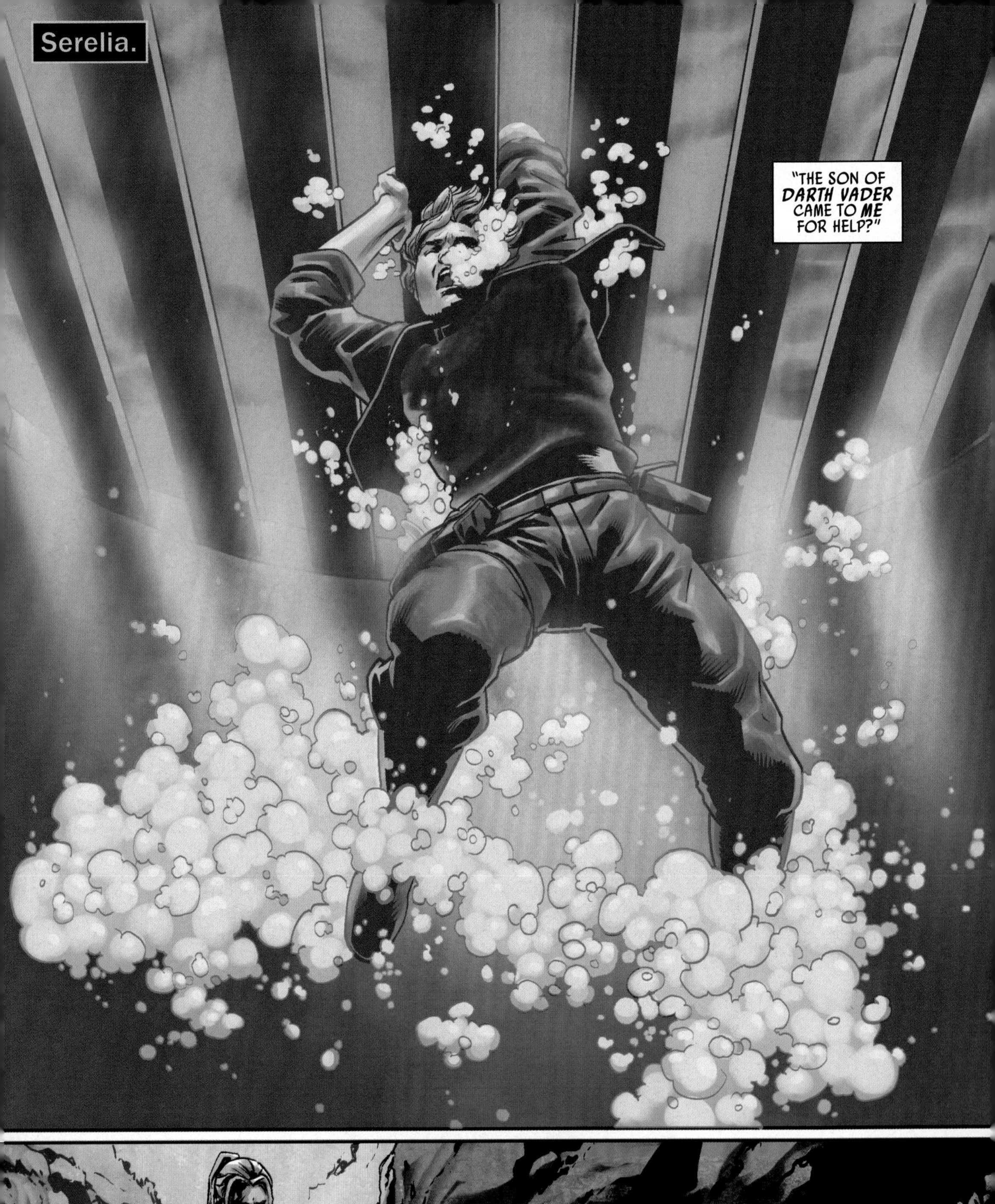
Serelia.
"THE SON OF DARTH VADER CAME TO ME FOR HELP?"

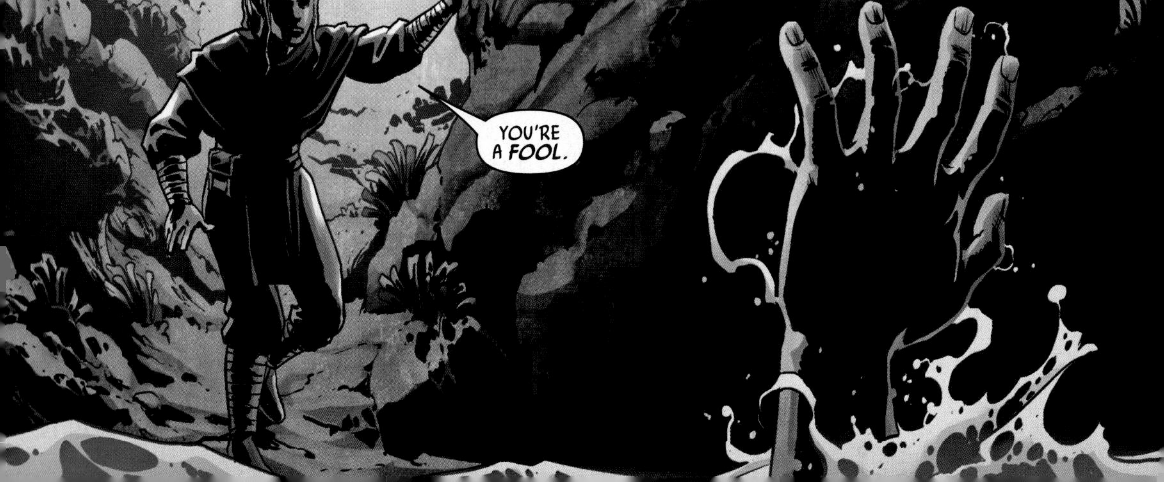
YOU'RE A FOOL.

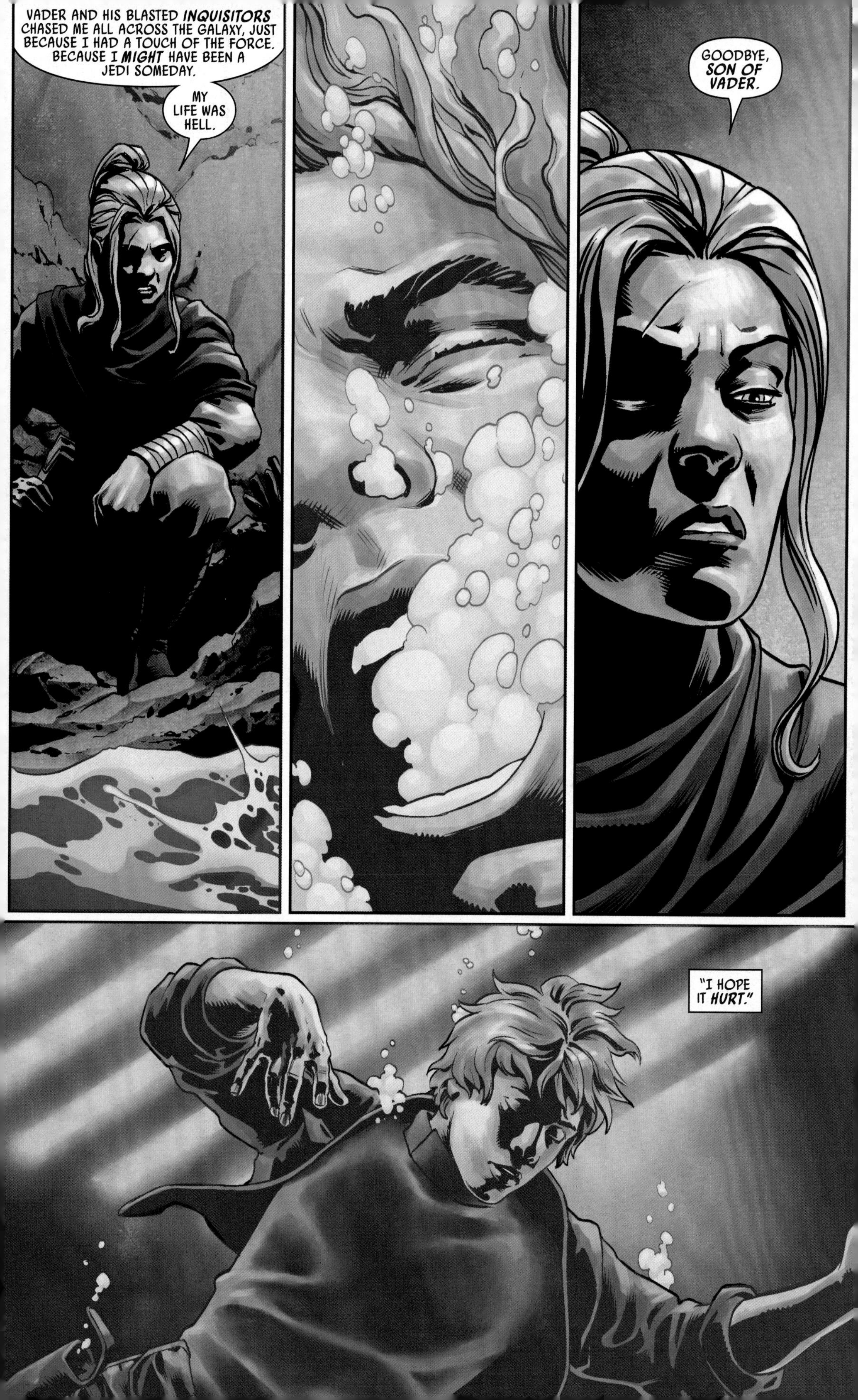
VADER AND HIS BLASTED INQUISITORS CHASED ME ALL ACROSS THE GALAXY, JUST BECAUSE I HAD A TOUCH OF THE FORCE. BECAUSE I MIGHT HAVE BEEN A JEDI SOMEDAY.
MY LIFE WAS HELL.
GOODBYE, SON OF VADER.
"I HOPE IT HURT."

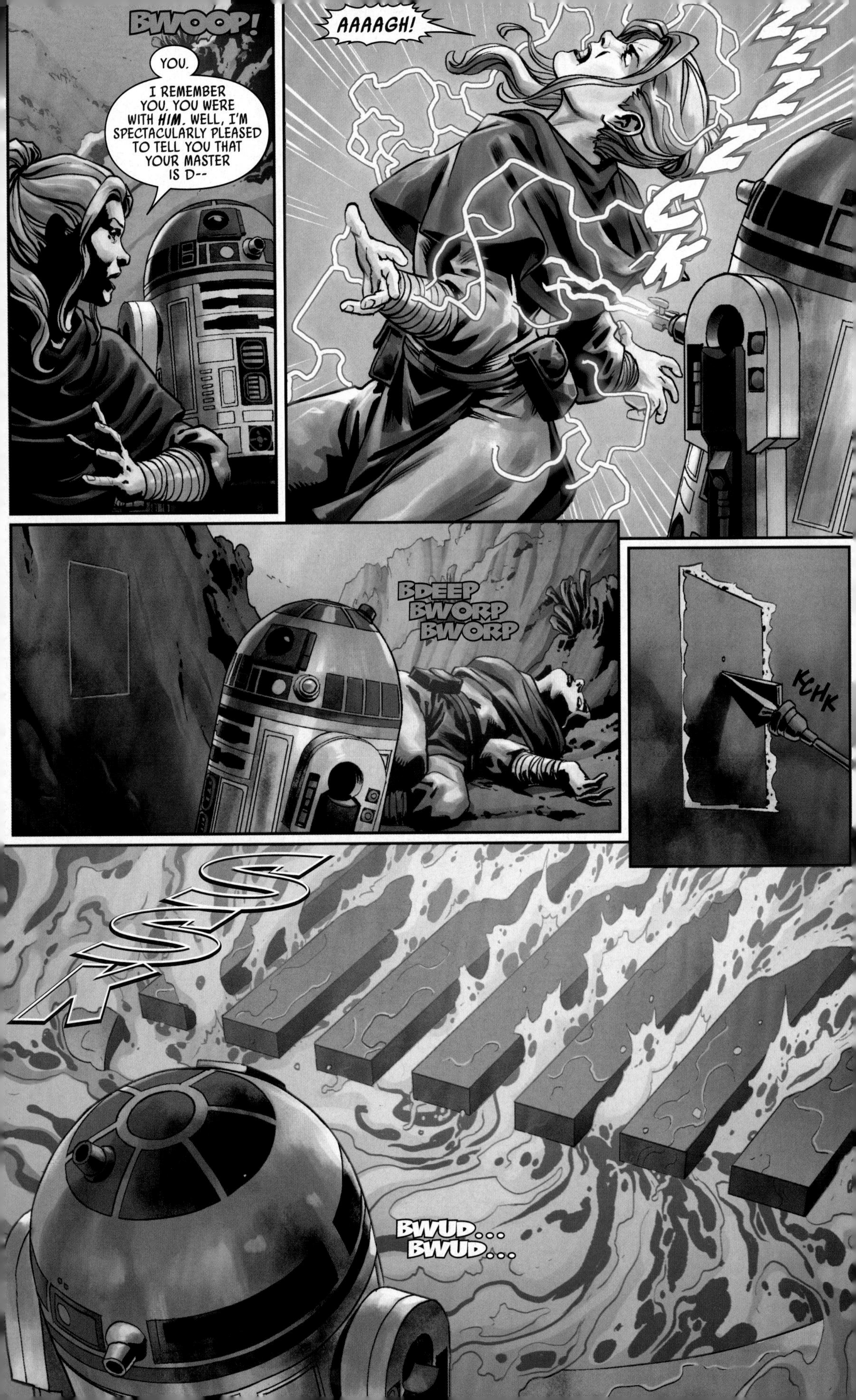
BWOOP!
YOU.
I REMEMBER YOU. YOU WERE WITH *HIM*. WELL, I'M SPECTACULARLY PLEASED TO TELL YOU THAT YOUR MASTER IS D--
AAAAGH!
ZZZZZCK
BDEEP BWORP BWORP
KCHK
SSSK
BWUD... BWUD...

TSH-KNLK

BBBPPP!

ZK

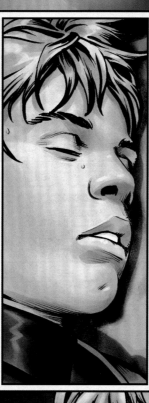

ZZK

ZZK

HRK!

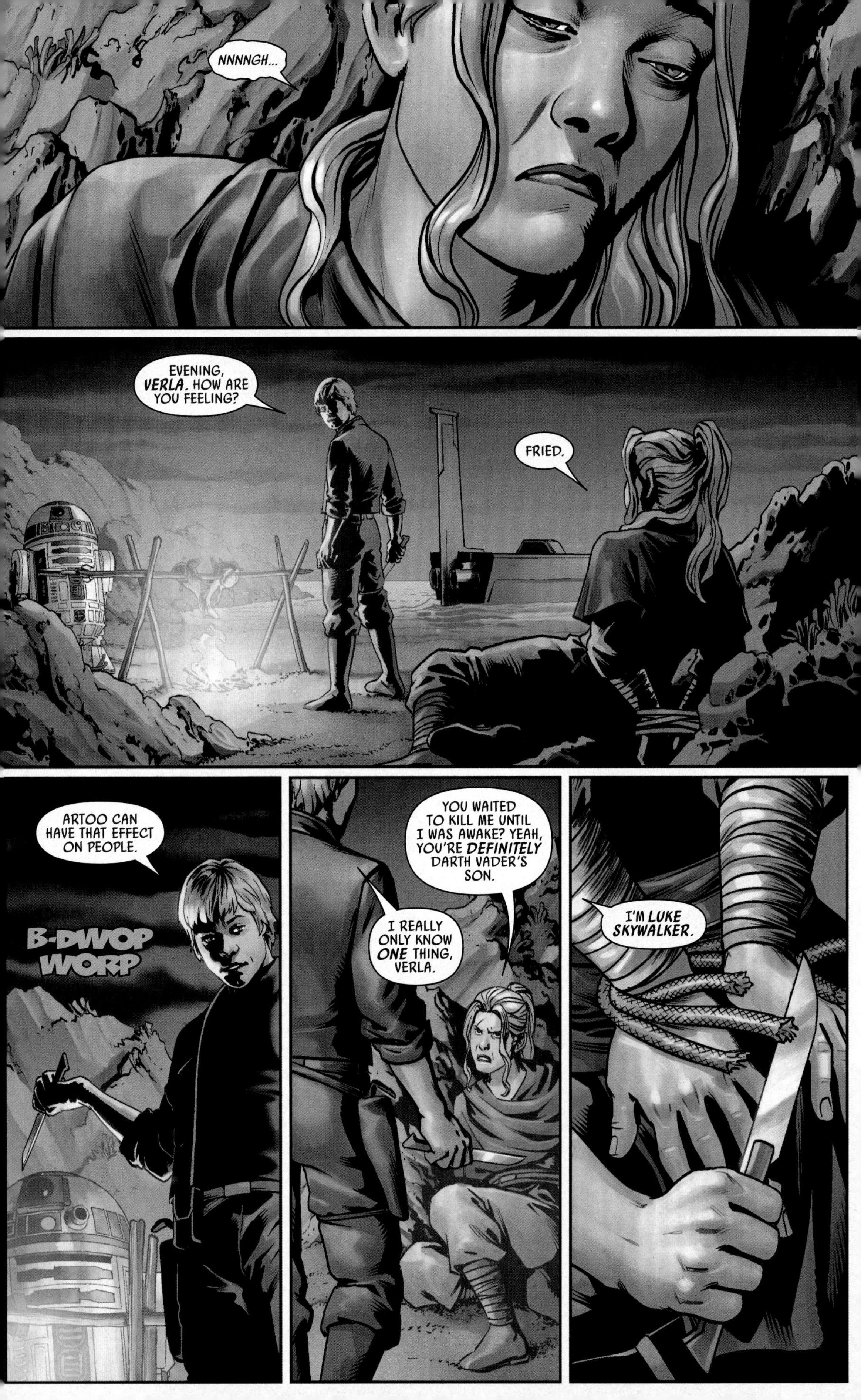

NNNNGH...
EVENING, VERLA. HOW ARE YOU FEELING?
FRIED.
ARTOO CAN HAVE THAT EFFECT ON PEOPLE.
B-DWOP WORP
YOU WAITED TO KILL ME UNTIL I WAS AWAKE? YEAH, YOU'RE DEFINITELY DARTH VADER'S SON.
I REALLY ONLY KNOW ONE THING, VERLA.
I'M LUKE SKYWALKER.

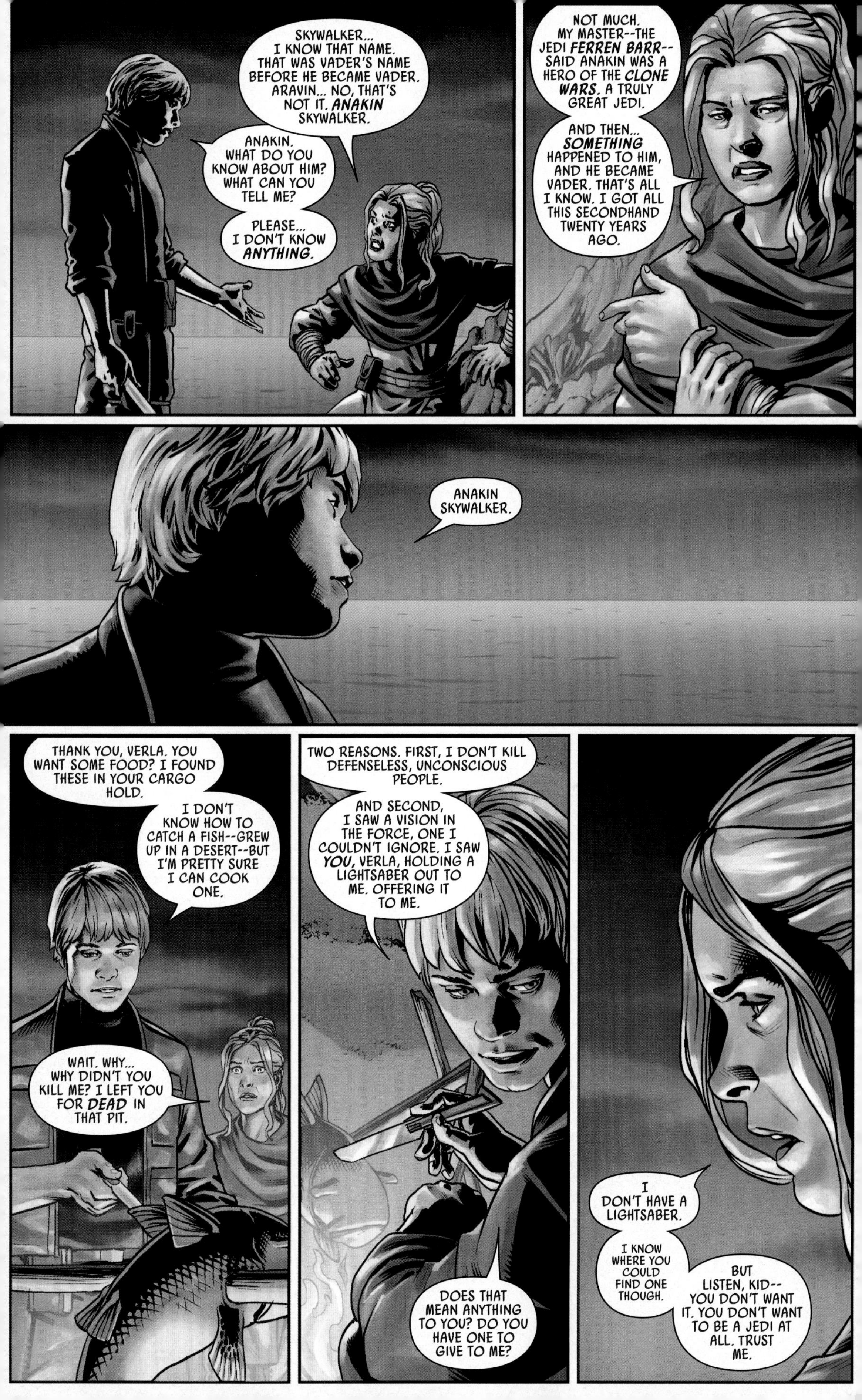
SKYWALKER... I KNOW THAT NAME. THAT WAS VADER'S NAME BEFORE HE BECAME VADER. ARAVIN... NO, THAT'S NOT IT. ANAKIN SKYWALKER.
ANAKIN. WHAT DO YOU KNOW ABOUT HIM? WHAT CAN YOU TELL ME?
PLEASE... I DON'T KNOW ANYTHING.
NOT MUCH. MY MASTER--THE JEDI FERREN BARR--SAID ANAKIN WAS A HERO OF THE CLONE WARS. A TRULY GREAT JEDI.
AND THEN... SOMETHING HAPPENED TO HIM, AND HE BECAME VADER. THAT'S ALL I KNOW. I GOT ALL THIS SECONDHAND TWENTY YEARS AGO.
ANAKIN SKYWALKER.
THANK YOU, VERLA. YOU WANT SOME FOOD? I FOUND THESE IN YOUR CARGO HOLD.
I DON'T KNOW HOW TO CATCH A FISH--GREW UP IN A DESERT--BUT I'M PRETTY SURE I CAN COOK ONE.
WAIT. WHY... WHY DIDN'T YOU KILL ME? I LEFT YOU FOR DEAD IN THAT PIT.
TWO REASONS. FIRST, I DON'T KILL DEFENSELESS, UNCONSCIOUS PEOPLE.
AND SECOND, I SAW A VISION IN THE FORCE, ONE I COULDN'T IGNORE. I SAW YOU, VERLA, HOLDING A LIGHTSABER OUT TO ME. OFFERING IT TO ME.
DOES THAT MEAN ANYTHING TO YOU? DO YOU HAVE ONE TO GIVE TO ME?
I DON'T HAVE A LIGHTSABER.
I KNOW WHERE YOU COULD FIND ONE THOUGH.
BUT LISTEN, KID--YOU DON'T WANT IT. YOU DON'T WANT TO BE A JEDI AT ALL. TRUST ME.

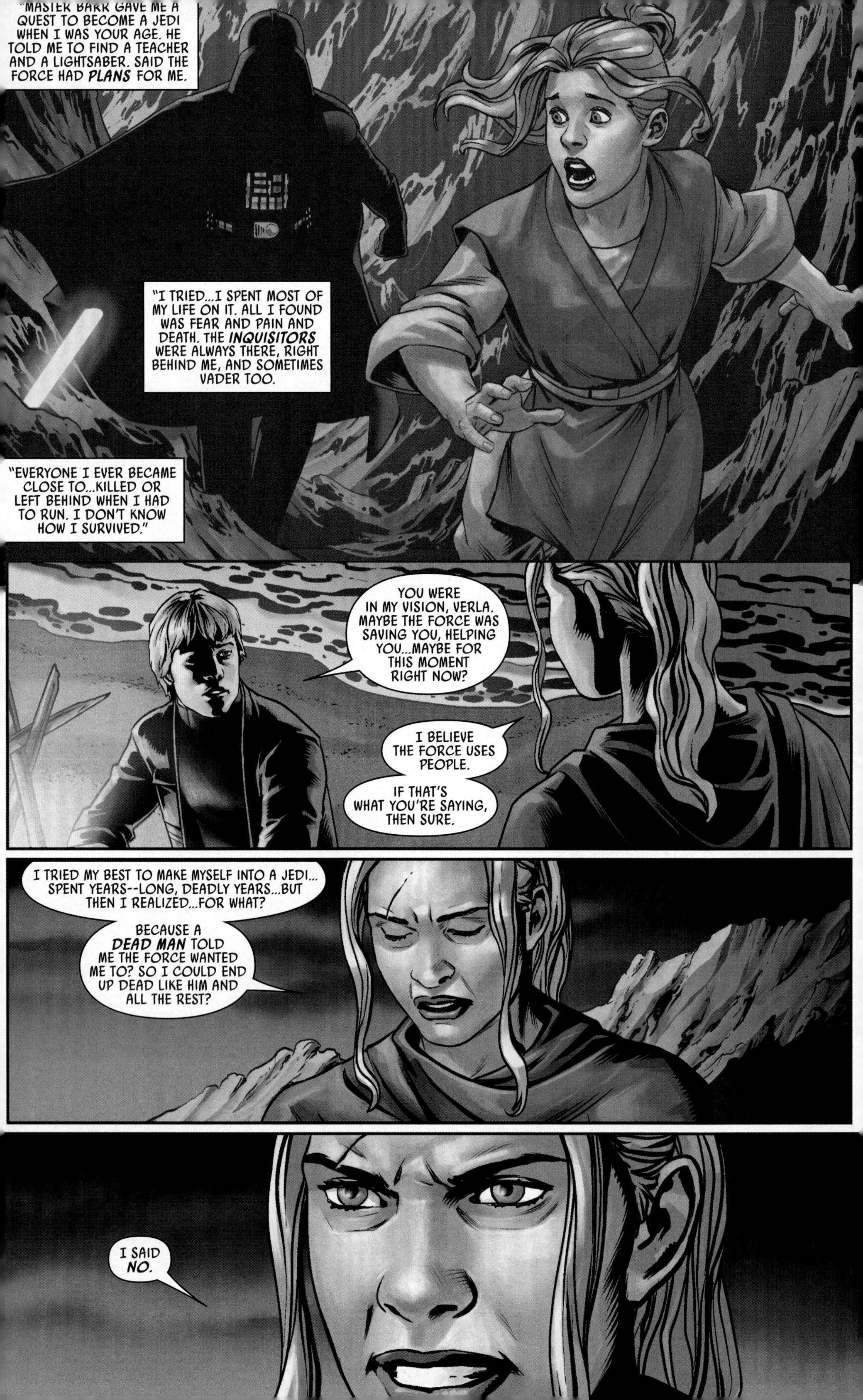
"MASTER BARR GAVE ME A QUEST TO BECOME A JEDI WHEN I WAS YOUR AGE. HE TOLD ME TO FIND A TEACHER AND A LIGHTSABER. SAID THE FORCE HAD PLANS FOR ME.
"I TRIED...I SPENT MOST OF MY LIFE ON IT. ALL I FOUND WAS FEAR AND PAIN AND DEATH. THE INQUISITORS WERE ALWAYS THERE, RIGHT BEHIND ME, AND SOMETIMES VADER TOO.
"EVERYONE I EVER BECAME CLOSE TO...KILLED OR LEFT BEHIND WHEN I HAD TO RUN. I DON'T KNOW HOW I SURVIVED."
YOU WERE IN MY VISION, VERLA. MAYBE THE FORCE WAS SAVING YOU, HELPING YOU...MAYBE FOR THIS MOMENT RIGHT NOW?
I BELIEVE THE FORCE USES PEOPLE.
IF THAT'S WHAT YOU'RE SAYING, THEN SURE.
I TRIED MY BEST TO MAKE MYSELF INTO A JEDI... SPENT YEARS--LONG, DEADLY YEARS...BUT THEN I REALIZED...FOR WHAT?
BECAUSE A DEAD MAN TOLD ME THE FORCE WANTED ME TO? SO I COULD END UP DEAD LIKE HIM AND ALL THE REST?
I SAID NO.

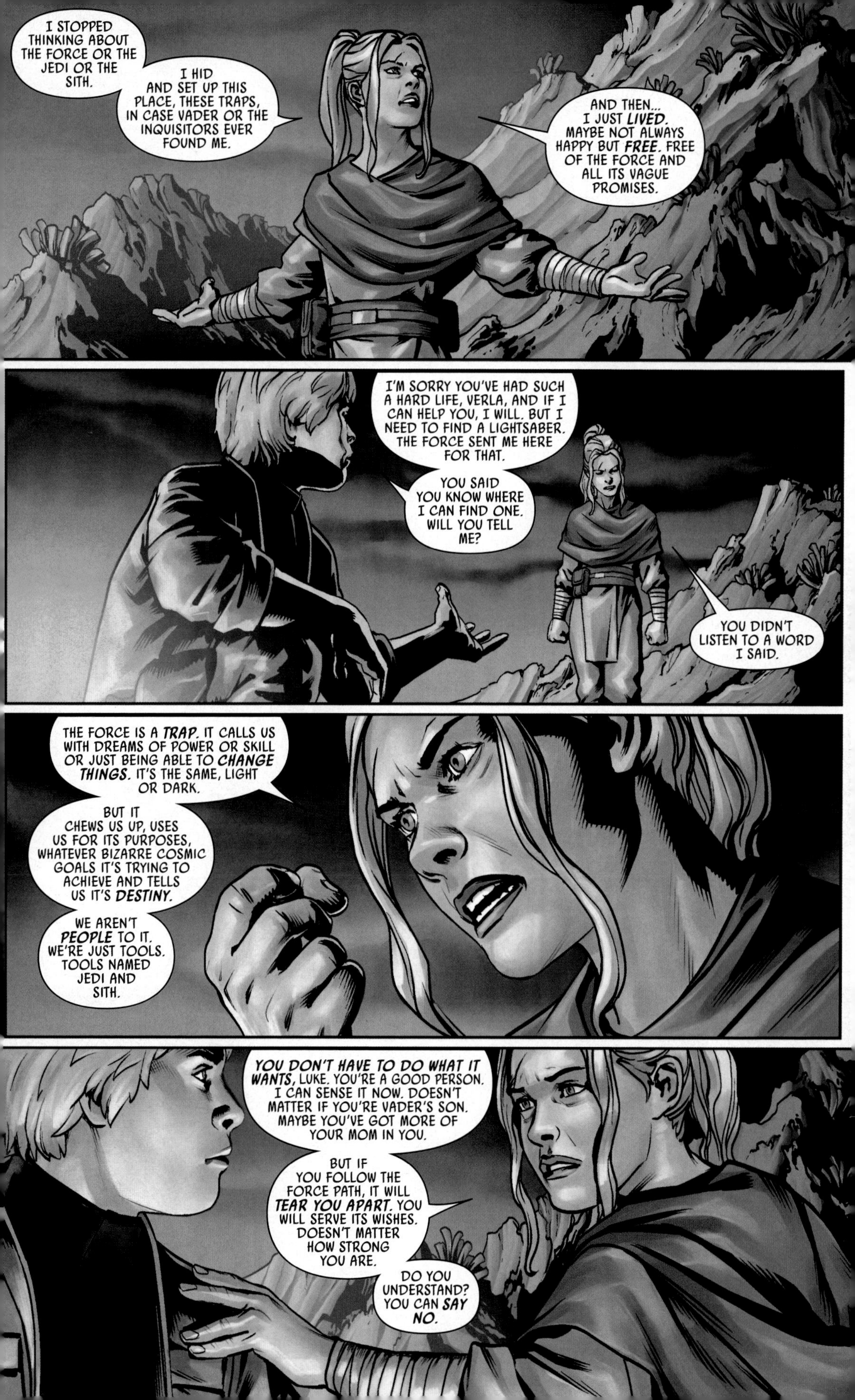
I STOPPED THINKING ABOUT THE FORCE OR THE JEDI OR THE SITH.
I HID AND SET UP THIS PLACE, THESE TRAPS, IN CASE VADER OR THE INQUISITORS EVER FOUND ME.
AND THEN... I JUST *LIVED.* MAYBE NOT ALWAYS HAPPY BUT *FREE.* FREE OF THE FORCE AND ALL ITS VAGUE PROMISES.
I'M SORRY YOU'VE HAD SUCH A HARD LIFE, VERLA, AND IF I CAN HELP YOU, I WILL. BUT I NEED TO FIND A LIGHTSABER. THE FORCE SENT ME HERE FOR THAT.
YOU SAID YOU KNOW WHERE I CAN FIND ONE. WILL YOU TELL ME?
YOU DIDN'T LISTEN TO A WORD I SAID.
THE FORCE IS A *TRAP.* IT CALLS US WITH DREAMS OF POWER OR SKILL OR JUST BEING ABLE TO *CHANGE THINGS.* IT'S THE SAME, LIGHT OR DARK.
BUT IT CHEWS US UP, USES US FOR ITS PURPOSES, WHATEVER BIZARRE COSMIC GOALS IT'S TRYING TO ACHIEVE AND TELLS US IT'S *DESTINY.*
WE AREN'T *PEOPLE* TO IT. WE'RE JUST TOOLS. TOOLS NAMED JEDI AND SITH.
YOU DON'T HAVE TO DO WHAT IT WANTS, LUKE. YOU'RE A GOOD PERSON. I CAN SENSE IT NOW. DOESN'T MATTER IF YOU'RE VADER'S SON. MAYBE YOU'VE GOT MORE OF YOUR MOM IN YOU.
BUT IF YOU FOLLOW THE FORCE PATH, IT WILL *TEAR YOU APART.* YOU WILL SERVE ITS WISHES. DOESN'T MATTER HOW STRONG YOU ARE.
DO YOU UNDERSTAND? YOU CAN *SAY NO.*

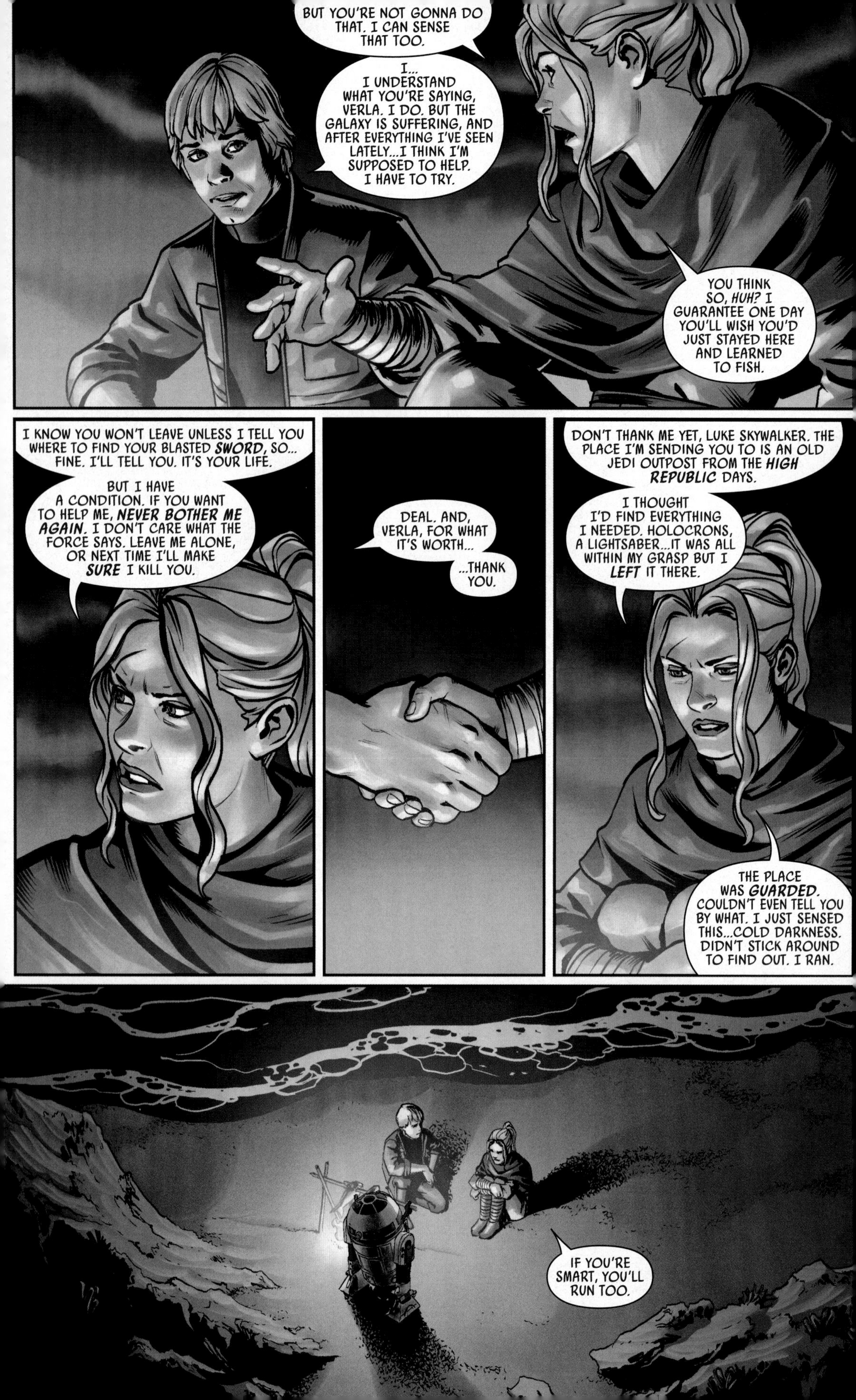
BUT YOU'RE NOT GONNA DO THAT. I CAN SENSE THAT TOO.
I... I UNDERSTAND WHAT YOU'RE SAYING, VERLA. I DO. BUT THE GALAXY IS SUFFERING, AND AFTER EVERYTHING I'VE SEEN LATELY...I THINK I'M SUPPOSED TO HELP. I HAVE TO TRY.
YOU THINK SO, HUH? I GUARANTEE ONE DAY YOU'LL WISH YOU'D JUST STAYED HERE AND LEARNED TO FISH.
I KNOW YOU WON'T LEAVE UNLESS I TELL YOU WHERE TO FIND YOUR BLASTED SWORD, SO... FINE. I'LL TELL YOU. IT'S YOUR LIFE.
BUT I HAVE A CONDITION. IF YOU WANT TO HELP ME, NEVER BOTHER ME AGAIN. I DON'T CARE WHAT THE FORCE SAYS. LEAVE ME ALONE, OR NEXT TIME I'LL MAKE SURE I KILL YOU.
DEAL. AND, VERLA, FOR WHAT IT'S WORTH...
...THANK YOU.
DON'T THANK ME YET, LUKE SKYWALKER. THE PLACE I'M SENDING YOU TO IS AN OLD JEDI OUTPOST FROM THE HIGH REPUBLIC DAYS.
I THOUGHT I'D FIND EVERYTHING I NEEDED. HOLOCRONS, A LIGHTSABER...IT WAS ALL WITHIN MY GRASP BUT I LEFT IT THERE.
THE PLACE WAS GUARDED. COULDN'T EVEN TELL YOU BY WHAT. I JUST SENSED THIS...COLD DARKNESS. DIDN'T STICK AROUND TO FIND OUT. I RAN.
IF YOU'RE SMART, YOU'LL RUN TOO.

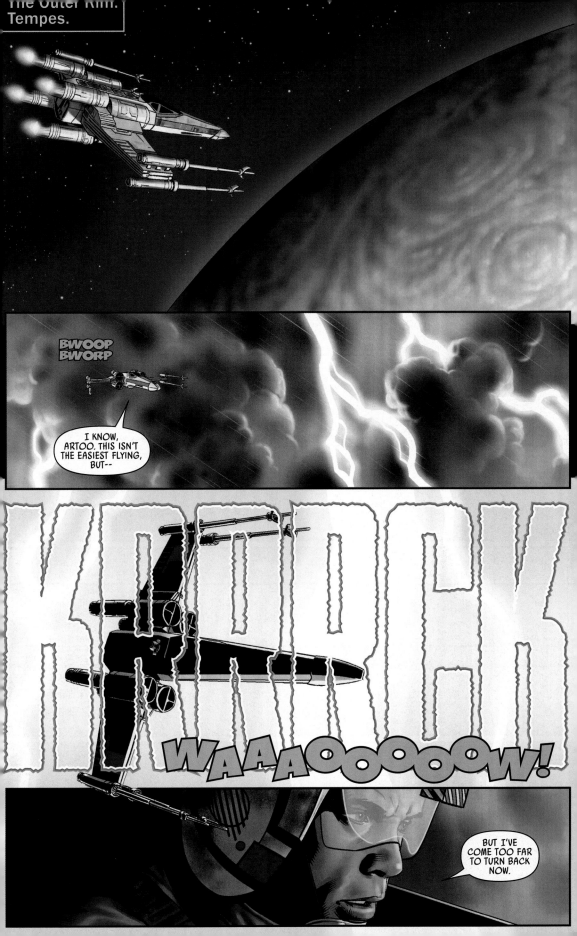

BWOOP
BWORP

I KNOW, ARTOO. THIS ISN'T THE EASIEST FLYING, BUT--

K-ROCK

WAAAOOOOOW!

BUT I'VE COME TOO FAR TO TURN BACK NOW.

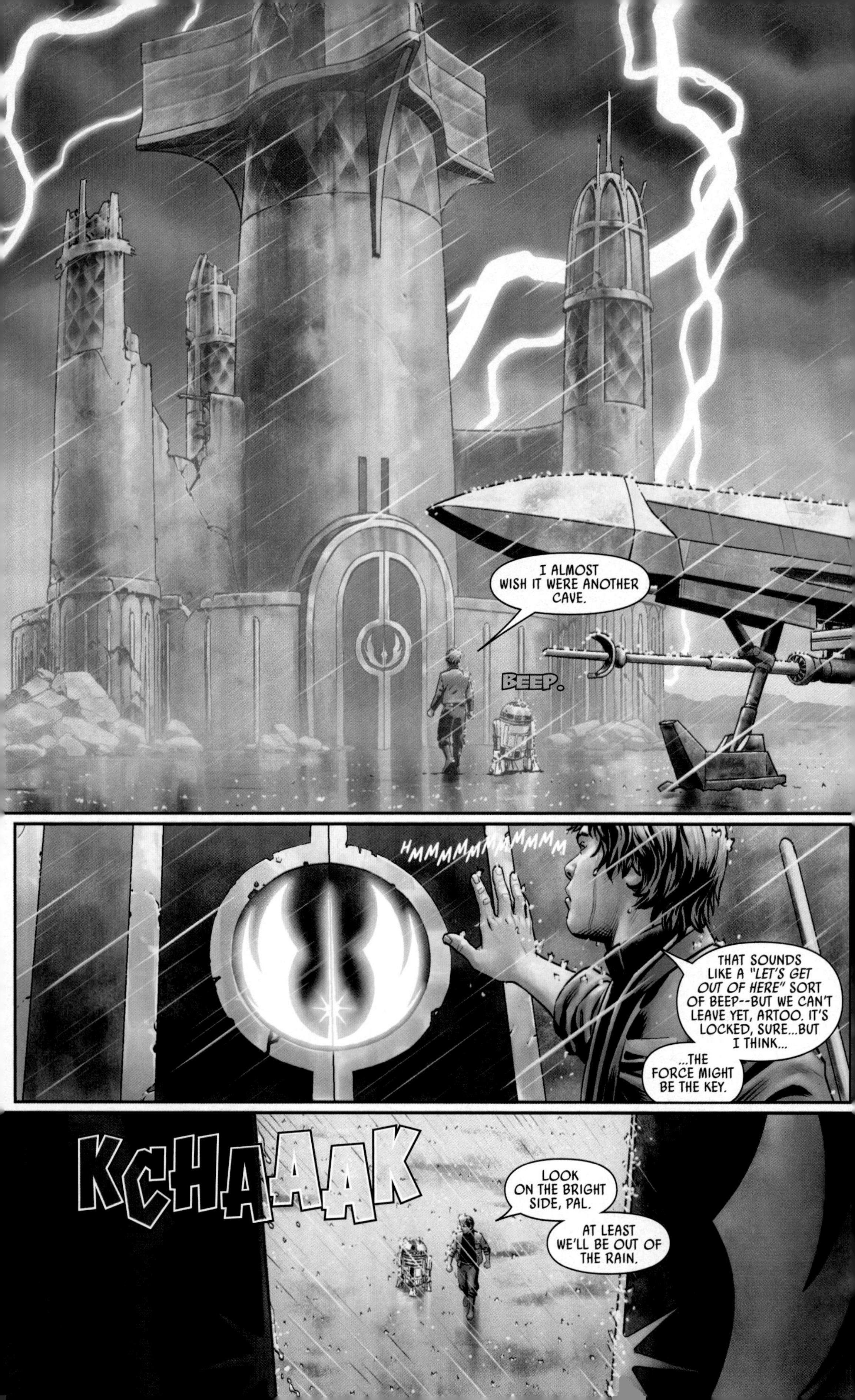
I ALMOST WISH IT WERE ANOTHER CAVE.
BEEP.
HMMMMMMMMMMM
THAT SOUNDS LIKE A "LET'S GET OUT OF HERE" SORT OF BEEP--BUT WE CAN'T LEAVE YET, ARTOO. IT'S LOCKED, SURE...BUT I THINK...
...THE FORCE MIGHT BE THE KEY.
KCHAAAK
LOOK ON THE BRIGHT SIDE, PAL.
AT LEAST WE'LL BE OUT OF THE RAIN.

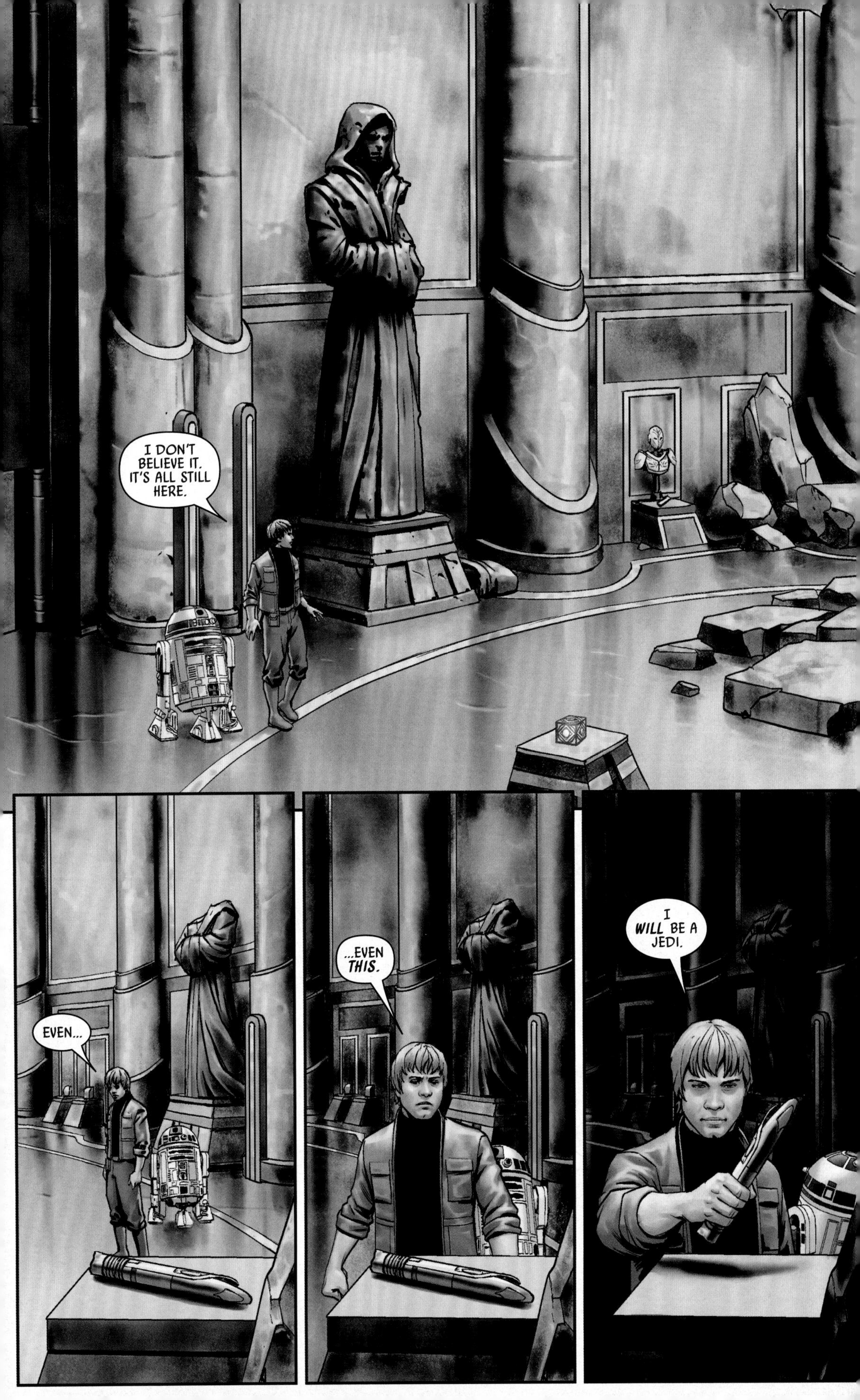
I DON'T BELIEVE IT. IT'S ALL STILL HERE.
EVEN...
...EVEN THIS.
I WILL BE A JEDI.

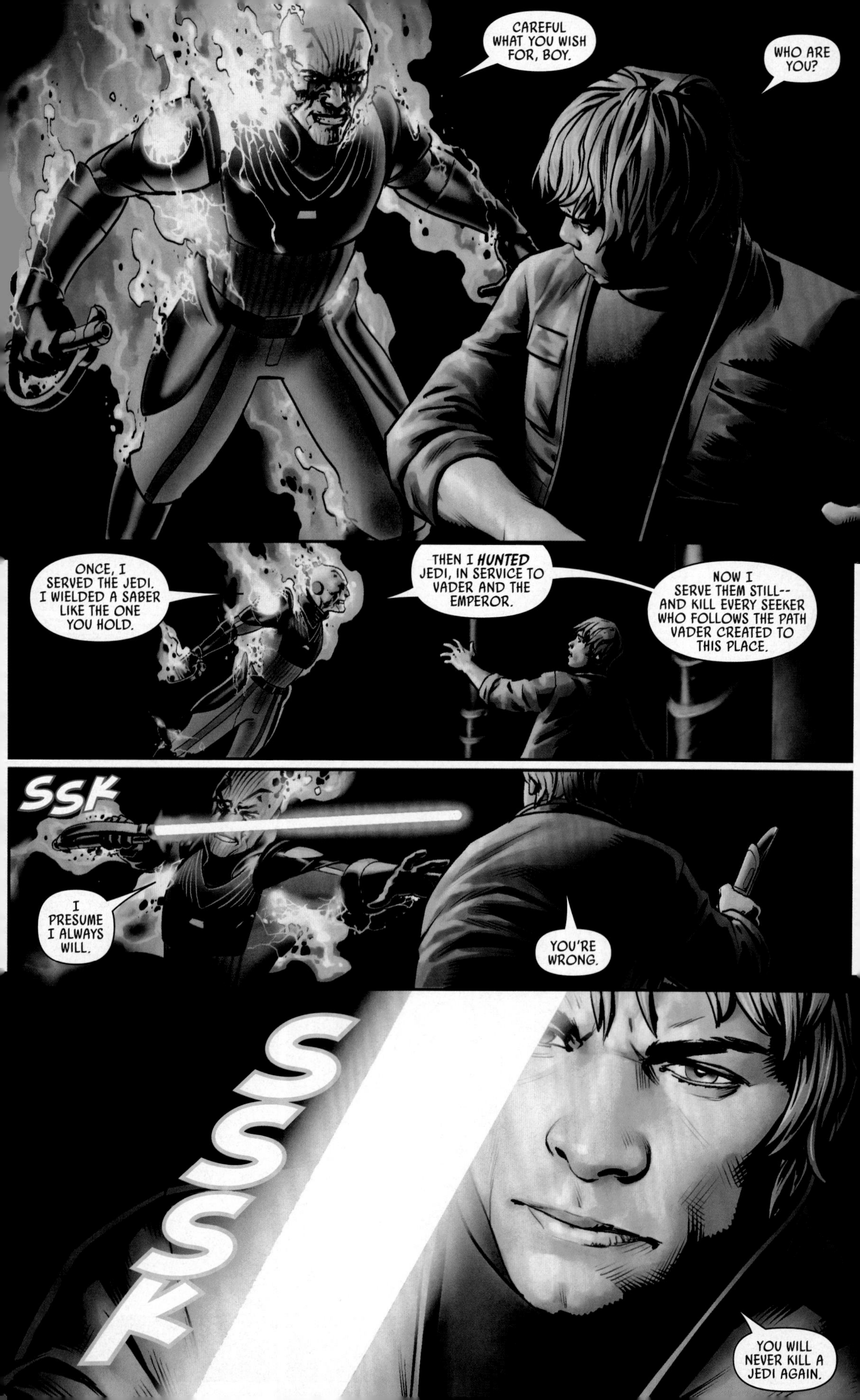
CAREFUL WHAT YOU WISH FOR, BOY.
WHO ARE YOU?
ONCE, I SERVED THE JEDI. I WIELDED A SABER LIKE THE ONE YOU HOLD.
THEN I HUNTED JEDI, IN SERVICE TO VADER AND THE EMPEROR.
NOW I SERVE THEM STILL-- AND KILL EVERY SEEKER WHO FOLLOWS THE PATH VADER CREATED TO THIS PLACE.
SSK
I PRESUME I ALWAYS WILL.
YOU'RE WRONG.
SSSSK
YOU WILL NEVER KILL A JEDI AGAIN.

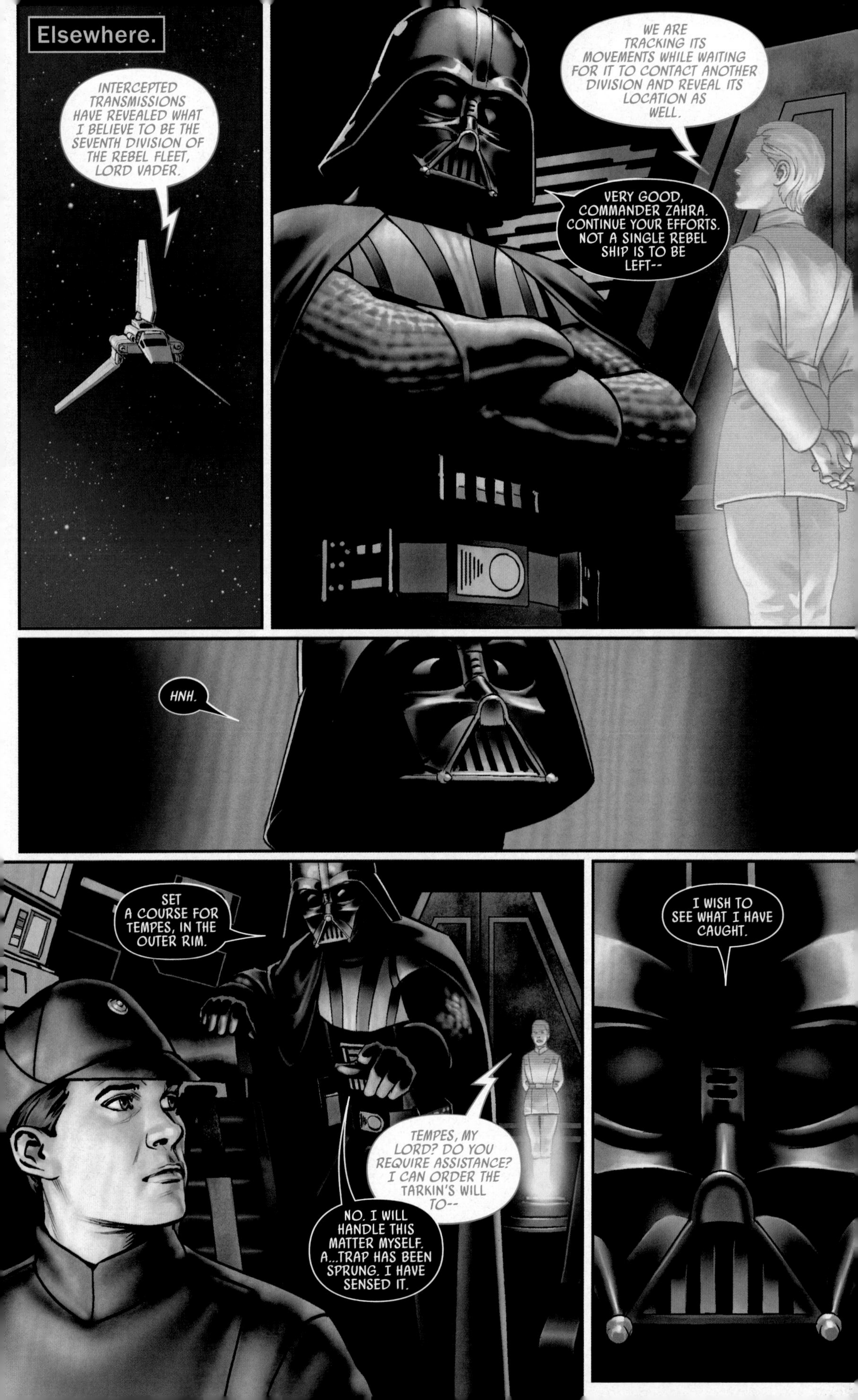
Elsewhere.
INTERCEPTED TRANSMISSIONS HAVE REVEALED WHAT I BELIEVE TO BE THE SEVENTH DIVISION OF THE REBEL FLEET, LORD VADER.
WE ARE TRACKING ITS MOVEMENTS WHILE WAITING FOR IT TO CONTACT ANOTHER DIVISION AND REVEAL ITS LOCATION AS WELL.
VERY GOOD, COMMANDER ZAHRA. CONTINUE YOUR EFFORTS. NOT A SINGLE REBEL SHIP IS TO BE LEFT--
HNH.
SET A COURSE FOR TEMPES, IN THE OUTER RIM.
TEMPES, MY LORD? DO YOU REQUIRE ASSISTANCE? I CAN ORDER THE TARKIN'S WILL TO--
NO. I WILL HANDLE THIS MATTER MYSELF. A...TRAP HAS BEEN SPRUNG. I HAVE SENSED IT.
I WISH TO SEE WHAT I HAVE CAUGHT.

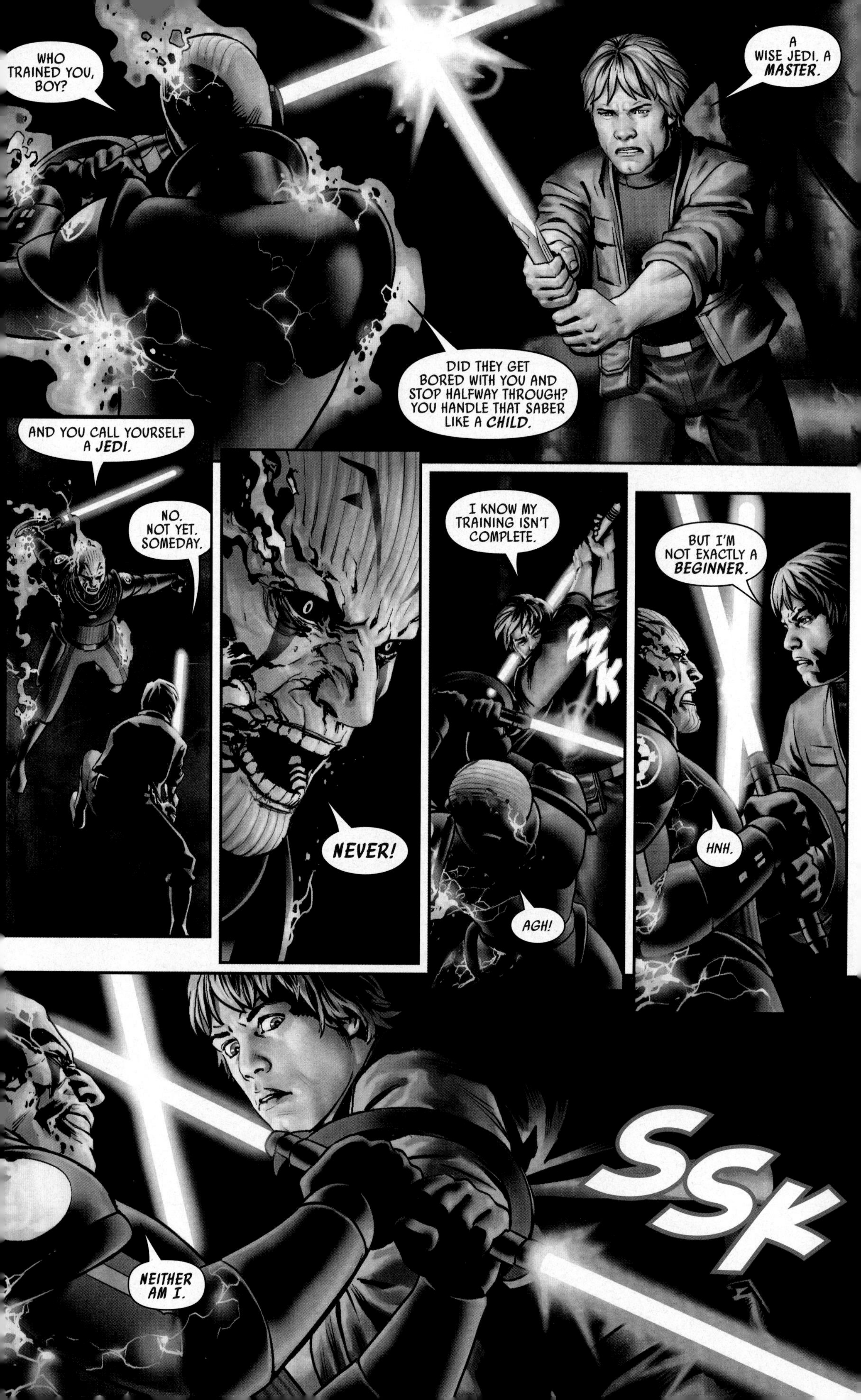

WHO TRAINED YOU, BOY?
A WISE JEDI. A MASTER.
DID THEY GET BORED WITH YOU AND STOP HALFWAY THROUGH? YOU HANDLE THAT SABER LIKE A CHILD.
AND YOU CALL YOURSELF A JEDI.
NO. NOT YET. SOMEDAY.
NEVER!
I KNOW MY TRAINING ISN'T COMPLETE.
ZZK
AGH!
BUT I'M NOT EXACTLY A BEGINNER.
HNH.
SSK
NEITHER AM I.

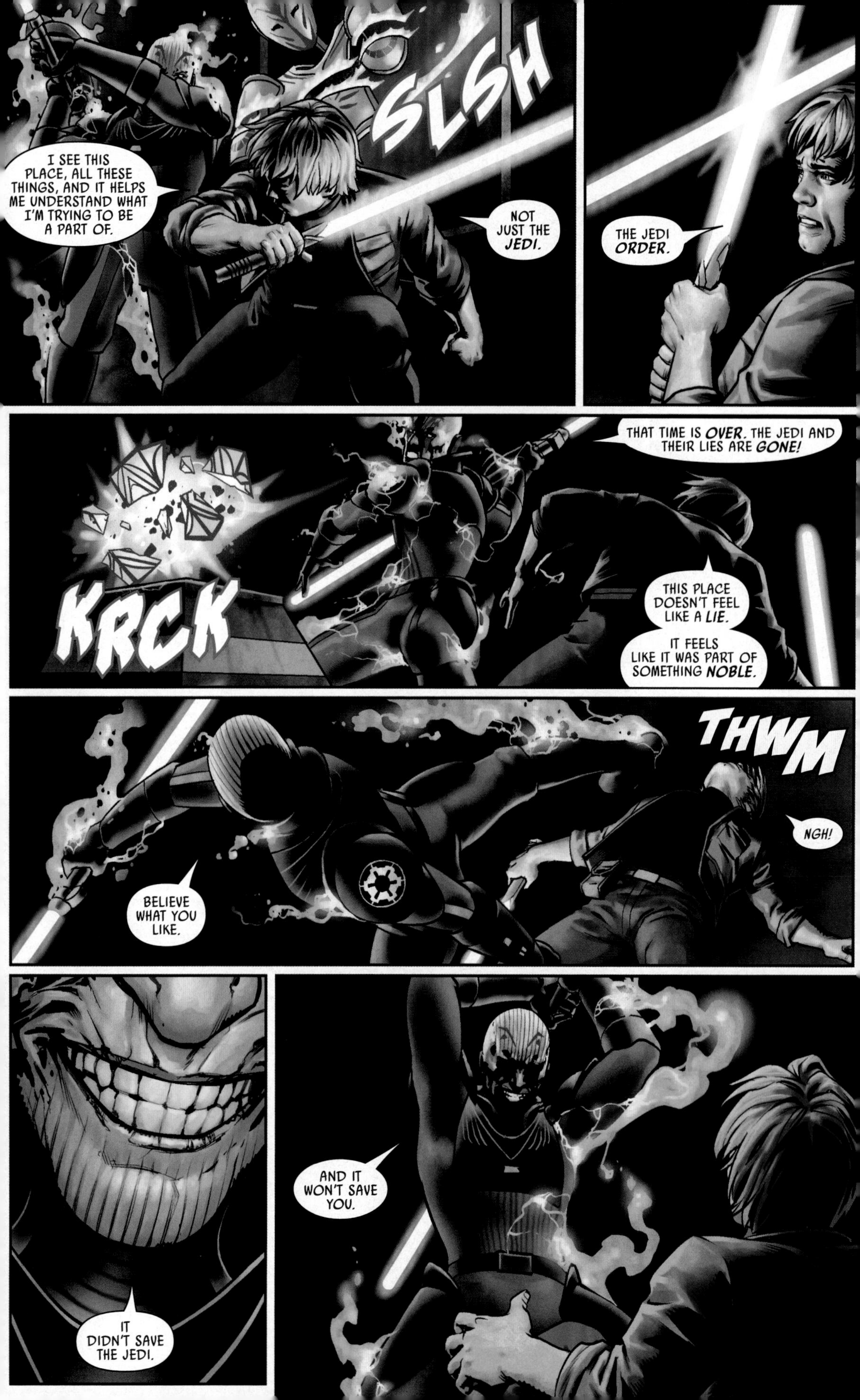
SLSH
I SEE THIS PLACE, ALL THESE THINGS, AND IT HELPS ME UNDERSTAND WHAT I'M TRYING TO BE A PART OF.
NOT JUST THE JEDI.
THE JEDI ORDER.
KRCK
THAT TIME IS OVER. THE JEDI AND THEIR LIES ARE GONE!
THIS PLACE DOESN'T FEEL LIKE A LIE.
IT FEELS LIKE IT WAS PART OF SOMETHING NOBLE.
THWM
NGH!
BELIEVE WHAT YOU LIKE.
IT DIDN'T SAVE THE JEDI.
AND IT WON'T SAVE YOU.

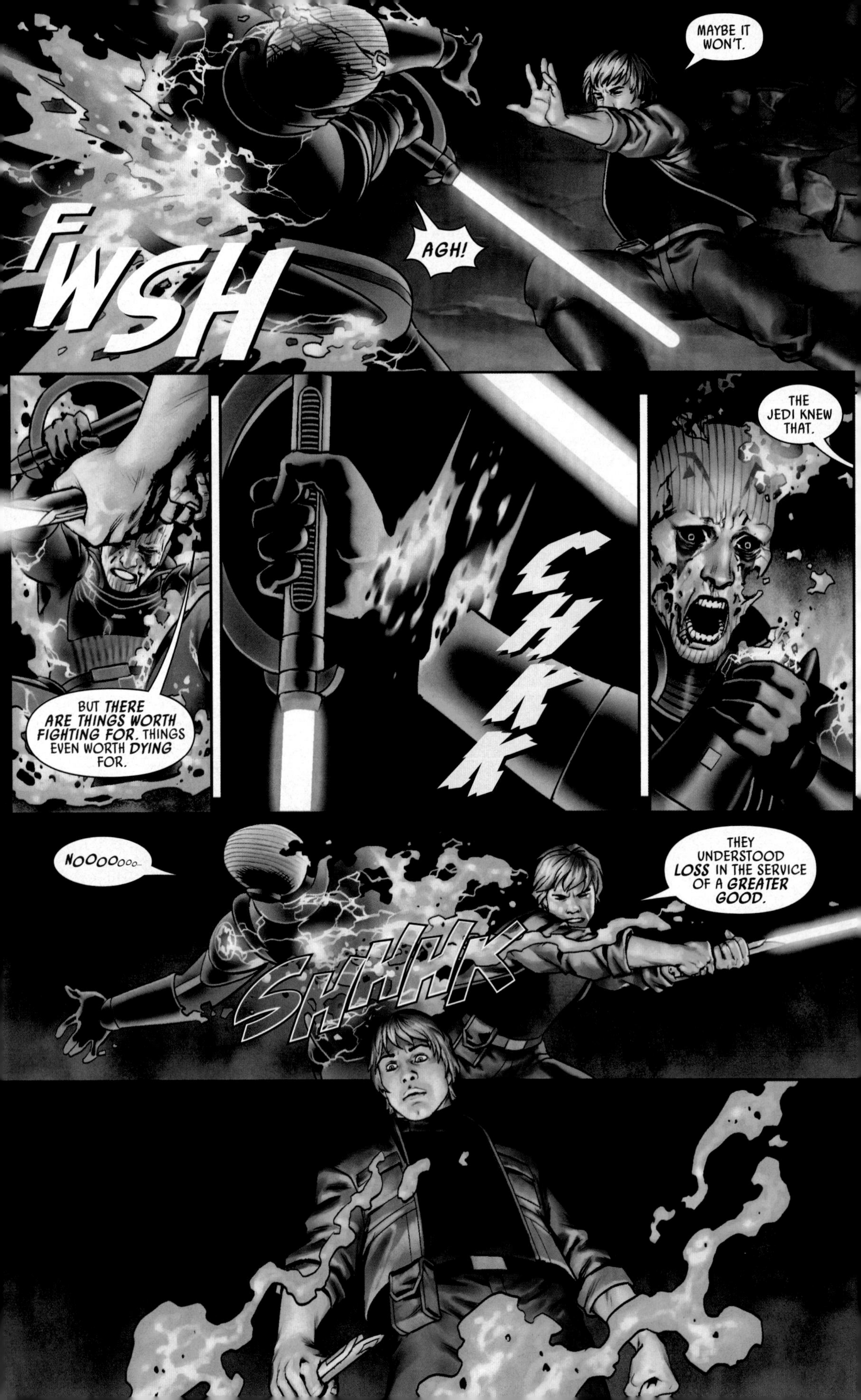
MAYBE IT WON'T.
AGH!
FWSH
BUT THERE ARE THINGS WORTH FIGHTING FOR. THINGS EVEN WORTH DYING FOR.
CHKK
THE JEDI KNEW THAT.
NOOOOooo...
THEY UNDERSTOOD LOSS IN THE SERVICE OF A GREATER GOOD.
SHHHK

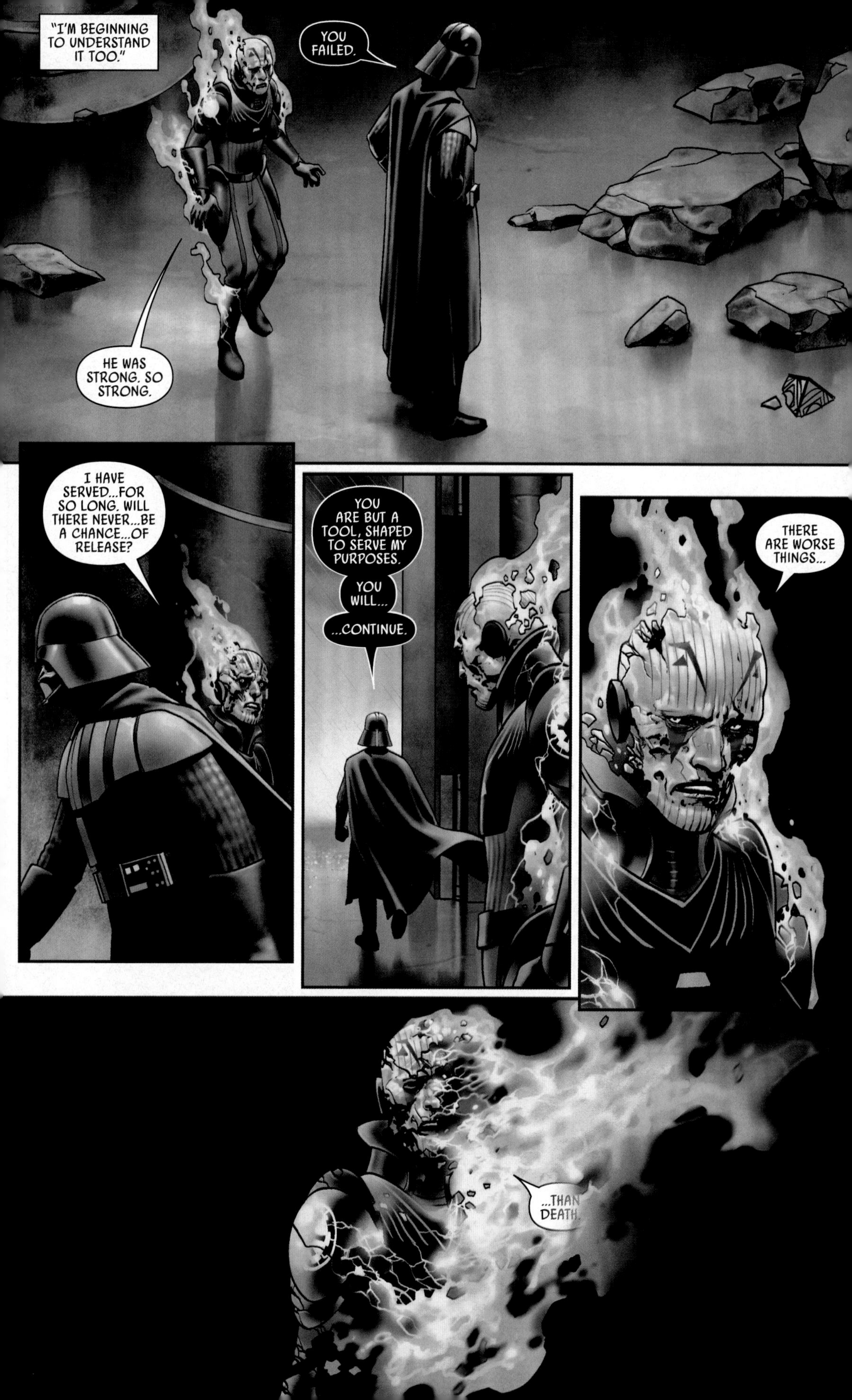
"I'M BEGINNING TO UNDERSTAND IT TOO."
YOU FAILED.
HE WAS STRONG. SO STRONG.
I HAVE SERVED...FOR SO LONG. WILL THERE NEVER...BE A CHANCE...OF RELEASE?
YOU ARE BUT A TOOL, SHAPED TO SERVE MY PURPOSES.
YOU WILL...
...CONTINUE.
THERE ARE WORSE THINGS...
...THAN DEATH.

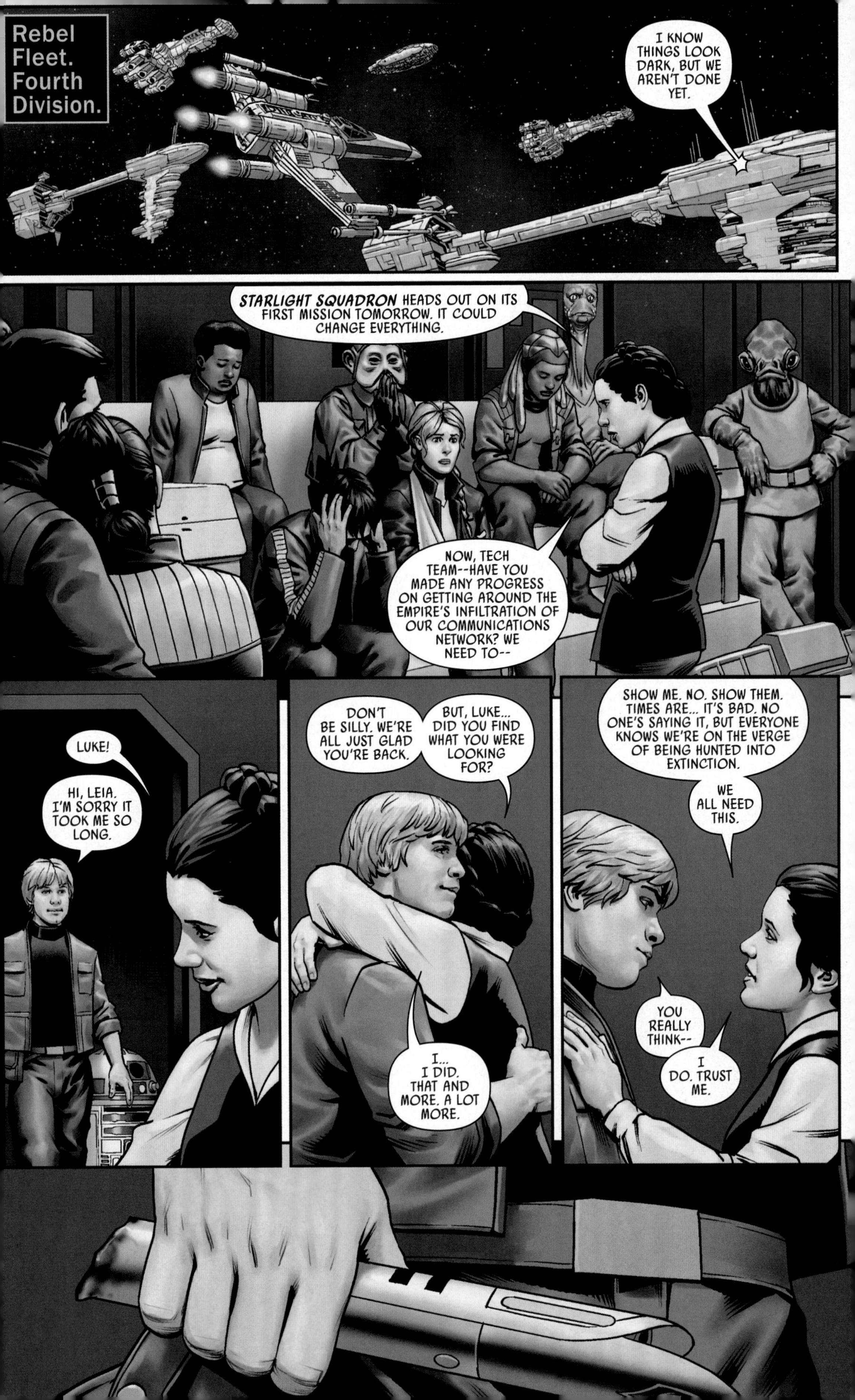
Rebel Fleet. Fourth Division.
I KNOW THINGS LOOK DARK, BUT WE AREN'T DONE YET.
STARLIGHT SQUADRON HEADS OUT ON ITS FIRST MISSION TOMORROW. IT COULD CHANGE EVERYTHING.
NOW, TECH TEAM--HAVE YOU MADE ANY PROGRESS ON GETTING AROUND THE EMPIRE'S INFILTRATION OF OUR COMMUNICATIONS NETWORK? WE NEED TO--
LUKE!
HI, LEIA. I'M SORRY IT TOOK ME SO LONG.
DON'T BE SILLY. WE'RE ALL JUST GLAD YOU'RE BACK.
BUT, LUKE... DID YOU FIND WHAT YOU WERE LOOKING FOR?
I... I DID. THAT AND MORE. A LOT MORE.
SHOW ME. NO. SHOW THEM. TIMES ARE... IT'S BAD. NO ONE'S SAYING IT, BUT EVERYONE KNOWS WE'RE ON THE VERGE OF BEING HUNTED INTO EXTINCTION.
WE ALL NEED THIS.
YOU REALLY THINK--
I DO. TRUST ME.

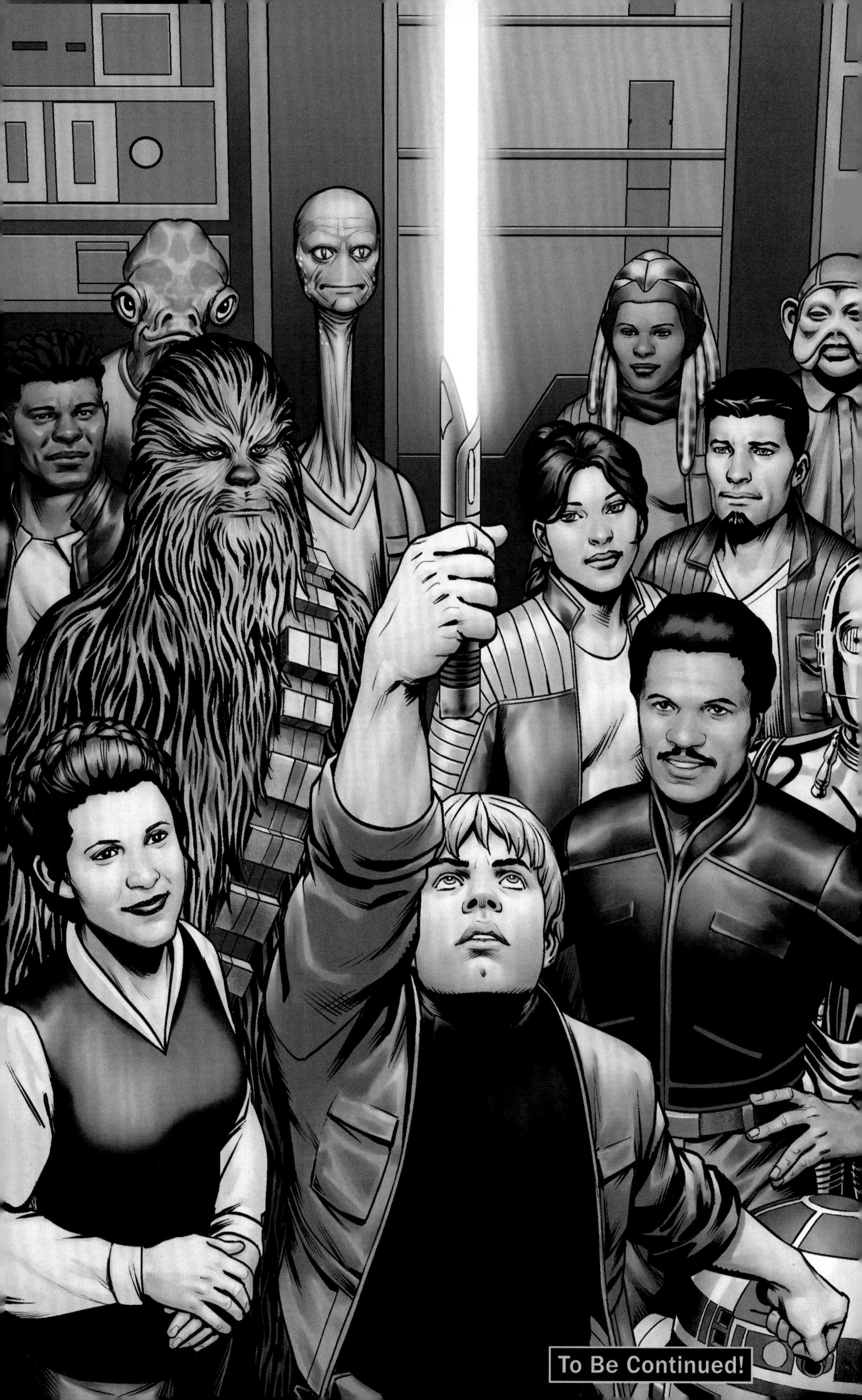
To Be Continued!

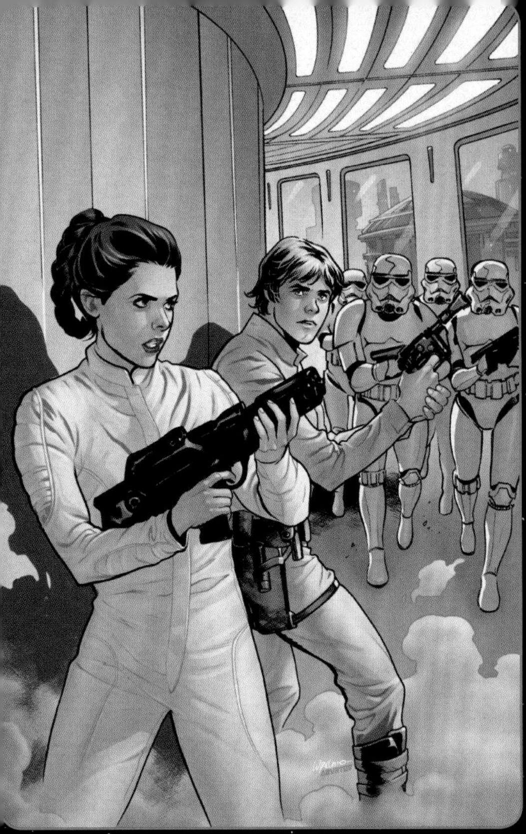

#3 Variant by
EMA LUPACCHINO & JESUS ABURTOV

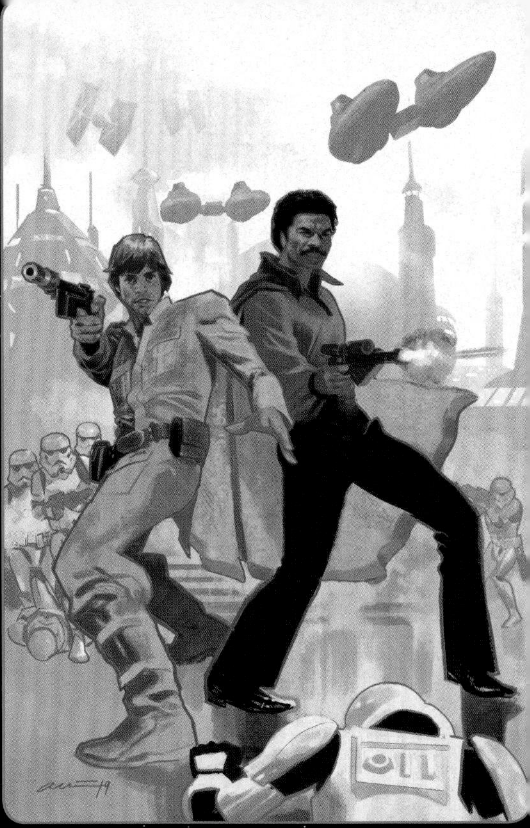

#4 Variant by
DANIEL ACUÑA

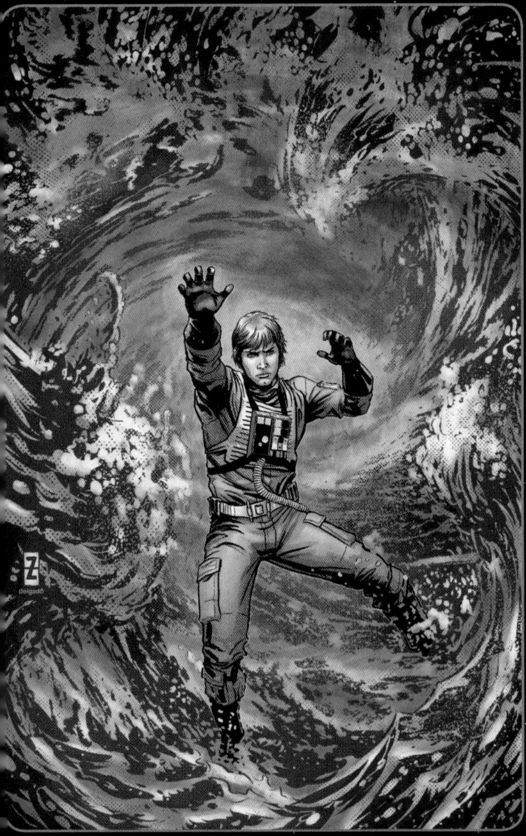

#5 Variant by

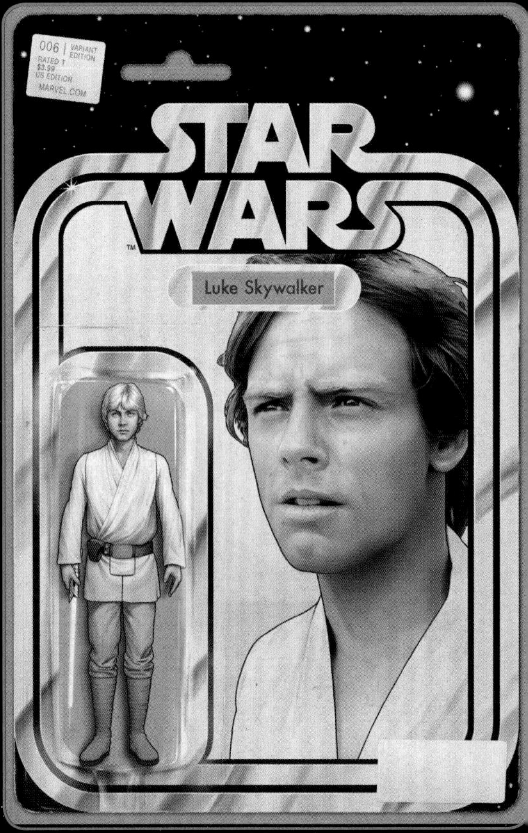
006 | VARIANT EDITION
RATED T
$3.99
US EDITION
MARVEL.COM
STAR WARS
Luke Skywalker

#6 Action Figure Variant by

STAR WARS COLLECTED EDITIONS

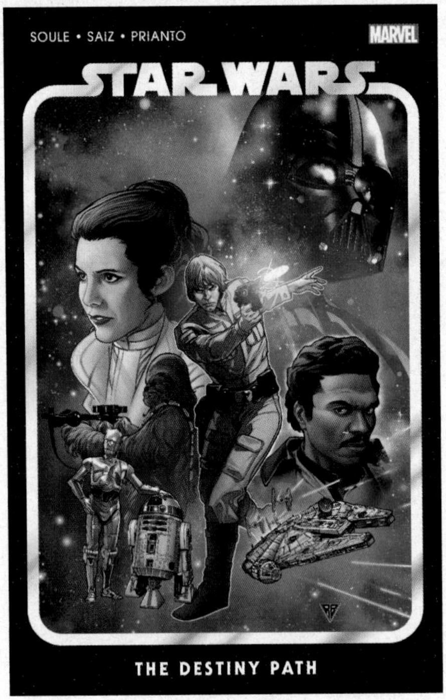
SOULE • SAIZ • PRIANTO
MARVEL
STAR WARS
THE DESTINY PATH

Star Wars Vol. 1:
The Destiny Path
ISBN 978-1-302-92078-4

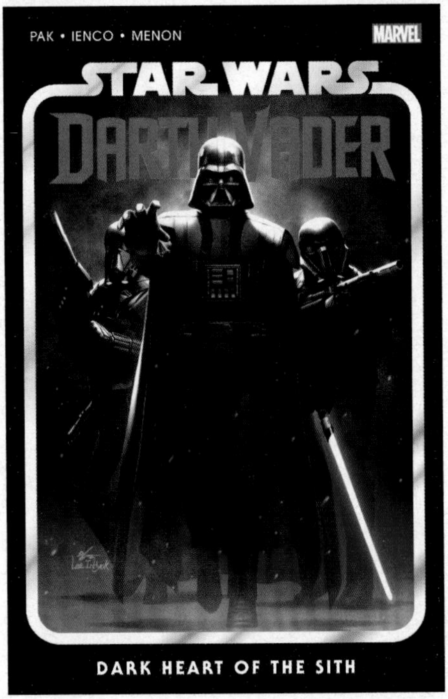
PAK • IENCO • MENON
MARVEL
STAR WARS
DARTH VADER
DARK HEART OF THE SITH

Star Wars: Darth Vader by Greg Pak
Vol. 1 — Dark Heart of the Sith
ISBN 978-1-302-92081-4

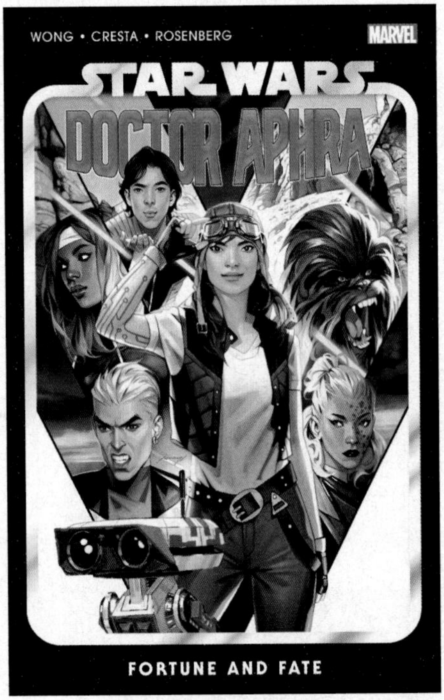
WONG • CRESTA • ROSENBERG
MARVEL
STAR WARS
DOCTOR APHRA
FORTUNE AND FATE

Star Wars: Doctor Aphra
Vol. 1 — Fortune and Fate
ISBN 978-1-302-92304-4

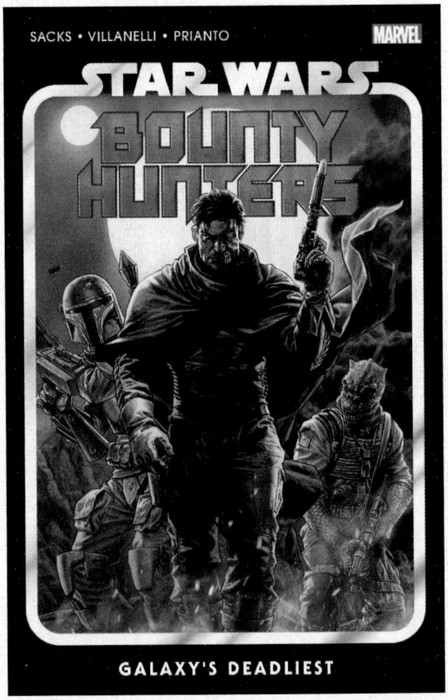
SACKS • VILLANELLI • PRIANTO
MARVEL
STAR WARS
BOUNTY HUNTERS
GALAXY'S DEADLIEST

Star Wars: Bounty Hunters
Vol. 1 — Galaxy's Deadliest
ISBN 978-1-302-92083-8

Disney · LUCASFILM MARVEL

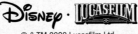